LIVINGSTONE'S
PRIVATE JOURNALS
1851–1853

Also edited by I. Schapera

*

DAVID LIVINGSTONE
Family Letters 1841–1856
(Vol. I 1841–48. Vol. II 1849–56)

LIVINGSTONE'S
Private Journals
1851-1853

Edited with
an Introduction by
I. SCHAPERA

1960
UNIVERSITY OF CALIFORNIA PRESS
BERKELEY AND LOS ANGELES

PUBLISHED IN THE UNITED STATES OF AMERICA
BY THE UNIVERSITY OF CALIFORNIA PRESS OF
BERKELEY AND LOS ANGELES, CALIFORNIA
*
PUBLISHED IN GREAT BRITAIN BY
CHATTO AND WINDUS LTD
LONDON

CONTENTS

EDITOR'S INTRODUCTION ix

AUTHOR'S NOTE xxv

I. FIRST JOURNEY TO SEBITOANE'S COUNTRY 1851

Reasons for leaving the Bakwains 1

Incidents in the first journey (from Kolobeng)¹ to Sebitoane 3

Particulars respecting Sebitoane 16

Sebitoane's illness and death 23

Sebitoane's character &c. 25

Visit Sesheke &c. 28

II. RETURN TO THE SOUTH

Return down Tamunakle R[iver] 51

Sebitoane's song 56

Rhinoceros 62

Tsetse 63

W. O. L. born 68

Different opinions. Providential kindnesses 70

Diseases of wild animals (&c &c) 74

Reach Kolobeng 78

Reach Kuruman 79

Reach Cape Town. Mr. O.'s kindness 80

III. SECOND JOURNEY TO SEBITOANE'S COUNTRY 1852–3

Leave Cape Town 84

Reach Kuruman. Sechele's letter 85

Detention at Kuruman. (Swallows) 91

Leave for Sebitoane's country second time 95

Growth of Boabob &c. 101

Poison of Ngoa. Fever 103

¹ Words in parentheses occur in Livingstone's lists of contents, but not in my sectional headings in the text; words in square brackets have been added by me.

v

CONTENTS

Grapes &c. 106
Find country flooded 113
Cross River Chobe 127

IV. AT SEKELETU'S TOWN
Arrive at Sekeletu's town 137
Fever 148
(At Sekeletu's town.) Demonstration 153
Condition of population (previous to contact with Europeans) 154
Proposal to visit Borotse. (Previous subject continued. Attempt to establish new relationships in the way of trade. Errors in Longitude detected) 160
Fever 163
Fabulous opinions about lion's roar 164
Facts about the people; their deportment 166
Ants and bees 170
Doctoring. Maps by Natives. (Nkalange Lake. Peculiarities of the climate) 174
Portuguese merchant Ferra arrives 176

V. VISIT TO THE BOROTSE
Leave for Borotse. Mpepe's death (and our return) 181
Types of Humanity. (Guyot's Earth and Man) 186
Vertigo. Arrival of Senor Porto. (Borotse serpent charming) 188
Second Departure for Borotse. (Liambae, Nambwe) 192
Falls of Gonye 195
Borotse country commences 198
Two men executed 200
Mamochisane 202
Naliele. Santuru 202
Senor Porto (at Katongo) visits Naliele. (Bakisi dancers. Rapidity of current of Leeambye) 204
Libonta 211
Fever 215

CONTENTS

Robbery by Mambowe 217

Confluence of the Loeti 219

Confluence of the Leeba or Lonta 219

VI. RETURN TO LINYANTI

Return to Libonta (and Mothibe's arrival) 222

Santuru's altar 224

Katongo. Arabs (&c) 226

Litofe. Sesheke 230

*Mpepe's character & intrigues. (Spears from Batoka.
 Anderson & Lake. Mothibe & Mamiré learning to
 read)* 231

Nokwane's illness 236

Borotse boatman's song 237

Dialogue shewing rain maker's arguments 239

VII. NOTES ON WILD ANIMALS &c.

Taste for the beautiful 244

Facts about elephants 244

Swallows 250

*African miseries (reproof beneficial) [and] barbarism
 (its causes. Old wet nurses)* 251

Notes about ants 254

Facts about the rhinoceros. (Drought in these parts) 259

Plasterer 264

Notes about giraffe 266

Eiland or pohoo 268

Absence of beauty in Native women 272

Hornets 273

Notes about buffaloes 274

Socialism among the MaKololo 276

Porto stealing 277

Scavenger beetles 277

Kokong or wildebeeste 278

Fascination by fire as of serpents 280

Habit 283

CONTENTS

Buceros Hydrocorax or khoroe   283

Facts about birds' nests   284

Insects   288

Preparation for departure   290

Mokhele's journey down the Sesheke   291

Notes about ostriches   292

*[Eve of departure]. (The rivers probably arms of one
great river)*   294

APPENDIX

I. *[Fragments of Kolobeng Journal 1848–9]. (Fragments of a journal lost in the distruction of Kolo-
beng by the Boers under Pretorious)*   297

II. *Observations on Latitude and Longitude by Mr
Maclear*   308

III. *[Native names of animals, &c]*   311

IV. *[Native names of plants]*   317

LIST OF REFERENCES   320

INDEX   327

LIST OF MAPS

1. Livingstone's routes in Southern Bechuanaland   52

2. Livingstone's routes in Northern Bechuanaland   138

3. Barotseland and the Upper Zambesi   182

EDITOR'S INTRODUCTION

(i)

THE original of the journal printed here is contained in two small notebooks, whose history Livingstone tells inconsistently. In *Missionary Travels and Researches in South Africa* (1857), he says that before leaving Dinyanti for the West Coast in November 1853 he gave the Kololo chief Sekeletu 'a volume of my Journal', to be sent, in case he did not return, to his father-in-law Robert Moffat. He was away longer than expected. Sekeletu accordingly delivered 'the book' to a trader, 'and', continues Livingstone, 'I have been unable to trace it. I regret this now, as it contained valuable notes on the habits of wild animals'.[1]

This version is supported by his correspondence. On returning to Dinyanti he wrote to Moffat (12 September 1855): 'I left a volume of notes to be given to any traveller in case of my being cut off. Sekeletu gave it to Mr S. Edwards. I suppose it will be delivered to you. Please send it to England. It is chiefly of a private nature.'[2] Moffat replied that he had not received it, and in October 1857 repeated: 'I have not seen nor heard of it. I have written to make enquiries.'[3]

But in *Narrative of an Expedition to the Zambesi and its Tributaries* (1865), Livingstone states that he had left with Sekeletu, not one, but 'two manuscript volumes. . . . One contained notes on the discovery of Lake Ngami, and on the Kalahari Desert; the other, notes on its natural history.' The MaKololo declared that these had been delivered 'to one of the only two traders who had visited them.' When

---

[1] *Op. cit.*, p. 229.

[2] *Family Letters* (ed. Schapera, 1959), vol. ii, p. 267; cf. *ibid.*, p. 274, for a similar statement to Mrs Moffat (26.ix.1855). Sam Edwards was a well-known adventurer who in the course of many journeys into the interior paid several visits to the MaKololo.

[3] Moffat to D. L., 29.x.1857 (Bruce collection). The earlier letter, which Moffat mentions there, does not seem to have been preserved.

Livingstone, on reaching them again in 1860 (from the East Coast), reported that 'the person in question' denied having received 'the books', one of Sekeletu's wives replied, 'He lies, I gave them to him myself.' 'Conscience seems to have worked', concludes the story, 'for the trader, having gone to Moselekatse's country, one of the volumes was put into the mail-bag coming from the south, which came to hand with the lock taken off in quite a scientific manner.'[1]

The obvious implication of this statement is that in 1865 one of the 'two manuscript volumes' was still missing. But in the very same paragraph of *Travels* where he mentions having left 'a volume' with Sekeletu, Livingstone says also: 'I find myself in my journal pondering over that fearful migration which lands us in eternity; wondering whether an angel will soothe the fluttering soul, sadly flurried as it must be on entering the spirit world; and hoping that Jesus might speak but one word of peace, for that would establish in the bosom an everlasting calm.' This passage is so unmistakably taken from Notebook I[2] that he must have had that particular Notebook at hand when he wrote; the words 'my journal' confirm that he could hardly have been citing some other record. It accordingly seems likely that what he says in *Narrative* was due to faulty recollection, and that he had in fact entrusted to Sekeletu only one volume, viz. Notebook II,[3] which ultimately came back to him in the manner there described. Notebook II, moreover, follows directly and uninterruptedly upon Notebook I, which does contain 'notes on the discovery of Lake Ngami.' It is highly improbable, in the circumstances, that there was yet another notebook, never recovered at all.[4]

(ii)

The journal starts with Livingstone's departure from Kolobeng in April 1851 for the country of Sebetwane, chief

---

[1] *Op. cit.*, p. 297. Moselekatse was chief of the MaTebele, and lived near the site of the modern city of Bulawayo, Southern Rhodesia.

[2] Cf. below, p. 97f.   [3] Cf. below, p. 295: 'This volume I leave in his charge'.

[4] Debenham (*The Way to Ilala*, 1955, p. 78) repeats the story that Livingstone's 'detailed notes and journal ... appear to have been lost'. But their recovery had already been mentioned by Blaikie in 1880 (*Personal Life of David Livingstone*, p. 151 n.).

of the MaKololo, and concludes on the eve of his leaving that
country for Luanda on the West Coast in November 1853.[1]
It describes the whole of his first journey to the MaKololo
(including the discovery of the Upper Zambesi at Sesheke),
his return south and visit to Cape Town to despatch his wife
and children to England, and his second journey to the
MaKololo, followed by an excursion from their capital (Dinyanti) into Barotseland proper. In Notebook I the main
narrative is interrupted (after the entry for 1 June 1853) by
a copy of 'Observations on Latitude and Longitude by Mr
Maclear'[2], following which is an 'extract from another
journal' (for the years 1848–9). The final pages of Notebook
II, similarly, contain miscellaneous notes, chiefly lists of
Native names of wild animals.

The opening passages of Notebook I show that Livingstone did not begin putting the journal into its present form
until on his way back from the first visit to the MaKololo (or
possibly even later). By that time he had already been in
South Africa for ten years and travelled much more extensively than any of his fellow-missionaries. While based on
Kuruman (1841–3), he made three journeys to the north
(two as far as Shoshong), and a fourth to initiate the mission
at Mabotsa. Thereafter he lived successively at Mabotsa
(1844–5), Chonwane (1845–7), and Kolobeng (1847–51),
from which he went on several eastward trips into what is
now the Transvaal, and then twice (1849, 1850) to Lake
Ngami in the distant north-west.

His contemporary accounts of these earlier travels are
found chiefly in his letters.[3] He does mention 'a journal, the
greater part of which was lost in the plunder of my house
[at Kolobeng] by the Independent Boers' in September
1852 ; but the salvaged portion of that journal (copied into
Notebook I) suggests that it consisted merely of sporadic

[1] His journey to Luanda, return to Dinyanti, and subsequent journey to the East
Coast, are described in another and much bulkier journal (now in the possession of
his grandson, Dr H. F. Wilson). Sebetwane, who died shortly after Livingstone
reached him, was the father of Sekeletu.

[2] Thomas Maclear (1794–1875) was astronomer royal at the Cape of Good Hope
1834–70.

[3] Two major collections have been published: *Some Letters from Livingstone
1840–1873*, ed. D. Chamberlin, 1940, and *Family Letters 1841–1856*, ed. I. Schapera,
2 vols., 1959.

and often sketchy memoranda. The 'notes on the discovery of Lake Ngami', for example, amount to only some 450 words, and apart from referring briefly to contacts with Natives contain little more than a few place-names and scanty remarks on rivers. Nor is it irrelevant, in this context, that the accounts published by the Royal Geographical Society of his two journeys to the Lake[1] were taken mainly (the second entirely) from his letters to Dr A. Tidman, Foreign Secretary of the London Missionary Society. And when, in April 1852, Tidman suggested 'that you keep a regular journal . . . more likely to prove of permanent interest and value than the more vague and general impressions conveyed in a hastily written letter', Livingstone replied curtly, and with no further reference at all to the subject, 'I cannot promise to keep a journal.'[2]

Unless he was being deliberately perverse, he must have understood by 'a journal' something more elaborate and systematic than he had already attempted; and it is surely no coincidence that from now on, and especially after he approached the country of the MaKololo for the second time, the entries become increasingly detailed and frequent. Even so, as late as September 1855 he wrote to Mrs Moffat that the 'volume of notes' he had left with Sekeletu 'is not intended for publication, but for my family. If I should try and make a book, it would be compiled out of such and similar everyday affairs, which *for the first time* I have begun to note down as they occur.'[3]

Despite its chronological arrangement, the present journal was thus evidently not intended by Livingstone to be a comprehensive record of his daily experiences. It omits many incidents mentioned in his letters of the same period, and, on the other hand, contains entries that seem to have no obvious connection with the dates under which they appear. The most striking examples are the synoptic descriptions of wild animals and insects. Some of these, as well as the section on animal diseases and the 'dialogue showing rain maker's

[1] *J.R.G.S.*, vol 20 (1850), pp. 138–42; vol. 21 (1851), pp. 18–24.
[2] Tidman to D. L., 14.iv.1852; D. L. (from Cape Town) to Tidman, 26.iv.1852 (L.M.S. archives). The relevant portion of Tidman's letter is quoted more extensively in *Family Letters*, ed. Schapera, vol. i, p. 16.
[3] *Family Letters*, vol. ii, p. 274; my italics.

arguments', are based on drafts found elsewhere in his papers[1]; similarly, the long list of places identifying the route of Sebetwane's migration from the Orange Free State to Barotseland must certainly have been copied from notes made several months previously. The Notebooks, in brief, are partly a chronicle, but partly also a repository of miscellaneous observations, reflections, and stray items of information, not all the immediate product of the journeys described.

The period and events with which the journal is mainly concerned are dealt with also in Chapters IV–XII (pp. 77–226) of *Missionary Travels*. But those Chapters contain much that does not appear at all, or is mentioned only very briefly, in the journal. This applies not only to many geographical and geological observations, but also, for example, to the story of the prophet Tlapane, who diverted Sebetwane into Barotseland (*Travels*, pp. 86–7), the note on migratory springboks (pp. 103–4), the account of diseases among the BaKwena (pp. 127–32), the remarks about serpents (pp. 143–5), and the descriptions of initiation ceremonies (pp. 146–8) and judicial procedure (pp. 183–4). Many shorter items could easily be added. Since his letters, too, rarely refer to them, Livingstone in writing about such topics must often have relied mainly upon his memory. That he is usually very accurate shows how remarkable were his powers both of observation and recollection.

On the other hand, the journal itself comprises much more than was published in *Travels*. Apart from describing Livingstone's residence at Cape Town in 1852 (barely mentioned in his book), it gives many additional details about the routes and incidents of his two journeys to the MaKololo, notably his attempts to cross the flooded river Chobe in 1853. It contains, what were omitted from *Travels*, a lengthy list of the places through which Sebetwane and his people passed on their gradual migration to Barotseland, portions of that chief's 'praise-poems', notes on the 'strange' illnesses of the

---

[1] For example, another notebook (now in the Livingstone Memorial, Blantyre) contains passages on the eland, bull frog, elephant, animal diseases, and the 'dialogue', all developed more fully in the journal (as well as an 'Analysis' of the Tswana language, a draft paper on 'Missionary Sacrifices', and various other oddments).

headmen Mahale and Nokwane, the 'Borotse boatman's song' (memorable chiefly as an example of Livingstone's poetizing), and the full texts of two important letters (one from Mrs Moffat reproaching him for taking his pregnant wife and small children 'on an exploring expedition', the other from Sechele to Moffat about the Boer attack on the BaKwena). It describes more minutely than in *Travels* the activities among the MaKololo of the Portuguese traders Silva Pôrto and Ferreira, the 'socialism' of the MaKololo, and such incidents as the execution of Mphephe's father and the robbery committed by Livingstone's Mbowe companions, with his own ingenious essay in detection ; gives a fuller version of the famous 'dialogue with a rainmaker' ; and, among notes on natural history not included in *Travels*, contains accounts of the giraffe and eland, a classification of species of ants, and lists of various trees and other plants eaten by wild animals.

The journal entries show also that what Livingstone published in *Travels* was sometimes embellished in the telling. For example, the descriptions he gives there of the Bushman guide Shobo, of his children's sufferings from thirst on the first journey to the MaKololo, and of how Sekeletu's rival Mphephe was killed, all contain details not found in the journal, and what he says about his last meeting with Sebetwane includes incidents occurring several days earlier. Occasionally the journal corrects dates given in *Travels*, for example for the discovery of the Zambesi at Sesheke and for Livingstone's departure from Kuruman on his second journey. Possibly, too, he may be thought to have treated his readers unkindly when, in writing about the tsetse fly, he substituted 'Is a man not as much a domestic animal as a dog ?' for the original 'Is a henpecked husband less domesticated than a sheep ?', and when, in writing about cattle-keeping among the MaKololo, he omitted the observation that 'If an ox is seen to be sick it is immediately slaughtered, in order, as an Irishman would say, to save its life.'[1]

The journal is thus not simply an earlier and sketchier draft of the corresponding chapters in *Travels* : it both supplements and occasionally corrects that famous book. It

Cf. below, pp. 66, 210.

therefore constitutes a distinct, and as indispensable, source of information about Livingstone's interests and activities for the period it covers.

It shows even more convincingly, for example, that his two journeys to the MaKololo, like all those he had made previously, were essentially what he himself called them—'missionary travels'. The first was undertaken in order to start a mission station in Sebetwane's country. When that proved impossible, for reasons mentioned in the text, he decided to send his family to England and return alone to seek both a site healthy enough for European settlement and a shorter route to the sea than the long trek from the south. His second journey, accordingly, was devoted specifically to exploration—but exploration in the service of Christ, and not for the sake of geographical discovery. Had discovery been foremost among his objectives he would hardly have ignored the opportunity in 1851 of visiting the Victoria Falls when he learned of their existence, only four days away, nor would he have written to Tidman from Dinyanti in 1853 that he did not 'feel it duty' to go in their direction[1]; in fact, he did not see the Falls until November 1855, when on his way to the East Coast.

Nor should it be forgotten that his journeys were not, like many Polar expeditions, ventures into completely untrodden fields. It is true that before himself no European had been to either Lake Ngami or the country of the MaKololo. But he was by no means the first person to travel there from the south. Letsholathebe's people at Lake Ngami were immigrants who at the end of the eighteenth century had seceded from the BaNgwato of Shoshong. Some thirty years later Sebetwane led the MaKololo, first to the Lake and then to Barotseland, all the way from the present Orange Free State. Lake Ngami had also been visited sporadically by parties of southern Natives, whose reports on their return had made its existence known to the outside world long before Livingstone came to South Africa. He himself before going to the Lake in 1849 and to the MaKololo in 1851 received messengers at Kolobeng from Letsholathebe and Sebetwane respectively, who invited him to visit them. His narratives

[1] *Letters*, ed. Chamberlin, p. 210.

show also that he was dependent all the way upon Native guides; his journal, especially, makes it clear that he and Oswell got to Sebetwane's country before Wilson and Edwards merely because they were fortunate enough, when at the Botletle, to find guides familiar with a more direct route than the one they had intended to follow. On both journeys, therefore, he and his companions were conducted over known paths to destinations already reached by many others.

What they really accomplished was to show that Europeans could also get to those places, despite such relatively cumbersome forms of transport as wagons, the perpetual need of sufficient water for large spans of trek oxen, and the occasional need of cutting through dense bush. The route taken to Lake Ngami by Livingstone, Oswell, Murray, and Wilson, immediately became established as the highway, and within a year several parties of European traders and hunters had successfully followed them over it. The route he and Oswell took to Sebetwane's country proved much more difficult, owing mainly to scarcity of water but partly also to the menace of the tsetse fly. Most later travellers therefore went up the Botletle and Thamalakane Rivers, following the trail blazed by Wilson and Edwards in 1851 and used by himself and Oswell on their homeward journey that year; alternatively, and increasingly, they took the Pandamatenka road much farther east. But it was he and his companions who had paved the way and so made possible the exploitation of the great wealth of ivory and other hunting spoils that was for many years the chief attraction of the north-west.

However, Livingstone was not simply a missionary who in the course of his vocational travels opened up regions previously unvisited by white men. What distinguishes him from all others who went into the interior about the same time is the nature of the scientific observations that he also made and recorded. Many of his contemporaries, among them Wilson and Edwards, seem to have left no written account of where they had been and what they had seen. Some, for example Hume, published nothing but sketchy itineraries. Still others, such as Methuen, Cumming, and Leyland, were concerned mainly with sport and natural history, and noted little else of much value. Livingstone stands alone in the diversity of his interests. He wrote voluminously and accurately on geography, botany, zoology, disease, linguistics, and what would nowadays be called anthropology, and for his own period he is by far the most comprehensive source of information on South-Central Africa.

It is usual in this context to think of him primarily as a geographer; Professor Debenham in fact calls him 'the greatest geographer that Africa has ever seen'.[1] But that aspect of his scientific work first became prominent after he had been to Lake Ngami, and especially during his journeys to the MaKololo. His earlier letters say much more about the Natives of Bechuanaland than about physical and natural features of the country. Even his initial report on the discovery of Lake Ngami is less detailed than Oswell's, published simultaneously with it by the Royal Geographical Society[2]; and it may be noted, incidentally, that neither tried to observe personally the size and shape of the Lake, about which they related merely what they were told by local Natives. It is only from the time of his first journey to the MaKololo, when he had already been ten years in South Africa and travelled extensively, that we find him making systematic records of latitude and longitude, temperature, and even distances covered, and paying careful attention to the compilation of maps.

The relatively late development of special concern with matters of geographical interest is apparent also in the nature of his literary activities while in Bechuanaland. He wrote several papers, not all accepted for publication, on missionary topics of various kinds and on the Native policy of the Boers; he also completed (though it was not printed until 1858) an 'Analysis of the Language of the Bechuanas.' He seems to have attempted nothing equally ambitious in the field of geography, though he does mention having written in 1843 to Professor William Buckland about the desiccation of Bechuanaland[3], and in other letters comments occasionally on climate, vegetation, rock formations, and kindred topics.

[1] *The Way to Ilala*, p. 15.

[2] 'Expedition to the South African Lake Ngami', *J.R.G.S.*, vol. 20 (1850), pp. 138–42 (Livingstone), 143–51 (Oswell).

[3] *Travels*, p. 528; cf. Blaikie, *Life*, pp. 61, 83. The letter may have gone astray; it was apparently never acknowledged.

His subsequent devotion to geographical inquiry may have been due partly to the knowledge that in contrast with the scenes of his earlier travels, where he had usually been preceded by others, he was now going into regions still completely unexplored. But he seems to have been influenced also by the recognition and encouragement he received from the profession. The cartographer John Arrowsmith sent him a map of Southern Africa to amplify and correct[1]; and the President of the Royal Geographical Society, in writing officially to congratulate him on the award of the Royal Premium for the discovery of the Lake, expressed the hope that he would persevere in his 'onward scientific course' and submit to the Society 'accounts of your future travels, and of the new regions which you will probably be one of the foremost in exploring.'[2]

'The Geographical Society', Livingstone wrote to a friend, 'has given me £26.5.0, but that will not procure a span of oxen, and I lost twelve last journey.'[3] He used the money to purchase not other oxen but a chronometer. The reason, he explained to Dr Tidman, was that 'the astronomer at the Cape' (Mr T. Maclear) had 'publicly invited any one to make observations on certain stars, [and] engaged to observe them simultaneously and make the calculations. As it would not require much time, and a small telescope kindly presented me by Mr Freeman with my own sextant are all that are required besides the watch, I felt anxious to comply with Mr Maclear's invitation.'[4] While at Cape Town the following year he also received personal guidance from Maclear, who likewise supplied him with written instructions that (as already indicated) were copied for ease of reference into the journal. He thus set out on his second expedition to the MaKololo better equipped than before with both technical knowledge and scientific instruments. The results are apparent in the greater abundance and improved quality of his observations.

[1] Cf. *Letters*, ed. Chamberlin, pp. 147, 148 (to Tidman); *Family Letters*, ed. Schapera, vol. ii, p. 129 (to Moffat). Both letters are dated April 1851.

[2] *J.R.G.S.*, vol. 20 (1850), p. xxx.

[3] D. L. to D. G. Watt, 10.i.1851 (L.M.S. archives).

[4] D. L. to Tidman, 30. iv. 1851 (Chamberlin, pp. 144–5). Mr J. J. Freeman, Home Secretary of the L.M.S., had visited Kolobeng at the end of 1849 during a tour of inspection in South Africa (cf. below, p. 306).

Even so, if one judges solely by what appears in the journal he was at the time of its writing still interested primarily in natural history. He himself, we may recall, mentioned as its main content 'valuable notes on the habits of wild animals'. Descriptions of mammals, birds, and insects, are indeed both more numerous and comprehensive than any other kind of scientific observation. Livingstone's accounts of the lion, giraffe, eland, buffalo, and other big game, compare very favourably with anything similar written by his contemporaries, and his almost unique lists of the plants eaten by some of those animals show how thorough an observer he was. Modern taxonomists confirm his conclusion that there are only two species of rhinoceros in South Africa; and it may be added, for the record, that as early as 1851 he recognized as new species of antelope both the puku (*Kobus vardoni*) and 'nakong' (sitatunga, *Tragelaphus spekei*)[1].

His interest was not exclusively scientific. 'The various forms of animated life', he says, 'present, to him whose heart is at peace with God, . . . an indescribable charm.' In several almost lyrical passages he indicates how much pleasure he got from watching the activities of ants and other insects, and these are by no means the only instances he gives of the enthusiasm inspired in him by 'the beauties of nature'. Ahead of his time, too, he deplored the ruthless destruction of game resulting from the introduction of firearms, and he makes it obvious that he himself hunted, and then very reluctantly, only when his people were short of meat.

The human inhabitants of the country he found less attractive to study. The journal does contain many observations on such Native beliefs and practices as religious conceptions, use of 'medicines' for magical purposes, divination, rainmaking, dances, tribal gatherings, infanticide, and certain aspects of marriage. But these are on the whole brief and sketchy. Livingstone was obviously far more interested in the languages than in the customs of the peoples he encountered. That is hardly surprising. He was after all a missionary, whose first concern must necessarily have been to find means of communicating the message he had come to preach. Indeed, soon after the discovery of Lake Ngami he wrote:

[1] Cf. below, pp. 37, 55.

'When I heard the new language and saw a few portions of the people, I felt that if I could be permitted to reduce their language to writing and perhaps translate the Scriptures into it, I might be able to say that I had not lived in vain.'[1] He never did attempt a translation, but the vocabularies he collected were until fairly recently the only data available on some of the local dialects.

It was no doubt partly also his missionary bias that made him condemn Native ways of life. Although he acknowledges gratefully the kindness and liberality shown him by the Ma-Kololo, he repeatedly expresses disgust at their behaviour in public, scanty dress, and eating habits; and there is little evidence of tolerance in such judgments as 'terrible depravity', 'moral impurity and degradation', 'the natural man presents few points of loveliness', and 'they possess neither courage, patriotism, natural affection, honour, nor honesty'.

But the specific instances he records of bloodshed, raiding, and other forms of brutality, show that he was not completely unjustified in his attitude. Together with what he also says about political intrigues, relations between rulers and subjects, and ramifications of the slave trade, they present a grim picture of social conditions. All this, however, at the same time makes his journal a most valuable source of information for the historian of Northern Rhodesia. Equally useful are his accounts of Sebetwane's battles and movements, and especially of the route taken by that chief in migrating from the far distant south to Barotseland; although many of the places named cannot be identified with certainty, it is at least evident that before crossing the Kalahari Desert to Lake Ngami the MaKololo must have gone much farther northeast in Bechuanaland than hitherto commonly supposed.[2]

The journal also adds much to our knowledge of Livingstone's personal characteristics. He himself described it to Moffat as being 'chiefly of a private nature'.[3] 'It is not intended for publication in any form', he likewise wrote in Notebook I, 'and not for any eyes but those of my own family.' He may

[1] D. L. to Freeman, 9.i.1850 (quoted in *Family Letters*, ed. Schapera, vol. i, pp. 17 f.).

[2] Cf., for example, D. F. Ellenberger, *History of the Basuto* (1912), pp. 307–14, and E. W. Smith, *Great Lion of Bechuanaland* (1957), pp. 375–406 *passim*.

[3] Cf. above, p. ix.

have been thinking specifically of Mrs Moffat's letter copied into it, of the doubts he expresses about the propriety of accepting Native gifts of cattle, and possibly also of entries like that in which he calls the Chief Justice of the Cape Colony 'an infamous hypocrite'.[1] Comparison of the contents with what he subsequently published shows too that in *Travels* he omitted the occasional prayers and toned down considerably some of his reflections on religion and death. Otherwise the journal seems to contain little of an intimate personal nature that he did not also mention in writing to his relatives and some of his friends.

It does, however, reveal more markedly than elsewhere his conviction that in all he did he was divinely guided and protected. A good, if rather pathetic, example is his attempt to answer Mrs Moffat's criticism by listing painstakingly the many incidents, some comparatively trivial, which were to him 'distinct evidences that our undertaking was smiled upon by Providence'. Of the hardships and deprivations he undoubtedly experienced he says relatively little, except when describing his attacks of fever. It is nevertheless evident that on his second visit to the MaKololo he was deeply distressed by the horrors of bloodshed and slavery to which he was an unwilling witness, felt acutely the lack of European companions, and was occasionally filled with forebodings about his own fate. But he was sustained by the belief that 'If God has accepted my service, then my life is charmed till my work is done.' His sense of vocation is emphasized in such statements as 'What an unspeakable mercy it is to be permitted to engage in this most honourable and holy work' and 'Had I a thousand lives they would all be dedicated to him who loved us and gave himself for us', and the spirit in which he sought to labour is reflected in his simple prayer, 'If success attend me, grant me humility; if failure, resignation to thy will.'[2]

In view of these and many similar passages, one can hardly agree with Professor Debenham's judgment: 'We are accustomed to say that David Livingstone was turned by chance from being a missionary into an explorer and geographer. I think that is the wrong way to put it; he was a geographer from the first and by nature, and became a mis-

[1] Cf. below, p. 82.   [2] Cf. below, pp. 132, 108, 111.

sionary as a sort of aside, or *en route*.'[1] Livingstone's own words provide perhaps the best answer. 'I am', he wrote to his sister Agnes in February 1850, 'a missionary heart and soul. God had an only son, and he was a missionary and a physician. A poor poor imitation of Him I am or rather wish to be. In this service I hope to live ; in it I wish to die.'[2]

(iii)

Together with other manuscript material, the notebooks comprising the present journal were presented in 1954 by Livingstone's great-grand-daughter, Miss D. L. Bruce, to the Central African Archives (now National Archives of Rhodesia and Nyasaland). Mr E. E. Burke, Chief Records Management Officer of the Archives, has kindly supplied me with the following description of them :[3]

Notebook I. Full calf, end-papers and edges marbled, fitted with a lock clasp, $7 \times 4\frac{1}{4}$ in. 355 pages, pale blue paper ruled feint. Inscribed on spine, 'Private Journal 1851-2-3'. Entries in ink. On the verso of the front end-paper, an inscription ; facing this, another inscription.[4] Pp. 1–353, the journal ; pp. 354–5, a list of the contents. Rear end-papers : a printed cutting of a letter entitled 'Discoveries in South East Africa', by Livingstone, pasted in.

Notebook II. Three-quarter vellum, end-papers and edges marbled, fitted with a lock clasp, $7 \times 4\frac{1}{2}$ in. 358 pages, pale blue paper ruled feint. Inscribed on front cover, 'Private Journal'. Entries in ink. Inside front board, a printed cutting of Thomas Hood's 'Bridge of Sighs' pasted in ; facing this, an inscription.[5] Pp. 1–330, the journal ; pp. 331–48, blank ; pp. 349–54, various notes ; pp. 355–8, a list of the contents. Between p. 358 and the rear end-paper is pasted a licence from the Resident Magistrate, Cape Town, authorizing Livingstone to remove 'from Cape Town to the Sebetwane country about 200 miles north of the Lake Ngami Seventy

---

[1] *The Way to Ilala*, p. 16.   [2] *Family Letters*, ed. Schapera, vol. ii, p. 74.
[3] I saw the notebooks at Salisbury (S. Rhodesia) in 1956, but as their publication had not yet been decided upon did not examine them carefully. My text is taken from photographic copies of the MS.
[4] These inscriptions are given fully on p. xxv below.   [5] Cf. below, p. 296.

five pounds of Gun Powder, One Hundred pounds of Lead and Three Guns'; dated 1852 May 22.

Many extracts from the journal were published in W. G. Blaikie's *Personal Life of David Livingstone* (1880). Some of the entries describing the first journey to the MaKololo were also quoted by Oswell's biographer (1900), and more recently brief extracts have appeared in biographies of Livingstone by G. Seaver (1957) and M. Gelfand (1957). The present volume, however, is the first in which the journal is published in full.

I have retained Livingstone's own spelling throughout, but to facilitate reading have occasionally normalized his punctuation and broken up some of his lengthier paragraphs. I have also supplied (in brackets) words inadvertently omitted, for example when starting a new page, and have likewise added transcriptions into the modern orthography, and translations into English, of the two long Tswana texts that he recorded ('Sebetwane's song' and Sechele's letter to Moffat). With these exceptions, the original style and wording of the journal remain unaltered.

However, again in order to facilitate reading, I have divided the main narrative into seven chapters, with titles supplied by myself, and have relegated to appendixes the intrusive matter in Notebook I (Maclear's 'Observations on Latitude and Longitude' and the 'extract from another journal') and the miscellaneous notes contained in the final pages of Notebook II. In each chapter I have also broken up the narrative into sections, following in the main Livingstone's own lists of contents, from which the appropriate headings have all been taken. The effect has been to give the present version a form not possessed by the original, but I hope this departure from normal editorial practice will be condoned if it succeeds in its purpose of making the text more convenient to consult.

(iv)

For permission to publish the journal I am deeply grateful to Mr V. W. Hiller, O.B.E., until recently Director of the National Archives, and to his successor, Mr T. W. Baxter. They were also kind enough to let me have a photographic copy from which to work, sent me similar copies of other Livingstone material in their custody, and responded generously to various queries that arose from time to time. I am indebted also to Rev. A. Sandilands and Dr E. Westphal for assistance in dealing with the Tswana texts, Mr E. Kedourie for translating and commenting on the Arabic inscription (p. 227), Miss I. Fletcher (Librarian of the London Missionary Society) for access to unpublished letters in the L.M.S. archives and for many other favours, Mr D. H. Varley (Chief Librarian, South African Public Library, Cape Town) for copies of Livingstone's Native vocabularies and of extracts from old South African periodicals, Dr H. F. Wilson for the very kind loan of Livingstone's MS journal for 1853–6, and Professor C. R. Boxer, F.B.A., for guidance to sources of information about Silva Pôrto and Angola. It is a pleasure to be able to record here my sincere thanks for the great help they have all given.

AUTHOR'S NOTE

[The following inscriptions, in Notebook I, occur respectively on the verso of the front end-paper, and on the page facing it. The second is a quotation from Coleridge's poem, *The Ancient Mariner*.]

In case of my being cut off, I beg those into whose hands this journal may fall to give it to my children. It is not intended for publication in any form, and not for any eyes but those of my own family. Please respect this.

D.L.

He prayeth well, who loveth well,
Both man, and bird, and beast ;
He prayeth best who loveth best,
All things both great and small ;
For the dear God who loveth us,
He made and loveth all.

I

FIRST JOURNEY TO
SEBITOANE'S COUNTRY 1851

Reasons for Leaving the Bakwains[1]

The Bakwains[2] tried for three successive years to raise corn on the banks of the Kolobeng but found the soil too spongy. The moisture was retained for only a short period after it had rained and the plants soon died. Some peculiarity too in the spot on which the station was built prevented as much rain falling there as on the ajacent country. To these unfavourable circumstances were superadded a series of remarkably dry years, the last or 1850–51 exceeding all the preceding in extent of country over which the drought prevailed, the Bamangwato, Botaoana, and the tribes in Sebitoane's country[3] suffering its severity as well as the Bakwains. The necessity for removal from the Kolobeng became apparent to both the people and ourselves. Most of the Bakwains inclined to proceed Northwards to Logageñ,[4] but a few including Sechele thought Limaoe, which is situated 8 miles higher up the Kolobeng than the old station, more eligible, the rocks of Limaoe[5] offering superior defences in case

[1] In substance and occasionally even wording this opening section echoes a letter D.L. wrote to Dr Tidman of the L.M.S. from Boatlanama on 30 April 1851 (cf. Chamberlin, pp. 145 f.). Some of the allusions suggest, however, that it was completed after he had been to Sebetwane's country.

[2] BaKwena, then living at Kolobeng (approx. 24° 45′ S., 25° 35′ E.) under Chief Sechele I (ruled 1831–92). D.L. had been with them as a missionary since 1845.

[3] The BaNgwato, northern neighbours of the BaKwena, were then living at Shoshong (approx. 23° S., 26° 30′ E., though the site of their town was changed several times); the BaTawana, an offshoot of the BaNgwato, lived in the vicinity of Lake Ngami; and Sebetwane was chief, c.1823–51, of the MaKololo, who after migrating from the far south had established themselves (c.1840) as the dominant tribe in Barotseland and neighbouring districts.

[4] Immediately adjacent to Molepolole (24° 26′ S., 25° 36′ E.), the present Kwena capital. Logageng means 'at the cave'; the cave itself, 'named Lepelole', is described in *Travels*, pp. 124 f.

[5] Dimawe, to which the BaKwena did in fact move during D.L.'s absence (cf. below, p. 78).

1

of an attack by the Boers, and the soil being red presenting the hope of being able to retain the moisture.

The proposal for removal had our entire approval, but the question arose as to whether it was our duty to follow them, and undergo the labour of building a new station. The Bakwains offered to build houses for Mebaloe[1] and ourselves if we should consent to go to the Limaoe.* But the Kolobeng was drying up even opposite the new location. If we sat down near the water we should be about two miles from the people. If we went near the town we should find great difficulty in procuring supplies of water and our healths would probably suffer. We should not even when near the water be able to raise any vegetables. And as there is no certainty of the people being able to raise corn themselves, there is a probability of their being compelled to remove thence again. This probability is heightened by the very threatening aspect of the Boers of late. They are more determined than ever to reduce all the tribes into subjection, and during our visit to Sebitoane they have given the Bakwains no rest.[2] The Bakwain mind even had we remained would not have been in a state favourable for attending to instruction. And as God in his good Providence had opened up for us an extensive region largely populated, I think there can be no doubt but that it is our duty to follow in the path He has indicated, although that involves separation from the people for whom I have laboured for nearly six years and of whom I endulged many sanguine hopes. I have much affection for them, and though I part from them I do not relinquish the hope that they will yet turn to Him to whose mercy and love they have often been invited. The seed of the living Word will not perish.

---

* This would involve less expense but just the same amount of manual labour for me. The men would be furnished but the buildings would be erected by my hands. [D.L.]

---

[1] A Native evangelist, originally from Kuruman, who was one of D.L.'s assistants. It was through his intervention that D.L. was saved when attacked by a wounded lion in 1844 (cf. *Travels*, pp. 11 ff.). He is mentioned repeatedly in *Letters*; cf. especially vol. i, p. 90 n.

[2] Leyland recorded in September 1851 a recent Boer threat to attack Sechele 'at his new town' (*Adventures*, 1866, pp. 204 f.).

Incidents in the First Journey to Sebitoane

I shall now proceed to note down some of the incidents of our journey to the country of Sebitoane. It being remembered that the journey was undertaken with the belief that it was our duty to embrace any favourable opening that might present itself, and certain hills mentioned by the people of Sebitoane who came to Kolobeng[1] offering a prospect of a salubrious residence for my family during the first season, I did not intend to return so soon as we have been compelled to do.

We left Kolobeng on the 24th of April 1851. Slept under the cave of Lepelole. The wolf only left the upper jaw of our sheep.[2] On the 26th passed Kopong[3] & got water at pond of Kholemarue.[4] Country excessively dry. Wherever we find water the place is remembered ever afterwards. Spent Sunday at the Pond of Sesasechoe[5] and thence went on to Boatlanama.[6] Left the usual road in order to get water at the Pond Selenye.[7] The water of this pond was very muddy. The blue matter held in solution was not deposited by alum.

Mr Oswel[8] in the mean time had digged wells at Lopepe[9] for us, and nearly lost his life by a lion while waiting for us. Four lions were exceedingly troublesome during several nights. This induced him to go out on horseback in the morn-

---

[1] Hearing of the attempts already made by D.L. and others to get to his country, Sebetwane had sent gifts of cattle to various chiefs along the route, 'with a request to each to assist the white men to reach him' (*Travels*, p. 77). His messengers came to Kolobeng in September 1850. They were still there when D.L. went to Kuruman in November, but not when he returned in March, Sechele having allowed them to depart; consequently he was unable to use them as guides (17.X.1851 Tidman; cf. *Letters*, vol. ii, p. 103).

[2] This incident is not mentioned elsewhere. 'Wolf' is an Africanderism for 'hyena'.

[3] A stream which the old road crossed about 17 miles north of Molepolole.

[4] Kgolomadue, 24° 6′ S., 25° 40′ E.

[5] Not identified.

[6] A well-known watering-place, 23° 37′ S., 25° 48′ E.

[7] Selinye, 23° 26′ S., 26° 1′ E. (GSGS 2871 Transvaal).

[8] William Cotton Oswell (1818–93), formerly in the Madras civil service; first visited Bechuanaland on a hunting trip in 1845, accompanied D.L. to Lake Ngami in 1849, and was his lifelong friend and benefactor. Cf. *William Cotton Oswell*, by W. E. Oswell, 2 vols., 1900, and Oswell's chapters (II–V) in *Big Game Shooting*, ed. C. Phillipps-Wolley, 1894, vol. i, pp. 26–153.

[9] Lephephe, 23° 20′ S., 25° 48′ E.

ing after them. His dogs having brought one to bay in a bush, he advanced in order to bring it within view, but the furious animal rushed forward, and the horse wheeling round brought his body into a 'wait a bit' bush.[1] This tore him out of his saddle. The horse springing away from under him, probably with a jerk in consequence of the talons of the lion tearing his hinder parts, made him fall on his head and stunned him. When he recovered his consciousness the dogs were still holding the lioness at bay about 30 yards from the spot on which he stood, and his eyes being dim he missed the beast with his shot. I thank God for preserving his life. May He have mercy on him and save him. When we reached Mashue[2] we found him waiting for us. Had very kindly taken the trouble to clean out the watering places for us. This kindness enabled us to water at once and proceed in the direction of Sekhomi, of whose sickness we had previous knowledge.[3] Mr O. went by way of Lobatane.[4]

Reached Sekhomi on the 8th [of May]. He had a large ulcer on the pit of the stomach, the result of an abscess having burst there. Administered medicine. He seemed very friendly, and treated us very kindly. He has a bad name, but we have always experienced kindness at his hands. He has in his intercourse with strangers been more sinned against than his detractors like to say. Those who have behaved well to him, as Mr O. &c, have no complaint to make. Counted the number of huts, but the nature of the ground on which I stood prevented me seeing all. Those within my range of vision amounted to 932, but there is a village of the Makalaka of Moloi[5] in the vicinity & I believe too another of the

---

[1] *Zizyphus mucronata*. Its popular name is due to its thorns, which tend to hook whatever brushes against them.

[2] Mashuwe, 23° 5′ S., 26° 4′ E. (GSGS 2871 Transvaal).

[3] At the end of March, 'A great sensation was caused at Kolobeng, by a rumour that Sechoma . . . had been poisoned by some of his own tribe; this, however, proved a false report. He had been seriously ill, but was now recovering' (Leyland, p. 128; cf. *Letters*, vol. ii, pp. 125, 129). Sekgoma I was chief of the BaNgwato 1834–57, 1858–66, 1873–5.

[4] Lobotani, 22° 59′ S., 25° 44′ E. (GSGS 2871 Transvaal).

[5] Chief of the BaTalaote, a tribe of BaKalanga (Tswana 'MaKalaka'), who had migrated to Shoshong from the N.E. some 20 years previously. They are still subject to the BaNgwato. Cf. Schapera, *Ethnic Composition of Tswana Tribes*, 1952, pp. 80 f.

Bapalleng.[1] A section of his people are Makalaka who have lately fled from under the rod of Mosilikatse.[2] Their language is different from the dialects with which I am familiar. They sow their corn in ridges and have some other peculiarities.

Having held a service in the Town we engaged one of Sekhomi's men to go with us instead of a Mokwain who fell sick and was obliged to return, and it was a happy circumstance that we did so, for he was of essential service to us afterwards. Reached Mr Oswel at Letlochwe,[3] and there being no water at Kanne[4] we remained two days at the former place.

14th. Passed Kanné after having found water at a pond called Sekemkené.[5] The pleasantest music in Africa is that made by the merry frogs, Tantalus like up to their chins in water. Esop was an African, and that is the reason he felt compassion for the frogs and put a tongue into their heads which speaks as much to the purpose as Balaam's ass did. 'What's fun to you is death to us'. No wonder Esop remembered them.[6] He must have heard them often as we have saying, 'What's fun to us, is life to you'. There is however a large frog called Matlametlo[7] which makes a noise where no water is near.

15th, 16th in the desert, and in the evening of 17 we reached Nkaoana,[8] a deep well in tufa by the side of a pan. There are several such in the vicinity. We think nothing of being three days without water, now that we know the way, but how much anxiety the same tract of country cost us

[1] BaPhaleng, a tribe of BaKgalagadi (early BaTswana) found at Shoshong by the BaNgwato and reduced to servitude; cf. Schapera, *op. cit.*, p. 72.

[2] The Tswana name for Mzilikazi, chief 1821–68 of the AmaNdebele (Tswana 'MaTebele'). An offshoot of the Zulu, they had first settled in the Transvaal and then migrated (*c.*1838) to the region now known after them as Matabeleland, S. Rhodesia. There they conquered and oppressed the indigenous Natives, mostly MaKalaka (whose language belongs to the Shona division of the Bantu family).

[3] Letlhotswe, not shown on modern maps; according to D.L. (*Travels*, pp. 151, 684) in Lat. 22° 38′ S., about 20 miles beyond Shoshong.

[4] Kane, also called Tlhabala; 22° 28′ S., 26° 20′ E.

[5] Not identified.

[6] D.L. is referring to Aesop's fable, 'The Boys and the Frogs' (cf. *Everyman's Library* edition, p. 74). For Balaam's ass, cf. Numbers 22: 22–35.

[7] Plural of *letlametlo*, bull-frog (*Rana Adspersa*).

[8] Nkowane Pan, 21° 55′ S., 25° 53′ E.

during our first trip, and how much the oxen suffered in consequence of being obliged to travel in the sun.[1] Mr Oswel's men opened another well, which from long disuse had become filled up. The droughts in this country are reported to be periodical or come round in cycles. How many years are required to complete a cycle it is impossible to know. But 1839 was a remarkably wet year, and many fountains which had dried up burst forth afresh after the copious rains. This well on being reopened afforded an abundant supply for all our cattle.

20th. Left Nkaoana. An old man informs us that the Natloa or Shoa river situated to the East of Nkaoane ends in a number of salt pans. The Shashe runs through the mountainous part of the Makalaka country and falls into the Limpopo.[2] Tlole is the chief of the Mashona.[3] Archbishop Whately & Bobby Fitzgerald, English sportsmen alias amateur butchers, shoot fieldfares.[4]

At Kokonyane.[5] Mr Oswel again opened the wells. Though I can't repay I may record with gratitude his kindness, so that if spared to look upon these my private memoranda in future years proper emotions may ascend to Him who inclined his heart to shew so much friendship.

27th. Left Nchokotsa[6] and proceeded N. to Maritsa.[7] A party of traders had preceded us by a few days, and being desirous of going to Sebitoane's they offered Tsapoe the Bakurutse chief 3 or 4 guns if he would furnish them with

[1] This happened during the journey to Lake Ngami in 1849; cf. *Travels*, pp. 59 f.

[2] The Nata R., rising near Figtree (S. Rhodesia), is called 'Shua' just before it enters the N.E. corner of the 'Makarikari Depression (or Great Salt Pan)' in the northern Kalahari. The Shashi, rising a little farther west, flows in the opposite direction and, as D.L.'s informant correctly stated, is a tributary of the Limpopo.

[3] In 1835 Andrew Smith was similarly told that 'Toli' was 'king' of the MaKalaka (*Diary*, vol. ii, p. 214). The name suggests 'Tuli' (in Tuli River, Tuli Block, etc.), but I have found no other mention of this man. MaShona is a generic name for the Native peoples of Southern Rhodesia (excluding MaTebele), of whom the MaKalaka are the western division.

[4] Richard Whately (1787–1863) was Archbishop of Dublin. The rest of the allusion I cannot explain; it may have been prompted by a newspaper report.

[5] Kokonyane Pits, 21° 26' S., 25° 37' E.

[6] Chukutsa Pan, 21° 17' S., 25° E.

[7] On modern maps called 'Madista', 21° 2' S., 25° 9' E.; correctly Maditsa (after a local Kalaka headman.)

guides. But he declined.[1] The gun of a Bamangwato man called Kamati[2] was accidentally broken after he parted with the traders. Coming to us at Nchokotsa he offered to give us a guide to lead us Northwards instead of going to the Tamunaklé[3] if we should give him one of our muskets in exchange for his broken one. To this we gladly consented, as the course he proposed was shorter than the other and it would enable us to reach Sebitoane before the trading party. This was of great importance, as first impressions are always strongest. The main spring of the gun of another Bamangwato man called Paku was broken. He volunteered to go with us as interpreter to the Bushmen if I should mend his gun. Mr Oswel furnished a gun for Kamati, and though we subsequently found that he had no power among the Bushmen to whom we were going, as a link in the chain of events which led us to go directly North he is entitled to some share of gratitude. We ascertained too that the traders had found a man at Tsapoe's who was left by Mahale (Sebitoane's messenger to Kolobeng) sick, but declined his guidance, thinking him a fool. We found however from Mahale that he would have been an excellent guide.[4] God seemed kindly to reserve the honour of reaching Sebitoané first for us. I thank him for his unmerited favour.

Crossed the dry bed of the Zouga[5] about 15 miles N.N.E.

[1] Tsapo was chief of the BaKhurutshe living along the Botletle River at or near Mopipi, 21° 8' S., 24° 51' E. The 'party of traders' consisted of J. H. Wilson, a trader at Kolobeng who had accompanied D.L. and Oswell to Lake Ngami in 1849; Samuel Howard Edwards (1827–1922), son of D.L.'s former colleague at Mabotsa and subsequently a well-known pioneer in South Central Africa; and the naturalist J. Leyland, author of *Adventures in the Far Interior of South Africa* (1866). Leyland does not record the incident mentioned by D.L., but says (pp. 152 f.) that soon after leaving Chukutsa on 18 May he and his companions met some of Sebetwane's people, who told them only that the direct road to that chief was impossible for wagons owing to drought and tsetse fly. The party proceeded as planned to Lake Ngami. Leyland then returned to the south, while Wilson and Edwards went on to Sebetwane's.

[2] 'Kamati or Kobati' (15.xi.1851 Oswell), 'Kabatie' (Chapman, vol. i, p. 97); owner of a cattle-post in that region.

[3] Thamalakane River, flowing towards Lake Ngami from the north-east.

[4] D.L. presumably heard this after reaching Sebetwane's country. Mahale, whom he described in 1860 as one of the most influential MaKololo (*The Matabele Mission*, ed. Wallis, p. 121), was still alive in 1883, 'and continued to take to himself a large share of the credit of bringing both the missionary and the trader into the country' (Arnot, ed. *Travels*, p. 433).

[5] Nowadays known as the Botletle River.

of Nchokotsa. The bed was stony, and there were small dykes of stones in it which are used for catching fish. Road hard, country terribly scorched. Reached Kubi or Koobe[1] on 27th. Several wells of fine fresh water, at which great numbers of game drink. This water is about 25 miles from Nchokotsa.

28th. Left Koobe at Midday, and in the evening 12 miles distant arrived at the well of the Mochweere tree.[2] This well is situated in a rocky part, and the water is strongly impregnated with sulphuretted Hydrogen gas.

On 29th still going nearly due North we entered on the salt pan of Ntwetwe,[3] which is 15 miles in diameter and about 100 long. At one part it is soft, and the wheels sinking through the dry crust on the surface up to the naves rendered it difficult to get them extricated. The crust breaking before the wheel, the weight was equal to a plough 2000 lbs weight working at subsoil ploughing of 2 feet deep. This would prove a barrier in wet weather, and indeed we were informed that it is in the wet season a barrier to men on foot. At each of these saltpans there is a spring of brackish water which may have been more abundant in former years. The continual deposit from these in the course of centuries would account for the thin efflorescence of salt and lime which covers them. But there are some of them covered over [with] a large quantity of recent shells & these may have been left by the Zouga, when it flowed into them. One salt pan called Cuantsa[4] has a deposit of salt nearly 2 inches in thickness on its surface. It being one of the lowest, the water of the Zouga with the salt of the other pans may have evaporated on it. The pans though apparently flat have an inclination to the N.E. After rain the water may be observed flowing in that direction.

Some aloes growing near our outspan place. Distance 23 miles, N & by East.

[1] Not on modern maps, though mentioned by several early travellers. Located in *Travels*, p. 684, at 20° 53′ S., 24° 52′ E., but the longitude is probably incorrect (on Passarge's map, 1904, it is 25° E.).

[2] *Combretum imberbe* (Tswana *motswiri*). I cannot identify the place. Tabler (1956, p. 38) suggests Odanakumadona, which, however, seems too far west (20° 53′ S., 24° 45′ E.).

[3] The western half of the Makarikari Depression.

[4] Not on modern maps; 'about ten miles to the north-east of Orapa', between Lotlhakane and Chukutsa (*Travels*, p. 159).

(Ipecacuanha rubbed on scorpion bite relieves pain. Watch key pressed firmly on the puncture extracts the poison. Strychnia is used by Irulloi in India[1] for snake bites.

Fever in India believed by the Natives to arise from the waters which they designate heavy and light. Some waters flowing over granite cannot be drunk for two days by any one without an attack of fever. The seeds of a certain kind of Lotus sown in a certain part produced it where it had not been known before.)

30th. Reach Tlomtla,[2] the cattle post of Moachoe. Here we found that we could not have Bushmen, in consequence of our having given the gun to Kamati and not to Moachoe, the latter being the true owner of the country.[3] His father was chief of a small tribe which on the occurrence of a marriage with the chief's daughter became incorporated with the Bamangwato. Here Moremi[4] stood boldly forward and advocated our cause, stating among other reasons for our being supplied with guides the entire approbation of Sekhomi to our proceeding to Sebitoané. After producing another gun it was arranged that a Bushman guide should go with us. We spent Sunday at Tlomtla. Met about 40 Bush & Bechuana, who seemed attentive. Then on Monday started for Horoye's.[5] About 12 miles beyond Tlomtla came to the spring or Lecha of Rapesh or Kiadjara.[6] On the west of it there is another called Kueta or Mohonono, on the East another

[1] The Irula of the Nilgiri Hills. Called 'Irulurs' in *Oswell*, vol. i, p. 151, where they are described as a jungle tribe, equal to the Bushmen 'in knowledge of wild animals and their ways'. (The other statements enclosed by D.L. in parentheses were presumably also derived from Oswell.).

[2] Called Thumtha by Chapman (vol. i, p. 64); probably at or near Tshoroga, 20° 21′ S., 25° 9′ E.

[3] Moatswi Kgomo was Sekgoma's 'overseer' (*modisa*) in the Botletle district. He belonged to the BaKubung (an early offshoot of the BaRolong), whose current tradition of how they joined the BaNgwato confirms D.L.'s version (Schapera, *Ethnic Composition*, pp. 70 f.).

[4] The man D.L. had taken on at Shoshong (cf. p. 5).

[5] D.L. describes him as a Bushman (*Travels*, p. 165). But Chapman speaks of 'Goroge, a nephew of Sekomi ... who has the superintendence of the district of the Madenisata [Bushmen], as other subordinate chieftains ... have over other districts' (vol. i, pp. 88, 93). Moatswi had a son named Goroje ('Horoye'), to whom Chapman is obviously referring. D.L. may therefore be mistaken, though it is conceivable that there were two men, one perhaps named after the other.

[6] Probably Segara, 20° 13′ S., 25° 18′ E. *Lecha* is a Tswana word meaning 'salt pan, shallow lake, vlei'.

called Mokolani or Kunehu. Oxen drank abundantly at these and at others around Tlomtla called Pitseperi.[1]

Morning of Tuesday we reach Horoye's spring called Kounjarrah,[2] about 11 miles beyond Rapesh. The whole of the ajacent country is hard, and covered over with Mopane[3] and Boabob trees. The underlying rock is white tufa, and springs called Macha[4] abound in it. There are so many to the East of Horoye's place the country recieves the name of Matlomaganyana or the 'Links', as of a chain. As the water in these springs comes independantly of the rains which fall in the district, are they not supplied by percolation from the numerous rivers in Sebitoané's country? Mosilikatse's cattle were reported to be feeding in Matlomaganyana.[5] On what rock does this tufa lie?

The Mopane tree leaves afford habitations for myriads of a small striped greenish insect not much larger than a pin's head.[6] It builds a minute dwelling shaped like a limpet's shell on the leaf of the mopane, of a sweet gummy substance. The people collect this gum in large quantities and use it as food. The boabob attains a circumference of from 50 to 70 feet, but the wood is very soft and I suppose even the very largest specimens to be, compared with some of the historical yew & oak trees of England, only big bloated babies.

The people of Horoye and indeed all the Bushmen were strong well fed looking men. The game abounds and they are reported to follow it in its migrations and live on the zebras gnus &c as if they were their domestic cattle.

Furnished with a Bushman guide from Horoye's, and with a glad heart that our difficulties had so far been removed or overcome, we set forward on Wedensday the 4th [June],

[1] Kueta is obviously Gweta, 20° 12′ S., 25° 16′ E., and Kunehu may be Konequa Pan, 20° 22′ S., 25° 22′ E. 'Mohonono' and 'mokolani' are Tswana plant names (for *Terminalia sericea* and *Hyphaene ventricosa* respectively). Pitseperi I cannot identify; the name means 'two zebras'.

[2] Kaungara Pan, approx. 20° 3′ S., 25° 17′ E.

[3] *Colophospermum mopane.*

[4] Plural of *lecha*. The whole district is often called by the locative form Macheng, 'region of salt pans'.

[5] Shown on modern maps as Matlamanyane, 19° 32′ S., 25° 57′ E.; but, as D.L. indicates, the name (derived from Tswana *lomaganya*, 'to join together') applies to a region rather than a specific place.

[6] Identified in *Travels*, p. 164, as 'a species of Psylla, a genus of small very active Homoptera'.

and after travelling about ten miles we reached Maila or Tsonarrah.[1] Found a Makalaka man called Kaisa who had fled from Mosilikatse living here.[2] Tetemba or Tlole is chief of the Mashona.[3] These people are interesting, for they are always spoken of by the other tribes as superior to them both in the arts of peace & war and they always prefer the former unless attacked.

Turn to the West at Midday and after travelling other ten miles we reached Unko or Gumkirreh.[4] Water from another of these springs excellent. Many buffaloes drink there.

Observed Altitude of Sun 5th June, 94° 40'.
Dec[lination]. 22° 31' Lat. 19° 54'

Friday the 6th. Pass through ten miles of thick bush and heavy sand, and next morning after going 5 miles more we reached Kamakama,[5] a fine pool of rain water standing near the well, which was quite dry. Leaving Kamakama we passed by a dried out leca or stoney depression similar to the other springs called liuli lipepe[6]—a long tract of bush, then three miles of a perfectly level and bushless flat covered with very short grass, the distance in all being about 12 miles. Found a beehive in an anthill, fine white combs.

On Saturday the 7th passed through 10 miles of well wooded country and reached a chain of ponds in a depression like the bed of an antient river. I counted 15 of them. There was a village of Bushmen near. The headman was named Mokuchoane[7] and the locality itself Gumtsouarah or Goosimjarrah.[8]

The Bush language is the most difficult of all human tongues. It abounds in monosyllables and Klicks. Hurree= iron, yee=a tree, jee=the fire, 'tsaa=water, Tsouga vulture, ata

---

[1] Tsaugara Pan, 19° 56' S., 25° 14' E.

[2] Chapman, who calls him 'Khaetsa' (and the locality 'Zoutharra'), says that his village 'mustered about 300 souls' (vol. i, p. 66).

[3] Cf. p. 6.

[4] Probably Kumsedisha Pan, 19° 36' S., 25° 5' E.

[5] Khama-Khama; located by D.L. at 19° 53' S., 24° 49' E. (*JRGS*, 1854, p. 302), on modern maps at 20° 2' S., 24° 59' E.

[6] Diolo diphephe, 'white ant heaps'. Not named on modern maps; called Lulupèpè by Chapman, who describes it (vol. ii, p. 59) as 'an extensive plain, sometimes covered with low bushes and white ant-hills, in other places with grass only'.

[7] Mokhutshwane; a fairly common Tswana (not Bushman) name, meaning 'a short person'.

[8] Not identified.

= yes, Quae = a man, Mbee = a horse, Tōra or Gama = God.[1]

What a wonderful people the Bushmen are. Always merry and laughing, and never tell lies wantonly like the Bechuana. They have more of the appearance of worship than any of the Bechuana. When will these dwellers in the wilderness bow down before their Lord? No man seems to care for the Bushman's soul. Often wished I knew their language, but never more than when we travelled with our Bushman guide Shobo. He could speak very few words of Sitchuana,[2] and these he frequently used in a wrong sense. When we enquired where the next water was his invariable answer was, 'Metse cotle, naga eotle', all water, all country.[3]

The most difficult part of the whole journey lay between Goosimjarrah & the river Mababe. The first 20 miles were heavy sand and thick bush. The axes were kept going constantly, and the course cut through was so winding we could scarcely ever see the front oxen. The trees were mohonono chiefly. This tree is remarkably sweet to the taste and elephants are very fond of it. On Monday the 9th[4] we were in 19° 38'. On Tuesday Shobo wandered, and as he followed the paths made by the Elephants in passing from one clump of mohonono bush to another our course was zigzag enough. We travelled chiefly at night, and felt contented when we had our heads towards the Northern Bear or Charles' Wain, but it was annoying when we found Shobo turned away round to the Southern Cross. Not a bird or insect could be seen during these three dreary days. As far as the eye could reach it was a vast plain of low thorny scrub. It was perfectly still. On the third day a bird chirped in a bush and the dog began to bark at it. On Wedensday the 11th Obs. Alt. ☉ 94° 56', Lat 19° 16'. We had been travelling for about 65 miles from Goosimjarrah in a Norwesterly direction. Shobo refused to go on at night and to our coaxing he replied with

---

[1] In the orthography used by Miss D. F. Bleek, *A Bushman Dictionary* (1956), D.L.'s list would read as follows (the symbols / and // represent 'clicks'): iron, /uri; tree, *jü* (*j* as in English *y*); fire, /e; water, *tsaa*; yes, *ata*; man, *kwe*; horse, *bie*; God, *thora*, //*gama*. The only word not identified is 'tsouga'.

[2] SeTswana, the language of the BaTswana.

[3] In the modern orthography, *metse tsotlhe, naga yotlhe*. The former should really be *metse aotlhe*, but the error may be an example of Shobo's broken speech.

[4] MS. has 19th, presumably a slip of the pen.

a good natured smile, naga eotle metse cotle, Shobo kia robega.[1] Do you know where you are, Shobo? Perhaps we are at Bitale,[2] perhaps somewhere else, I don't know; and then double himself up like a dog on his side to sleep, leaving us to look on in utter dumfounderment at his coolness.

At last we began to observe the presence of birds, then the footprints of animals, particularly of the Rhinoceros, which we knew never lives far from water, then a broad footpath made by animals in going to drink; so we unyoked the oxen and put them on the path. They went off at a hard trot and never stopped till they reached the water in the River Mababe or Dodobe.[3] Some of them diverged into another path, and we have reason to suspect that they were bitten by the Tsetse in consequence. We never saw the animals so much distressed by thirst, though we have seen them go longer than three days without a drop of water. Mr O. & I remained with the waggons while all the people went after the oxen. As is always the case the children drank more than usual as the water became less, and their mother sat crying over them as she saw the precious fluid drawing to the bottom of the bottle. It was no wonder. We did not know for certain that the men would return with water, and the very idea of little ones perishing before one's eyes for thirst is dreadful.

On Thursday morning Mr O. & I went forward in search of the people, and after walking three or four miles met them returning. No one knows the value of water till he is deprived of it. We never need any spirits to qualify it or prevent an immense draught of it from doing us harm. I have drank water swarming with insects, thick with mud and putrid from Rhinoceros urine and buffaloes' dung, and no stinted draughts of it either, yet never felt any inconvenience from it. Have those who find that good water does them harm not wasted[4] their stomachs by fermented and other liquors so

---

[1] In *Travels*, p. 79, Shobo's reply is rendered as: 'No water, all country only; Shobo sleeps; he breaks down; country only'. '*Kia robega*' actually means 'I am (become) broken', but Shobo may have been trying to say, *Ke robetse*, 'I am sleeping', hence D.L.'s use of both verbs. The same confusion between *robega* and *robetse* is quoted by Chapman (vol. ii, pp. 74 f.) as an example of the 'comical' SeTswana spoken 'in these parts'.　　　　[2] Not identified.

[3] A watercourse in the general vicinity of 19° S., 24° E.; connects the Ngoga River (a branch of the Okovango) with the Mababe Depression to the north-east.

[4] 'washed' (Gelfand, p. 51).

that they are incapable of bearing their natural fluid? Are their stomachs in the same state as diseased eyes which cannot bear the stimulus of light?

Moyeiye[1] chief lived near to the spot where cattle found water, his name Morotse.

12th. After the people returned with the cattle we turned from our Westerly course to the N.N.E. and went parallel with the river. Reached a Bushman village. A very old Bushman called Shamayama came to see us. Lat. 19° 16'.

13th. Went about two miles and came to the village of Chombo or MoroaMadzane.[2] The people are a portion of the Banajoa.[3] They live on the banks of a swamp 10 or 11 miles in breadth into which the Mababi flows. It contains a great deal of reed but much more Tsitla,[4] the root of which being full of starch affords a nutritious meal of which they make porridge. The root tsitla or Tseetla is excellent when roasted in the ashes, and those who have access to it are never so miserably lean as the inhabitants of the Desert are.

The people of Chombo build their huts with a sort of second storey in which they sleep. When Mosquitoes are troublesome they make a fire below and lie in the smoke.[5] The insect must be very numerous on the swamp, but at the time we passed there was a sharp frost & we were not troubled by them.

Chombo volunteered to be our guide to Sebitoané and informed us that there were two paths, one of which was short viz. only three days, but it had Tsetse, the other was longer but we should be three nights or four days without water and no tsetse. Understanding from him that we could

---

[1] The BaYeei, called MaKoba by the BaTswana, were immigrants from N.W. Rhodesia who had settled in Ngamiland early in the 18th century. There they divided into many small groups, each with its own 'chief' (like Morotse).

[2] 'The head man of this village, Majáne, seemed a little wanting in ability; but had had wit enough to promote a younger member of the family to the office. This person . . . was called Moróa Majáne, or son of Majane' (*Travels*, p. 80). Chapman refers to him as 'a petty chief named Murimajani, a great rascal' (vol. i, p. 183).

[3] BaNajwa or BaNanzwa. Of Kalaka stock, they formerly lived much farther east, but fled from the MaTebele and settled on the Mababe Flats. Majane is said to have been killed there by Sebetwane. Cf. Nettelton, 'History of the Ngamiland Tribes', 1934, p. 356.

[4] 'The flag or rush plant' (Brown); *Prionium serratum*.

[5] 'Their huts were built on poles, and a fire is made beneath by night, in order that the smoke may drive away the mosquitoes' (*Travels*, p. 80; cf. Chapman, vol. i, p. 183).

travel in the tsetse district by night in safety we chose the shorter path, and after spending Sunday the 15th with the Banajoa crossed the swamp. The frost was severe on Monday morning, but the pumpkin leaves were untouched by it when we were at the village. This leaf shews frost sooner than any other in this country. Sleep 8 or 9 miles beyond the marsh under Mopane trees.

After travelling other 16 or 17 miles we reached a fine large pond called Tsatsara,[1] in all from Chombo's 34 or 35 miles.

18th. Went to a small pond called Tsara.[2] Obs. Alt. 95° 24' 30", Declination 23° 25' = Lat. 18° 37'.

In approaching the Tsetse district in the evening saw for the first time the Tsetse.[3] We unyoked and sent the cattle back till it was dark, and then rode forward. Crossed the river Sonta[4] about 8 miles beyond Tsara or Mokhalo[5] pool. The Sonta was about 3 feet deep, full of Tsitla & reed and about forty yards broad. It was filling when we crossed it.

27 miles from Tsara we struck the Chobe or Turoga river[6] and found ourselves still in the midst of the Tsetse.

Obs. Alt. 95° 56'
————————
47 58
89 44
————————
41 46
23 26 Dec.
————————
18° 20' Latitude South

opposite the village of Matlape.[7]

[1] Chat-Garra, 18° 46' S., 24° 3' E. (Passarge).

[2] Not named on maps. The latitude given suggests the vicinity of Gubatsa (long. 24° 5' E.).

[3] The Tswana name, now in common use, for *Glossina morsitans*, a fly whose bite is usually fatal to cattle and other domestic animals.

[4] Now known as the Savuti channel, linking the Linyanti River with the Mababe, though it has been dry 'since about 1888' (Wellington, *Southern Africa*, Cambridge 1955, vol. i, p. 415).

[5] Tswana *mokgalo*, buffalo-thorn (*Zizyphus mucronata*); evidently used here as synonymous with Bushman *tsara*, 'thorn-tree'.

[6] Also called the Linyanti River; a major tributary of the Zambesi, which it joins at Kazungula.

[7] Not identified; presumably a minor headman.

Matlape brought us two immense dishes of milk and an ox as food. As our cattle would not swim over they were kept in the reed during the day, it being believed that the Tsetse does not fly thither. Next day some of the beautiful little cattle of the Makololo or Basuto[1] were brought to precede our cattle in crossing the river. They take to the water readily.

On 20th Ponuane[2] one of the chief men of Sebitoane was sent with Mahale to us. Many of the people were clothed in European manufactures, one had a dressing gown on & a red worsted nightcap.

21st. Went down the river about 25 or 30 miles in a canoe to the village of Maunko.[3] The canoes are thin & light, and being propelled by five paddlers they go along at the rate of about six miles an hour. Saw date trees for the first time. A hippopotamus started up close to the canoe. They frequently overturn them and drown people in them. When we came to Maunko's village we heard the chief and all the people singing very nicely, their voices good and the tune quite different from the Eee, æ, of the Bechuana. They continued their song even after we approached them.

Particulars respecting Sebitoane

Having saluted Sebitoane we retired to a little distance. He was a thin wiry framed man about 5 ft 10 in height and slightly bald. A little flurr[i]ed at first but soon regained complete selfpossession. Having stated the object of our visit —the preaching of the gospel, their elevation in the scale of humanity, Peace, and the avoidance of murder and the barter in slaves—he expressed his pleasure in meeting us, that he had heard of our wish to see him and our unsuccessful efforts to reach him, that though our cattle had been bitten by Tsetse and would certainly perish he would supply their place by others. He had the idea that our teaching was chiefly the art of shooting and other European arts, and that by our

[1] The MaKololo were of diverse origins, but Sebetwane's own people were BaFokeng-baPatsa, a branch of the BaSotho (Basuto).

[2] Ponwane, also called Ngwanangombe ('Nuanañompe', cf. below, p. 29), was a Lozi tribesman who had become one of Sebetwane's indunas; he subsequently served Sekeletu in the same capacity, but died of fever in 1860 (Jalla, *Litaba za Sicaba za Ma-Lozi*, 1934, p. 30; *Narrative*, pp. 272, 274).

[3] Mmanku, one of Sebetwane's wives. She lived on an island about 12 miles south of Linyanti (cf. below, p. 35).

giving him guns he would thereby procure peace, the peace he so earnestly longed to possess. The people of Mosilikatse who frequently come in order to steal cattle would be deterred from continuing their unwelcome visits, & he would be able to come out of his fastnesses in the rivers, live on the plains, and visit his relatives the Basuto & other tribes like other people.

He then presented us with a pot of porridge, a calabash of honey containing upwards of two gallons, and an ox for slaughter. Everything we needed, as mats to sleep on &c, he presented in quite a royal style, and when we declined a gift he never recieved it back again but presented [it] to some one else.

His people are much more savage in appearance and modes of eating than any we have seen. In the evening he came to sit by our fire, and when a pot of porridge was brought he invited us to partake of it, but so many hands were thrust in at [the] same time with our own we did not get three mouthfuls before it was finished. If an ox is killed each one cuts off a long slice and throws it on the fire, and when still half raw it is devoured. A whole ox is finished in the course of half an hour and every bit of it broiled in the above way. They have domestic and guinea fowls in abundance, and know the process of transforming the former into capons. Monkeys too were running about Maunko's village.

Two men were drowned during the night by the overturning of a canoe. The event did not excite much surprise: they were 'lifted by the Morena',[1] they said. This 'lifting' is used in the sense the word was put to by the Highlanders of Scotland when they lifted or stole cattle. Lifting among Bechuana is no[t] considered stealing.

Early in the morning Sebitoane came to our fire and related many of the adventures of his most eventful carreer. The following notes of his course will shew how chequered the scene is through which even poor natives pass in their way to Hades.[2]

[1] *Morena* usually means 'lord, master', but here evidently refers to God.

[2] As the gaps in the footnotes show, I have not been able to identify, even tentatively, many of the places mentioned. One reason is that Sebetwane sometimes used Sotho names, which are unlikely to prevail locally, especially in Northern Rhodesia; for example, Lithabana (No. 46), Lithabeng (No. 49), Thabaneng (No. 63), Thaba enca (No. 66), and Thabana ea basari (No. 71), are all derivatives of *thaba*, mountain.

1. He was attacked and driven from his own country in the first instance by Sikonyelo, his patrimonial lands being situated by the hill Kurutleri or 'Metse a ba bañue'. It is situated south of the Marikwe and not far from Thaba uncu.[1]

2. He then fled to Sekonyelo's present country.[2]

3. Thence returned to the Marikwe.

4. Thence to Mokolobata.

5. Thence to Puchweng.

6. Thence to junction of Lekwa & Linta rivers.[3]

7. Thence to the Moretele or upper part of River Lekwa.[4]

8. Thence to Mañope, West of the Oorie.[5]

9. Back again to the Marikwe and there lost all by an attack of Matibele.

10. Thence to Bapuchweng hills without any cattle.

11. Thence went to Liribeng and took the cattle of the Bakwains under Moreakhomu[6] and afterwards returned to Puchweng.

12. Thence to Mekwaring.[7]

13. Thence towards Kuruman but was driven back by the Griquas in 1824.[8]

[1] Sekonyela, chief of the BaTlokwa 1821–56, attacked Sebetwane's people in June 1822 (Ellenberger, *History of the Basuto*, p. 306). Kurutleri (Kurutlele) is situated between the Sand and Vet Rivers in the Orange Free State, near Winburg (Ellenberger, *loc. cit.*; Chapman, vol. i, p. 167). Thaba Nchu is less than 100 miles to the south; the Marico rises much farther away and flows northward into the Crocodile (Limpopo).

[2] The upper valley of the Caledon River (near Ficksburg, O.F.S.).

[3] The 'Lekwa' (Vaal) and 'Linta' (Vals) join a few miles west of Bothaville, O.F.S.

[4] The Moretele (Pienaar's) River is a tributary of the Crocodile, not 'part of' the Vaal.

[5] 'Oorie' (Odi) is the Crocodile River; Mangope was a Hurutshe chief living at Borutwe (Mangope Siding, near Groot Marico, Western Transvaal).

[6] Moruakgomo was chief of the BaKwena *c*.1822–8. They themselves say that they were living at Dithubaruba, near Molepolole, when driven by Sebetwane's advance into the Kalahari Desert (Schapera, *Ditirafalô tsa BaTswana*, p. 45). 'Liribeng' (Didibeng) means 'at the wells'.

[7] Possibly the Matlhwareng River, north of Kuruman.

[8] Kuruman, 27° 28′ S., 23° 26′ E., was an L.M.S. mission station, founded 1817, and since 1821 under the direction of Robert Moffat (1795–1883), D.L.'s father-in-law. The Griquas, originally called 'Bastards', were mostly mixed-breed descendants of Hottentots and Europeans, and lived farther south in and around the region now known as Griqualand West. In June 1823 (not 1824), a horde of 'Mantatees', advancing on Kuruman from the north, was defeated at Dithakong (27° 5′ S., 23° 59′ E.) by a combined force of BaTlhaping and Griquas, the latter armed with guns that proved irresistible. Sebetwane's people were among the invaders, who however consisted mainly of BaPhuthing and BaHlakwana. Cf. *Apprenticeship at Kuruman*, ed. Schapera, pp. 91–103.

14. Back to the Marikwe.
15. Went & took the cattle of the Bakhatla and Bahurutse and thence proceeded to settle on the Molopo.[1]
16. Thence to Chueling.[2]
17. Seretsaneng.
18. Matlakaneng.
19. Junction of Marikwe & Oorie.[3]
20. Borumatau.
21. While at Borumatau the Bamangwato attacked his town while he was absent and killed his women. He proceeded to the Bamangwato & took their cattle in revenge.
22. Limpopo.
23. Khucoe, a hill West Nor West of Bamangwato.[4]
24. Serōe, N. of Bamangwato.[5]
25. Mabele a puri.[6]
26. Selepeng.[7]
27. Bokalaka.[8]
28. Maritlokweng.
29. Tutumane.[9]
30. Matlabuke.
31. Ratlabani.
32. Shōe.[10]
33. Charime.
34. Makokotlong.
35. Tlomtla.[11]
36. Botletli & Bakurutse ; took all their cattle.
37. Sebitoane's ford.[12]

[1] The BaHurutshe (of Marico district, Transvaal) and BaKgatla-bagaKgafêla (of Pilansberg district) both have traditions of being attacked by Sebetwane. The Molopo River rises south-west of their territories, near Mafeking, and flows to the west.
[2] Possibly Motswedi, 25° 17′ S., 25° 53′ E.
[3] At approx. 24° 12′ S., 26° 53′ E.
[4] Kutswe, approx. 22° 42′ S., 26° 37′ E., in the Makhware hills north of Shoshong.
[5] Serowe, 22° 23′ S., 26° 43′ E., the present capital of the BaNgwato.
[6] Mabeleapodi ('teats of the goat'), twin peaks about 10 miles north of Serowe.
[7] A hill about 20 miles north of Francistown.
[8] 'The country of the MaKalaka', around the upper reaches of the Shashi River and south of the Maitengwe.
[9] Presumably somewhere near the Tutumi, a tributary of the Nata.
[10] Probably Shua, where the Nata enters the Makarikari Depression (cf. p. 6).
[11] Cf. p. 9.
[12] Where he crossed the Botletle, at 20° 55′ S., 24° 28′ E. (GSGS 2871 Transvaal).

38. Makala maberi, on Zouga.[1]
39. Tamunakle.[2]
40. Namanyane.[3]
41. Kuabi nami.[4]
42. Gaila ; attacked Matibele of Rasipipe and then crossed the Zouga.[5]
43. Went with all his people on an expedition against the Damaras or Matluma[6] & lost most of his cattle by want of water.
44. Matseng.[7]
45. Lotlakaneng.[8]
46. Lithabana.
47. Moraraecu.
48. Makukushung.
49. Lithabeng.
50. Ngami.
51. Cross Ragatsinatsi.
52. Antariloge.[9]
53. Makotlong.
54. Lichuaneng.[10]
55. Kumpakumpa.[11]
56. Mokwele.[12]

---

[1] Makalamabedi, 20° 19′ S., 23° 53′ E.   [2] Thamalakane River.

[3] Motlhaba wa Namanyana, nowadays called Mochabeng (Motlhabeng); the belt of land, immediately N.W. of Lake Ngami, where Sebetwane defeated the BaTawana (cf. Ellenberger, p. 310).

[4] Possibly the Kgwebe Hills, approx. 20° 38′ S., 23° 4′ E. The BaTawana were living there when Sebetwane arrived in their country.

[5] Gaila may be Gaina Hill, 20° 43′ S., 23° 27′ E. The 'Matibele of Rasipipe', also invading marauders from the south-east, have not been certainly identified, but were apparently fugitive BaTlokwa (cf. Wookey, *Dicò tsa Secwana*, Tiger kloof, 1929, pp. 56 f.).

[6] OvaHerero (Tswana 'MaTlamma') of South West Africa. For Sebetwane's disastrous expedition against them, in the course of which his son and heir Kgwanyane was killed, cf. Ellenberger, pp. 310 f.

[7] Macheng, 'the region of salt pans'; a Tswana name for Ghanzi district, S.W. of Lake Ngami.   [8] Possibly Rietfontein, 21° 55′ S., 20° 54′ E. (Tswana *lotlhaka*, reed).

[9] Possibly Andara, 18° 4′ S., 21° 27′ E., where Sebetwane crossed the Okovango after proceeding northwards from Lake Ngami along the Taoge (Ellenberger, pp. 310, 311).

[10] Possibly the village of 'Lichuane' (Ditshwaane), a Subia chief living on Mpalela island immediately west of Kazungula.

[11] A Tonga chief living N.E. of the Victoria Falls (*Narrative*, p. 233). The hamlet of Kumbe-Kumbe, approx. 17° 52′ S., 25° 58′ E., may be named after him.

[12] Possibly either Makoli, 17° 29′ S., 26° 4′ E., or Mukwela, 17° 2′ S., 26° 39′ E.

57. Litlabateng.
58. Moetse.[1]
59. Seretsaneng.
60. Hapori.[2]
61. Kabungka.[3]
62. Motering.
63. Thabaneng.
64. Melale.
65. Nyakane.
66. Thaba enca ; attacked by Matibele.
67. Lekologeng ; took thence large horned oxen.
68. Hanyati.
69. Gasialobi.[4]
70. Spopa.
71. Thabana ea basari.[5]
72. Liphokung.
73. Sashoko.[6]
74. Matsa.[7]
75. Noka ea Teketu.
76. Noka ea likota, or the Bridge.
77. Noka ea Marile.[8]
78. Then into the island of the Borotse after they had killed his women. Seunturu built the island.[9]
79. Sesheke.[10] There attacked and defeated the Matibele of Licuano[11] whom the Borotse subsequently drowned.

[1] Possibly Mwenze, approx. 17° 7′ S., 27° 4′ E.

[2] Kapoli (near Kalomo, 17° 1′ S., 26° 58′ E.), where the MaKololo are known to have settled temporarily (cf. Smith and Dale, *Ila-Speaking Peoples*, vol. i, p. 29).

[3] Kabanga, 17° 34′ S., 26° 46′ E.

[4] Possibly 'at (the home of) Shaloba', an Ila chief living in Lubwe, Namwala district (approx. 15° 45′ S., 26° 30′ E.).

[5] 'The women's mountain', close to Sachitema (in Chiyobola, Kalomo district), where Sebetwane was attacked by Moselekatse's MaTebele. The place was so named because 'even the women joined furiously in the fight' (Smith and Dale, vol. i, pp. 30 f.).

[6] Possibly connected with Shasokwe, an Ila headman living in Lubanda, Namwala district.   [7] Probably Macha, 16° 22′ S., 26° 48′ E.

[8] Marile River, the eastern channel of the Zambesi in the general vicinity of Mongu (15° 16′ S., 23° 8′ E.). *Noka* means 'river'.

[9] Identified in *Travels*, p. 216, as Naliele, 15° 24′ S., 23° 6′ E. 'Seunturu' (Santudu, better known as Mulambwa) was chief of the MaLozi (BaRotse) c.1780–1830 (Gluckman, 'The Lozi of Barotseland', 1951, p. 2).

[10] The town of this name was moved several times; its position in 1853 was approx. 17°32′ S., 25° 13′ E. (*Travels*, p. 203).   [11] Cf. below, p. 26.

80. Sekota,[1] near the Waterfall.
81. Moremeri.
82. Linyanti[2] & Nalieri.

His towns are

1. Litofe.
2. Magariku.
3. Lifale.
4. Choku.
5. Khaola.
6. Mamochisane.
7. Nalieli.
8. Sekeletu.
9. Mpollo.
10. Basaribagolu.
11. Palinyane.
12. Mothibe.
13. Likokong.
14. Libonta.

These are Makololo towns and are not to be confounded with the towns of the subjected tribes, which are all much larger. Those specified are however the aristocratic towns.[3]

They questioned me as to why the White men had attacked and killed so many of them at Litakong in 1824. I replied by asking if they did not see a white man beckoning them to come to a parley before the attack. Yes we did, said an old man, there were three men on horseback capering before the others. On my explaining their object, he replied, 'then we killed ourselves by not understanding their language.'[4] Another old man had his shoulder dislocated by a bullet striking his shield in a slanting direction with such

[1] Sekute, a Leya chief living on Kalai island immediately above the Victoria Falls ('the Waterfall'). Cf. *Travels*, pp. 517 f.

[2] Dinyanti, approx. 18° 17′ S., 23° 50′ E. (*Travels*, p. 203). The site has long been abandoned.

[3] Some are obviously named after their headmen, e.g. No. 6 (Sebetwane's daughter), No. 8 (his son), No. 9 (his brother), No. 12 (Sekeletu's father-in-law), and possibly No. 11. Others (Nos. 1, 3, 7, 14) are places mentioned elsewhere in the journal. The rest I cannot identify; No. 10 means 'old women'.

[4] The only Europeans at Dithakong (p. 18) were Robert Moffat and John Melvill (Government agent at Griquatown). Some of the Griquas, however, were also mounted. Moffat describes how before the battle started he and 'another of our number' vainly tried to reason with the invaders and prevent any fighting (*Apprenticeship at Kuruman*, ed. Schapera, pp. 91 ff.).

force as to force the humerus downwards out of the socket. The same bullet killed a man behind him.

We had a long discussion and explanation of the likualo (scriptures)[1] in the morning. Mr Oswel then returned to the waggons but I remained, and right thankful I am now that I did so, for the services of that day were the only ones Sebitoane was ever well enough to attend. We returned together on Monday morning. His canoe was propelled by six picked paddlers and quick work they made. At each stroke of the paddle the stern dipped under the water. We landed at a clump of Date bushes in flower to eat a pot full of porridge which he presented to me. The course of this river, called the Mbonta or Chobe,[2] is exceedingly winding, and its general direction is N.E. or N.N.E. Sebitoane thought he could ferry our waggons accross by means of canoes, but he had no idea what ponderous lumber these were. He felt anxious to place us on the Northern side of the Chobe, as the Southern bank is infested by bands of Matibele who frequently come in search of cattle. When he saw the waggons he felt convinced that his light canoes were unable to convey them accross.

Sebitoane's illness and death

He then gave orders to remove his town to the vicinity of the waggons, and while this was in process of accomplishment he was taken ill of inflammation of the lungs. He applied for medicine and I gave a little but it was not used. He had three doctors in attendance. Had been very ill of same complaint at the Borotse town last year. The Borotse cured him by about fifty long incisions on his chest similar to those the Bangwaketse employed to number the number they killed in battle.[3] He lingered a fortnight under the com-

---

[1] Tswana *dikwalô*, from *kwala*, to write.

[2] 'Mbonta' is probably a local name; the river is commonly known as Linyanti or Chobe.

[3] 'He had been cured of this complaint during the year before by the Barotse making a large number of free incisions in the chest. The Makololo doctors, on the other hand, now scarcely cut the skin' (*Travels*, p. 89). For the use of such marks as a tally of men slain (among the BaKgatla of Mabotsa), cf. also Methuen, p. 266, and Cumming, vol. i, p. 207. The BaNgwaketse are the southern neighbours of the BaKwena, whom they (like the BaNgwato) regard as their parent tribe.

plaint. I visited him daily. He seemed to have placed entire confidence in us from the beginning. I endeavoured on one occasion to introduce the subject of death by rema[r]king, when he appeared to be getting better, that yesterday I was afraid he was going to die. 'Die', said one of the doctors, 'Do you think Sebitoane will ever die? Why do you speak of death to Sebitoané?' I felt I should not be allowed to proceed farther with that topic. Think I yielded too easily, ought to have made another effort.[1] But the doctors gave him up and two others were called. These thought that as Mrs L. was in the family way my presence in his court was unfavourable to his cure.[2] The people told me but seemed afraid I should be offended. Here if a woman menstruates she retires to a hut and lives alone. The flow is very profuse and prolonged. Probably the malaria is carried off by this means, for fewer of the women die of fever than of the other sex, and they complain that they have the discharge more profuse &c among the rivers than elsewhere. Laban did not seek the images long after Rachel told him her condition.[3] Here it is believed that the women may kill a man by not telling him when he approaches that they are menstruating.

I did not like to offend their prejudices and only went to the door of the court and saluted him. I spoke to the doctors as to the propriety of offering my assistance as a medical man, but they candidly told me that my fears of his ultimate recovery were well founded, and also that there was a chance of blame in case of that event occurring while he was under my treatment.[4]

[1] In *Travels*, pp. 89 f., this conversation is transferred to the occasion of D.L.'s final interview with Sebetwane.

[2] The BaTswana believe that should a pregnant woman or her husband visit a sick person they will 'trample' upon him (contaminate him with their ritual impurity) and thus greatly retard recovery. Mrs Livingstone gave birth to a son on 15 September (cf. below, p. 68).

[3] Cf. Genesis 31: 34 f.

[4] Cf. *Travels*, p. 89. Chapman, who visited the MaKololo in 1853, says however that 'Sebetoane's doctors attribute the chief's death to the white men coming amongst them, and whenever Dr. Livingstone preaches in the presence of or visits a chief, the doctors burn something as a charm to protect them from his witchcraft. Being, as they find, a doctor, he has also the reputation of being a wizard. This makes him either feared or admired, and gives him a certain influence. They give him credit for being a good doctor, and say he has cured many, but killed some natives' (vol. i, p. 171).

July 6th. Sebitoane very ill of Pneumonia ; expectoration profuse, seems to consist of greenish pus.

After preaching on Sunday the 7th he called me to see, as he said, 'if he was still a man'. I went to the door of the court as usual, he lifted himself up, saluted, and then when we parted told one of the people to 'take Robert to Mauñko's house and get some milk for him'.[1] I saw him no more, for on the same evening his people removed him towards the Linyanti town and when still on the way, just at the clump of date bushes at which we stood,[2] he expired in his canoe. The morning was very cold and the exposure may have hastened the fatal event.

Poor Sebitoane, my heart bleeds for thee, and what would I not do for thee now that nothing can be done. Where art thou now? I will weep for thee till the day of my death. Little didst thou think, when in the visit of the white man thou sawest the long cherished desires of years accomplished, that the sentence of death had gone forth. Thou thoughtest that thou shouldst procure a weapon from the white man which would be a shield from the attacks of the fierce Matibele ; but a more deadly dart than theirs was aimed at thee, and though thou couldst well ward off a dart, none ever better, thou didst not see that of the King of Terrors. I will weep for thee, my brother, and I would cast forth my sorrows in dispair for thy condition, but I know that thou wilt recieve no injustice whither thou art gone : shall not the judge of all the earth do right? I leave thee to him. Alas ! Alas ! Sebitoane ! I might have said more to him. God forgive me. Free me from blood-guiltiness.[3] If I had said more of death I might have been suspected as having foreseen the event and guilty of bewitching him. I might have recommended Jesus and his great atonement more. It is however very difficult to break through the thick crust of ignorance which envelopes their minds.

Sebitoane's Character &c.

He came from the Borotse to Sesheke, a distance at least

[1] In *Travels*, p. 90, these are described as 'the last words of Sebituane'. Robert was D.L.'s eldest son, then aged about five. [2] To have breakfast together; cf. p. 23.

[3] Cf. *Letters*, vol. i, pp. 82 f., for a similar apostrophe evoked by the death of a former Native attendant. It too contains the prayer, 'Let me not be guilty of the blood of souls'.

300 miles, in order to be nearer to the white man, and then removed to the Linyanti 100 miles farther South, and would had he been spared [have] gone down to the river of the Bapalleng or Tsō[1] in order to be at a convenient distance for the visits of white people. He was much emaciated, I think hurt himself by smoking wild hemp, the cannabis sativa or as it is called in India 'Bang'. Had a wound just over the region of the liver which he recieved from the Wanketse of old. The man who killed old Makabba was constantly by him, his name is Mosari oa tau (Wife of a lion).[2]

He always went very slightly clad. Esteemed by all as very wise. He has been fighting almost constantly for the last 30 years. Must have possessed great natural abilities. Was very politic. Married Maunko, a Letibele, in order to induce the Basuto & Bakwain under him[3] to marry the black races in subjection to him. Tutañka[4] the son of Seunturu, the chief of the Borotse whom he expelled, lived with him and he gave him a gun before he had given any to the Basuto.

A few years ago a large party of Matibele under one called Mpakane came against him. He placed a few goats on an island, & then appointed them a ferryman who took them accross in his canoes. But as soon as they were all over he according to previous instructions left them. When nearly starved they fell an easy prey to him, and having put the principal men to death he sent the commander with a message to Mosilikatse. The Borotse however who ferried him over, thinking to do Sebitoane a still further favour, overturned the canoe in which they were carrying him and

---

[1] The Ngoga River in Ngamiland. The BaPhaleng (related to those at Shoshong, cf. p. 5) lived to its north, in Kabamokoni district.

[2] Makaba II, chief of the BaNgwaketse since c.1795, was killed while resisting a raid by Sebetwane late in 1824 (Schapera, *Short History of the BaNgwaketse*, 1942, p. 6).

[3] Sebetwane's followers consisted of his own BaSotho (p. 16) and many aliens, notably BaKwena and BaNgwato, whom he had enlisted while in Bechuanaland. The 'black races' were the people he conquered in Northern Rhodesia. Cf. *Travels*, p. 197.

[4] Called Lutango by Silva Porto (*Viagens*, p. 111) and Lotanku by Mackenzie (p. 244), but better known as Sipopa. After the overthrow of the MaKololo in 1864 he became the first king of the restored Lozi dynasty.

drowned him.[1] The majority of the people he incorporated into his own tribe.

He prohibited the Matoka[2] knocking out the upper front teeth.

Was extremely generous to all strangers, no matter who they were, and felt anxious to renew intercourse with his relatives, the Basuto of the South. He must have possessed great natural abilities, for he has often lost all he possessed, yet kept his people together, and not only so but ended his days richer in cattle and having more people under his sway than any chief we know in the Southern part of Africa. Many hairbreadth escapes he has had. Only last year he was nearly killed by Matibele. A party of them, sent by Mosilikatse, were endeavouring to cross the river. Sebitoane, having obtained notice of their whereabouts, did not wait for the assembling of his people, but went to attack them with the handful of people near him. Thinking to pounce upon them before they saw him, he approached warily to the shore under a cover of reed, but the Matibele were lying in ambush behind the screen of reeds, and no sooner did the canoes touch the land than in jumped the Matibele, and in the confusion several of the boats were overturned. Sebitoane was caught hold of by a Borotse man and borne ashore, while many of the people were killed in the water.[3]

He perhaps hurt himself by smoking wild hemp, but most of his people are addicted to the same noxious weed. It is impossible to overstate the importance all attached to him. He was so sensible, quite unlike a native, and so frank withal. When Lechwee came from the Bamangwato on a visit he enticed one of Sebitoane's wives to follow him. She had ten attendants, and after wandering about among the rivers for some months they were discovered in the reeds, unable to get away. Eight of them were put to death, and then the wife was

[1] According to other versions, the MaLozi drowned not Mpakane (or 'Licuano', p. 21), but Ngabe (Nxaba), a Tebele chief who was independent of Moselekatse (cf. Jalla, *Litaba*, pp. 50 f.; Ellenberger, pp. 315 f.). Their account of this episode differs from D.L.'s in various other details.

[2] BaTonga ('BaToka'), living east of Barotseland in Southern Province, N. Rhodesia. Sebetwane's prohibition was unsuccessful; cf. *Travels*, p. 532.

[3] Although not mentioned in *Travels*, this incident is related by Ellenberger (pp. 317 f.) and other sources.

delivered to her father. He replied that she was no longer his daughter and he must just do to her as he had done to the others. She too was executed, but the tenth person, a woman, came while we were at the Chobe. She refused to go near untill I offered to speak to Sebitoane in her behalf. She was in wretched plight when she arrived, and in dispair wished to jump into the river. When I besought Sebitoane to spare her he said, 'Shall I kill her after you prayed for her? O No.'[1] I do not wonder at the Roman Catholics praying for the dead. If I could believe as they do I would pray for them too.

The Judge of all the Earth will do right, and all His Providential dealings are for the furtherance of his own cause. Let me try & say from the heart, 'It is well'.

Visit Seshéke &c.

In the afternoon Mr. O and I went over to the village to condole with the people. They recieved our condolences very kindly and took our advice in good part. 'Do not leave us, though Sebitoane is gone. His children remain, and you must treat them as you would have treated him. No blame can be attached to you'. We agreed to remain. This was my plan previous to his death, and Mr O., though tired [of] waiting in a state of inactivity, very frankly agreed to remain also. We proposed now to go to Sesheke, but the people had, they said, no power. We must wait till they heard [from] Mamochisane.[2] They then all left us in order to attend to Sebitoane's property.

9th. Ice ½ inch thick and hoar frost on the grass in the morning but in the middle of the day the sun feels hot.

10th. Very few people near us. Built a hut for children to play in. Put up smith's bellows. Saw two date trees about 20 feet high, they were in flower. Very small owl abounds here, also Paroqueets & small monkeys.

13th. Mahale and Kuenane[3] returned from the Linyanti,

---

[1] This incident is not recorded elsewhere, nor can I identify 'Lechwee'.

[2] Mma-Motsisane ('mother of Motsisane'), alias Dikuku; Sebetwane's daughter by his chief wife, and full sister of Kgwanyane (p. 20). She was then living at Naliele.

[3] Kwenane, one of Sebetwane's indunas; apparently of Lozi stock (cf. Jalla, *Litaba*, pp. 64, 66). Coillard in 1886 mentioned a village headman of that name (*Sur le Haut-Zambèze*, p. 257).

others expected. Hear that Mamochisane, Sebitoane's daughter, is successor to him in the chieftainship. She was installed while her father was still alive—recieved the tribute and distributed the plunder; and all the presents we had given to Sebitoane were laid aside in order to pass through her hands. Her husbands or rather paramours, for she does not confine herself to one, have no power. It was so arranged by her father. Pity some one was not there to suggest that a husband should hold the same position as Prince Albert.[1] She has three children, the two younger are boys. Her other name is Likuku. A son or stepson by an inferior house is called Sekeletu or Litaba,[2] and he will lead the army to battle. Women are usually less practicable in dealing with white men than the opposite sex. It may be otherwise with Mamochisane.

14th. When out walking in the evening came unexpectedly on an elephant drinking. Fired over his head in order to drive him off. He runs very quickly and is very dangerous, as he seeks a person out. A pitfall is a secure refuge from him, he wheels off immediately from one. This however did not give us chase. We were startled by its coming a little way in the direction in which we were standing. I have had many escapes. We seem immortal till our work is done.

Mahale presents an ox as food.

16th. Nuanañompe or Ponuane returned today and brought a good supply of corn for us. We rece[i]ved five large bundles of it and Mr O. an equal number.

The rivers are all said to come from one source called Lobale. What is Lobale? Is it a Lake or river?[3] One branch

[1] 'Sebituane installed his daughter Mamochisáne into the chieftainship long before his death, but, with all his acuteness, the idea of her having a husband who should not be her lord did not seem to enter his mind. He wished to make her his successor, probably in imitation of some of the negro tribes with whom he had come into contact; but, being of the Bechuana race, he could not look upon the husband except as the woman's lord, so he told her all the men were hers, she might take any one, but ought to keep none' (*Travels*, p. 179). Albert, Queen Victoria's husband, was 'Prince-Consort' of England.

[2] Sekeletu's mother, Setloutlou, was a widow captured in war, who had became the wife of Letshai (a Kololo nobleman) but was subsequently taken from him by Sebetwane (Ellenberger, p. 307; cf. *Travels*, p. 179). In Native law the original husband would normally have been considered legal father of all her children, no matter by whom begotten.

[3] It is the region, immediately north-west of Barotseland, inhabited by the tribes collectively termed BaLovale.

forms the Borotse river[1] and another the Bashukulompo river or river of Matoka.[2] These join and form the Zambesa.

Sebitoane has been attacked three times by the people of Mosilikatse and twice by other parties of Matibele. On the first occasion he beat them off and recovered his cattle in the field. On the second he prevented them getting any cattle into their possession, fighting them at the entrances of his town. On the third occasion he served them out by taking them on to an island and starving them.

19th. Languages of the black race which inhabits the river seem to be all dialects of one tongue. They differ from each other as much as an English provincial dialect does from broad Scotch, and they bear the same relationship to Sichuana as the Latin does to French or English. The Bakoba or Bayeiye speak one of these dialects, but they have adopted some of the Bushman Klick from the Masaroa[3] on the banks of the Zouga. The Bayeiye up here seem to have fewer Klicks than those on the latter river. The different dialects are the Bayeiye or Bakhoba

Bashubea & Banyeti or Baloi
Batōka & Bashukulompo
Borotse
Bamaponda or Baponda
Banyeñko
Balojazi.[4]

Collected at different times from different individuals of the above named tribes about 300 words of each of the dia-

[1] The Zambesi above Sesheke.

[2] The Kafue, draining the regions inhabited by the BaIla ('Bashukulompo') and BaTonga.

[3] MaSarwa, the Tswana term for Bushmen. On the occurrence of 'clicks' (injective consonants) in Yeei, cf. Schapera and van der Merwe, *Notes on . . . some Bantu Languages of Ngamiland*, Cape Town 1942, pp. 4 f.

[4] Nowadays generally written: BaYeei or BaYeye (Tswana 'MaKoba'); BaSubia (BaSubiya), BaNyeti, ALuyi; BaTonga (Tswana 'BaToka'), BaIla (Lozi 'MaShukulumbwe'); MaLozi (Tswana 'BaRotse'); MaMbunda; BaNyengo; BaLuchazi. These peoples all speak Bantu languages, which however are not always as much alike as D.L. implies. In Doke's classification (*Bantu*, 1945, pp. 31, 101, 105), Yeei belongs to the 'Western zone', Subia, Luyi, Tonga, and Ila, to the 'Central zone', and Mbunda, Luchazi, and Nyengo, to the 'West-Central zone'.

lects.[1] There are several sounds in these dialects which do not exist in the Sichuana, viz. the hard sound of G as in Langebongo, the sound of the θ as in Ka*th*ingongo.[2]

A Motoka man whom Sebitoane saved gave the words in that dialect. He says the Bashukulompo speak the same dialect as the Batoka.[3]

A Balojazi man named Shokolo, whom Mpepe[4] captured when he attacked the company of elephant hunters from the Balojazi tribe,[5] furnished the words of that dialect. He says he slept 45 times before he reached the town of the Borotse. His chief is called Monachahela. He drew a sketch of the rivers of his country and stated that the[y] run N.N.W. This may mean that they come from that direction. They flow into the sea on the West coast, he knew. The Babirikwe[6] live near to the mouth of the Langebongo,[7] which is the 'mother' of all the other rivers in that quarter. They possess horses oxen sheep & pigs, build boats, and have waggons which make a clinking noise as they go. They marry from the Balojaze. The Basindele or Babindele[8] live on the sea coast and are the servants of the Portuguese. The Tsetse exists in their country and all their rivers are navigable.

Mistakes in the words collected are no doubt to be found, for when I asked for the meaning of the word to teach he

[1] These vocabularies were entered on pp. 212–43 of a quarto notebook, the same word being given in parallel columns across the open page for 'Bakhoba, Bashubea, Balojazi, Maponda, Borotse, Batōka, Banyeñko, Bechuana' and English. The volume, now in the South African Library, Cape Town, was described by W. H. I. Bleek, *Catalogue of the Grey Collection*, vol. i, part I (1858), p. 186, item 280.e. (For this information I am indebted to the Librarian, Mr D. H. Varley, who was also kind enough to furnish me with a photostat copy of the vocabularies.)

[2] The English equivalents are *g* as in 'go', and *th* as in 'then'.

[3] The 'BaToka' (BaTonga) live chiefly in the enclave between the Zambesi and Kafue Rivers, extending westwards to Sesheke. The 'Bashukulompo' (BaIla) are to their north, on both sides of the Kafue River, mostly in Namwala district. Their languages are very similar.

[4] Mphephe, Sebetwane's 'nephew' (*Letters*, vol. ii, p. 219) and governor of the Barotse valley.

[5] The BaLuchazi live chiefly in S.E. Angola, between the Lungwebungu and Luanginga Rivers, and nowadays also in N.W. Rhodesia, notably Kabompo district.

[6] Not identified.

[7] Lungwebungu, a major tributary of the Zambesi, which it joins from the north-west at approx. 14° 19′ S.

[8] Not identified. In *Travels*, p. 359, D.L. says 'the Babindéle or Portuguese' had been at war with one of the local tribes.

took it to be the word rota, instead of ruta, and the translation was shuza, to micturate !¹

A Matoka man gave the words in that dialect, and he informed us of the junction of the Bashukulompo or Maninche river with the Sesheke² being about a month distant. The women are said to go in puris naturalibus. One came to the waggons in that state, but was seen in time to be sent off. The Bashukulompo wear their hair raised up in the centre of the head. Possess a herd of very small but beautiful cattle. They keep them in their houses and the little animals become remarkably tame. They do not drive them, but the herd goes before and when he wishes them to come along he makes a few antics and the whole herd run along gambolling. In the evenings they come and lie down near the fire and stretch themselves out like dogs.³ They give plenty of milk and might be an improvement on the lap-dog system of England. A pet cow would be more useful than a pet dog. They have very neat cow & sheep bells of native manufacture. The Batoka & Bashukulompo knock out the upper front teeth at the age of puberty.

Mokantju a Mokaponda man furnished the Maponda⁴ dialect. He was taken captive by the Borotse while still young, and had the address to ingratiate himself with Seunturu the chief. He was the constant attendant on Seunturu when he was in his boat, and that being built of planks sewn together, roofed in with white cloth and requiring twenty men to paddle it,⁵ the river even up [at] the Borotse town must be of considerable size. Mokantju managed to get installed into the same position with Sebitoane, and though an ungainly fellow has a great deal of knowledge. He was of

¹ Tswana *rota*, micturate; *ruta*, teach. In D.L.'s MS. vocabularies, the Luchazi word for 'I teach' is given, in parentheses, as '*shusha*, to piddle'.

² *Scil.*, the junction of the Kafue with the Zambesi.

³ This account suggests that some of D.L.'s remarks about those cattle in *Travels*, p. 192, are based on hearsay. Both Chapman (vol. i, p. 174) and Oswell (*Big Game Shooting*, vol. i, p. 149) say the animals were only about 'three feet high'. Faulkner and Epstein (*The Indigenous Cattle of Africa*, 1957, pp. 68 f.) classify them as the 'Tonga type' ('small to medium size') of the Sanga group.

⁴ The MaMbunda live chiefly in S.E. Angola, between the Luanginga and Kwando Rivers, and in the northern districts of Barotseland.

⁵ This was presumably 'Nalikwanda', the ceremonial barge of the Lozi kings (cf. Turner, *The Lozi Peoples*, 1952, p. 28).

much use in drawing maps, and Mr O. and I drew or had drawn for us upwards of sixty. The tablet was frequently only the ground but the agreement of different individuals in their dileneations of rivers &c shews that what we furnish on their authority is worthy of credit.

The Bamaponda knock off the inner corner of the central incisor teeth so as to leave a triangular space in front.

Only the ground but the agreement of different individuals in their dileneations of rivers &c shews that what we furnish on their authority is worthy of credit

The Bamaponda knock off the inner corner of the central incisor teeth so as to leave a triangular space in front

One of the Banyenko[1] gave the words of the dialect of his tribe. He was an expert fisherman with a long thin spear. Peering down into the deep Chobe he seldom ever missed to transfix a fish. Whether it was from his unerring aim, or from a curious propensity in the fish to turn and look at the point of the spear as it approached, I was unable to determine. Some use hooks, for he knew them perfectly. The Banyenko file their front teeth to points in order to be like tigers.

A Bashubea[2] man gave the words in that dialect. They have more of the $th \theta$ sound in their language than any other. They have never been a warlike tribe. Nor indeed do any of the river tribes appear to have been warlike, they have always

[1] BaNyengo, found chiefly west of the Luanginga River in Kalabo district, N.W. Barotseland.
[2] BaSubia or BaSubiya, found chiefly on the Chobe River in Sesheke district, and southwards in the Caprivi Strip and northern Ngamiland.

trusted in the defence which their deep reedy rivers afforded. They have all been addicted to overturning their canoes and drowning those who were obnoxious to them.

Some Barotse people furnished that share of the dialect which they speak. Sebitoane has been the means of diffusing the Sichuana in all that region. Providence seems to have been opening up our way for us and probably a good expressive language will spring up out of the materials now brought together.[1] It is much better that all these tribes should be under one strong government than under their different petty rulers. Their former disunion seems proved by the differences of dialect of people living within short distances of each other.

22d. Took Altitudes for Longitude. The error of the watch, a very indifferent one, was two or 3 minutes.

$\odot$ 78° 34'　Upper Limb, Oswel's
$($ 66° 20'　Lower Limb, Livingston's $\Big\}$ good

$\odot$ 81° 59' 30"　Upper Limb Oswel's
$($ 61° 29' 50"　Lower Limb Livingstons $\Big\}$ good

$\odot$ 87° 33'　　Livingston's
$($ 52° 17' 50"　Oswel's $\Big\}$ doubtful
$\odot$ 90° 40' 10"　Liv.
$($ 47° 32' 30"　Osw.

Began observations about 20 minutes to ten and concluded them about 25 minutes past ten—22 July 1851.

Sun rising, Moon setting
Latitude 18° 20' South
Moon of artificial Horizon　　$)$
　D⁰　of sextant　　　　　$)$
Sun of sextant　　　　$\odot$
Sun of artificial Hor.　　$\odot$

Observations 23 July 1851. Lat. 18° 20' S.
　　Hour 9..31..15
　$\odot$ Alt. 77° 14' 40"　upper Limb Oswel's
　$($ Alt. 82° 1' 30"　Lower Limb Livingstons

[1] D.L. was right. The MaKololo themselves were overthrown in 1864, but their language was retained in modified form and, known as Lozi, is now the official tongue of Barotseland.

Hour 9..39..51
⊙ 78° 25′ 50″ Oswel's Upper Limb
☾ 80° 39′ 20″ Livingston's Lower D°.

Lunar distances
Hour 9..43..3—67° 55′ 50″
Nearest limbs=☾⊙ Moon West, Sun East

Hour 9° 49′ 39″
W E
☾ ⊙ 67° 53′ 50″ Livingston's

Hour 9..54..53
W E
☾ ⊙ 67° 52′ Livingston's
Hour 9..59..34   Error of
W E   Oswel's 1′ 20″
☾ ⊙ 67° 50′ 10″ Livingston's D° L's   10″

Observed Alt ⊙ 102° 4′ 50″ Livingston's
  D°   D° D° 102° 0′ 50 Oswel's

102° 4′ 5″
51 2 2
89 44

38 41 58
20 22

18 . 19 . 58 being Latitude of Chobe where waggons
                stood 1851.

Saturday 25th. Went over to the town of Linyanti, about
12 miles distant N.N.W. Crossed Linyanti river at the town,
about 5 feet deep and 35 yards wide. Contains a good many
people. The poor wives of Sebitoane in deep mourning.
Theirs seems no fictitious sorrow.

26th. Water of Chobe rose one inch. Probably the effect
of wind somewhere above. Hear that Sebitoane died at the
very spot where we went ashore in coming up from Mauñ-

ko's, and this was at the date trees where we had our breakfast of porridge.[1] Some of the oxen are sick and others are dying of the bite of the Tsetse. People say they will all die.

Mokantju gives the names of a great many rich towns and tribes.[2]

Thursday 31st. Recieve a message by Ponwane that it was the will of Mamochisane that we should be treated exactly as if Sebitoane were alive, and that we should be taken wherever we wished to go.[3] The man who went express to tell her of her father's death slept nine nights and reached the Borotse town on the tenth day. It must be 350 miles from where the waggons stood.[4] Very glad now that we had urged our friend Oswel to stay. The pleasure of seeing the Seisheke will be so much increased by his presence, and he who is so liberal with his means, never sparing if he can promote discovery, ought & I hope will be gratified.

1st August. Leave the town of Linyanti on our way to the Seisheke. Proceed N.E. and enter into a number of cattle posts. People very liberal in their supplies of milk. Sleep at Pogo's, a Moyeiye, where Tsitla was supplied to us in abundance.

2d. Pass along a large broad cattle path. Enter Motongka's station.[5] He is remarkably frank & generous; offers to slaughter an ox, which we decline. Country quite flat, clumps of date bushes. Sleep by a bush.

3d. The country presents all the appearance of being occasionally under water. The raised spots appear to be the work of ants. And now the farther we go North the larger do the date bushes become. In the evening they were full grown trees, and there were also large groves of Palmyras.

[1] Cf. p. 23.

[2] Not listed in the journal, but shown on the facsimile map in *Oswell* (vol. i, facing p. 262).

[3] 'She was reported to be in childbed at the time, but sent the chief next in authority to herself to visit us on her behalf' (*JRGS*, 1852, p. 166).

[4] But in *JRGS* (*loc. cit.*) D.L. says that Mma-Motsisane was 'still at the head town of the Borotse, a distance of 12 days, or nearly 200 miles, from the waggons'.

[5] Motonka, better known as Lebeola (cf. below, p. 130), was one of Sebetwane's companions from the south. During Sekeletu's reign he was accused of sorcery and fled to the BaTawana at Lake Ngami. There he and several compatriots were later killed for conspiring against Letsholathebe, the local chief, but his descendants are still in the tribe and constitute the nucleus of Shwanka ward, named after his son. (Schapera, field notes, 1940; *Ethnic Composition*, p. 97.)

When the country is overflowed the seeds of the date &
palmyra seem to have been borne to the hillocks on which they
now grow. Both the fruit & inside of the stem of the root are
eaten, also the rind of the Palmyra seed, and it is very good.

We entered into a Bakalahari village in the afternoon.
They presented us with a goat. Waited near a patch of tsetse
with the Kalingo river[1] on our right till sunset. We then proceeded through the infested district and slept by a bush on
the other side. Our stock of provisions were getting low &
many of the people who had come with us were reduced to
short allowance of tsitla, mosibe[2] &c. During the night Mr.
O. heard the Kitchen commenting on our not killing game.
'Are these men barena[3] or gentlemen? They are not men.
What is the use of their guns? The Mambari[4] *were* Barena,
but these are things only'. A whole torrent of abuse was
showered down upon us, much to the annoyance of the only
hearer of their scorn, but to the amusement of us both in the
morning. Mr O. rode down a quagga or zebra in the morning to the very great delight of the spectators, and our characters were perhaps placed on a par with the Mambari. The
latter however were better or more gaudily clothed than we,
and killed a good many wild animals for the Makololo.

During most of this day, the 4th, we passed over a country
bearing evidence of being frequently under water. We saw
a number of antelopes called poku,[5] very much like the reed
buck but probably different, also a very small antelope like
a stein buck but different in its conduct & habits. There is
also a small antelope, Seangu or 'Kama.[6] The Sesheke over-
flows most of the country over which we travelled on this
day. The grass is exceedingly rank & tall (country very
marshy), the grass in moist places reaching up to the shoul-

[1] The Lilonga, a stream flowing from the N.E. into Liambezi Lake; called 'Kal-
engue' on Streitwolf's map (1911).

[2] Central Bantu *mushibe*, Rhodesian copalwood (*Guibourtia coleosperma*).

[3] Plural of *morena*, 'lord, master'.

[4] Commonly identified as the OviMbundu of Central Angola (cf. *Travels*, p.
218), though Dr J. T. Tucker says that correctly the name refers to 'individuals,
either slaves or descendants of slaves, who acted as agents for white traders' (*Africa*,
vol. 26, 1956, p. 187).

[5] Puku, *Kobus vardoni* Livingstone (cf. *Travels*, p. 256; *Narrative*, p. 265).

[6] Not identified; called *sanku* in *Journal*, p. 80, and described as 'a very prettily
spotted antelope'.

der of a man on horseback. Trees evergreen. One, a splendid tree, has an edible fruit the stones of which are like those of a peach, but all were broken by some animal. The people extract an oil from the fruit. We saw for the first time in South Africa two specimens of Orchideous plants.

In the afternoon we came to the beautiful river Sesheke, and thanked God for permitting us first to see this glorious river.[1] All we could say to each other was to express our great pleasure by saying to each other, How glorious! How magnificent! How beautiful! And grand beyond discription it really was. Such a body of water, at least 400 yards broad, and deep. It may be stated as from three to five hundred yards wide. There are numerous banks of white sand, and on these we saw crockodieles. One hippopotamus appeared in the middle. The town of Sesheke appeared very beautiful on the opposite bank. The waves were so high the people were afraid to venture accross, but by & bye a canoe made its way to where we stood. They always keep the broadside of the canoe to the wind in crossing, so it is not surprising that accidents frequently occur. We went up the river some way in order to take an island in our passage. When there the space passed over seemed 300 yards, and there was an equal distance before us. The banks are from 16 to 20 ft high yet the annual overflow extends fifteen miles out. The period of its stated rise was said to be the month of September, and this being the end of a remarkably dry season it is not likely any one will come after us and find it lower. The water is hard and does not form a lather with soap. The water of the Chobe being quite soft, their sources are probably different.

We observed swallows flying about the banks, though this was winter in these parts and all these birds have left the country which may be called South Africa.

In crossing this beautiful river the waves lifted up the canoe and made it roll beautifully. The scenes of the Friths of Forth and Clyde were brought vividly back to my view, and

---

[1] In *Travels*, p. 90, D.L. writes that he and Oswell discovered the Zambesi 'in the end of June, 1851'. The date, as given above, was 4 August. He says also (p. 208) that the river 'is called by the whole of the Barotse the Liambai, or Leeambye. This we could not ascertain on our first visit, and, consequently, called the river after the town, "Sesheke". This term Sesheke means "white sandbanks", many of which exist at this part'.

had I been fond of indulging in sentimental suffusions[1] my Lachrymal apparatus seemed fully charged. But then the old man who was conducting us accross might have said, 'What on earth are you blubering at? Afraid of these crockodiles, Eh?' The little sentimentality which exuded[2] was forced to take its course down the inside of the nose. We have other work in this world than indulging in sentimentality of the 'Sonnet to the moon' variety.

On landing we were welcomed by many. The prevailing idea was that our presence was a sure precursor of abundant intercourse with Europeans and peace or 'sleep' by the possession of firearms. One of the chief wives of Sebitoane saluted us rather too freely. She seemed tipsy. Between three & four hundred persons collected around us. Moriantsané, the principal person,[3] shewed us round the town. Shewed us also three English guns which they had procured from the Bajoko or Bagatsaeri, who are either bastards or true Portuguese;[4] they had hair like ours, but it was cut short. The Makololo had gone on an expedition against the Bashukulompo, and when they met these slave dealers on the Maninché they had numbers of captives and gave about thirty of them as a present for the 3 muskets. They were well satisfied with their new customers, for they promised to visit Sebitoane in the course of 1851. We protested against the trade in the bodies of men, and they seemed to understand that it was wrong. They cordially agreed to the statement that it was not right to break up the family ties.

As we had tasted nothing since the night previous to this, and then only two buiscuits each, we were rather hungry. The question was at last put, What do these people eat? 'Everything except an alligator' being the reply they had latitude enough, but still they sat and feasted their eyes while

[1] 'effusions' (Blaikie, p. 113).　　　　　　　　　[2] 'exceeded' (Blaikie, p. 113).

[3] Morantsiane (Lozi 'Mulanziane') was the official name assumed by every successive headman of the town of Sesheke (cf. Coillard, pp. 154, 240). The man referred to here, Sebetwane's brother-in-law (*Travels*, p. 234), was killed by Sekeletu c.1860 on a charge of witchcraft (*Narrative*, p. 270; *Zambesi Expedition*, p. 257).

[4] BaJoko or BaZonko (MaZungu) was a name applied to Portuguese, Arab, and half-caste traders from the East Coast (cf. *Narrative*, pp. 217, 331). 'Bagatsaeri' means 'the people (or followers) of Tsaeri', i.e. of the Arab slave-dealer Ben-Habib (cf. below, p. 292).

our stomachs were starving. At length Sebitoane's sister[1] brought some milk. Then a sickly looking man gave a piece of meat, & the drunken lady a dish of 'mothuohatse'.[2] With these we returned to the other side and prepared to sleep on account of the horses being there.

5th. I went over early in the morning in order to hold a service in the town. About 400 collected and behaved better than usual on first occasions of the kind. They listened attentively. The water was quite smooth when I went over, but when the time for taking an altitude of the sun approached the river had become so rough it was with difficulty I could get boatmen to take me accross. When they consented I stripped and prepared for a plunge but we got safely over and found the altitude to be—

5th August.

    L's 110° 24′ 40″

    O's 110° 17′   Mean= Lat. 17° 29′ South

People presented about 5 gallons of honey, meal, & an ox in the morning. We took the former but declined the latter, and as soon as we had taken the latitude prepared to depart.

Ñuanamoari & Nuanabotale are the two chiefs of the Bashubea who live at Sesheke.[3] They are large men. They draw the river nearly North & South, and say when you look up the Borotse river as far as it is known 'the sun rises on one cheek & sets on the other'. Two days above Sesheke the rapids of which there are four begin, and four days below Sesheke is situated the waterfall of Mosioatunya or resounding smoke. It is so named because of the spray rising with great noise so high as to be visible ten or twelve miles off. Immediately beyond the falls the river is narrowed by means of rocks and the water is rapid untill it again spreads out and

---

[1] Mantshonyane, wife of Morantsiane. D.L. met her again when he revisited Sesheke in 1860 (cf. *Narrative*, pp. 273 ff.).

[2] Probably *Arachis hypogoea*, the ground-nut. 'The natives raise, besides their usual grains, considerable quantities of a bean which bears its pods underground. They are called "motu o hatsi" (earth-man), and are sweet when roasted' (*JRGS*, 1852, p. 168).

[3] 'Nuanamoari' (Mwanamwali) is the official name of a particular Subia chief in the Sesheke district; 'Nuanabotale' may be Monibothale, described by Coillard (p. 257) as 'quite an inferior village chief'.

becomes placid.[1] The Portuguese never came up the Sesheke, at least such is the testimony of Ñuanamoari and
Ñuanabotale, who are both old men and must have heard of
white men had such visited their river during any portion
of the last hundred years. We were the first white men ever
seen by the Bashubea. Seunturu, the chief of the Borotse
whom Sebitoane expelled, was said by his son[2] to have been
in the habit of sending men up to Lobale in order to purchase articles of European manufacture there. These he en-
umerated as clothing, crockery and beads.

This part of the Sesheke river is named so from numerous
banks of white sand in the river. We saw no rocks, but a
fragment picked up from the river bed was hard limestone.
There were numbers of trees quite new to us, and the people
say that up at the Borotse it is never cold. The sugar cane
grows there and also sweet potato and another kind of potato
(probably yams). They have also a low sort of grain, perhaps
buckwheat. The cattle attain maturity very soon and bring
forth when mere calves.

A party of Sebitoane's people went up the river to attack a
chief called Sekilenke.[3] They crossed a river called Lonta which
contains white or lightcoloured water. The water of the Liambae is clear, but when the Lonta flows into it the two waters flow
together for some distance unmixed.[4] The people of Sekilenke
had a stockade and defended themselves in it untill their powder was expended. The Makololo fought untill this took place,
then entered easily into the stockade and killed or dispersed
the people.[5] They have never been farther in that direction.
The information respecting the Moeng or Moenye river,[6]

---

[1] This is possibly the earliest authentic description of the Victoria Falls (which
D.L. first saw in 1855). On Oswell's map they are marked, fairly accurately, as
'Waterfall; spray seen 10 miles off', and the Zambesi below them is called 'R. of
Mosi oa tunya'. [2] Presumably Sipopa (p. 26).

[3] A Mbunda chief who had fled with his people from Angola and was living (in
December 1853) as a vassal of the Lozi chief Imasiku (cf. below, p. 201) near the
confluence of the Zambesi and Kabompo Rivers (*Travels*, p. 269).

[4] 'Lonta', as used here, is the Zambesi above its junction with the Kabompo
(D.L.'s 'Liambae', cf. the map in *Travels*).

[5] This may refer to the siege of Imasiku and his followers at Lukulu (cf. Jalla,
Litaba, p. 43; Ellenberger, p. 317).

[6] The Luanginga, which joins the Zambesi from the N.W. at approx. 15° 12′ S.
'Moenye' (Mwenyi) is the name of a tribe living in its basin near Kalabo, N.W.
Barotseland.

Lobale &c &c, was derived from Mokantju, Shokolo, & others. They report that nearly all the people on the rivers put down in our sketch possess boats and are rich. There is no want of food. Many of the tribes possess guns, and many more are well supplied with clothing and beads. These must come from the Portuguese, for we never heard of any people manufacturing cloth or beads. They all have the idea that those who are sold to the whites are eaten. One tribe situated far to [the] North West is called Bayibathu,[1] but they probably have this name from the circumstance of their purchasing slaves. Another is called Kalonda maeo which means 'tusk seekers'.[2] The guns of the Mambari are of very antient manufacture ; the stocks are grooved or fluted, and the locks apparently 100 years old. The words Legitimo de Braga & Lazaro Lazaretto seem to prove that they are of Portuguese origin.[3] They make bullets of common iron about the size of a large pea. They use cartridges too. Those the Mambari left with Sebitoane were bought for a boy each.

These Mambari were slave dealers from another tribe of that name. Their hair was like that of other natives but their complexion was lighter. They were all clothed in gaudy coloured apparel, and had a large assortment of English manufactured goods in their possession. When they came to the hill Libompa,[4] which is about one day beyond the Borotse gardens, they encamped and were afraid to come near the Makololo. Sebitoane went over to them in a canoe, the whole of the plain between the gardens and Libompa being under water, and persuaded them to come near the town. They hoisted a white flag as an indication of their pacific intentions. But the visits of slave dealers are never welcomed by the poorer classes. With the English trader it is different. All classes rejoice at his coming and all readily acquire the habit of keeping goods for his return. The Mambari must have been aware that their visits were not welcomed generally. They remained many months with Sebitoane, and when the Makololo offered to barter with cattle and ivory they de-

---

[1] Not identified; Tswana *baja-batho*, cannibals (lit., 'eaters of people').
[2] Not identified; possibly the BaLunda?
[3] Braga is a town in Portugal, about 30 miles N.N.E. of Porto.
[4] Libonta, 14° 59′ S. (*Travels*, p. 685).

clined, saying they wanted boys only. Sebitoane gave them 8 boys for the same number of guns, and four as presents. There was one person with them having a large mass of hair on his head and rather lighter in colour than the others. He described himself as a half caste, his mother having been a Balojazi woman and his father a Portuguese.

After remaining some months with the Makololo they proposed to attack some other tribe which might be at enmity with them, and stipulated that in consideration for the use of their guns in the attack the Mambari should recieve all the captives while the Makololo should take all the cattle. The command was entrusted to Ponuane and it was while on this foray they met with the Bazoñko or Bajoko, who are in the habit of frequenting the Maninche or Nakalañka, which are said to be the large rivers of the Bashukulompo.[1] The Mambari rivetted the chains on the hands of the youths whom they procured, and departed with about 200 of them. They call a chain Lewinge.[2] They promised to return again to Sebitoane. They made very neat shoes, jackets, & managed to kill a good many Lechwee[3] &c with their guns.

They went away towards the N.N.W. Some of the Makololo went with them but soon returned, probably from not liking the fatigue of the journey. They reported that the Mambari ordered them to turn back. The[y] made a tour through the different towns named by Mokantju and collected very many slaves. They gave a piece of cotton cloth about 28 yards long for a man or boy.[4]

The usual size of a mantle or cloak of striped cotton was 57 inches long and 66 inches broad. They had abundance of blue green and red baize.

Pity the market is not supplied with English manufactures in exchange for the legitimate products of the country. If English merchants would come up the Zambesi during the months of June July and August the slave trader would very

---

[1] 'Maninché or Loenge' (*JRGS*, 1855, p. 229), i.e. the Lunga, a major tributary of the Kafue, which it joins at approx. 14° 35' S., 26° 25' E.

[2] Lozi *liwenge*, 'chain, fetter' (Jalla, *Dictionary*). The word also occurs in Luchazi, Mbunda, and Nyengo (D.L., MS. vocabularies).

[3] *Kobus leche*, the lechwe waterbuck.

[4] 'The price of a boy was one old Portuguese musket or about 9 yards of cotton or baize' (17.x.1851 Tidman, in Chamberlin, p. 155).

soon be driven out of the market. That the country drained by the Sesheke is not a small portion of the slave producing region may be inferred from the fact that the Borotse town is situated about 8 days beyond the town of Sesheke, and the people know it as a very large river at least 8 days or other 200 miles beyond. The natives too mention the existence of a water or Lake called Sebolamakoa,[1] and if this is Lake Maravi[2] most of the Slaves exported on the East Coast come from that part. The people of Sebolamakoa are said to be rich in cattle and to possess many beads and much cloth.

Mr O. thinks that agents or commissioners situated in different parts in that region would in the course of ten years extirpate the slave trade. I imagine that the existence of a salubrious locality must first be ascertained, and if that is of easy access by the Sesheke, then mercantile men may be invited to carry their enterprize into that region. If it is profitable for those who are engaged in the coast trade to pass along in their ships and pick up ivory, bees wax &c, those who may have enterprise enough to push into the interior and recieve the goods at first hand would surely find it much more profitable. The returns for the first year might be small, but those who for the love of their species would run some risk would assuredly be no losers in the end. The natives readily acquire the habit of saving for a market. Honey abounds in the country but all the wax is thrown away. Ivory has only been used to form armlets, and the saw employed is so thick it distroys half an inch each time it passes through the tusk. Ostrich feathers are only used for adorning the head in the dance. All these and other articles would be preserved for the legitimate trader. The people have abundance of cattle. They are unlike the poor starvelings to the South, whose every thought must be directed to, What shall we eat and what shall we drink and wherewithall shall we be clothed? Give a people the opportunity they will civilize themselves, and that too more effectually than can be done by missionary societies. The slave dealer must have his due.

---

[1] In *Travels*, pp. 502 f., D.L. says that Ben-Habib had 'visited Sebola Makwaia, and found that the chief town was governed by an old woman of that name'. She lived 'far to the N.E.', in the vicinity of Lake Suye (approx. 14° 25′ S., 27° 35′ E.).

[2] An old name for Lake Nyasa.

All the Mambari came decently clothed. We never saw a party of Bechuanas or Griquas of whom so much could be said. Perhaps civilization as the duty of Missionaries is a thing taken for granted, yet still requiring to be proved. We ought to preach the gospel. Some will believe and some will reject. If we are faithful we shall stand in our lot in the latter day and hear the sentence which will wipe away all tears from our eyes.

5th. Our horses were brought up as soon as we had taken the Latitude, and we soon set off on our return to the waggons. We slept on the spot usually selected for the purpose by people before going through the Tsetse.

6th. Early in the morning we passed through it and breakfasted at the Bakalihari village.[1] They supplied us with the fruit of the Palmyra tree. It is the rind which is eaten and it tastes like sponge buiscuit. A meal is extracted from the fibrous root of the date bush, but it is not good. They make a kind of sack with the fibres surrounding the root of the date tree.

Passing along we entered the cattle post of Motoñka, but before reaching it we passed by a great number of people sent on an expedition to the Sekota[2] for corn. One of them hand-[ed us?] a cup of beer, his name   .[3] John[4] had nearly lost his voice with hunger. Leaving Motoñka's about 12 we proceeded, intending to sleep at Pogo's village, but we were misled by John believing a certain tree visible in the dark was Pogo's Palmyra or Moporotla[5] tree, but when we went several miles through cold damp reedy places we found out our mistake and had to sleep with very little firewood. We met in one day more people carrying corn, honey &c, than we should have met in ten in any part of the Bechuana country already supplied with missionaries. We saw between 4 & 500 people in our way to Sesheke. We met Mpepe by the river, he was borne on a sort of couch and clad

---

[1] Cf. p. 37.

[2] The Zambesi, immediately above the Victoria Falls, is called 'R. of Sicota' on Oswell's map. For 'Sekota', cf. p. 22.

[3] D.L. left a blank space for the missing name.

[4] Probably William John Thomas, familiarly known as John, a Cape Coloured man who was Oswell's favourite servant (cf. *Oswell*, vol. i, pp. 117, 211, etc.).

[5] *Kigelia pinnata*, the 'sausage tree'.

in cotton trowsers &c. Having reached Linyanti we were welcomed back and heard that Mrss Wilson and Edwards had arrived.[1] Proceeded same evening to the waggons and found all well. The traders had come on horseback.

Resolve to return on Tuesday 12th because the moon was at its full, and if we did not return then we must wait another month for next moon. Next month the Tsetse would bite in the night. If the Chobe filled so would the Sonta behind us and any delay in crossing the Sonta would be fatal to all our oxen for that is the very midst of the Tsetse habitat.

Because nothing definite could be settled without the presence of Mamochisane, and she was 350 miles distant,[2] we could not come to any arrangement with the subordinates; and even though she had been present, the strong defence of their deep reedy rivers ought not to be abandoned for my convenience, and the hilly parts are so far off, either to the Eastward on one hand or to the Northward beyond the Borotse on the other. They are so plagued by Mosilikatse the North seems the only likely place for peace. That we were obliged to return was a source of unfeigned sorrow to me, for we had nothing before us but a long dreary way back, and we had come in with the expectation of being allowed to remain for at least a twelvemonth. Our hopes respect[ing] Mr Oswel were that he would proceed along one of the numerous rivers of which we had heard, perhaps to the sea, and thereby open up a path to us for supplies, but the immense marshes which abound everywhere and the Tsetse presented insuperable barriers.

It is almost impossible for one who has not seen the country to form an accurate idea of it. It is intersected by numerous and deep rivers, and these are very winding in their courses. They are, too, flanked by extensive reedy bogs, and the whole country is perfectly flat besides, the only exceptions being patches on which stand the towns and gardens. At the period of the annual flow of the rivers the whole of the lower parts are covered, and the district for hundreds of miles must present the appearance of one vast marsh with numerous islands on its surface. Almost every one has a boat, and in these they traverse the country in every direction.

[1] From Lake Ngami; cf. above, p. 7.   [2] But see above, p. 36.

They generally go to their gardens in their canoes. A root of the waterlily called Kankalla[1] forms a pleasant article of diet. It is the potato of these parts, and is found in abundance when the water subsides. The water of the Chobe is quite soft. It rose one inch while we were there in July but gradually fell one inch and a quarter. The Tsō or river which supplies the Teoge, Lake, Tamunakle &c had its annual flow during the same period. This would indicate different sources, but the natives were not agreed in their accounts of it. It must rise from 8 to ten feet before it reaches some fish dykes which we observed ajacent to the river and about a mile from the waggon. The annual flow of the Sesheke occurs in August, but 1851 was an exception in the case of the Chobe. The rains and rise of the Chobe are nearly contemporaneous, but they are said by some to have a rise independantly of rains in the parts inhabited by Makololo.

The fever prevails in a very virulent form among the Makololo. Indeed the majority of the people whom Sebitoane brought into these parts have been cut off by it. The women escape better than the men, but they are troubled by an excessive menstrual discharge. The malarious poison is probably carried out of the system by this means.[2] The River races do not suffer so severely. They are quite black, and their muscular system is strongly developed. They possess much animal life, are deep chested, and the muscles of the arms & chest are very large. Some parts of the country are not so much infested by fever as others. I offer myself as a forlorn hope in order to ascertain whether there is a place fit to be a sanatorium for more unhealthy spots. May God accept my service and use me for his glory. A great honour it is to be a fellow worker with God.

The people have distinctly the idea of a supreme being, to whom every thing supernatural is ascribed. He is called Nyampi or Reza. The latter word agrees with Oreeja of the Bayeiye.[3] If a man dies he is said to have been 'lifted by Nyampi' or by the Morena (Lord), the word lift, 'Gapa',

[1] Not identified; possibly *Nymphaea calliantha*.
[2] Cf. above, p. 24.
[3] The names Nyambe ('Nyampi') and Leza ('Reza', 'Oreeja') are widely used for the Supreme Being in various parts of Central Africa; cf. *African Ideas of God*, ed. E. W. Smith, 1950, pp. 75-77, 156-61.

being used in the same sense as the Highland 'lift' in stealing cattle.[1]

There is a peculiar kind of divination employed by all the river race. It consists of a form of enquiry at an axe handle which is laid on the ground for the purpose. In the case of a sick man they ask, is the sickness caused by (naming a number of persons in succession), all the while attempting to lift up the axe handle with the fingers. It comes readily untill the proper name is pronounced, and then by a little art it is made to appear sticking fast to the ground, the fingers slip off with a jerk, and a little sand falling in the direction of the person named is confirmation of the original verdict.[2] When this point is settled they take a little meat and place it on a little river grass, and place it with a prayer before the departed spirit which has caused the sickness.

Amongst the Bamaponda the doctors take beads &c, & present them to the spirit of the departed who is believed to be inflicting sickness on the patient, and a prayer is uttered, 'Moejenkodjo, Moejenkodjo' (Let him alone). This is accompanied by a whistling sound, 'Shatoka celanda' (we give beads). Though they fear these superior spirits occasionally, they have neither reverence nor love to them. They hate God. This is evident in their thoughts concerning him. For if a man is supremely wicked they say of such a one, 'He has God'. If pain in any part they say God is here, or if twinges in their stomach God is here, placing their hand on the part. When the chief Libebe[3] was asked why he had not any cattle he replied, 'because cattle have God', they are the source of evil.

When a man dies among the Batoka his son stabs all the grown cattle and leaves only the younger ones. Of this we were informed by Guantu.[4]

The Batoka have also the strange custom of knocking out

[1] Cf. above, p. 17.

[2] According to White (*Africa*, vol. 18, 1948, p. 88), this method 'is most commonly used to divine the names of ancestral spirits reincarnated in children, or to ascertain troubling spirits in case of illness'.

[3] Chief of the MaMbukushu living in western Caprivi Strip at and around Libebe (18° 1' S., 21° 29' E.), which is named after him.

[4] Not mentioned elsewhere. He may have been the man who furnished D.L.'s Toka vocabulary (cf. above, p. 31).

the upper front teeth at the age of puberty. They do so in order to be like oxen. But the Babimpe knock out both upper and lower front teeth. This is said to have arisen from a quarrel in which the wife of a chief bit his hand. He ordered her teeth to be knocked out, and his people followed his example.[1] When the under teeth are relieved from the pressure and attrition of the upper they grow long and press out the under lip. The upper lip too falling inwards gives an antient look to the countenance. The custom seems universal among both men & women, though considerable resistance is made to the infliction of so much pain as is implied in having the teeth knocked out with a hatchet.

11th. People very anxious for our stay. Promise to return. They propose to make a garden for us. Gave them seeds— maize, millet, English corn, peach & apricot stones, beans (French), melons, pumpkins &c &c. They seem very desirous to have new kinds of grain. Leave 9 oxen & a calf & Lady the dog.[2] Spoke in behalf of Chombo or Moroamatsane, and again as we have done repeatedly against the traffic in slaves. They promise to abstain from it, but the surest way of securing a fulfillment of their engagement would be to supply the market with English manufactures in exchange for the natural produce of the country.

Promise Mpépe the chief an iron pot next time we come into the country, also a larger breed of fowls & a larger breed of sheep & goats. They promise to fulfill Sebitoane's intention of supplying us with cattle in lieu of those killed by the Tsetse. Is it right to recieve them? They have probably been stolen. But according to the laws and customs which have been in operation from time immemorial, the cattle have always gone into the hands of the strongest. They are esteemed the rightful property of those who have had the power to get & keep them, & if we examine the sources whence the different tribes have derived their cattle we find there are none honestly come by in the country. Most of the Boors' cattle

[1] A fuller version is given in *Travels*, pp. 532 f., where it is said to be a 'facetious explanation' of the custom advanced by 'some of the Makololo'. The 'Babimpe', according to D.L.'s map (cf. also *Narrative*, p. 214), live on the north bank of the Zambesi just below the confluence of the Kafue. Modern sources do not show or mention a tribe of that name.

[2] Possibly the animal mentioned above, p. 12.

were stolen from the Hottentots. Even Lechulathebe's cattle were taken from the Bakalihari.[1]

We come among them now as propagators of a better system, Harbingers of peace. We do not come as judges to condemn the past, but [as] messengers of reconciliation, believing that in reference to both the past and future there is one who judgeth, and that judge says 'vengeance is mine, I will repay', saith the Lord. If they offer I shall recieve without reference to the source from which they have taken them. Ministers of the Church of England take their tithes &c., though many of those from whom they are exacted believe themselves robbed.

With respect to eating the meat of these animals, the rule seems to be, 'Eat what is set before you, asking no questions for conscience sake'.[2] We might do without, but take what is offered in order to make the people feel that we are theirs, and if we give them our all it is no great matter in them to feed us for a time. If we impart unto them spiritual things is it a great matter if we reap their carnal things?

[1] Letsholathebe was chief c.1840–74 of the BaTawana at Lake Ngami. The BaKgalagadi are reputedly the earliest Bantu settlers in Bechuanaland; most of them were conquered or driven into the Kalahari Desert (whence their name) by later invaders, and in D.L.'s time many were serfs of the ruling class in such tribes as the BaKwena, BaNgwato, and BaTawana.

[2] 'Whatsoever is set before you, eat, asking no question for conscience sake' (1 Corinthians 10: 27).

II

RETURN TO THE SOUTH

Return down Tamunakle River

Tuesday 12 [August]. Brought the cattle over the river Chobe and inyoked after sunset, then proceeded onwards to the Sonta. One waggon fell behind, and when we reached the Sonta we were unable to get out of it. Remained in the middle of the river till about nine o'clock, having sent back the cattle to bring the other waggon on. The other waggon then came up and we were obliged to stand in an open space all day. The Tsetse abounded on all sides of us. We managed to keep the cattle away from the trees & in the evening recommenced our journey, reaching Tsatsara pond early in the morning.

Chobe to Sonta	12 miles
Sonta to Tsatsara	14 —
Tsatsara to sleeping place	16
Sleeping place to Chombo's	23
	65 miles
(Path to Sesheke from the waggons	
Chobe to Linyanti	10 miles
Pogo's village	17 —
Date bush sleeping place	23 —
Setlagana's village[1]	10 —
To other side of Tsetse spot	13
To Sesheke town	20
	93 miles at least)

Sunday 17th. Spent at Chombo's village.[2] Attendance 250. Very large proportion of them are children. Crops having failed, they live mostly on Tsitla or Tseetla, which seems to contain a large amount of starch. It abounds in large quantities in all the rivers. They are a branch of the Banayoa

---

[1] The 'Bakalahari village' (p. 37); cf. below, p. 130.   [2] Cf. above, p. 14.

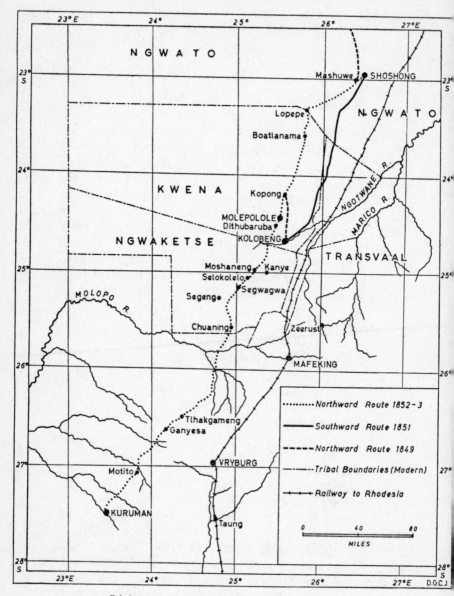

1. Livingstone's Routes in Southern Bechuanaland.

or Makalaka. Many shave the whole head. Their huts are made so as to admit of a fire underneath the sleeping place. The mosquitoes abound in their swamps.

head . Their huts are made so as to admit

of a fire under neath the sleeping place

The mosquitoes abound in their swamps

18th Left on monday - Passing

along to the west of our old path accross

the part where we allowed our oxen

to run along the Rhinoceros foot path

18th. Left on Monday, passing along to the west of our old path accross the part where we al[l]owed our oxen to run along the Rhinoceros foot path for water.[1] There the oxen which died at the Chobe may have been bitten by the Tsetse, for the guides now inform us that the insect exists all along the river near Morotse's.[2] Road soft & through Mopane trees. Slept near enough the river for oxen to be led to it for water after dark.

19th. Through large Mopane trees, till we strike river about a mile south of Matsaratsara's village.[3] Two palmyra trees close by the village. Tsetse abounds on the Western side of the Mababe ; saw some brought over by the Makoba. Pass on in the evening, with the intention of sleeping with Mr Oswel before entering on a patch of tsetse which we intended to go through by the light of the moon. It being dark we came upon some pitfalls (Mr O. saw Tsetse here) when some one called out, 'An ox in a pitfall'. This induced me to

---

[1] Cf. above, p. 13. [2] Cf. above, p.14.
[3] At 'Mabokwe' (not identified), on the eastern bank of the Mogogelo River. Its inhabitants subsequently moved to the Botletle. (Schapera, field notes, 1940; *Ethnic Composition*, p. 83.)

stand, and having burned all the grass which covered the pit-falls we remained there during the night; and being perplexed in the morning what to do, our guide refusing to go farther, and suppose we went after Mr O. we should light upon the spot of Tsetse just in the heat of the day, we resolved to go along the river and in the event of seeing the fly turn our oxen into the reed. This step to which we were providentially led proved our safety, for Mr O. after travelling five hours through deep heavy sand and thick bush found himself just abreast of us, and his oxen were probably bitten by the Tsetse at the same time. Many of his oxen died subsequently to this, but none of ours, except such as were sick when we left the Chobe. Saw three tigers[1] in the morning. River generally flat and apparently shallow. Flows Nor-East & East. Shoot a hippopotamus which came up to breathe close by the waggon. Matsaratsara comes up. A pleasant old man & very frank. He is the paramount chief of the Bayeiye.[2]

Pass along a few miles & wait till moon rose about 4 A.M., then pass through a thick belt of Mopane trees. Early in morning see a large dry Pond on our left. Another long tract of large Mopane trees with a hillock of Tufa, near which we saw some Tsetse. Road rather heavy. Pitfalls; a horse falls into one. We then unyoked at an open space by the river by a Bushman and Bakoba village. Tsetse all about in the trees. In the evening having gone about 3 miles we reached Lingalo's.

22d August 1851, at Lingalo's village, Lat. 19° 42'.[3]

Hour 8..28

☉ 58° 21' 40" Upper Limb

☽ 94° 33 Lower Limb

Sun East Moon West near Meridian

Moroa Manchunyana,[4] a Makololo man sent after us with

[1] Africanderism for 'leopards'.

[2] He was the great-grandson and namesake of the chief under whom the BaYeei had migrated from the north; but as they had become divided into many politically separate groups in Bechuanaland, he was 'paramount' only in acknowledged seniority of birth. (Schapera, field notes, 1940.)

[3] Dingalo, hereditary head of Mepakwana ward, was one of Letsholathebe's chief retainers and 'overseer' of the BaYeei in eastern Ngamiland. His village was at approx. 23° 45' E.

[4] Morwa-Mantshunyane, 'son of Mantshunyane'; not mentioned elsewhere.

a present of eight small oxen, came up to us at Chombo's and to my regret turned round at Lingalo's village.

From Chombo's to Matsaratsara's	20
To the pitfalls	3
To the Hippopotamus	5
To Mopane bush	5
To Lingalo's	15
To Sumagow's	13
	61
To Makheto's on Zouga	16
	77
From Chombo's to Chobe	65
	142

Pass on on 22d to Moroamokondi's.[1] The Nakon a new antelope[2] abounds here. It lives in the reeds, and is well adapted by the length of its feet for walking on soft mud. The horns are like those of a Khoodoo[3] but smaller. When pursued it submerges itself all except the point of the nose, and is usually killed by the Bakoba while in that position. When the reed is being burnt it often allows its horns to be burned rather than come out of them.

In evening go about four miles and sleep where Harstflee[4] fell into a pitfall.

23. Reach Sumagow's village[5] and remain there on Sunday. Mr O. passed on with guides towards Makheto's.[6] Hearing from him that the distance was about 16 miles, we proceeded forward on Monday & reached the Zouga by Makheto's village, 8 miles from the junction of Tamunakle, on Tuesday morning.

[1] Not identified.   [2] *Tragelaphus spekei,* marshbuck or sitatunga.
[3] *Tragelaphus strepsiceros.*   [4] Apparently the name of an ox.
[5] Samaxao was a Yeei headman living close to Maun (20° S., 23° 25′ E.), the present Tawana capital.
[6] Makgetho, also a Yeei headman, lived at approx. 20° 10′ S., 23° 32′ E. (TSGS 1539, Kalahari).

Sebitoane's song

Sebitoane's song

Sekhosi sa Laoeya tlotloko
Tlotlo sa mothu a sa lule Hae
Sekhosi sa laoeya liyo tse
Liyo tsa mothu a sa lule Hae
Mosari oa bathu botle
Antse a tsamaea mo nageñ
Pelesa tona ea ba lisebana
Ea matlamela rure
Ea sita ea lifola hela lioma
Le moyi oa eona ga o ko o shuta
Ga o ko o bo o leba magetleñ
Khomu ea gañoa lisebana
Le Banyana ba e gama
Ga ki tlole ki nyala lifurutse
Lifurutse la ga manyane
Khomu ea teñ e ema hela
Khomu ea Mañope ea Lifurutse
E sita le banyana ba e gama
Ea sita le mengañ ba e gama
Khomu ea Mangope ea Lifurutse
Khomu se lelela sekhosi
Mothu a kile a tlabana entua
A lelekisa Matibele
A lonakeñ loa Chuéta a Laka
A Chuéta a ga Laka
Go tue u bone a ñuana
A ikhamela

*

Go tla tlatsa khueri mañ
Selemo tsega e coa ka morago
Go tla tlatsa ñuanatsele
Tsega e coa ka morago

*

Seashokoe
E lese ea shokoe
Ba re bolaile ki makorocoanyane
Ga rea luñua ki mothu boloi
Re bolailoe ki makorocoanyane
Re yeloe ki khomu gare ea eona
Ga rea lōa ki makorocoanyane
Cuara fupa ga leakoe
— a tenane
Lehakoa la ga kuñka
Luana fupa lekañka
— Legakoe

The above are some of Sebitoane's songs, and important as specimens of pure idiom or [at] least of idiom untouched by European influence.[1]

*

[Transposed into the modern orthography:

(a) *Sebetwane's song*

Segosi, sala o e ja tlotloko(?)
tlôtlô la motho a sa dule gae ;
Segosi, sala o e ja dijô tse,
dijô tsa motho a sa dule gae.
5 Mosadi wa batho botlhe
a ntse a tsamaya mo nageng.
Pelesa-tona ya badisa-bana
e a matlamêla ruri,
ya sita ya difola(?) fêla diôma,
10 le moji wa yônê ga o ko o šuta,
ga o ko o bo o leba magetleng.
Kgomo e a gangwa [ke ba-]disa-bana,
le banyana ba e gama.
Ga ke tlhôle ke nyala LeHurutshe,

---

[1] Even if D.L. recorded the texts correctly, which is doubtful, they are of a kind whose interpretation is by no means easy (cf. p. 59). I am much indebted to Rev. A. Sandilands and Dr E. Westphal for help in dealing with problems of orthography and translation.

15 leHurutshe la ga Manyane ;
kgomo ya teng e êma fêla,
kgomo ya [ga] Mangôpê, ya leHurutshe ;
e sita le banyana ba e gama,
e sita le mengang ba e gama,
20 kgomo ya [ga] Mangôpê, ya leHurutshe,
kgomo e lelêla Segosi.
   Motho o kile a tlhabana ntwa,
a lelekisa maTebele,
a lonakeng lwa Tšwêta a Laka,
25 a Tšwêta a ga Laka ;
go twe, o bônê, a ngwana a ikgamêlê.

(b)

Go tla tlatsa kgwedi mang ?
Selemo tshega e tswa kwa moragô.
Go tla tlatsa Ngwanatsele,
tshega e tswa kwa moragô.

(c)
Seašôkwe

E lesê, e a šôkwe.
Ba re bolaile ke makorotswanyane ;
ga re a longwa ke motho boloi,
re bolailwe ke makorotswanyane,
5 re jelwe ke kgomo gare ga yôna ;
ga re a loiwa ke makorotswanyane.
   Tshwara fupa, ga le akwe,
      [le] a tenane,
lehakwa la ga kunka,
10 lwana(?) fupa lekanka
      [ga] le gakwe.

Translations:

(a) *Sebetwane's song*[1]

Segosi,[2] stay here and eat . . .
the prosperity of a person still at home.
Segosi, stay here and eat the food,
the food of a person still at home.

5 The wife of all the people[3]
is still going about in the veld.
The big pack-ox of the child-tenders
it has departed for good (?)
it has even . . .

10 and he who eats it moves not away,
nor does he look back over his shoulders.
The cow is milked by the child-tenders,
and even the children they milk it.
I shall no longer marry in Hurutsheland,

15 Hurutsheland of Manyane;
where the cow just stands still,
the cow of Mangôpê of Hurutsheland,[4]
so that even the children milk it,
even cowards they milk it.

20 The cow of Mangôpê of Hurutsheland,
the cow is bellowing for Segosi.
A man once fought a battle
and drove away the maTabele

---

[1] This 'song' is evidently part of Sebetwane's *mabôkô* (praise-poems). Such poems, a characteristic and common element of Bantu traditional literature, 'consist of phrases and sentences in praise of some tribe, clan, person . . . They narrate, in high-pitched adulatory style, deeds for which the subject has acquired fame. . . .' Two noteworthy features are 'the extraordinary difficulty of their language, which . . . is often so archaic as to be only partly intelligible', and 'the highly figurative and allusive nature of words and expressions used, which require a considerable amount of extensive and intensive historical as well as ethnographical knowledge for their understanding' (G. P. Lestrade, in *The Bantu-Speaking Tribes of South Africa*, ed. Schapera, 1937, pp. 295 f.).

[2] 'Royal one', apparently addressed to Sebetwane.

[3] A common praise-name for a chief, because 'he provides the people with sustenance'.

[4] Mangope was chief of the BaHurutshe-booManyane, whom Sebetwane had attacked c.1824–6 (cf. above, pp. 18, 19 and Breutz, *The Tribes of Marico District*, pp. 58, 59).

       of the . . . of Chweta, son of Langa,[1]
25 of Chweta, son of Langa ;
       it was said, Look, let the child milk for itself.

(b)
Which month will make it full ?[2]
In summer Tshega comes out afterwards.
November will make it full,
Tshega comes out afterwards.

(c). It is twisted[3]
Leave it, it is twisted.
They defeated us with small canoes ;
no one harmed us by witchcraft,
we were defeated with little canoes,
5 we were eaten by an ox in its midst (?)
we were not bewitched by the little canoes.
    Seize the divining-bone, one does not lie to it,
      [it] causes disgust
the praised one (?) of . . .
10 .   .   .   .   .   .
     [it] cannot be forgotten.

I add the following instances of his circumstances inducing certain courses of conduct. The people of Sekhota who live at the Waterfalls sent for the Matibele to attack him, and when they came ferried them over the river as they could outflank him. Sebitoané retired before them and directed his way towards the Borotse, but this people made free with his cattle in the march and even killed some of the advanced body. When informed of the circumstance he said, 'You see I flee in my affliction to these Borotse, and they kill me, I thought to find an asylum but I find murder'. On the following day the Borotse came again, and Sebitoane coming in front of the cattle killed great numbers of them. The whole tribe turned out against him on the third day, and were com-

---

[1] Reputedly the first chief and eponym of the BakaLanga (Tswana 'BagaLaka'), a 'Tebele' (Ndebele) tribe living in Potgietersrust district, Transvaal.

[2] This seems to be part of a children's song about the sequence of the months. 'Tshega' I cannot explain; Dr Westphal thinks it may be the name of a star.

[3] This may be another fragment of Sebetwane's praises, but I cannot make much sense of the text as recorded or explain the allusions.

pletely routed & great numbers slain. They [were] then reduced to be tributary. Having repulsed the Matibele too, he went down to the Sekota and expelled them, putting one of their number in the place of the tribe because this man had spoken against inviting the Matibele, saying, Why invite the Matibele to attack Sebitoane with whom we are living in peace?[1]

The Borotse are not very submissive subjects to Sebitoane. They have several times broken out into rebellion, killed women & children, and not unfrequently kill those whom they dislike by overturning the canoes in which they are sailing.

Koma is the name of the Papyrus plant.

Tula an edible fruit tree.

Mosibe a bean, edible.

Motsikiri a beautiful fruit-bearing tree, people extract oil from its seeds.[2]

Jesus came not to judge, κρινω, condemn judicially or execute vengeance on any one. His was a message of peace and love. He shall not strive nor cry, neither shall his voice be heard in the streets.[3] Missionaries ought to follow his example. Neither insist upon our rights, nor appear as if we could allow our goods to be distroyed without regret; for if we are righteous over much[4] or stand up for our rights with too great vehemence we beget dislike, and the people see no difference between ourselves and them; and if we appear to care nothing for the things of the world, they conclude we are rich, and when they beg our refusal is ascribed to niggardliness and our property too is wantonly distroyed. 'Ga ba tloke' they are not in need, is the phrase employed when our goods are allowed to go to distruction by the neglect of servants. The principle propounded in the bible ought to be kept in view: 'the laborer is worthy of his hire'.[5] They who

---

[1] Sebetwane's conquest of Barotseland was by no means as simple as D.L. implies; cf. Jalla, *Litaba*, pp. 41 ff., Ellenberger, pp. 313 ff. His attack on Sekute (p. 22) is described more fully in *Travels*, p. 517.

[2] Koma = *Cyperus papyrus*; tula (Tswana *morula*) = *Sclerocarya caffra*; mosibe (cf. p. 37) = *Guibourtia coleosperma*; motsikiri = *Trichilia emetica* (the 'splendid tree' mentioned on p. 38).

[3] Matthew 12: 19.   [4] Ecclesiastes 7: 16.   [5] Luke 10: 7.

preach the gospel should live off the gospel.[1] In South Seas the first question put to a chief who applies for a missionary is, Can you support him? In Africa the idea somehow or other has become prevalent that he who allows a missionary to live with him confers a benifit upon the missionary. In coming among a savage people we ought to make them feel we are 'of them'. We seek not yours but you.[2] But while ever careful not to make a gain of them, we ought to be as careful to appear thankful & appreciate any effort they may make for our comfort or subsistence. When ye enter into a village &c., eat such things as are set before you.[3] Acting otherwise in order to feel that we are independant, or because the people are impure, or may have lifted the cattle they slaughter, seems like 'Stand by, come not near me, for I am holier than thou'.[4] 'Whatsoever is sold in the shambles, that eat' &c.[5]

Rhinoceros

Left Sumagow's on Monday morning. Proceed along the bank for about three miles. Leave river and go 9 miles. Sleep about five miles from Zouga. See a Rhinoceros, Keitloa. There seems after all to be only two kinds of Rhinoceros, the White and the black. Of the white[6] there are the common Mohohu and Kuabaoba as varieties, and there is not a particle of difference in them except in the shape & direction of the horns. Of the black[7] there is the Keitloa, or long horned variety, the two horns being of same length, and the borile, or little short horned variety which has not yet attained its full size. There is not a particle of difference between these varieties except in the matter of age & growth. The Keitloa is only the full grown black Rhinoceros. The colour of both white & black is the same.

Held service at Makheto's and proceeded 18 miles along the bank, the last 8 very heavy with thick bush, the branches meeting overhead. About opposite to the honey tree, saw several Bushmen and Bakhoba villages on the Southern bank.

27. Came out of the thick bush and passed along very

---

[1] 1 Corinthians 9: 14.   [2] 2 Corinthians 12: 14.
[3] Luke 10: 8.   [4] Isaiah 65: 5.
[5] 1 Corinthians 10: 25.   [6] *Diceros simus* (Tswana *mogohu*, *kôbaôba*).
[7] *Diceros bicornis* (Tswana *kgwêtla*, *bodile*).

heavy sand for about 2 miles, then crossed the Zouga at Mak-hetonyane's. A very good ford.[1]

Passed on about three miles. Horse fell into a pitfall. Great numbers of ostriches killed in pitfalls this year. The drought must be intense in the desert when these are compelled to come to the river for water.

28th. Proceed onwards & sleep at Cheeta village.[2] Weather still cold in mornings. Came over hard ground with low trees.

29th. Over very heavy sand to a hollow 4 miles on Lake side of Palane's.[3] Remain Sunday. What a comfort it is to be out of the Tsetse. It is said to abound nearly all the way down from Matsaratsara's or rather from Chombo's to Sumagow's. The road however is generally hard & could be travelled easily during the night. There is always plenty of water upon it, which makes it preferable to the route of Shobo.[4] There are several other fords on the Zouga.

Tsetse

This insect is about the size of a common blue bottle fly, and is similar in appearance to the dog fly, having yellow bars accross the after part of the body. The wings project beyond the body backwards, and the[y] seem slightly to overlap each other. It abounds over extensive tracts of country in the Interior of Africa, and as its bite is certainly fatal to domestic animals numerous and large tribes are compelled to live on grain and the flesh of game. Its farthest progress Southwards is the banks of the Limpopo, but it seems to extend as far North as the vicinity of Abysinia and is probably the Zimb described by Bruce.[5]

1 Probably Chanokha Drift, 20° 9′ S., 23° 39′ E. Makgethonyane was presumably a petty local headman.

2 Not identified; evidently somewhere between Chanokha Drift and Makalamabedi.

3 Phalane was a Yeei headman, living at or near Makalamabedi, whom D.L. had met on the first journey to Lake Ngami in 1849.

4 From Goroje's to Chombo's; cf. above, pp. 10 ff.

5 James Bruce (1730–94), author of *Travels to Discover the Sources of the Nile* (5 vols., 1790), explored Abyssinia in 1769–71. He describes *zimb* as a fly, 'very little larger than a bee', which appears in dense swarms as soon as the tropical rains begin to fall. 'All the cattle [then] forsake their food, and run wildly about the plain, till they die worn out with fatigue, fright, and hunger' (*op. cit.*, vol. i, p. 388).

As we lived for two months on the Southern bank of the Chobe where this insect abounds in great numbers, and both our children and selves have been bitten repeatedly, we can testify that the poison which produces such fatal effects in cattle is perfectly innocuous to man and wild animals. When undisturbed the Tsetse thrusts his proboscis into the skin apparently farther than necessary to reach the true skin. He then slightly withdraws it. A reservoir is probably made by the manoeuvre, for his mandibles are presently seen at work, and the proboscis becomes of a purple colour and his shrivel- ed belly very soon expands, & when quite full he flies off to the nearest tree. The bite produces less irritation than that of the Mosquito. If on the back of the hand or anywhere where the skin is thin, there is no inflammation or irritation, but on the palm of the hand an inflamed point of about a quarter of an inch in diameter having a tingling sensation lasts for a few days. One happened to insinuate himself into the bosom of my shirt one evening, but though I heard him buzz I thought it was one which I had secured in my pocket, and allowed him to remain in contact with the pit of my stomach during the night. Three inflamed spots each about an inch in diameter appeared on the part in the morning, but no other consequences followed except local uneasiness of pain & itchiness combined.

Our children too were repeatedly bitten, but with so little even local disturbance it was difficult to believe that the same bite could produce such terrible effects in cattle, horses, dogs &c., as we know from the testimony of the natives and the experience of several Europeans do certainly take place. Several Englishmen have lost all their cattle horses & dogs by being led into a Tsetse district. Captain Vardon of the Indian army,[1] doubting whether it could be the Tsetse which distroyed the animals, rode one of his horses up a hill on which the tsetse prevailed, remaining only so long as to take a sketch of the surrounding country. He caught about 50 on the horse, and in eleven days the animal was dead. It

[1] Frank Vardon, after whom D.L. named the puku (cf. above, p. 37), was Oswell's companion in South Africa during 1846–7, when they hunted together along the Limpopo River. There they encountered the tsetse (described also in *Oswell*, vol. i, pp. 136–8), of which Vardon brought the first specimens to England (cf. *JRGS*, 1850, p. 149 n.).

immediately began to fall off & exhibit the usual symptoms of the bite.

All domestic animals begin to lose flesh & strength as soon as bitten by the insect, and if no rain falls may linger for two, three or five months and then perish in a state of extreme emaciation. If rain falls soon after the infliction of the bite the fall of temperature consequent thereupon proves speedily fatal. A horse however in my possession lived five months after being bitten, and rain fell frequently during that period. Dogs live but a short time after being subjected to the poison. But a remarkable feature in the case is the perfect immunity of the wild animals. Elephants, buffaloes, Rhinoceros, Wild hogs, zebras, gnus, pallahs, Waterbuck, Lechwee, Jackalls, live undisturbed in the very habitat of the Tsetse. The pallah[1] is quite as thin skinned as the goat, yet we often observed them feeding quietly while scores of Tsetse were buzzing round our ears. And what is more remarkable still, calves so long as they remain with the cows, which they do in this country till they are ten or twelve months old, are not killed by the bite of the Fly, while dogs which have been reared on milk as certainly die if bitten, and dogs which have been reared on the meat of game live even though employed to hunt in the tsetse district.

The insect, too, is confined to certain districts or tracts of country. These are well known to the natives. A river is the usual boundary which separates an infested from a non-infested part. A broad open part without trees also may form a boundary, or a patch of reed. And though the tsetse is taken in the hair of buffaloes or on the cloaks of the people over the natural boundaries, the insect does not seem to increase in the non-infested parts. They are generally to be met with on trees, and during the winter one may safely travel through the habitat of the Tsetse by night, but in August they begin to bite during the darkness as well as during the day. The natives usually drive their cattle into the reed or keep them in an open flat during the day when travelling. One may travel with safety during the night in May, June, July, but when the weather becomes hot people are obliged to refrain from going through a tsetse district altogether. They are re-

---

[1] *Aepyceros melampus*, the impala (Tswana *phala*).

ported to disappear after the first rains. Where do they go to? Is it true?

We met them most frequently along the banks of rivers, but along the Limpopo one may travel with perfect safety near the river, though the hills on which the Tsetse lives in great abundance be only a quarter of a mile distant.

It seems to prevail over large and thickly populated districts, for huge tribes are mentioned which cannot rear a single domestic animal. Their country though well adapted in other respects for the rearing of cattle is only inhabited by game. They have tried, but invariably found when the calves which have been brought up in the district attain the age of puberty they die. Even now it is not uncommon for a herd to lead his flocks into a Tsetse locality by mistake, but the result is the loss of all the full grown cattle. Why should domestic animals alone be obnoxious to the poison, and animals so nearly allied as the Zebra (to the horse), the buffalo (and ox), the wild (& tame) hog, &c be free?

What is there in domestication which renders cattle horses dogs &c more subject to be acted on by the poison? Is man not a domestic animal? Is a henpecked husband less domesticated than a sheep?

The symptoms observed were swelling under the jaw & over the eyes. Running at the eyes (& mouth). The coat stares. There is a peculiar flabbiness or flaccidity of all the muscles. The animal walks crossing the hind legs over each other. General emaciation commences, and should the animal live steadily advances, untill he is unable to rise from weakness in the loins. Some however have died quite fat.

The Post mortem appearances are, all the cellular membranes under the skin distended with air, presenting the appearance of a great number of soap bubbles scattered over the surface of the body, these bubbles being about half an inch or an inch in diameter & the same in height above the flesh. The fat has a peculiar oily, gelatinous look, and is generally of a greenish yellow colour. Muscles quite flaccid. Heart generally flabby or soft & pale. Lungs diseased in patches of red or yellowish grey[1] colour. Liver always deranged either

[1] MS. has 'grew'. Gelfand, p. 53, reads it 'green', but cf. *JRGS*, 1852, p. 172: 'pink or grey'.

functionally or organically. Gall bladder distended with bile of a clear oily consistence. Small intestines pale & empty. The blood remarkably destitute of colouring matter and very small in quantity. If the hands are dipped in it, it does not stain them.

The poison seems to be of a zymotic nature & propagates itself, and the organs through which the poisoned blood passes are most affected—the lungs, heart, liver. And occasionally the brain was affected, for some appeared to become blind and giddy as if drunk. This symptom induced us to believe that the disturbance was caused by the circulating fluid, & that the poison was of the nature of a ferment gradually affecting the whole mass of the blood & distroying some one or more of its constituents.

A very few Tsetse seem capable of killing an ox. Horses are not liable to be killed by a few, but if a sufficient number settle on a horse his death is much more speedy. We never saw any settle on our oxen though we looked carefully, and many of them died, while two horses which were ridden through the midst of the tsetse seemed to get fat in consequence. The Tsetse may prefer the ox to the horse, for the cattle & horses were never separated and the oxen alone died. The cattle too which were fattest were more obnoxious to the poison than those which [were] lean.

The river Zouga has not risen to within three feet of what it did last year. Drought seems to have prevailed at its sources. The Chobe fell an inch and a quarter during the period of the annual flow of the Tamunakle Teoge &c. This indicates different sources. The country of Libebe is an interesting one. There is a hill called Sorila, very high, & a waterfall near it.[1] The country is so swampy & boggy there is a stratum of mossy stuff which covers water and shakes as people tread upon it. The Zo divides into two or three rivers. One branch the Mababe flows N.E., the other the Tamunakle South to fill the Zouga. The Teoge[2] is very winding.

Glad to see Palane our old friend. Shewed that he was un-

[1] Tsodilo Hill, approx. 18° 46′ S., 21° 46′ E., and, presumably, the Popa Falls, approx. 18° 7′ S., 21° 40′ E.
[2] Taoge, the main channel on the western side of the Okovango delta.

happy under Lechulathebe. That foolish chief sent a long & friendly message. Advise him not to provoke Sebitoane's children by his foolish talk & joy at his death. He promises compliance. Pass down river, but very slowly in consequence of the oxen being very weak.

10th. Recieve letters by Hans Hae & Mrss Bushe & Shelley, also by Dolman.[1] Mend a wheel for Bush & Shelly at the Rapids[2] on the 11th. They present two bottles of Port Wine, very kind and quite providential.[3]

W.O.L. born

15th September. A son, William Oswel Livingston, born at a place we have always called Bellevue.[4] Weather very hot. Past the bend where many trees were cut first year.[5] Saw Joseph Aron's[6] horse in pitfall, for which he captured 3 of the Bakhoba who were afterwards redeemed by Tsapoe. Saw Bakhoba with about 60 eggs of an alligator.

(Natives of India much weaker internally than Europeans, Natives of Africa much stronger internally than Europeans. Ipecacuanha famous in dysentery if given frequently.)

17th. Letters from Directors approving general course pursued & from Steele,[7] he has purchased a gold watch for me. God's goodness to me very great.

---

[1] Hans Hae was a Griqua from Danielskuil, south of Kuruman, who often went on hunting and trading expeditions into the Interior; H. Bushe and Ernest Shelley were Englishmen hunting in the country for sport; and Alfred Dolman (1827–52) was a wealthy young traveller, who soon after leaving D.L. died mysteriously near Kolobeng (cf. his journals, *In the Footsteps of Livingstone*, ed. J. Irving, 1924, pp. 226–46). These men are all described more fully in *Letters*, vol. ii, pp. 7, 136, 137.

[2] Slightly east of Matebele Drift, at approx. 20° 19′ S., 23° 58′ E.

[3] Blaikie, misreading 'Mrss [Messrs] Bushe & Shelley', says (p. 118 n.) that 'the wine was a gift from Mrs Bysshe Shelley, in acknowledgment of his aid in repairing a wheel of her wagon'!!

[4] D.L. had originally intended to name the boy Charles, after his younger brother, but then decided to pay Oswell the compliment instead (cf. *Letters*, vol. ii, pp. 142, 159). 'Bellevue' I cannot identify.

[5] In 1849, on the way to Lake Ngami. 'In one 5½ mile stage upwards of 100 trees were cut down, from the size of my arm to that of a blacksmith's — the distance took 6½ hours to accomplish' (Oswell, in *JRGS*, 1850. p. 147).

[6] Joseph Arend, a Coloured inhabitant of Kuruman, who also went periodically into the Interior to hunt and trade (cf. *Letters*, vol. ii, p. 7).

[7] (Sir) Thomas Montague Steele (1820–90), an army officer who, visiting Bechuanaland in 1843 on a hunting trip, had become and remained very friendly with D.L. Cf. *Letters*, vol. i, p. 80.

Cumming's book[1] a miserably poor thing. Hear from Watt.[2]

18th. Thomas[3] attacked by river Fever. Removed a few miles to a high part on his account. Better on 19th. A change of locality is very beneficial in this fever. Wrapping in a wet sheet and administering water by the mouth soon produces perspiration ; then quinine. Thomas was seized with fever three times at about an interval of a fortnight.

Left Bellevue, & went 3 miles along the river, then accross great bend 13 miles to Ngabisane,[4] then to Sebitoane's ford. Good grass on other side of river, which is decreasing daily. Remained at Sebitoane's ford nine days.

Thomas taking fever again we left on 10th [October] and went towards Tsapoe's.

During the nine days at Sebitoane's ford the Thermometer stood at 104° in the coolest part we could find. Kumadow[5] dry. 'Kuma' means a particular plant which forms a stratum on the water sufficiently strong to bear up a man, and 'dow' means path.

19th. A very heavy thunder storm occured in the evening and filled all the ponds. Being compelled to leave the river in consequence of another attack of fever in Thomas, this rain fell most opportunely. I thank God for it.

20th. Go forward to Kamati's ponds.[6] Oxen need much less water since rain fell. The moisture in the atmosphere seems to refresh them.

21st. Grass has sprouted out $\frac{1}{16}$ of an inch already. Game all very lean this [year]. Hear two traders fired at immense herds of buffaloes but could not keep them from the water.

23d & 24th at Orapa. The well here is salt & purgative.

---

[1] *Five Years of a Hunter's Life in the Far Interior of South Africa* (2 vols., 1850), by Roualeyn Gordon Cumming (1820–66). Cumming had made several expeditions into Bechuanaland 1845–9, and often refers to D.L. in his book.

[2] David Gilkinson Watt (1817–97), a pastor at Northwich, Cheshire, and previously a missionary in India. D.L. had become very friendly with him when they were fellow-students in London.

[3] D.L.'s second son, born March 1849.

[4] 'Namissan' on modern maps; approx. 20° 24′ S., 24° 23′ E.

[5] Nowadays generally called Lake Dow, approx. 21° 15′ S., 24° 40′ E. Bushman *dau*, 'path, spoor, road'; for 'kuma', cf. above, p. 61.

[6] Not identified; possibly at or near Macana Pan, 21° 13′ S., 24° 57′ E. For Kamati, cf. above, p. 7.

Another well called Thutsa exists to the N.E. of Orapa, also a salt-pan called Chuantsa having about 1½ inches of salt on its surface. It is about 10 miles distant from Orapa.[1]

Different Opinions. Providential Kindnesses

About 22,000 Bechuanas enjoy the instructions of 10 European and 6 Native teachers. The following extracts will shew in what light our efforts are regarded by those who as much as we do desire that the gospel may be preached to all nations.

My Dear Livingstone   (no date)[2]
Before you left the Kuruman I did all I dared to do to broach the subject of your intended journey, and thus bring on a candid discussion, more especially with regard to Mary's accompanying you with those dear children. But seeing how averse both you and Father were to speak about it, and the hope that you would never be guilty of such temerity (after the dangers they escaped last year), I too timidly shrunk from what I ought to have had courage to do. Mary had told me all along that should she be pregnant you would not take her, but let her come out here after you were fairly off. Though I suspected at the end that she began to falter in this resolution, still I hoped it would never take place, i.e. *her going with you*, and looked and longed for things transpiring to prevent it. But to my dismay I now get a letter, in which she writes, 'I must again wend my weary way to the far Interior, perhaps to be confined in the field'. O Livingstone, what do you mean? Was it not enough that you lost one lovely babe, and scarcely saved the others, while the mother came home threatened with Paralysis?[3] And will you again expose her & them in

---

[1] Orapa is approx. 21° 17′ S., 25° 24′ E. (GSGS 2871 Transvaal). The other places named are also between Chukutsa Pan and Lotlhakane (*Travels*, p. 159).

[2] This letter, from Mrs Moffat, was probably written in April, when the Livingstones, who had left Kuruman in February, were about to start for Sebetwane's country. (It will be noted that, unlike D.L. himself at that time, she gives his name the final 'e'.) Gelfand, p. 58, mistakenly quotes the opening sentence as part of a separate letter from Robert Moffat.

[3] On his second journey to Lake Ngami (1850), D.L. had been accompanied by his wife and children. Soon after their return to Kolobeng late in July, Mrs Livingstone gave birth to a daughter, who died on 18 September. She herself also became seriously ill, the right side of her face being temporarily paralysed. Cf. *Letters*, vol. ii, pp. 100–1, 103, 116.

those sickly regions on an *exploring* expedition? All the world will condemn the *cruelty* of the thing to say nothing of the indecorousness of it. A pregnant woman with three little children[1] trailing about with a company of the other sex, through the wilds of Africa, among savage men and beasts! Had you *found a place* to which you wished to go and commence missionary operations, the case would be altered. Not one word would I say, were it to the mountains of the moon. But to go with an exploring party, the thing is preposterous. I remain yours in great perturbation

M. Moffat

(a true copy by D L)

In another, dated May 12th, the following sentence occurs: 'Much prayer has been made for you, that if the thing were not in accordance with Christian propriety you might in great mercy be prevented by some dispensation of Providence, and I still hope these prayers have been heard'.

On the other side we can mention many distinct evidences that our undertaking was smiled upon by Providence. When we applied to Sechele for guides which had been at Sebitoane's with Mutlanyane,[2] he informed us that he had none. One of them however called Moremeri was with Mr Oswel, but instructed we believe to pretend he had not. Sechele boasted after we left that we should not succeed in reaching Sebitoane except through him, & he had planned by sending Sebitoane's messengers back[3] that they must bring down the ivory to his waggon at Palane's. His waggon was sent forward, and the two traders, who were exceedingly anxious to reach Sebitoane first, offered Tsapoe several guns (3 or 4) if he would furnish them with guides. A man whom Mahale left sick at Tsapoe's here offered to guide them, but though as we ascertained afterwards quite competent they rejected him as a fool.[4] When we reached Nchokotsa two links in the chain of events which enabled us to reach Sebitoane first

---

[1] Robert (1846–65), Agnes (1847–1912), Thomas (1849–75).

[2] Sechele had sent a party of messengers to Sebetwane in 1850 (cf. *JRGS*, 1851, p. 19). Mmutlanyane was presumably their leader.

[3] Cf. above, p.3.

[4] Cf. above, p. 7. In the MS., '(3 or 4)' comes between 'would' and 'furnish'.

came to our notice. Kamati's gun broke, and so did Paku's. We had by attending Sekhomi & engaging one of his men Moremi got the Bamangwato on our side, Moremi always insisting that there could be no objection on Sekhomi's part to our succeeding. Then Shobo was lately come out and knew of the water at Kamakama & Goosimjarrah in consequence. We had another route in our minds[1] untill the Northern route was proposed by Kamati. Then though Moremeri denied all knowledge of the path we succeeded admirably. Again, the opening up of the way to Sesheke, the detention for two months affording us so much more time to collect information respecting the whole country ; the Chobe not rising at its usual time, the saving of our oxen notwithstanding our detention on the Sonta, the precaution of our following Mr O. at the pitfalls into the midst of the Tsetse which distroyed so many of his oxen ; the better health of Mrs L. during this confinement than any previous one, the quick & safe confinement, the healthy child, the two bottles of Port Wine presented by Mrss Shelley & Bushe ; the approbation of the Directors, the present of a gold watch by Captain Steele, the kind attentions of Mr Oswel & the cookery of George[2] ; the recovery of Thomas while a Thomas at Kuruman[3] was cut off ; the commencement of the rains just as we were leaving the river and its continuance accross the desert, the cattle even becoming fat though worked every day ; Rains again at Bamangwato ; and then the request of Mr Oswel that we should draw for as much money as we should need from him.

While at Lotlakane[4] we had three days rain. This made the Mokoko assume the appearance of a large river, flowing Northwards.[5] The old people remember the time when it

[1] Probably via the Botletle, Thamalakane, and Mababe, which was in fact the route taken in returning.

[2] George Fleming, a West Indian negro, one of Oswell's servants. He went north again with D.L. in 1852–3, in order to trade with the MaKololo; D.L. then wrote of him, 'He thinks his forte lies in cookery' (*Letters*, vol. ii, pp. 212 f.).

[3] Presumably young William Ashton (son of a missionary at Kuruman), who had died of croup in June 1851 (*Letters*, vol. ii, p. 155).

[4] Lotlhakane, 21° 24′ S., 25° 35′ E.

[5] The Mokoko, extending N.W. from Lokokane Pan (22° S., 25° 54′ E.), is marked 'old river bed' on some modern maps.

flowed so through the whole year, so the country seems to have been much better watered in comparatively modern times.

A very large kind of frog called Matlametlo[1] is found in pools as soon as rain has fallen. The natives believe that they fall with the rain, but on enquiry I found that the Bushmen are well acquainted with the habits of the animal. As soon as the ponds of rain water are dried up they retire into holes at the roots of trees. A particular sort of spider takes advantage of the hole and makes his web accross its mouth. The Bushmen know this spider's web, and when they light upon it usually dig up the Matlametlo. They make a croaking noise in their holes in damp weather and may decieve travellers as to the vicinity of water. When a shower falls they are instantly out, and seem to make up for their long inactivity during the months of drought by great diligence in the work of propagation. The males are extremely pugnacious. Walking at some distance from the waggons one day in the Mokoko, I heard a loud grunting & snorting and fancied I had stumbled upon a litter of young lions at play. Advancing, as Cumming would say, 'with extreme caution' under cover of an anthill, I was amused to see three pairs of Matlametlo in furious combat. They snorted at each other and struck out like game cocks and ever and anon one caught the other and threw him clean over him, making him light with a splash on his back. They continued fighting for hours afterwards.

The tortoise continues to live though for centuries. Every one seen by either Bushman or Bechuana is picked up and killed. When she is about to deposit her eggs she digs herself into the ground, untill only the top of her shell is visible. When the rains begin to fall the young ones come out and are unattended by their dam. They are strong enough to attend to themselves. Their food is grass, Thotona, ashes & loobu.[2]

The Porcupine eats Sekaname, Licuge & Makatane.[3]

[1] Cf. above, p. 5.

[2] 'Their food is tender grass and a plant named thotona, and they frequently resort to heaps of ashes and places containing efflorescence of the nitrates for the salts these contain' (*Travels*, p. 135). *Thotona* is a species of *Silene*, and *loobu* brackish soil.

[3] Sekaname = *Urginea burkei*, 'licuge' (*ditshuse*) are small edible bulbs (*Babiana spp.*), and makatane wild melons (*Citrullus caffer*).

Diseases &c of Wild Animals

Immense herds of eilands[1] have been seen all along our route. They have been compelled to come out of the desert by the drought being unusually great, and all were very lean. Many had mange or scab. On enquiry at Mathuluane we find that wild animals are affected by nearly all the diseases of the tame. I know of 25 Khoodos which died at Chonuane[2] of a disease called Quatsi or malignant carbuncle,[3] and one gnu from the same complaint. The meat having been eaten by two Bakwains the disease was communicated to them. I found a buffalo blind at Ootse[4] from ophthalmia, and all the game are liable to a scabby disease called Mange when they become lean. Great numbers of quaggas are found dead occasionally of horse sickness,[5] the foam exuding from the mouth as when the horse is the subject of it. Bisons die quite out of a district in one season in India.

All wild animals too are subject to intestinal worms. Tape, short, & thread worms are often found existing together in one Rhinoceros, the thread worm is often found under the peritoneum of quaggas,[6] and a curious flat thin leechlike worm with 2 eyes is observed in the stomach of Lechwee, also a redish worm of about a quarter of an inch long. Also a worm is frequently found on the conjunctiva of Rhinoceros. This however is not the cause of this animal's defective sight. His horn being in the line of vision prevents him seeing as well as other animals, but the variety Kuabaoba, having a horn below the line of vision, sees as well as any other animal.

All the game become lean and emaciated & perish miser-

---

[1] The eland, *Taurotragus oryx*.

[2] Chonwane, 24° 52′ S., 25° 58′ E. (about 47 miles N. of Zeerust). Sechele's Ba-Kwena were living there when D.L. started mission work among them in 1845.

[3] Anthrax (Tswana *kwatsi*).

[4] Approx. 25° 1′ S., 25° 44′ E., and about 25 miles S.E. of Kolobeng.

[5] *Oedema mycosis*, 'an acute or subacute, febrile, seasonal, infectious disease' of equines that is peculiar to Africa (M. W. Henning, *Animal Diseases in South Africa*, 2nd ed., Cape Town 1949, p. 581).—Gelfand, p. 54, combines this and the preceding sentence as follows: 'All game are liable to a scabby disease called Mange, and the giraffe may die of horse-sickness in large numbers'.

[6] *Equus burchelli*, Burchell's zebra. '. . . the peritoneum of the giraffe' (Gelfand, p. 55).

ably by reason of the teeth decaying. If a lion becomes too old to catch game he frequently takes to killing goats or men, otherwise he eats grass, and when the natives see undigested vegetable matter in his droppings they look out with the expectation of finding him under some tree unable to move and he will soon die.[1] Giraffe, eilands & Kukama[2] are frequently found dying of hunger & mere skeletons.

Passed Tlabala's.[3] The country all green. Wells full, but had all been built round with strong hedges. The drought had been greater this year than during any of the years preceding it since we came into the country. See a new tree

'Msava covered with reddish blossoms
and smelling like violets
Morule the name of an edible root
Martinus says there are those kinds of
it. one of which if eaten produces a
pain in the head as if it were splitting

Reach Sekhomi's A heavy thunder
storm fell in the evening. S. promises

called 'Msava[4] covered with reddish blossoms and smelling like violets.

Morule the name of an edible root. Martinus[5] says there

---

[1] 'The natives, observing undigested vegetable matter in his droppings, follow up his trail in the certainty of finding him scarcely able to move under some tree, and despatch him without difficulty' (*Travels*, p. 137).

[2] *Oryx gazella*, the gemsbok.

[3] Kane (cf. p. 5). Tlhabala, whose name is given to the village on some maps, was chief of the BaKgalagadi living there.

[4] Not identified; possibly *Securidaca longipedunculata*, the violet tree (cf. Miller, *Woody Plants*, p. 41).

[5] Presumably one of D.L.'s servants; cf. *Letters*, vol. ii, p. 221.

are two [?] kinds of it, one of which if eaten produces a pain in the head as if it were splitting.[1]

Reach Sekhomi's. A heavy thunder storm fell in the evening. S. promises to secure the gun for us which Kamati got by falsehood.[2] Hints pretty plainly his wish that we should settle with him, by saying if we came to him he would call all his people together and build a house for us; but his idea seems to be that we might come & live at some little distance and visit him frequently, he at the same time reciprocating our visits. He does not speak of being taught. Confesses that he compelled Green Bushe & Shelley to give him a horse &c.[3] '*He will not deny it, he will tell me all about it so that I may not be able to say he was guilty of "boherehere" or "swindling"* '. Boherehere seems to be in his mind worse than extortion.

Parted with Moremi, has been a good servant. His wife died during our absence, and a process of charming was necessary. Besides an emetic he was enjoined to wash himself with certain medicines mixed with cow & goat's dung, and then the remainder of the mixture was scattered by him over some goats & oxen as they said that he might be identified with them. (The idea seems to be that being so identified he may not be noticed by the evil influence which distroyed his wife.) If not charmed they feared he might feel unprotected & waste away & become imbecile in consequence.[4] The process of charming involves considerable expense.

Leshonya, the ant which emits a strong & disagreable effluvium when irritated,[5] exists in great numbers here. Saw a dead body exposed in the field.[6]

[1] This suggests that 'morule' may be a species of *Solanum* (Tswana *morola*).

[2] Cf. above, p. 7. 'Kamati or Kobati left the gun at a cattle-post. Sekomi promises to seize it' (15.xi.1851 Oswell).

[3] Because they would not sell him gunpowder, Sekgoma had made them give him some, and also a horse, for nothing. (*Travels*, p. 146). Frederick J. Green, born in Canada, hunted and traded in Bechuanaland from about 1850 onwards, and then settled in South West Africa, where he died in 1876 (Tabler, in *Africana Notes and News*, vol. 11, 1954, pp. 35–42).

[4] Purification ceremonies like those described are still observed by newly-bereaved spouses among the BaTswana (Schapera, *Married Life in an African Tribe*, 1940, pp. 310 ff.).

[5] *Palothyreus tarsatus*, the 'stink ant'.

[6] The BaTswana normally buried their dead, but the corpses of people executed for sorcery or other serious crimes were sometimes left exposed in the veld as 'food for the vultures'.

By mistake we took the road which goes to Boshuela khosi[1] and thus missed Mr Oswel, whom we knew would kindly wait for us at Mashue ; but we got a man to go to him & inform him of our position.

Spend Sunday at a pond about 4 miles South of the Bamangwato range, Monday at another pond, & Tuesday at Midday reach Serinane,[2] a warm salt water bath. The water is extremely salt, and the temperature upwards of 100°. It rushes up perpendicularly in a strong stream of about 2 inches in diameter. The hole from which it boils up is full of sand and admits of one sinking down about three feet. Very pleasant to lie in. I enjoyed it about an hour. The skin becomes as if macerated, yet has a greasy feel. Many plants which absorb salt grow about. Pity one cannot secure it for public benefit. I discovered the warm bath down at Morimolole, Bamapela country, and the Boers have since appropriated it to themselves and levy a toll on all who need its therapeutic aid.[3]

18th. Saw nest of the bright redbreasted bird with three youngs newly hatched. Nest is formed of inner bark of thorn tree partially decayed & lined with some hair & fine roots. It seems an affectionate bird.

An immense oval tuber called Longañaale.[4] It has beautiful pink flowers.

19th. Passed pond of Shokotsa.[5] Many bulbs called Naka loa tolo[6] in flower here. Also a cotton nest. The birds are the smallest I have seen in Africa ; light yellow bellies & darkish

[1] A hill about 25 miles east of Molepolole, at approx. 24° 25' S., 25° 57' E. The name means 'the place where the chief died'; tribal traditions mention two different chiefs who were slain in the immediate vicinity.

[2] Not shown on modern maps; described in *Travels*, p. 134, as 'east of Lopepe', and in *Journal*, p. 462, as 'about 20 miles south' of Shoshong. I have found no other record of a thermal spring in that region.

[3] Modimolole is a hill close to Middelfontein, 8 miles east of Nylstroom (24° 42' S., 28° 24' E.), but the description suggests Warmbad (17 miles south of Nylstroom), well known for its hot radio-active springs. D.L. had visited the BaMapela (BakaLanga, p. 60) in 1846, but makes no contemporary reference to any 'warm bath' in their country, nor have I been able to confirm his statement about its exploitation by the Boers.

[4] Not identified. The name is normally used for 'dried strips of vegetable marrow' (Brown).

[5] Probably Sokoswe, 23°34' S., 26° 10' E. (GSGS 2871 Transvaal).

[6] Not identified. In Southern Sotho the name (meaning 'kudu's horn') is used for *Sonchus integrifolius* (Mabille and Dieterlen, *Dictionary*, 1950 ed., p. 229).

backs. The mouth of the tube was closed and two tiny young ones, naked, were enclosed in the nest ; short bills. The stand is for the bird's convenience when opening & shutting the tube. Thursday morning reach Kuruchoe pond[1] (sandy & a thicket on North side of it). Sleep at a pond where we hear a tiger. Mopipi tree[2] at midday. On Saturday morning come along Molapo oa likhoñ,[3] pass a Bushman village, & go on as far as we could, but were obliged to spend Sunday without water.

Monday at Boshuela khosi.

Observed at Kuruchoe seeds of Rosewood moved by insects inside them.

'He who has to act on his own responsibility, is a slave if he do not act on his own judgement' (Lieutenant Edwardes).[4]

Instance of the power of imagination : A man who could not breathe in a square in London if the gates were shut.[5]

Serotologana[6] or Koma a very good twine.

Reach Kolobeng

On reaching Kolobeng we found all the people had removed to Limaoe, which was just as we expected.[7] It was trying to see the deserted station, but we have done our duty to the Bakwains. Sechele came down the day after we arrived and presented us with an ox, a great thing among so poor a people. He said to Paul[8] previous to his removal that he must just cast the dirt off his feet and remove. If in so saying he meant to include us, then he may be said to have left us. If not, then we have left him, for we gave him to understand distinctly that our work was done amongst them when they

---

[1] Not identified. [2] *Boscia rehmanniana.*

[3] Not identified; the name means 'valley of firewood'.

[4] Blaikie says (p. 115) that D.L. 'highly valued' this saying. (Sir) Herbert Benjamin Edwardes (1819–68) was an Indian official, who in 1848 'twice routed, on his own responsibility, the rebel . . . prince of Multan' (*D.N.B.*).

[5] I cannot explain the allusion; it may be something D.L. had read in the newspapers he found awaiting him at Shoshong.

[6] Possibly *seropologane*, 'a species of ground creeping plant with longish smooth fruit' (Brown).

[7] Cf. above, p. 1. Leyland had found Kolobeng 'nearly deserted' at the end of August (*Adventures*, p. 196). D.L. got there on 27 November (*Letters*, vol. ii, p. 154).

[8] A Native evangelist who was one of D.L.'s two assistants at Kolobeng; cf. *Letters*, vol. i, p. 116, etc.

declined being taught, and that we should certainly leave them.

Large horned ox died on the way out, the length from tip to tip nine or $8\frac{1}{2}$ feet.[1]

Reach Kuruman

R. M. Junior at Kuruman.[2] ☞ Marriage is not the end of life.

Spent last week of December[3] and two weeks of January 1852 at Kuruman. Passed through Griquatown[4] on 19th–20. Curious instance of the transference of vitality from a young wife to an old husband. He had not felt so well for forty years.[5] It sometimes occurs in cases where a child sleeps with its grandmother. David's physicians were knowing rogues when they recommended Abishag to be laid in the king's bosom.

The country South of Griquatown is destitute of trees and grass. The whole landscape for days South of the Orange river is covered by a low bush containing great quantities of salts, alkalies perhaps. Some stain the tires of the waggons blue as if they contained a large amount of gallic or tannic acid. Sheep & goats thrive on them all. Very few ants or other insects. Hills generally exhibit marks of denudation rather than of igneous agency.

Bushmen carry off herds of cattle numbering 50 or 60, and kill them all without eating more than a mere morsel. It must be revenge for injuries, either real or imaginary, which incites them to these reckless deeds.

Boers generally rich and content with the English Government. The opening of Mitchell's Pass[6] has given them easy

---

[1] These animals (described in *Travels*, pp. 85 n., 192, and *Oswell*, vol. i, pp. 212 f.) are classified by Faulkner and Epstein (pp. 63 ff.) as the 'Setswana type' of longhorn Sanga cattle. The words 'or $8\frac{1}{2}$' are an interlineation.

[2] Robert (1825–62), Moffat's eldest son, was 'spending the honeymoon' at Kuruman 'with a wife he picked up at Natal, a good looking lady' (*Letters*, vol. ii, p. 162). [3] MS. has 'January', an obvious slip of the pen.

[4] The principal settlement of the Griquas, and an L.M.S. station since 1801; located at 28° 51′ S., 23° 15′ E., about 100 miles south of Kuruman.

[5] This refers to Isaac Hughes (1798–1870), a missionary at Griquatown, who in 1850 had married, as his second wife, a woman 33 years old; after seeing him, D.L. wrote, 'The Abishag system seems to have been successful in his case' (*Letters*, vol. ii, p. 164). Cf. 1 Kings 1: 1–4.

[6] The mountain road, opened in 1848, which connects the Tulbagh valley with Ceres (Western Province, Cape Colony).

access to the Cape market and increased the value of their farms amazingly. If viewed only as a stroke of policy, none could have [been] better adapted for rivetting their loyalty to the English Government. The like might be attempted for the more distant farmers.

A bush called 'Pissgoed'[1] is said if eaten by oxen to cause retention of urine and death. It is a kind of solanum and bears small brownish red berries about the size of a pea. The Jackall's bloemje[2] kills oxen ; it resembles the dandelion in shape and size.

Reach Cape Town. Mr O's kindness

Reach Cape Town 16th of March. Find our friend Oswel here before us. The outfit ordered, and he presented £50, £20, then £80, £20,=£170, with the remark that as the money had been drawn from the preserves on our estate (elephants) we had as good a right to it as he. God bless and preserve him. 'O Divine Love I have not loved thee strongly deeply & warmly enough'. He embarked on board the 'Harbinger' screw steam ship on Thursday.[3] The best friend we had in Africa.

Constrained by importunities to give a copy of letter to Royal Geographical Society for publication in Advertizer.[4]

Got my uvula excised,[5] which I hope will enable me more freely to preach unto the gentiles the unsearchable riches of Christ. Saw a double star α centauri, one of which revolves round the other & completes the revolution in 60 or 75 years.

---

[1] The Afrikaans name for *Euphorbia genistoides*. 'So called because when eaten by castrated animals it produces severe urethritis, which unless treated in its early stages results in death' (Pettman, *Africanderisms*, p. 375).

[2] Possibly *Dimorphotheca zeyheri* (Afrikaans 'jakkalsbos').

[3] The 'Harbinger' sailed from Cape Town on 2 April 1852 (*Letters*, vol. ii, p. 167).

[4] 'Notes of a Tour to the River Sesheke, in the Region North of Lake Ngami, by Dr. Livingston', was published in the *S.A. Commercial Advertiser*, 7 April 1852, pp. 4–6. It contains almost verbatim the account that afterwards appeared in *JRGS*, vol. 22, 1852, pp. 163–73, but has a long introduction, in the course of which D.L. says that he consented to its publication 'only in consequence of the urgent wishes of friends whom I cannot otherwise favour, being incapacitated by a disease in the throat for public speaking'.

[5] D.L. had for some time past been troubled by his uvula (cf. preceding note), and only his wife's illness had prevented him from going to Cape Town in 1850 to have it seen to; cf. *Letters*, vol. ii, pp. 89, 109.

By Mr Maclear's[1] calculations, the part of the Chobe on which we stood for two months is in Long. 26° East, or within ten minutes of our own reckoning.

The Cape heart is chafed & irritable. Its rancour and rage are sometimes directed against Earl Grey, or the Hottentots or the Caffres, or Mr Montague, or the Missionaries, or Botha.[2] The blame of everything wrong is hurled everywhere. In the mean time merchants become rich, and England must pay the piper. The Natives generally learn to despise us. The follies of Govt officials over which we have no control teach the natives their own power. The mass of the people, and natives too, are stumbling on to developements which God alone can plainly foresee.

Recieved Portuguese Passports from the Chevalier A. Duprat.[3]

Found great difficulty in getting a supply of gunpowder. Went to the Lieutenant-Governor Darling and asked permission from him, & also requested him to take a copy of our map to be used in case of any future dispute as an authority. He kindly granted both requests.[4] But I can plainly percieve that we are in bad odour at Cape Town. The London Society's agents are especially obnoxious to the Government. The

[1] (Sir) Thomas Maclear (1794–1879) was Astronomer Royal at the Cape of Good Hope, 1834–70. He strongly encouraged D.L. to persevere in making observationsand gave him considerable assistance (cf. *Travels*, pp. 93, 168), including a short memorandum of instructions, which was copied into this journal (cf. below, Appendix II).

[2] At the end of 1850 the Xhosa tribes on the eastern border of the Cape Colony had attacked several nearby European settlements. This led to the 'Eighth Kaffir War', which lasted until March 1853. It was aggravated by the rebellion of many Hottentots, including some living on L.M.S. stations. Henry George Grey (1802–1894), third earl Grey, was Secretary of State for the Colonies 1846–52, and John Montagu (1797–1853) was Colonial Secretary at the Cape of Good Hope 1843–1853. For Botha, cf. below, p. 82.

[3] Alfredo Duprat (1816–81), created viscount in 1870, represented Portugal at Cape Town on the 'Mixed British and Portuguese Commission' for the suppression of the slave trade to America; he was also the local Portuguese consul, and subsequently consul-general in London (*Grande Enciclopédia Portuguesa*, vol. 9, pp. 355–6). The reference to passports shows that D.L. intended to travel from Barotseland through Portuguese territory to the coast.

[4] D.L.'s difficulty in obtaining gunpowder was due to the fear, aggravated by the Kaffir War, that some might find its way into Native hands and be used against Europeans. However, as he indicates here, he ultimately got all that he had requested, which was considerably more than the 'ten pounds' mentioned in *Travels*, p. 106; cf. above, pp. xxii f., and *Letters*, vol. ii, p. 179. Charles Henry Darling (1809–70) had been Lieutenant-Governor of the Cape Colony since January 1852.

illfeeling was especially manifested against poor Botha, a field cornet of forty years standing. I attended the trial of eight days' duration.[1] The Lord Chief Justice[2] is an infamous hypocrite and gave abundant evidence of having prejudged the case. The conduct of the court was extremely indecorous through[out], and at last a bottle of wine was brought in. Sir John Wylde took several swills, pretending he was so much fatigued he needed it, pursed up his mouth after each glass as if he did not like it, and then when he passed sentence, which had been previously written, he brightened up till even the foam came out at the corners of his mouth. His tirade in passing the sentence was $\frac{1}{2}$ an hour in length, and was the most horrid exhibition I ever witnessed. Old Botha made a sensible speech afterwards. The jury, a stupid looking set, gave a verdict of guilty on all the counts, though the third count had been given up by the Attorney General.

Botha in prospect of death spoke nobly afterwards in the prison. He forgave those who had witnessed against him falsely. I admired the old man's composure and faith in requesting Mr Read[3] to take charge of his clothes for his children.

His sentence has since been commuted to hard labour on the roads for life.

Saw Sir Harry Smith returning, recalled by Earl Grey; a worn-out old man.[4] He found, he said, the Caffre war to be like that of the Circassians & Russians. The infusion of a few Hottentots is enough to make the war formidable enough. So much for the alledged incapacity of the Hottentots. San-

[1] Andries Botha, the Hottentot field-cornet (magistrate) of the Kat River Settlement, an L.M.S. institution, was tried at Cape Town for high treason in May 1852. He was found guilty and condemned to death, but the sentence was commuted, 'and he was ultimately pardoned, after serving a period in prison'. It seems certain that he took part in the rebellion, but, says Marais (*The Cape Coloured People*, 1939, p. 244), 'The way in which the Chief Justice conducted the trial was not altogether satisfactory: in his charge to the Jury, for example, he appeared to be more eager than the Public Prosecutor to explain away weaknesses in the evidence.'

[2] Sir John Wylde (1781–1859), Chief Justice of the Cape Colony since 1827.

[3] James Read junior (1811–94), L.M.S. missionary at the Kat River Settlement 1837–51, and subsequently elsewhere.

[4] Sir Harry George Wakelyn Smith (1787–1860), a veteran of the Napoleonic wars and several Indian campaigns, was Governor of the Cape Colony, December 1847–January 1852. Recalled because of his apparent inability to end the Kaffir War, he sailed from Cape Town on 17 April 1852.

dillah[1] made a noble speech to Mr Renton,[2] and in it he plainly stated that the missionaries have been made tools of oppression by the Government, for converts have been brought out of Caffreland by missionaries on pretence of refraining from war, and these men have been forced by the Government to bear arms against their own countrymen. The gospel must hence appear to the Caffres as an instrument in the hands of politicians to draw men off from their legal chiefs. And how despicable our Government must appear, when they reflect that after a solemn promise of safe conduct made by Colonel Somerset[3] to Sandillah, as soon as he made his appearance he was thrown into jail.[4] He remarks in his speech to Mr Renton that the Caffres who believe ought to remain and teach their fellow countrymen ; that God sent his son into the world and white men killed him, He was not killed by black men. God had made boundaries and white men crossed them. It was they who broke God's laws. He was a chief made so by God, but Smith the Governor was made a chief by the Queen.

The Graham's Town Journal[5] said our watchword is, 'Send away Sandillah', and Sir Harry Smith was fool enough to try it. After spending 2 millions of money in the attempt, he himself was recalled with dishonour.

[1] Sandile, chief (1840–78) of the AmaNgqika, a Xhosa tribe, whom he led in the war against the Colonists.

[2] Rev. Henry John Renton, of the United Presbyterian Church, had visited South Africa in 1850–1 to inspect the stations of the Glasgow Missionary Society.

[3] Henry Somerset (1794–1862), commander of the Cape Mounted Rifles; subsequently governor of Bengal.

[4] Sandile had also fought against the Cape Colony in the 'Seventh Kaffir War' 1846–8. He surrendered in October 1847 on condition that his life would be spared, and was held at Grahamstown until the end of the war. He subsequently maintained that, far from 'surrendering', he had been treacherously seized by some British officers at a parley (C. Brownlee, in *Bluebook C. 2220*, 1879, pp. 11 f.). D.L. must be referring to this, since Sandile remained at large throughout the Eighth Kaffir War.

[5] The organ of the frontier Colonists, and hostile to the work of the L.M.S.; published weekly at Grahamstown since 1831.

III

SECOND JOURNEY TO SEBITOANE'S COUNTRY 1852–3

Leave Cape Town

Left Cape Town on the 8th of June. Boers along the road are very kind, and great rogues. Have very small regard for truth, and if one swears he is doing you a favour you may take his oath as meaning that he is cheating you. Their talk is entirely on rix dallers, scaap, guilders, Uithaalder, paarde, moi dick vrowen &c.[1] They are more like Jews than any people I know. They have respect for religion but not enough to be religious themselves. Visited Scheit fontein and felt pleased with Mr & Mrs Alheit.[2] The plant with which the Hottentots ferment their honey beer is very difficult to get. Are they under an oath not to divulge it?[3] It makes an excellent ferment for bread.

Kau goed[4] is a good remedy for tooth ache. It is fermented before it is fit for use, in the same manner as tobacco is sweated.

Davidjes wortels[5] is a purgative, also an emetic.

When the pith of vines is removed & they grow and the fruit has no stones in it.[6]

Reached Griqua Town 15th August, Kuruman about a fortnight afterward.

[1] The 'rix daller' (rix-dollar, worth 1s. 6d.) and 'guilder' (worth 6d.) were old forms of currency, survivals of Dutch rule at the Cape; Willem Uithaalder was a leader of the rebel Hottentots (p. 81); and the other words mean, respectively, 'sheep', 'horses', and 'nice fat women'.

[2] Rev. Christoph Alheit, since 1847 in charge of the Rhenish mission station at Skietfontein (now the town of Carnarvon, about 360 miles N.E. of Cape Town).

[3] 'Try and discover the root and plant by which the Hottentots make their mead to ferment', wrote D.L. to J. S. Moffat in 1858 (*The Matebele Mission*, ed. Wallis, p. 11). Pettman says (*Africanderisms*, p. 253) that the plant, 'concerning which they are very secretive', is probably *Mesembrianthemum stellatum*.

[4] *Mesembrianthemum tortuosum* (Afrikaans *kougoed*, 'something to chew').

[5] *Melothria punctata* (Afrikaans *Dawidjieswortel*, 'little David's root').

[6] The '&' is a marginal addition; possibly D.L. also intended (but omitted) to delete 'and' after 'grow'.

The follies of men make the world interesting. What a dull drivelling affair it would be if the Universe were regulated according to the dicta of heavy Dutch Predikants for instance. Who would not wish to escape from a chaos of everlasting humdrum—schaap, rix dallers, moi dik vrowen &c?

Reach Kuruman. Sechele's letter

Was delayed much longer on the road than I anticipated, but soon after reaching Kuruman I discovered that these delays were the means by which a kind Providence saved my life. For on the 28 August a large commando of 600 Boers and a great number of natives came against Sechele and distroyed the town, carrying off my cattle and goods, also those of the Bakhatla & Wanketse,[1] and if I had succeeded in getting along according to my wishes I should have been at Kolobeng in the very thick of the fight. The Boers often expressed a wish to have had me in their power, and hoped they would yet catch me.

The following letter was recieved from Sechele in the beginning of October.[2]

Limaoe

Tsala ea me ea lorato loa pelu ea me, le boikanyo yotle yoa pelu ea me, ki na Sechele ki paletse ka eintla ea Maburu a 'ntlasetse ki sina molatu le bona, mi ba botsa gore ki ne mo bogosiñ yoa bona, mi ka gana mi ba re ki thibe Makoa le moseteri le Botlapiñ mi ka re botle ki tsala tsa me ga 'nkake ka thiba ope, mi ba re ki ea go bua le bona, mi ka re ga ki utlue puo ea lona, mi ka re ha lo lerile Mr Edwards o riha toloko, ki gona ki tla bua le lona, mi ba tla ka Saturdag mi ba ikitletsa go tlabana ka Sabata mi ka ba rapela gore ba si tlabane ka Sabata mi ba retsa, mi ba simolola ka mantaga ka phepahalo ea mosho mi ba hula ka thata eotle ea bona mi ba cuba motse ka molelo, mi ba re halatsa mi ba bolaea bathu ba me ba le 60 mi ba thopa basari le bana le banona le Mabalerileñ ba mo thopa le likhomu cotle le mahumo aotle a Bakuena le

---

[1] The BaKgatla-baMmanaana at Mabotsa, who with their chief Mosielele (c. 1840-73) had recently fled to Sechele because of trouble with the Boers; and the BaNgwaketse at Kanye, whose aid Sechele had sought on learning that the Boers were coming to attack him.

[2] It was addressed to Robert Moffat, and brought to him by Sechele's wife.

eintlu ea ga Livingston ba cula thoto eotle gague, ba cula cotle tsa gague, mi palo ea bontsi yoa Makoloi a bona a le 85 le Kanona. Mi erile ba sina gapa Koloi ea me le ea ga Macabe mi yana palo ea Makoloi a bona ea na 88. Mi lilo tsa Bacomi tsa cubeloa cotle le motse mi ba halatsa Sentuhe le Mosielele mi ba ikaeletse go senya Lehatse yeotle. Mi Maburu a bolaoa a le 28. E Moratioame Moffet. Mi yana mosari oa me o ea go bona bana. Mi ka rapela Kousi Hae go cula mosari oa me mo Koloiñ mi ka bona yalo, mi Ma sebele o le Koloiñ ea ga Kousi mi o tla mo lere go uena Moruti oa me. Masebele oea go bona bana kua go uena Monare Moffet mi ki tla romela Koloi go ena go mo cula.

Mi gape ki lebetse go gu raea, mi ka raea Bakuena ka re A re tsabeleñ kua hatsiñ ya boroa mi Bakuena ba gana mi ki tla lebelela pele pele ha Ba tla agañ gona mi ba boiha Magosi a hatsi yeno mi ba re Magosi a boroa ga a na kagisho epe.

Mi lo rumele lotle baruti ba me mi le bana ba rumela botle.

Ki na Sechele
Moroa Mocoasele.

[*Transcription into modern orthography.*][1]

Dimawê

Tsala ya me ya loratô lwa pelo ya me, le boikanyô jotlhe jwa pelo ya me, ke nna Setšhele. Ke paletswe ka ntlha ya Maburu ; a ntlhasetse ke se na molato le bônê, mme ba botsa gore ke nnê mo bogosing jwa bônê, mme ka gana. Ba re ke thibê Makgowa le Masetedi le Batlhaping, mme ka re, botlhe ke tsala tsa me, ga nkake ka thiba opê. Mme ba re ke ya go bua le bônê, mme ka re Ga ke utlwe puô ya lona ; mme ka re, Ha lo lerile Mr. Edwards go dira tôlôkô, ke gônê ke tla buang le lona. Mme ba tla ka Satartaga ba iketleetsa go tlhabana ka Sabata, mme ka ba rapêla gore ba se tlhabane ka Sabata, mme ba reetsa, mme ba simolola ka Mantaga ka phêpafalô ya mosô, mme ba hula ka thata yotlhe ya bônê, ba

---

[1] I am much indebted to Rev. A. Sandilands for the basic draft of this version. 'The letter', he comments, 'is written in extremely unidiomatic Setswana, in the stilted and untypical language which presumably Sechele acquired as he learned to read and write with the inadequate written material of that time. The repeated "mi" ("mme") seems taken from early scriptures, which reproduced the "wau consecutive" of Hebrew literature of the Bible.'

tshuba motse ka molelô, mme ba re halatsa, mme ba bolaya
batho ba me ba le 60, mme ba thopa basadi le bana le banona,
le Mma-Balerileng ba mo thopa, le dikgomo tsotlhe le ma-
humô aotlhe a Bakwena, le ntlo ya ga Livingstone ba tshola
thoto yotlhe ya gagwê, ba tshola tsotlhe tsa gagwê. Mme palô
ya bontsi jwa mokoloi a bônê e le 85, le kanona. Mme e rile
ba sena go gapa koloi ya me le ya ga Macabe, mme jaana
palô ya makoloi a bônê ya nna 88. Mme dilô tsa batsomi tsa
tshubêlwa tsotlhe le motse, mme ba halatsa Senthufe le Mosielele, mme ba ikaeletse go senya lefatshe jotlhe. Mme Maburu a bolawa a le 28. Ee, morati wa me Moffat. Mme jaana
mosadi wa me o ya go bôna bana, mme ka rapêla Kousi Hae
go tshola mosadi wa me mo koloing, mme ka bôna jalo. Mme
Mma-Sebele o le koloing ya ga Kousi, mme o tla mo lere go
wêna, Moruti wa me. Mma-Sebele o ya go bôna bana kwa
go wêna, Monare Moffat, mme ke tla romêla koloi go ênê go
mo tshola.

Mme gapê ke lebetse go go raya, ka raya Bakwena ka re,
A re tshabeleng fatshing ja borwa, mme Bakwena ba gana,
mme ke tla lebelêla pele ha ba tla agang gônê. Mme ba boifa
magosi a fatshe jeno, mme ba re magosi a borwa ga a na
kagisô epê.

Mme lo dumêlê lotlhe, baruti ba me, le bana ba dumêlê
botlhe.

Ke nna Setšhele, morwa-Motswasele.

Translation[1]

Limaoe (on the Kolobeng)
(no date)

My Friend of my heart's love and of all the confidence of
my heart. I am Sechele. I am undone by the Boers, who have
attacked me (though) I had no guilt with them. They re-

---

[1] The version printed here was sent by D.L. on 12.x.1852 to Rev. William
Thompson (1811–89), L.M.S. agent at Cape Town, with the comment: 'A true
copy. All the words added to bring out the meaning are in parentheses.' Another,
virtually identical but for slight differences in the glosses, was sent by Moffat on
22.xi.1852 to Dr Arthur Tidman (1792–1868), Foreign Secretary of the L.M.S.
in London. I cannot determine who actually made the translation. It was subsequently published almost verbatim (though with a few proper names mis-spelt)
in the L.M.S. *Chronicle*, vol. 17, 1853, p. 34. The version in *Travels*, pp. 118 f.,
omits the second paragraph and several sentences of the first.

quired that I should be in their kingdom, but I refused.[1]
They demanded that I should prevent the white people ('Makoa', English are so named; Boers are called Maburu[2]), the
Griquas and Batlapi[3] from passing me (towards the North).
I replied, all these are my friends, and therefore I can prevent no one (of them). They said that I must go and speak
with them, and I replied I do not understand your language,
but I said if you bring Edwards[4] to be an interpreter (between us) then I shall speak with you. They came on Saturday and prepared to fight on Sabbath, but I besought them
that they should not fight on the Sabbath, and they assented.
They began on Monday morning at twilight[5] and fired with
all their might and burned the town with fire and scattered
us. They killed sixty of my people, and captured women and
children and men.[6] And the mother of Balerileng* they also
took prisoner, they took all the cattle and all the goods of the
Bakwains, and the house of Livingston they also plundered,
taking all his goods. The number of their waggons was
eighty five and a cannon, and after they had stolen my wag-

---

* A former wife of Sechele, & the mother of two children. She has since escaped
from the Boers, but one of her children was given to another Boer than he who
recieved her as his captive, and is now in a state of hopeless slavery to one of these
'*Christians*'.[7] [D.L.]

---

[1] More idiomatically, ' . . . though I had done nothing to them. They wanted
me to be under their rule, and I refused' (Sandilands).

[2] *MaKgowa* is nowadays still often used for English-speaking people only, though
sometimes also for Europeans generally; *MaBuru* is an adaptation of 'Boer'.

[3] BaTlhaping, the southernmost Tswana tribe, then living mostly at and around
Taung, about 90 miles east of Kuruman.

[4] Rev. Rogers Edwards (1795–1876), L.M.S. missionary at Mabotsa 1843–52;
father of Sam Edwards (p. 7).

[5] 'on Monday at morning twilight' (Moffat).

[6] In October 1852 Sechele gave his losses as 'sixty-eight men killed of his own
tribe, besides a number of women, and between 200 and 300 children carried away
captives' (Chapman, vol. i, p. 113); in January 1853, at Bloemfontein, as 88 men
killed and 200 women and 400 children captured, 'among them his own son' (*P.P.
England 1852–3*, LXVI, p. 790); and in April, at Cape Town, as 89 men killed and
200 women and 1,000 children captured (*P.P. England 1854*, XLIII, pp. 523 f.). D.L.
himself recorded the names of 124 children who had been taken away (cf. *Letters*,
vol. ii, p. 200).

[7] The child referred to was Kgari, Sechele's son by Mokgokong (one of the
wives whom he had discarded on becoming baptized in 1848). 'Barileng', not found
in any existing list of Sechele's children, was presumably another name for Mokgokong's daughter Bantshang.

gon and that of Macabe[1] then the number of their waggons (counting the cannon as one) was eighty eight. Also the goods belonging to the hunters (viz. Webb, Codrington, Green, Macabe, English gentlemen exploring the country) were all burned with the town,[2] and they have also scattered Sentuhe's (people)[3] and Mosielele's (people, viz. Wanketse and Bakhatla), and they have determined to distroy the whole country. And of the Boers were killed (28) twenty eight.[4] (Several, both Boers and Bakwains, have since died of their wounds, both parties leaving several of their dead unburied.) Yes, my beloved friend, now my wife goes to see the children, and Kobus Hae will convey her to you.[5]

I forgot to mention that I said to the Bakwains, Let us flee to the South country, but they replied. 'the kingdoms of that country have not a bit of peace'. I shall therefore wait and see where they will settle.[6]

[1] Joseph McCabe (1816-70), hunter and itinerant trader; subsequently a store-keeper among the BaKwena at Molepolole. Cf. *Letters*, vol. ii, p. 200 n. 9.

[2] Elsewhere D.L. explains that owing to the distance between Cape Colony and the northern parts of Bechuanaland, relays of cattle were 'absolutely necessary. It has therefore become customary for travellers to leave a portion of their stores at my house and half of their cattle in charge of Sechele' (29.ix.1852 Darling, in Campbell, *Livingstone*, p. 146). William Frederick Webb (1829-99) and William Codrington were army officers. The former became very friendly with D.L., and was a pall-bearer at his funeral in Westminster Abbey. Cf. *Letters*, vol. ii, p. 216.

[3] Senthufe, who had in 1844 succeeded his father Sebego (son of Makaba II), ruled over a large section of BaNgwaketse living independently of the main body (to which they were forcibly reunited in 1857).

[4] The Boers reported their own casualties as four men killed and five wounded (cf. *Letters*, vol. ii, p. 185). Sechele may however have included Native auxiliaries.

[5] D.L.'s version is here incomplete. Sechele actually wrote: 'Yes, my beloved Moffat. And now my wife is going to see the children. I asked Kousi Hae to take my wife in his wagon, and he agreed, so Mma-Sebele is in Kousi's wagon, he will take her to you, my teacher. Mma-Sebele is going to see the children at your place, Mr Moffat, and I shall send a wagon to bring her back.' Mma-Sebele (Selemeng) was the wife Sechele had retained on becoming baptized. Her son Sebele, with three of Sechele's daughters by other wives, had been sent to Kuruman in March 1852 to be educated under Moffat's supervision. 'Kousi' (Jakobus) Hae was presumably a kinsman of Hans (p. 68).

[6] Here again D.L.'s version is incomplete. Sechele wrote: 'Also I forgot to tell you, I told the BaKwena, "Let us flee to the country in the South"; but the BaKwena refused, so I shall watch first to see where they will settle. They fear the chiefdoms of that country, they say the chiefdoms in the South have no peace at all.'

Salutations to all the teachers and to my children.

(signed) I am Sechele,

son of Mochoasele.[1]

The Boers were commanded by Peit Scholz.[2] Many of them were drunk. Two of them were shot with one ball. Some were left unburied. Several have died of their wounds. They told the natives that they had now got the whole country from Victoria and would abolish chieftainship.[3] This is the first movement of Pretorius after being feasted at Bloemfontein and Natal.[4] They evidently intend to stop up the way into the Interior, but the Lord reigneth.

The Bakhatla and Wanketse never fired a shot.

With respect to the effects of this most unprovoked attack on the developement of God's Providence, I cannot but look on the whole as likely to be productive of good. The Bakhatla have had the gospel for upwards of eight years but turned a deaf ear to all God's invitations of mercy, and though they had some excuse in an unfortunately tempered missionary[5] yet their conduct has been outrageous to him, and the gospel has been the but[t] of their ridicule. The Lord has seen it. When the bell was rung for school or service the

---

[1] Motswasele II, chief of the BaKwena c.1807–22; assassinated at a tribal meeting by his cousin Moruakgomo (p. 18), who then usurped the chieftainship, but was himself subsequently killed in battle by Sebetwane's people.

[2] Pieter Ernest Scholtz, commandant of the Marico district. His report on the campaign is published in *Transvaalse Argiefstukke 1850–1853* (Pretoria 1949), pp. 233–5.

[3] By the Sand River Convention, 17 January 1852, the British Government had *inter alia* recognised the independence of the Boers beyond the Vaal River and disclaimed alliance with 'coloured nations' in those parts (*op. cit.*, pp. 163–5, especially clauses 1 and 3).

[4] Andries Willem Jakobus Pretorius (1798–1853) was Commandant-General of the Boers in the Western Transvaal. In 1848 he and others had joined many of the Boers in the Orange Free State in resisting, unsuccessfully, the British annexation of that territory, and a reward had been offered for his capture. Subsequent developments changed the situation, and in May 1852 he visited the British colony of Natal, and towards the end of June was also in Bloemfontein (capital of the O.F.S.), 'where he was received by the government with every mark of honour' (Theal, *History of South Africa*, vol. vii, p. 333).

[5] Rev. R. Edwards. He and D.L. had jointly started the mission at Mabotsa in 1843. They subsequently quarrelled (1845), and D.L. moved to Chonwane, leaving him in sole charge. Ever after D.L. always referred to him disparagingly (cf. *Letters*, vol. i, pp. 112 ff., 124 ff., etc.).

whole of the children of the town were accustomed to run down to the church and commence a noisy game with a long rope just at the door, and they have all been repeatedly ordered from the public place of proclamation[1] on no account to enter the meeting house. Upwards of £1000 have been spent on this small and insignificant tribe. It is high time they were given up, for we cannot [but] look on money spent on those who deliberately reject the gospel as so much abstracted from the Heathen beyond and given to those who deserve it not.

The Wanketse of Sentuhe have also wilfully rejected the gospel and they are punished. They had the gospel from the lips of Sebubi, formerly their enemy and an example in his own person of the transforming power of the truth.[2] And most of the Bakwains are in exactly the same position with respect to God's offers of mercy. They have refused them wilfully. There is nothing mysterious in these dispensations. God has dealt graciously with them for years and now suffers them to feel the rod of his anger. May they have wisdom granted to them to look up to him who chastens in mercy.

Detention at Kuruman

October 7th. As the Boers have resolved to stop up the way into the Interior and express great hatred to me personally, I think I am in the way of duty in remaining till the several parties of Boers who have gone to the countries beyond the Bamangwato have returned[3]. Several of them may be cut off, and should I meet them it would be like meeting a bear bereaved of her whelps.

Mr Webb and Codrington came from the interior in the

[1] *Kgotla*, the open air council-place or forum found in every Tswana village; briefly described in Schapera, *The Tswana*, 1953, p. 47.

[2] Sebubi, a Tlharo tribesman (from the vicinity of Kuruman) who at one time had fought against the BaNgwaketse, worked among them from 1848 onwards as an L.M.S. evangelist. He settled at Ranaka (near Kanye), where some of his descendants are still living. Cf. *Letters*, vol. i, p. 259; Schapera, 'Short History of the BaNgwaketse', pp. 10 f.

[3] They were hunters who had gone to Lake Ngami (cf. Chapman, vol. i, pp. 99 ff.). In *Travels*, pp. 119 f., D.L. says he was 'detained for months at Kuruman' because owing to Boer threats of violence he was unable to get servants 'willing to risk a journey to the north'.

end of October. They have been down the Limpopo and about four days North of it. They say the river runs East. They turned about the Shashe. Mosilikatse sent invitations to Mr Moffat to visit him.[1]

2d Novr. Send off paper on Caffre war to Dr Vaughan.[2]

Novr 22d. Still at Kuruman, but two drivers have providentially been provided and I hope to proceed to the North in the course of next week. The attempts of the Boers to block up the path into the Interior of the Continent make me more determined to open up a new path to either the East or West coasts. May God enable me to accomplish it.

Send off a reply as to the necessity of abandoning the Colonial stations, in answer to a circular of queries on the subject dated 30 September, also a statement to the Temperance Society of our ability to perform the severest labour without the stimulus of intoxicating drinks. This in answer to a circular was as follows.

Revd T. Spencer[3]

Sir   Having acted on the principles of total abstinence from all alchoholic drinks during upwards of twenty years, my experience as a missionary is all on one side of the question. Whether I could have performed my duties better had I been in the habit of using alchohol as a daily beverage I cannot from my own experience say, and though I do not consider that such an experiment would be sinful, I have no intention of putting the matter to the test. My individual opinion is that the most severe labours and privations may be undergone without the alchoholic stimulus, because those who have endured the most had nothing else but water, and not always enough of that.

[1] 'Some Griqua hunters have approached the outposts of Mosilikatse, and he sends a message to Mr Moffat, "Why don't you come and see me? Be sure and come, and bring a chair for me"' (12.x.1852 Thompson). Moffat did again visit Moselekatse, for the third time, in 1854; cf. *Matabele Journals*, ed. Wallis, vol. i, pp. 139 ff. (and, for their previous meetings in 1829 and 1835, pp. 1–138).

[2] Robert Vaughan (1795–1868), editor of the *British Quarterly Review* 1845–1865 (*D.N.B.*). D.L. had contributed an (anonymous) article on South African missions to that journal (vol. 14, 1851, pp. 106–13), but three others subsequently submitted (including the one he mentions above) were all rejected.

[3] Possibly Thomas Spencer (1796–1853), described in *D.N.B.* as 'writer on social subjects' and 'a keen opponent of slavery, the corn laws, intemperance, and pauperism'.

The introduction of English drinking customs and English drinks among the natives of this country inevitably proves the destruction of both soul and body.

Kuruman 22d November

In reference to certain queries propounded by you in your circular of 30 September[1] we beg leave to submit our decided conviction, in so far as support by our Society is concerned, that the whole of the Colonial and Griqua missions ought immediately to be abandoned. We believe that the Colony has ceased to present the temporal & spiritual destitution which are understood to entitle a country to be treated as a missionary field by our Society. And the prompt establishment of the Pastoral relationship in all its bearings is the only measure which either here or at home is likely to secure a continuance of public confidence and support.

Viewing such a procedure as one of justice to the Constituents of the Society and also to the real heathen nations beyond, we can attest from our own personal observation that the members of the Colonial & Griqua churches are in point of temporal comfort and educational advantages decidedly better provided for than the majority of the members of Independant churches at home, and consequently no shyness need be experienced by them in accepting the honour of the entire support of their Pastors. To those of our bretheren who prefer the work of evangelists in connection with the Society to the settled pastorate there is sufficient work in really heathen lands.

The above with some remarks on District Committees was signed by
D. Livingston
Robert Moffat

Mr Ludorf[2] visited Kuruman in beginning of November. Things worth remembering picked up from him. A small

[1] This was a printed circular, sent out from Cape Town by Rev. W. Thompson, which asked *inter alia* for expressions of opinion about the present conduct and future policy of the L.M.S. missions in South Africa. The reply, of which the journal entry is a partial draft, is not in the L.M.S. archives in London.

[2] Rev. Joseph Ludorf, Wesleyan missionary to the BaRolong-boorraTshidi at Lotlhakane (Rietfontein, near Mafeking). The people having abandoned their village because menaced by the Boers, he was now on his way to Bloemfontein with his family (*P.P. England 1854*, XLIII, pp. 524-6).

branch of a tree will grow if a barley corn is inserted in a slit made at the lower end ; keep ground moist.

If a tree runs too much to wood, cut a circular [piece] out of another and insert it into a spot of similar size in the too luxuriant tree. The bark of an apple may be exchanged with a pear with great advantage, the part being tied firmly on & plastered over with cow dung.

A piece of bark cut off completely round and plastered with cow dung for a year will so far change the nature of the part that when the tree is cut off below the incision and planted it gives roots, so that instead of one tree we have two exactly alike.

Take about 8 inches of the stalk of a potato & plant it upside down, the result is larger potatoes & good too, as if it were a kind of grafting.

Graft a vine on the root of another, the flavour is improved by it.

Graft a branch on to a piece of root of a tree, it propagates soon.

Twist an apricot, plum and peach together, a medium sort of fruit is obtained in some of the branches.

Paying native teachers invariably spoils them—Wesleyan experience.

If vines are frosted pull off the fruit, they bear well again but late.

The Society de propaganda fide collected in 1847 throughout France Austria Italy & other countries of Europe and throughout North and South America the sum of

	£155,843
Church of England & Ireland	£190,291
Dissenters of England	£199,490
Protestants of other countries of Europe including Scotland and America	£159,174
Protestant Missions	£548,965
R. Catholic Missions	155,843

Protestants give much more than three times more than

the £160 millions of Roman Catholics, though a penny a week is forced from the latter in some countries.[1]

Last week of November, Simpson the trader brought back for stealing Webb's cattle & fined £60 at Kuruman.[2]

End of November, while waiting for my driver who has gone to Campbell,[3] I wrote an analysis of the Sechuana for the Asiatic Journal. Sent it to Watt.[4] The comparative expressiveness of the Greek, Sechuana and English may be understood when it is known that the Septuagint version of the Pentateuch contains about 140,000 words, the Sechuana 156,000 and the English 182,000.[5]

Leave for Sebitoane's Country second time

14th December. Start for the North.[6] Have written to Sir John Pakington about the seizure of the English path by the Boers.[7]

Sunday 17th at Setloñuaneñ.[8]

[1] The figures for the Protestant collections were evidently taken from L.M.S. *Chronicle*, vol. 16 no. 1, January 1852, p. 13 (where the total is given, correctly, as £548,955). D.L.'s source for the Roman Catholic figures I cannot trace; the *Chronicle*, p. 12, gives only those for 1850, which amounted to £138,488.

[2] J. Simpson (of whom little is otherwise known) had on his way back from a trading expedition to the MaKololo lost all his oxen through tsetse bite (Chapman, vol. i, pp. 98 ff.). Sechele then asked him to take to Moffat at Kuruman some cattle which the Boers had failed to loot; instead of doing so, he apparently tried to make off with them. 'The people here pursued them, overtook . . . Simpson, fined him, and the price of the missing cattle and such as remained are in custody here for the owner' (12.xii.1852 Tidman, from Kuruman; in this letter D.L. says the animals belonged to Codrington).

[3] A Griqua settlement at 28° 49' S., 23° 44' E., about 110 miles south of Kuruman.

[4] The original 'Analysis of the Sitchuana', dated 'August 1852', is on pp. 6–47 of a quarto notebook now in the Livingstone Memorial, Blantyre. It was never published in the *Asiatic Journal*, but 25 copies were privately printed in 1858, as a booklet of 40 pages entitled *Analysis of the Language of the Bechuanas*, for the use of members of the Zambesi expedition. Substantial extracts are given in *Dr Livingstone's Cambridge Lectures*, ed. W. Monk (1858), pp. 106–24.

[5] On p. 24 of the MS. 'Analysis' (see previous note) D.L. painstakingly calculated, multiplying the number of words per page by the number of pages, that the Tswana version of the Pentateuch contains 156,792 words, the English version 182,024, and the Septuagint 140,956.

[6] In *Travels*, p. 120, the date is given as 20 November.

[7] Sir John Somerset Pakington (1799–1880), created Baron Hampton in 1874, was 'secretary for war and colonies under Lord Derby in 1852' (*D.N.B.*). D.L.'s letter to him, dated 'Kuruman, December 12, 1852', was published in *P.P. England* 1852–3, LXVI, pp. 803–4.

[8] Setlhongwane, not on modern maps; according to early sources, approx. 27° 9' S., 23° 47' E.

19 at Motito.[1] Hear Sechele had come to Setlonuañeñ. He came by night to Motito. Said he would have followed me back to Setlagole.[2] Wished much I would go with him to the Colony.[3] As I had much to talk to him about, I went back with him to Kuruman. He has given Mokokoñ to Basiamañ.[4] Had only 36 men on the hill with him in the fight.[5] Moikabi[6] was wounded in the fight in both knees and left. He was killed in the morning when the Boers came to destroy the wounded. Perhaps he thought and prayed on that dreary night. Sechele did not wish to kill any Boers afterwards lest the English should be influenced by that circumstance. He pleads for his children. It was thought best for him not to go at present to the Governor but wait till an answer should come from Green the British Resident.[7] I left and came back to Motito. Hear of the Barolongs having stolen 4 or 5 large troops of cattle. This in December 1852 is the very [first] instance in the memory of man in which Bechuanas have plundered Boers or white men. Pretorius must now proceed in pursuit of the stolen cattle. He intends to collect the blacks again and punish the tribes which stole. The Barolongs led the stolen cattle towards Mahura's country[8] in order to lead the Boers to believe that he was guilty.

24th spent at Nyisa.[9] Old Mocuara blind and apparently

---

[1] Bothitong, 27° 4′ S., 23° 49′ E., about 35 miles N.E. of Kuruman; at that time a French (P.E.M.S.) mission station under Rev. Jean Frédoux (1823–66), husband of Moffat's daughter Ann.

[2] Setlagodi, 26° 17′ S., 25° 6′ E., on the road usually taken between Kuruman and Kolobeng; D.L., however, was now travelling farther west to avoid the Boers.

[3] Sechele had decided to appeal in person to Queen Victoria for redress against the Boers. He reached Cape Town on 11 April, but turned back homewards on 16 June (C.G.H. Almanac, 1854, pp. 297, 300): 'his resources being there expended', he had had to abandon his hope of proceeding to England (Travels, pp. 120 f.).

[4] Sechele's agnatic half-brother. He was in fact 'given' not Mokgokong (p. 88) but Motshipi, another of the four wives Sechele had discarded on becoming baptized.

[5] 'The tribes whom I had called to my assistance fled at the first fire. I was surrounded on a hill, with only a few men, by the boers. I fought till it was dark, and retreated to another hill' (Sechele, at Cape Town, April 1853; P.P. England 1854, XLIII, p. 523).

[6] An agnatic kinsman of Sechele, and headman of Ntsono ward.

[7] Henry Green, brother of the hunter (p. 76); Resident of the Orange River Sovereignty, July 1852–March 1854.

[8] Mahura was chief, 1825–69, of the BaTlhaping at Taung.

[9] Ganyesa, 26° 35′ S., 24° 11′ E.

demented, a sad sight to see.[1] A boy drowned in a well. His old father uttered a most piercing bitter cry. No hope. Sorrow without hope must be bitter indeed.[2]

27. Made a good deal of Easting to get to the road. Pass Tlakameñ[3] at night.

28. Meet Kobopuri's party[4] in morning.

Milk of figs turns milk thick.

Little bee Mōka stings.[5]

An immense number of swifts pass along the plains north of Kuruman. I counted about 4,000 one evening in November passing down the Kuruman river. They do not breed in this country, for this is the breeding season and there are not 20 nests in Kuruman, these chiefly of the house swallow too. There is no place near where they can build too. They don't appear to be influenced by the sexual desires at all. No chasing each other and no appearance of having paired. There are many birds which continue in flocks though this is the breeding season. Do migratory birds come to Africa simply to pass the winter and then return to breed in more temperate climes? The breeding time is chiefly the periods between the cold & very hot seasons.

Am I on my way to die in Sebitoane's country? Have I seen the last of my wife & children? The breaking up of all my connections with earth, leaving this fair & beautiful world & knowing so little of it? I am only learning the Alphabet of it yet; and entering on an untried state of existence, following him who has entered in before me into the cloud, the veil, the Hades, is a serious prospect. Do we begin again in our new existence to learn much by experience, or have we full powers? My soul, whither wilt thou migrate to? Whither wilt thou lodge the first night after leaving this body? Will an

[1] Motshwari, chief of the Mariba section of BaRolong-booRratlou, was already 'aged, blind, and very deaf' in 1849 (Freeman, *Tour*, p. 269). Breutz mistakenly says that he died 'between 1830 and 1835' (*The Tribes of Mafeking District*, 1955, p. 171).

[2] In *Travels*, p. 131, this incident is said to have happened 'when we were passing one of the deep wells in the Kalahari'. [3] Tlhakgameng, 26° 28' S., 24° 22' E.

[4] Koboyapudi was a convert from Kuruman attached to the mission at Mabotsa. That station also having been attacked by the Boers (August 1852), he and several others were now returning to Kuruman. Cf. *Letters*, vol. ii, pp. 196, 201.

[5] But Pettman says (*Africanderisms*, p. 353) that the 'Small Moka bee' (*Trigona sp.*) is stingless; cf. also below, p. 171, and Chapman, vol. ii, p. 156.

angel soothe thy flutterings, for sadly flurried thou wilt be in entering on Eternity? O if Jesus speak one word of peace that will establish in thy breast an everlasting calm. O Jesus, fill me with thy love now, and I beseech thee accept me & use me a little for thy glory. I have done nothing for thee yet, and I would like to do something. O do, do, I beseech thee, accept me and my service and take thou all the glory.[1]

28th. Thermometer 95° in a cool box inside waggon.

31. Remain a day searching for a lost ox. Find it & move on to Logagen or Litubaruba.[2]

1st & 2 January at Logageñ. 1853.

30th Decr 1852. The very first cases of cattle stealing from the Boers by Bechuanas took place this month. The Barolongs of Montsioe were the people, and they stole five lots.[3] This is of course what they themselves have taught them. They plunder Sechele, and then other Bechuanas plunder them.

1st & 2d January 1853. Remain at Logageñ in order to avoid travelling on Sunday. Heavy rains. Therm. at Midday 96°.

3 Monday. Reach Molopo.[4] See two lions in morning.

5th. At Choaneñ.[5] Many tortoises come to the pan to lick. Is it the lime they need?

7. At Seguagua.[6] Mr Macabe kindly lends a horse. He crossed the desert and his oxen were 20 days entirely dependant on melons.[7] They did not seem to care for water when they got them. Every animal eats them. Wild dogs. There are at least twelve days hard trekking by desert path without water.

---

[1] Blaikie, p. 139, dates this paragraph 'September'.

[2] Logageng, 25° 56′ S., 24° 43′ E.; 'a cave on the Maritsani river, in a most romantic and lovely spot, with a pretty variety of rocky and wooded scenery' (Chapman, vol. i, p. 135); not to be confused with its namesake at Molepolole (cf. above, p. 1).

[3] See above, p. 96. Montshiwa was chief, 1849–96, of the BaRolong-boorra-Tshidi.

[4] The route he was taking suggests that D.L. reached and crossed the Molopo River at or slightly east of Tshidilamolomo, 25° 50′ S., 24° 41′ E.

[5] Chuaning (Tswaneng) Pan, 25° 31′ S., 24° 59′ E.

[6] Segwagwa, 25° 9′ S., 25° 5′ E.

[7] Cf. Travels, p. 122, and, for McCabe's own account of his great journey across the central portion of the Kalahari Desert to Lake Ngami and thence to the Ma-Kololo (June–September 1852), W. C. Holden, History of the Colony of Natal, 1855, pp. 413–34. The melon referred to is the well-known 'tsama' (Citrullus vulgaris).

8th. After ten hours ride we came to Selokolelo,[1] a beautiful valley, in which we spend Sunday the 9th. It is a dry river bed embosomed in trees.

10th. Went a little way along the road to Segeñ,[2] then turned off to the East N. East & went towards Moshuaneñ.[3]

Tuesday sleep West of Kolobeng.

Wedensday pass Loale,[4] where there are rents in fine new red granite filled up by a dark blue porphory.

Milk of Tola a solanaceous plant makes goats milk curdle.[5]

It is 14 hours from Moshaneñ to Litubaruba, Sechele's new place, = 42 miles.

Found the Bakwains where I first saw Bubi.[6]

Obs. Alt. of Aldebaran   16° 12 34

R[ight] A[scension] of D°   4° 27 22

Maleke a former chief of Bakwains died on Litubaruba of the bite of a mad dog.[7]

Remained 5 days with the Bakwains.

Khari[8] was restored to his mother by the Boers. Many tears were shed. Ordered my house to be burned.[9] Several readers among the Bakwains. I have still hopes of them.

18th. Reach Khopong.

19th. Kholemarue pond. Saw real cactus in long valley South of Boatlanama.

---

[1] Selôkôlêla, 25° 3′ S., 25° 8′ E.   [2] Segeng, approx. 25° 12′ S., 24° 50′ E.

[3] Moshaneng, 24° 56′ S., 25° 13′ E.

[4] Not identified; evidently somewhere near Moshupa (24° 45′ S., 25° 26′ E.), and not the Lwale at 23° 18′ S., 25° 40′ E.

[5] 'The milk of goats does not coagulate with facility, like that of cows, on account of its richness; but the natives have discovered that the infusion of the fruit of a solanaceous plant, Toluane, quickly produces the effect' (*Travels*, p. 160). *Thola*, dimin. *tholana*, is the fruit of the *morola* bush (*Solanum sp.*).

[6] Half-brother and successor of Moruakgomo (p. 18); accidentally killed by an explosion of gunpowder in 1845 (cf. *Letters*, vol. i, pp. 137 f.). D.L. had visited him in 1842 at Dithubaruba in the Dithejwane Hills (about 30 miles N.W. of Kolobeng). The BaKwena settled there again after vacating Dimawê, but in 1864 moved 7 miles N.E. to Molepolole.

[7] Maleke was acting chief of the BaKwena c.1803-5, during the minority of his nephew Motswasele II (p. 90).   [8] Sechele's son by Mokgokong (p. 88); died 1895.

[9] D.L. had hoped to visit Kolobeng and see for himself 'the destruction made by the savages', but on learning that some Boers would be there to hand Kgari back changed his mind ('I must not put myself in the way of being caught without reason'), and asked Sechele's brother Kgosidintsi 'to burn the house rather than let it be a receptacle of Boers' (*Letters*, vol. ii, p. 200). Everything he wrote about the damage done to his premises at Kolobeng was therefore based entirely on hearsay.

21st. No water in Boatlanama pits.

22. No water at Lopépe. Proceed to Mashue & spend Sunday 23d there.

Monday 24th. Pass Koribelo[1] & reach Sekhomi's on 25th. Leave Bamangwato on the 26th.

28th. Pass on to Letlochee & spend Sunday there. Slow travelling.

February

The oxen seem weaker in summer than in winter. 29th, 30th at Letloche, Kanne 31st, Mathulane[2] 3d February.

5th. Finish a paper on Trans Vaal Boers and slavery, for Quarterly.[3]

6th. Sunday. At Motlatsa.[4] Oxen sent accross country to Nkowane for water. Half of them were lost and remained without water five days.

8th. Leave Motlatsa. Wedensday sleep at Mañgana.[5] Thursday 10th at Lotlakané.

11th. 12th. 13th. At Lotlakané. Leave on Monday 14th. Beyond Mokolane trees at Midday. Therm. in shade 96°

    In sun on leathern cushion   122°

    on green painted box in sun 126°

    Two inches beneath soil   128°

Tuesday 15th. Reach Nchokotsa.

Wedensday 16th. Maritse. Country parched more than in winter.

Thursday 17th. Koobe. Dig for water, & remain 18th. 19th. 20th. Leave Monday 21st.

We have killed on the journey, 2 Bustards & one zebra, three stein bucks,[6] three Redbucks or Palahs, one eiland, two giraffes and two black Rhinoceros. The black Rhinoceros were 5 feet four inches high at the shoulder and 10 feet from point of nose to the insertion of the tail. The Giraffe

---

[1] Kudibela, 23° 1′ S., 26° 14′ E. (GSGS 2871 Transvaal).

[2] Not named thus on modern maps; identified by Passarge (1904) as Batshukudu, 21° 52′ S., 25° 49′ E.

[3] Cf. above, p. 92. This paper, rejected by the *Quarterly Review*, was published posthumously in the second edition of Blaikie (1881), pp. 490–511.

[4] Identified by Passarge as Malachwai, 21° 47′ S., 25° 46′ E.

[5] Mangana Vlei, 21° 38′ S., 25° 43′ E.

[6] *Raphicerus campestris*.

females were fourteen feet high from forefoot to point of horns. Six serpents.

22d. At large Mouana tree[1] about 2 miles beyond pan Ntwetwe. It consists of six branches on one bole, and at three feet from ground is 85 feet in circumference.

23 Wedensday. At Mokolane trees West.

24. Pass T'lomtl'a & sleep near Rapesh.

25 Friday. Horoye.[2]

26 Saturday. Maila or Kaisa's.

27th Sunday.   Do.

28th. Pass Unku. Country exceedingly lovely. All the ponds are full of water, the grass in seed, and the flowers of the forest in full blow.

The Thermometer 88° protected in shade at 3 o'clock
                       98° in waggon   Do.

Growth of Boabob &c

29th Tuesday.

One foot of the Moana tree gives 72 rings
     Do   at another part   90
           Do Do   Do   80
     Do   at another part   84
                                    4)326
                                  81½ mean

The Bark as seen growing is from 2½ to 3 inches in diameter. In the inner bark 20 rings may be observed in an inch. These are apparently composed of a single lamina of tubes, and they in the wood arrange themselves into rings of 2, 3 & 4 in one lamina. I think the bark laminae ought to be considered as the growth of years.[3] Assuming the centre to be in the middle of a tree 40 feet in circumference

[1] Tswana *mowana* or *moana*, the baobab (*Adansonia digitata*). The tree mentioned was the first to be seen on the road from the south; and Mackenzie says (p. 145) that in 1860 he observed, among the many names carved on its trunk, 'the initials "L. and O.", with a date which I have forgotten; but no doubt commemorative of one of Livingstone and Oswell's visits to the interior'. The letters, he adds, were 'nearly closed by the growth of the bark'.

[2] Kaungara, 'Horoye's spring' (cf. above, p. 10).

[3] '. . . supposing each ring the growth of one year . . .' (*Travels*, p. 163).

2) 17 feet in diameter

8·6 Diameter from centre

12

102

20

2040 years

But taking one having 6 distinct trunks united into one bole as having only one centre for its concentric rings instead of six, as that near Ntwetwe, 85 feet in circumference or

ft

2)36·5 inches in diameter

18·2 Diameter from centre

12

218·0

20

4360 years

But it is so spongy the axe can be struck into it to the head with a good blow, and though [it] has great vitality it is difficult to believe that such a baby looking thing is as old as the pyramids. It however possesses amazing vitality.

Tuesday 1st March. Remain & bleed all the horses. Two of them evidently very sick. They recover.

2d Wed. Thermometer at five A.M. 68° p[rotected]. In current 65°. At one P.M., p. 92°, unp. 91°. On deal plank in sun 148°. 3 Inches below surface of ground 138°. In sun 5 ft. from ground 104°. In shade 98°.

3d March Thursday. Reach Kamakama, where old Horoye & his son Mokantsa are at present living.[1] Friday 4th, Leave Kamakama & sleep in bush abreast of Lurilophépe. Therm. 93° p., 94° unp., surface of soil 125°. Yet ants were busy working on it. Water of pond 100°. People killed 4 zebras, 2 gnus.[2] Then one buffalo & 2 zebras.

5th & 6th Sat. & Sunday. At Pond where Mokhutsane & Selokisho[3] live. 2 zebras.

[1] Mokantsa may still have been living in 1909, when A. W. Hodson met at 'Gumkede' (Unku) a man of that name, who was chief of the MaDenasana and 'the most influential Bushman in these parts' (*Trekking the Great Thirst*, 1912, p. 230). [2] *Connochaetes taurinus*, blue wildebeest or brindled gnu.

[3] Not identified. For 'Mokhutsane', cf. above, p. 11.

7th Monday. Pass through very thick Mohonono bush, & sleep in it. Axe constantly in operation in hands of three men.

Poison of Ngoa. Fever

8th. Thick bush again but emerge onto the plain & sleep on it. See some Bushmen at Midday, and first see the N'goa, a caterpillar the internals of which the Bushmen use as a poison on their arrows.[1] They say that a small portion of it introduced under the nails or under the cuticle has an effect exactly similar to that of morbid matter in dissection wounds. The agony produced is so great that the person cuts himself and flies from human habitations a raving maniac. The effects are equally terrible when animals are wounded by it. The lion becomes furious and bites trees in his rage, uttering at the same time moans of distress. The remedy employed is the caterpillar itself and fat of eilands. The Bushmen say it kills only when unmixed with fat.

9th. Find water at T'loga[2] and at a number of large ponds East of it. Lat 19° 16′ 11″, Long 24° 24′ East.

10th Thursday. At another Pond. One zebra.

11th. Remain at Pond, Friday, Saturday, Sunday & Monday in consequence of four of people being seized with fever.[3] It seems caused by malaria arising from a great number of ponds around us drying up.

The Bushmen make ropes of the bark of the Moana and catch game with them. Stripping the bark completely off a portion of the entire circumference six feet in diameter or height does not kill the tree. It puts forth new bark. Portions even detached from the upper side retain their vitality, & when a side is burned even there large knobs of new matter are developed. It possesses great vitality undoubtedly, yet credulity which can assert these great baby looking veget-

[1] Identified by J. Waterston (*Natural History Magazine*, vol. 2, 1929, pp. 74-80) as the beetle *Cladocera nigroornata*. It 'appears to be toxic at all stages, but for arrow poisoning only the grubs or the pupae are employed. Injection of the venom is fatal to all mammals' (*op. cit.*, p. 75).

[2] Not shown on modern maps.

[3] In *Travels*, pp. 167 f., D.L. says this happened 'when in lat. 19° 16′ 11″ S., 24° 24′ E.'. Elsewhere he gives the position of the 'fever ponds' as 19° 15′ 53″ S., 24° 55′ E. (*JRGS*, 1854, pp. 302, 303; *Travels*, p. 684). He was therefore probably in the vicinity of what is now called Sayo Pan.

ables to be older than the Pyramids throws the faith of Christians into the shade.

Breezes come accross us occasionally carrying with them a pleasant odour, but they cause sneezing in self & people.—Monday 14th.

15th. People complain of headache chiefly. Tongues furred, pulse generally slow, vomit much bile. Resembles bilious attacks more than fever. Bushmen quite well.

Khā the prickly melon.[1]

Wedensday 16th. People somewhat better. Some relapses.

Friday 18th. People very ill. In most cases it began as a bilious attack. Pulse slow & full. Face anxious. Some perspire profusely, others not. All complain of pain, violent generally, in head & neck. Great heat in back of neck & down spine. The rest of the body cool. Many complain of feeling of weight in head & great pain in muscles which bend head back. The feet have feelings of heat & violent throbbing sickness. Pain at pit of stomach. Vomiting of much bile. Headache sometimes relieved by spontaneous bleeding, yet bleeding from the arm does not assist. Swoon. Stimulants did good in one instance. One had Intermittent fever. Fever seemed to leave him thus. It is difficult to ascertain their real condition for they keep on pretending to great illness when weakness alone remains.

Sat. 19th. Oxen ran away during the night. On getting up, I found all the people down except Kibopecoe,[2] who had gone after the oxen. He continued away all day & all Saturday night. When going off on Sunday morning in search of him I found him near the waggons. He had been driving them all night. A large wolf had set them off.

Sun. 20th. Intend to leave tomorrow 21st.

Mon. 21st. Went about 8 miles & came to a hollow of 'Wait a bit' thorns containing water. People seem better in general.

Tuesday 22d. 12 miles through forest and scrub to Mariba,[3] where road turns off to West for Matsaratsara's. Resolve to go straight towards Sebitoane's country. Course N. 3° west.

[1] Identified by L. Schultze (*Aus Namaland und Kalahari*, Jena, 1907, p. 670) as *Cucumis heptadactylus Naud.*, Bushman //gān.

[2] Kebopetswe, a Kwena youth (cf. *Travels*, p. 168).   [3] Not identified.

23 Wed. Pass through about 8 miles of forest & scrub. Very difficult in consequence of fallen trees and deep sand. All cutting of trees & driving done by Kibopecoe & self. People seem worse. A Bushman takes fever. Secure an ant eater which catches its prey with its tail while its head is under ground.[1] It is a hairy worm an inch and a half in length. The claspers of the tail yellow. General colour of body black.

Think much of my poor children.

Thur. 24. Still toiling through forest. Very difficult on account of trees being so close a passage has to be cut through almost every part. I have been employed almost constantly cutting Mosu trees.[2] A great deal more of leafiness in trees here than farther South. The leaves are chiefly of the Pinnate kind, but so large they afford a fine shade & are exceedingly beautiful when seen against the sky. All the berries much larger than in the south. A great variety of the papilionaceous family grow in this country.

Bushman takes oxen Eastward to water.

25th Frid. George knocks up. Inspan his oxen for him. Oepeñ[3] says he will try & drive. Cannot come on so we resolve to go on & come back for them. Divide the water with them, only half a cask full. I was employed the whole day in felling trees for waggons to pass. Heavy rain commenced at 1 o'clock. Passed on all wet to skin. Every stroke of the axe brought down a thick shower on me. Water ran down into my shoes. Thoroughly wetted we outspanned not more than 2 miles from water. Our course had been N.E. Several Bushmen came to us. It is pleasant to see the human face even though there can be no mental communication. One of them took out his dice[4] and after throwing them said God told him to go home. He threw again in order to shew me the command, but it said the opposite & he remained.

Remain over Saturday & Sunday, 27th.

People all very weak. Kibopecoe & I alone well.

Kibopecoe hurt his leg. It festers, so I alone am in a sound

---

[1] Described in *Travels*, p. 170, as 'probably a new species of ant-lion (*Myrmeleon formicaleo*)'.   [2] *Acacia litakunensis*.

[3] A Kuruman native employed as wagon-driver by George Fleming; cf. *Letters*, vol. ii, p. 236.

[4] Divining-pieces of bone or wood, usually four in number and roughly triangular in shape; cf. Schapera, *Khoisan Peoples*, pp. 200 f.

condition. Water in the pond drying up so we must move on. Thick mists occur. Haloes round the moon, & immense masses of clouds which frequently discharge their treasures on the earth, all shew another climate than that from which we have come. We are not forgotten by God's good Providence. Our Redeemer will not forget our work in his service. May he guide so that our efforts may result in his glory.

Grapes &c

28th Mon. Kibopecoe and I still driving. Others complain of weakness only. Many trees knocked down by Elephants present obstacles to our progress. Had to cut our way through the forest and drive too. In the afternoon discovered vines with clusters of grapes on them. Could scarcely believe my own eyes.[1] I sat on the waggon chest for some time looking at them before I could put the idea in words, there are really grapes growing in the wilderness. George however had put a lot round his hat, and when I looked at the Indiginous plant I believed it really & truly is the vine. But how it got there? The country has never had rivers so far as I can percieve. There are no remains of civilization, but perhaps these may be met with farther on. There are different varieties of leaf, some very much rounded, others very much divided & pointed, but tendrils, stalk and clusters shew it to be the vine. The seeds however are different, they are broad & flat, resembling split peas. Aliquid semper novi ex Africa. The Bushmen know the grapes & eat them. They call them Madzampi.[2] Cotton also of a remarkably strong staple grows wild. Was this an antient river & the ancestors of the Bushmen living on its banks planted those vines? There seems to be more than one sort. One is bright red, another bears bunches of grapes. A dark purple grape grows in South America quite black or dark purple.[3] There is a hollow channel in which a great many pools occur. Such hollow is called 'Dom' and the present one is called T'lomha.[4]

---

[1] Chapman (vol. i, p. 279) also describes wild grapes found 'growing luxuriantly' beyond Khama-Khama in December 1854.

[2] Bleek's *Bushman Dictionary* does not list this word.

[3] Last three words added at beginning of new page.

[4] The name suggests a connection with Kumha Pits, 18° 42′ S., 24° 41′ E. *Dum*, 'riverbed', is a Bushman word.

29. Waiting for the oxen. A Kukama shot.

30th. Oxen brought by two Bushmen who were sent after them. They had run very far. Lions very tame here. Bushmen often shoot them when asleep. Walked about ten miles from waggon on evening of 29th to seek water for the sick ones. Politeness not confined to civilized society. The Bushmen whom I met near the water went before me & picked the bushes out of the way, breaking branches & pointing out fallen trees.

31st. Will remain & wash today. People are improving. Sneyman[1] was incoherent during the night & grows weaker. Sleeps much, a bad sign. Will endeavour to move on tomorrow.

1st April, Frid. Broke a waggon pole. Called up at night by Sneyman fainting; very weak.

Sat. 2d April. Sand excavated everywhere by mice. The waggon & oxen sink in so much we move on with great difficulty. Came to a large tree bearing a nut covered with a peel like almond. George says it is bastard Betel nut. It is eaten by Bushmen. Leaves palmated. Oxen tired out. I went forward to look for water. Found none and was obliged to return after dark. The Bushman guide we have now seems very stupid. Lat. of Tlomha 18° 56 South.

Sun. 3d. Must go with oxen for water, we have very little at the waggons. Went & found water $2\frac{1}{4}$ hours off. We ought to have gone up the Tlomha farther East. Several Bushmen came up to us. They eat a root very much like a kidney potato, white oblong & having eyes. George thinks it manihot. Bechuanas call it Motsia.[2] A bush having leaves like the Peach abounds, so does another leafy kind. It bears berries not eatable.

Mon. 4th. Came to water in a hollow evidently the bed of of an ancient river. It is called Kuadzou[3] & is in Lat 18° 46'. Obs. Alt. ⊙ L.L. 130° 24'. People do not become stronger. Have to lift the driver out & into the waggon. Kibopecoe has had several boils. I am spared in health while all the company

[1] A coloured man employed by D.L. mainly as a hunter to help feed the expedition. Cf. *Letters*, vol. ii, p. 233.

[2] Not identified.

[3] Not shown on modern maps. D.L.'s latitude suggests that it may be Wia Pan, long. 24° 22' E.

have been attacked by the fever. If God has accepted my service then my life is charmed till my work is done. And though I pass through many dangers unscathed while working the work given me to do, when that is finished some simple thing will give me my quietus. Death is a glorious event to one going to Jesus. Whither does the soul wing its way? What does it see first? There is something sublime in passing into the second stage of our immortal lives if washed from our sins. But O to be consigned to ponder over all our sins with memories excited, every scene of our sinful lives held up as in a mirror before our eyes, and we looking at them & waiting for the day of Judgement.[1]

Tues. 5. At Kuadzou, and will remain here on the 6th too on account of the people. A wolf uttered its cry during the night exactly like a dog in agonies, and then moved off with his howl. Many swallows here. First we have seen since leaving Molopo.

Thur. 7th. Leave Kuadzou. Pass Kingushe[2] and several pools containing water. Spoor of elephants everywhere. Sleep at a large pool. Kibopecoe complains of pains in back, first symptoms of Fever. Pass on on Friday 8th & come to Mopane trees with hard ground & much water. A tree like Walnut seen. Much game about. Vines. Heavy rain. Had I a thousand lives they would all be dedicated to him who loved us and gave himself for us. Swallows whiter breasted than those at Kuruman & black heads. Saw many birds black with white stripe on side of head & on shoulder. Are these Nutha[t]ches?

Sat. Sun. 9th & 10th. Detained at Mopane trees by heavy rains. Many vines. Much game. Bushmen every where, finely formed men. The swallows are small, and seem to belong to the country. One came into the waggon to roost at night. It seemed to shiver with cold consequent on the fall of the rain, though the temp. was upwards of sixty F. Back head and wings steel blue colour, a quarter of an inch above the bill dark brown, & half an inch under bill brown of a lighter colour. Below this and going quite round the neck a black

---

[1] Blaikie, p. 139, dates this entry 'February'; Gelfand, p. 61, has 'March'.

[2] Not shown on modern maps; apparently at or near Tsotsoroga Pan, 18° 43' S., 24° 22' E.

ring about $\frac{3}{4}$ inches broad. Under front part of wings pale yellow with a little lead colour in it. Belly white. Under part of tail beyond vent yellow. Under part of eight feathers of tail contain white spots size of peas.[1] It perished during the night from cold.

11th Mon. Passed through a lovely country of Mopane trees chiefly. It is like a gentleman's park. Much water and game. Vines festoon the trees. The grapes are about equal to Bramble berries at home. Rhinoceros buffalo & elephants abound. Bushmen eat the Lotus (Lotofagi). When young it is somewhat like a potato but a slight degree of bitterness exists. Two Koroe (Buceros Hydrocorax)[2] taken out of their nest. Feeds on nux vomica & so do natives. The female plasters up the hole with her own droppings. She comes out before her young are able to fly. Country richly furnished with excellent grass. Passed a very large pond and breakfasted at another called Tsaeheriga.[3] Lat. 18° 41' 12", Obs Alt 126° 23' 20", 11th April. Ducks have young now.

Slept at a little pond to the left of the Mopane trees. It would have been better had we gone among the mopane as it is hard ground & plenty of pools.

12th Tues. Passing along by the side of the Mopane belt we came to a part full of marks of game. Shot five zebras. The reason of so many being shot was having fired three bullets none fell, & having loaded the two guns again & fired 4 fell, and Kibopecoe had killed another at the same time. The Bushmen guides now wished to turn and tried to lead us to the West to a village. Proceeding Northwards they prepared to leave us. As it was of no use to contend with these independant gentlemen I paid them, and rode forward about 7 miles to see if I could find the road which I knew to be near from a hill called N'gwa appearing in the North, and to the East of which Kibopecoe had passed last year. (Magasimetsa, Matseka & Mabodo, names of Bushmen who left us here.

[1] D.L. first wrote, 'Under part of two longest feathers of tail two white spots', which he then altered to the version printed.

[2] Called *Tockus erythrorhynchus*, 'red-beaked hornbill', in *Travels*, p. 613. Roberts (*Birds*, p. 226) prefers *Lophoceros erythrorhynchus*. The words placed in parentheses are interlineations.

[3] Not shown on modern maps. The latitude given is approx. that of Kakoaka, long. 24° 22' E.

Good obliging fellows.[1]) We do not go to our old stand on the Chobe. The grass grows so rank & high, it was impossible to see a path. Great quantities of vines grow here & grapes in abundance. The seed is very astringent. The game is very tame. Khoodoos and giraffe stood looking in amazement at me. I came to a wady or bed of an antient river.[2] Returning to the waggon I went back to the spot where the zebras were shot and found the guides busy cutting up the meat. Some of their friends had come. I paid a boy and man who had remained by the meat in their presence. This operated as a charm, and two fresh guides volunteered immediately.

15th. On Frid. went forward & came on the road. It was scarcely visible. Rains are heavier in this country than in the south. Guides will always be necessary. A lion came to us when at the Mopane trees at daybreak. He went round & round at a distance of 30 yards and roared at the top of his voice, but seeing the oxen remained still he would not attempt to attack them. We could catch a glimpse of him occasionally among the long grass. He went off very angry & roared for a long time at a distance. Took Lunar distances of Aldebaran & Pollux on evening of 14th, Lat 18° 38. Breakfasted at Palmyra trees, Lat. 18° 31'. Hill N'gwa 5 miles N., 15° East. Kibopecoe took fever yesterday, is very ill today 15th.

16th. K. very ill. Took medicine twice and seemed much relieved, but on 17th refused 'because he has nothing in his bowels'. It affects the lungs in some, and all complain of much pain in the head, back of neck, and down the spine. The hill N'gwa[3] is composed of limestone tufa. It is covered over with dense forest, and on the North has a most beautiful valley, equal to that of any gentleman's park in England. The loveliness was increased by a White Rhinoceros sauntering accross it and a gnu standing under a tree. A magnificent Boa-

[1] These two sentences were added in parentheses at the head of the page (whic starts, 'a part full of marks of game').
[2] Possibly the 'Ngwezumba' of modern maps.
[3] 'Called by the Bushmen Ngwa . . . [and] Dowgha by the Bechuanas' (*JRGS*, 1854, p. 303); nowadays commonly known as Goha. Located, according to D.L. (*op. cit.*, p. 302; *Travels*, pp. 172, 684) at 18° 27' 50" S., 24° 13' 36" E. Modern maps place the central peak at 18° 26' S., 24° 12' 30" E. D.L.'s observations were thus on the whole accurate enough for the various identifications suggested above to be considered plausible.

bob on one side added enchantment to the scene. We spend Sunday in this lovely valley. Andenoé the Bushman guide declares that there is no tsetse in the path we now traverse. There is none on Ñ'gwa. We are now about due East of our stand on the Chobe. Some Lotuses have no bitterness and are quite mealy and good. The stalks are boiled & eaten too. Oxen have swelled feet which makes them quite lame. Many bleed at the nose too. It is different from the Hoof disease of the Colony, for that happens when the roads are dry. Here we have plenty of water. The grass is green, and some of it is higher than the waggon. In looking for the oxen at a distance of 200 yards one can only percieve the tops of their horns though standing on the waggon chest. The country could support millions of cattle & horses.

17th Sunday. 'Kandehy' on the North of the N'gwa[1] (name of worm used in poisoning arrows). One bird utters a clear loud melodious song very much like that of our blackbird.

It is not the encountering of difficulties and dangers in obedience to the promptings of the inward spiritual life which constitutes tempting of God and Providence, but the acting without faith, proceeding on our own errands with no previous convictions of duty & no prayer for aid and direction. Purify my motives, sanctify all my desires. Guide my feet and direct my steps so that the Great and Glorious Jesus may be glorified. What a mercy it is He favours me with health while all my people have been sick. It is not so much the attack of the fever itself but the subsequent weakness which would hinder me in my movements. I thank thee, Lord of all, for this much of an intimation that thou dost not reject my unworthy services. If success attend me, grant me humility. If failure, resignation to thy will.[2]

18th Mon. Went to a pond surrounded by large trees. Lat. 18° 16'. Country begins to undulate and have the appearance of that ajacent to the Chobe. The vallies contain a great deal of water. The grass excessively rank & high. Bush-

---

[1] 'A most lovely valley, about half a mile N. of Ngwa' (*JRGS*, 1854, p. 303). Streitwolf, who was there in 1909, says that the Bushmen with him did not know the name given by D.L., but called the valley Kasinka (*Der Caprivizipfel*, 1911, p. 48). Modern maps show Kasinka as a village at 18° 12' S., 24° 20' E.

[2] Blaikie, p. 139, dates this entry 'February'; Gelfand, p. 62, has 'March'.

men here call the vine 'Temere.[1] Expected an occultation of
γ Leonis but moon went down when it was quite near taking
place. Lions came very near & roared in order to frighten the
oxen, but when they saw all remained still they retired. They
had killed an eiland a few hundred yards off a few days before.
The Bushmen got the bones. Cold very severe, the first we
have had this season. It is so favourable for me, and will help
the invalids. Kibopecoe solicited medicine, feels considerably
better this morning to[o].

19th Tuesday. Bushmen took us too far East. Passed real
Banyans, date trees, and several others which I do not know.
I am the only driver of the waggons now. Sneyman is re-
covered from fever but very weak. Slept at George's kraal.

Wed. 20th. Came to numerous branches of a river. Passed
through two about 4 feet deep & 20 yards broad. Stuck fast
in a third & broke waggon pole. Made another. First mosquitoes. Very many at night as I slept alone, the waggon being in the water. Date trees tall.

Thursday 21st. Accross another 40 yards wide, 4 feet
deep. Having got through that came on to plain strewed
thickly with shells. Date trees and palmyras abound. Slept at
date bushes of the gnu & . . . . .[2]

Frid. 22d. Went about three miles and then forded another river about 50 yards wide and 4 feet deep. It was very
difficult on account of numerous foot marks of a troop of elephants which had passed the ford & sunk about two feet
every step. When walking we always tumbled into them,
which wet us all over. The oxen too tumbled & floundered
desperately. We were in the water all the morning. Having
got the last waggon through at one o'clock I had been wet
to the skin $3\frac{1}{2}$ hours, & had been frequently wet during the
greater part of the day, yet suffer no injury. Thank God.

The Bushmen eat the rind part of the young Palmyra.
The[y] cut down the whole of course, and then the bole used
is a cone about 2 feet long and 10 inches in diameter at the
base. It is slightly bitter but good as a vegetable. The mornings are cold now. The country is intersected by rivers everywhere, the grass rank & strong.

[1] Not in Bleek's *Dictionary*.
[2] I cannot decipher the final word, an interlineation that looks like 'sewana'.

Find Country Flooded

Sat. 23d. On getting up this morning and preparing to inspan I found the Bushmen determined to return home. The number of rivers in front and the slow progress made were the reasons urged for wishing to abandon us. It is difficult to put down an idea of what are called rivers here. They are branches of the Chobe and fill up low winding hollows in vast prairies. There are numerous basins of five or six miles diameter which too are filled with water, and all are covered with reeds or course sedgy grass about six feet high. The surface of the water is covered with the broad leaves of the Lotus and there are fishes in it, generally small, and the current is slow. Shells abound and frequently there is a strong smell of sulphuretted hydrogen when certain parts are stirred. The depth generally is from three to four feet, but there are holes which seem to have been made when the parts were dry, into which both men & horses sink overhead.

The Bushmen declared these rivers were so numerous there was no possibility of going farther. I then proposed to go forward with them on horseback to Moremi's, one of the Makololo, and after offering them each an iron spoon as compensation for an extra effort they agreed and we went off in a N.W. direction. After travelling through a swamp for three hours in water three feet deep we came to an island and then tried to go to the North, but we found that the N. & W. were flanked by a deeper river than any we had yet seen, and it extended Eastwards & westwards as far as the eye could reach. We tried to ford it on the North, because there we could see trees which seemed to grow on high ground, but after proceeding half a mile we found the water gradually deepening untill we came to a channel about 30 yards wide without any reeds. This was so deep we were obliged to turn. We tried it at various points along the Western side of the Island but always came to the same deep channel and at last on the island we found the bones and several pieces of skin of the Hippopotamus thrown on a bush for future use by those who had killed the animal in these waters. This disheartened us, for if deep enough for that animal it was not likely that Bushmen who could not swim could cross it. I had my watch with me too & having had my legs in water about six hours, the water having frequently been up to the saddle, and having forgotten to take breakfast before starting,[1] my ardour was somewhat cooled.

Returning to the waggon we slaughtered an ox and gave the Bushmen a good filling in order to brace them up for another trial on the South West on Monday. If the Bushmen left us we should only have one effective man for work besides George and self. George is frequently troubled with the 'all overs', and on these occasions he puts on a visage so utterly mock-cadaveric I can scarcely avoid a guffaw when I look at him. Kibopecoe has no pain in head but his lungs seem much affected at night. He has regular remissions each day.

Having forgot to take breakfast before starting, I was somewhat sore on the weak point when two enormous pigs stood still before me at 5 yards distance till I had taken a leizurely aim. The gun missed fire. Then two buffaloes ran off when I was within ten yards of them. I did not see them untill at that distance they were making off at full speed. The reed & grass was so tall & thick we could not see many yards in front. Then some Lechwees stood close by, but my bullets were raised up by the grass, for I heard them rush along and quite over the animals.

The fascination produced by fire on some animals & insects must be of the same nature with that of serpents. I have seen toads come to the fire in the evenings and rush right into the middle, the heat only making them redouble their efforts & never deviate from a straight course into the centre, the coagulation of their fluids & roasting of muscles alone arresting their course. Various beetles do the same, and though rescued and conveyed back to the dark, after feeling its scorching power will return again to the flame.

Elephants dig up the bole of young Palmyras and eat the same part as the Bushmen. They also shake the large Palmyras by moving them backwards and forwards and then pick up the fruit, which is about the size of a small orange.

In crossing one of these sedgy rivers we find difficulty in managing the oxen, for they get restive from frequently sinking and stumbling in soft places and manifest an especial

[1] This clause is an interlineation.

tendency to turning completely round in the yoke and breaking skeys [and] neck bands and getting over the trektow.[1]
They usually stand quiet after getting their heads where their
tails should be, and when putting one to rights four or six
usually go wrong. It is very difficult to make them move in
the water to their proper places, but by pushing driving beating and twisting and biting their tails they are at length got
into that position that when they move forwards they must
come right. Then there commences such a shouting screaming yelling & beating as make the ponderous vehicle move
on, but ten to one the trektow breaks or whatever may have
been going to break for a month before then takes the opportunity. The tamest and best oxen take fits of jumping or
stubborness or mule-head[ed]ness, and when we get ashore
all wet and dripping we wonder again what pleasure the
Boers can have in driving. The elder Boers almost always
drive themselves though they have grown-up sons in the waggon. Latitude of place where waggons stand is 18° 4′ 27″.[2]
I make an effort to get to people tomorrow Monday 25th.

The Norther[n] constellation Ursa Major is now seen well
above the horizon. Nothing gives a much better idea of the
immense distance one is from his native land than the consciousness of having a new firmament overhead, the Southern
Cross supplying in some measure the place of the North pole
star. Yet welcome is the sight of the well known pointers. I
shall not soon be so far North as to see the Pole star again.
Pity but the immense prairies I now traverse were the pleasant haunts of man. The lands of the world are sufficient for
all its population. The population can never outgrow the
means of subsistence.

25th Mon. We went South West seeking a fordable place.
It was rather cold. The Bushmen poor fellows felt it much,
for in addition to the cold and wet they had to bear the ab-
rasion of their skin by the serrated edges of the Palmet.[3] It
grew so thick & high we had to part it & force it down at
every step. Though on horseback I could not see more than a

[1] Afrikaans *skei*, yoke-pin; *trektou*, tow-rope.
[2] 'We at last came to the Sanshureh, which presented an impassable barrier, so
we drew up under a magnificent baobab-tree (lat. 18° 4′ 27″ S., 24° 6′ 20″ E.), and
resolved to explore the river for a ford' (*Travels*, p. 174).
[3] *Prionium serratum* (Afrikaans *palmiet*).

few yards in front. The reed & sedge was much higher than I. After working our way through several miles we came to the same broad deep sheet of water which obstructed us on Saturday. We wound our way along the edge of this till tired & saw at different parts the trail of the hippopotamus to & from this the main channel. We then went farther West but could find no passage to the North.

Going along with the design of continuing our Westerly course till we should find a ford or people, we found a large branch turned to the South. This formed a river about 200 yards wide. We then went Southwards, but when we entered a belt of jungle we saw two Tsetse. These induced me to turn home resolving to make a trial to the North East tomorrow. We saw one or two elephants, and some deserted Bayeiye huts. The Elephant digs the roots of the vine and the Bayeye eat dates. We saw the seeds round their huts, some of them sprouting. On the water in some of the more stagnant parts there were immense quantities of a dirty greyish slime in roundish lumps exactly resembling scybalæ of fæces.

26th Tuesday. We tried the country to the East of this and came to the same deep river which hinders us on the West & North. The Bushmen having given us the slip during the night I went with Connat, who is the most recovered. Thebe can work a little.[1] All the rest are quite useless. I shall try the Pontoon[2] tomorrow. Though I have had my legs almost constantly wet during these efforts no bad result has followed. The waters seem drying up. Date trees and many others which seem fruit bearing abound. I plant date [and] other seeds everywhere. What a different world this would now have been had all men been trying to improve instead of spoil it.

Wed. 27. Went Northwards and crossed the Sanshuré, a reedy river or rather swamp $\frac{1}{2}$ a mile wide and very deep.[3] Packing up the pontoon on the other side Connat carried it on his head, and I, with my coat slung over my gun and a

---

[1] Connat (Konate) was D.L.'s wagon-driver, and Thebe the leader of his oxen; both were BaTswana from Kuruman. Cf. *Letters*, vol. ii, pp. 216, 233.

[2] 'Kindly presented by Messrs. Webb and Codrington' (*JRGS*, 1854, p. 292).

[3] Curson says that whereas in D.L.'s time the Sansureh 'was an arm or channel flooded from the Kwando (Chobe) River and situated on the *south* bank of that river', nowadays it is on the north, 'indicating that the river has changed its course towards the south' ('Notes on Eastern Caprivi Strip', 1947, p. 139).

haversack containing half a loaf and a little coffee and sugar & a piece of meat, marched on in front of him in a course a little to the west of North. Towards sunset we approached a mass of reed stretching away to the N.N. East which I felt persuaded was the Chobe. But before coming to this reed we found the country flooded to the depth of about 8 inches, and covered with a dense crop of rushy grass three feet high. The water contained fishes, generally small. Pushing on vigourously we reached the reed as the sun was set, & seeing a mass of forest to the South West we spent the night in a bower which bore marks of having been the day before been the shady retreat of buffaloes during the noontide heat.[1]

In the morning many Rhinoceros birds[2] flew past. Both these and the other Buphagidæ of this country seem to attach themselves to buffaloes and Rhinoceros from the same instinct that dogs attach themselves to man. They do not derive all their food from the parasitical insects which at certain seasons infest these animals, for at other seasons not an insect can be detected on them. In some parts of the Colony & in Natal the parasites are exceedingly numerous, but in this country the Buphagidæ would starve if they trusted entirely to these. They are usually seen feeding on the ground near the animals as well as perching upon them. Both buffaloes and Rhinoceros feed during the night and it is on this account that the Buphagidæ may frequently be seen searching for their companions in the morning.

Having inspected the country from a tree, it seemed probable that we should find a passing through the reed into the river in the forest with which its banks were covered in the South West. As we could see the trees on the other side about three miles distant, while up on the Nor-East we could see nothing but a horizon of reeds as far as the eye could reach, we went about 7 miles towards the West, and when mounted on a tree saw a large sheet of water on the Nor West. Believ-

[1] At the foot of this page (237 of Notebook I), D.L. wrote: 'A note respecting Buphagidae hydrocorax read here, it is to be found on page 315.' That page is headed: 'Mem. to be inserted at page 237 two lines from bottom.' In the text as printed above, the 'note' has been inserted accordingly.

[2] Two species occur in South Africa: *Buphagus africanus*, the yellow-billed oxpecker, and *Buphagus erythrorhynchus*, the red-billed oxpecker; both are known in Afrikaans as *renostervöel*, 'rhinoceros bird' (Roberts, *Birds*, p. 402).

ing this to be the river we made for an island nearest to it. There were three islands in a line and the farthes[t] off was distant a little more than a mile. The intermediate space was closely planted with a coarse sedgy grass six feet high & armed with a double row of serrated teeth which cut the hands most cruelly. It cut only at certain angles, and stray ones seemed more dangerous than masses. The work of forcing our way through this with the water up to our middles made the perspiration stream from every pore. In addition to the sedge the space between the second & third islands contained a dense mass of reed mixed with the other. This exhausted us both so much we were obliged to deposit our burdens on the bent mass & work our way forward unencumbered. This we effected by putting a staff against the reed & pressing against it with all our might, & when it reached the water we mounted on it & bent it down farther.

When we reached the island the first object that arrested our attention was bramble berry bushes in full blossom, and the island consisted of limestone tufa. The trees had vines intertwined among their branches up the Top. A solitary hole in the dense mass of vegetation (reed papyrus &c &c) which surrounded the island on all sides for about one hundred yards induced me to enter in so that I might see if any thing could be seen after I had passed beyond the range of the light. The first step took me up to the middle in water and another to the breast, but nothing could be discerned in the dark cavelike hole from which the overhanging dense vegetation excluded the light of day. Connat & I attempted to make a passage by the side of this by both mounting on a mass of vegetation which we had slightly bent, but our united weights could only bring it down to an angle of about 45°. The mass consisted of bramble Papyrus nearly as thick as the wrist, reeds vines and sedgy grass bound together by a kind of creeper so strong to break it seemed like trying [to] snap whip cord. When the foot became entangle[d] in it we were completely hampered till we stopped & broke it.

Giving up the attempt to force a way into the sheet of water we set forth on our return, and found it nearly as difficult as when making the passage, for nearly all we had with so much labour bent down had risen up again, and that which was still bent presented the points to our eyes and more cutting edges than before. With our hands all raw and bloody and knees through our trowsers we at length emerged & proceeding North East again rested in our bower. The serrated edged sedge which had inflicted much injury on our persons and clothing is I believe the tsitla, from the root of which an excellent and nutritious flour is extracted and [the] root itself is excellent and refreshing either raw or roasted. Whole villages subsist for several months each year on this root alone. A great deal of starch could be extracted from it with little trouble.

Many plants which are of essential use to man and animals are armed with thorns and spikes as a defence against annihilation. They form part of the original curse, and in this as in many other instances the curse is turned into a blessing. The thorns form a sort of defence to plants, restricting their use to a limited number of animals and thereby securing them from extinction, as in animals horns, fleetness, quickness of scent &c. (& Kala[1] or Buphaga seeking their friend Rhinoceros). The young Palmyra would be eaten by buffaloes, oxen &c &c, as they shew a strong inclination to it, but the spikes restricts it to the elephant and man. Thorns too form a safe defence for small birds. They at once fly to thorn trees for protection and roosting sit secure where no bird of prey can approach.

Having rested an hour we proceeded North East in search of an opening into the river. The most part of the day (Thursday) had been spent in hard but fruitless labour. Connat fell behind a little, and when I called him a buffalo which was lying about three yards from the spot where I stood rushed out between us. We then killed a Lechwee and hanging up the meat spent our second night not far from our first.

In our bower of Hydrangea we saw a curious little nest, the second I have met composed of spider's web woven to a few leaves. The bird thrusts it through the leaves with its bill. The inside is coarse hair.[2]

---

[1] The Tswana name for the oxpecker. (The words placed in parentheses were added at the foot of the page.)

[2] 'While collecting wood that evening, I found a bird's nest consisting of live leaves sewn together with threads of the spider's web. Nothing could exceed the airiness of this pretty contrivance; the threads had been pushed through small punctures and thickened to resemble a knot' (*Travels*, p. 175).

29th Friday. We went on in the Nor East direction and with much toilsome labour discovered that we had as yet come to no opening. As nearly the whole of this day's march was performed in water and high grass, which rendered it necessary to lift our feet very high and then force our way through with our knees, their bare and abraded surface was very painful. Connat by frequently falling down with his load and always [lagging] behind shewed evident symptoms of knocking up. We resolved to leave the Pontoon on a tree and if we found an opening come back for it. Proceeding onwards and searching many bends in vain, we at length at sunset reached a Makoba hut & fishing weir apparently deserted some months previously. After firing repeatedly in order to make people hear us we went into the hut to sleep.[1] The dew being very heavy and our clothes all wet it proved a most welcome [shelter]. A large whitish-brown mouse seemed to be in possession, and crops of date seeds vegetated round the door.

An insect called Tampan,[2] which seems one of the human pediculae, bit me during the night, and as its custom is filled itself full of blood. It then resembles a small blue soft berry with a few sprawling legs. Its bite remains painful & partially itchy for many days afterwards. It is common in Bechuana huts and I have swelled all over in consequence of their bites. It is remarkable that the bites of these insects should present indications of a strong poison. Its effects are not merely those necessary to warn the animal of the presence of a noxious neighbour. They are seen more when the tipulae are allowed full swing. Sucking blood seems to afford them intense enjoyment, for when fully engaged in it one may put his finger with ease upon them, while at other times they fly off at the slightest movement. They usually make a movement as if they would alight on a part, humming at the same time as loud as possible and striking the part, then retire allowing many a slap to be driven to the place. If no move-

[1] 'At one time something came near us, making a splashing like that of a canoe or hippopotamus: thinking it to be the Makololo, we got up, listened, and shouted; then discharged a gun several times; but the noise continued without intermission for an hour' (*Travels*, p. 176).

[2] '*Onithodorus savignyi, var. cæcus.* A species of large tick the bite of which is particularly painful and irritating' (Pettman, p. 493).

ment is made the next approach is made more quietly & to alight. The immense swarms may be looked upon either as embodiments of happiness or living plagues. If however we view them as the production of a Benevolent Father the plague must be considered as the necessary effect of our being parts of one grand system, in which each ministers to the gratification of the other. We can by ingenuity prevent any undue plague or evil influence as in other general effects of the laws of nature—cold, heat, rain, &c., wind, fire, water &c.

In the country we had traversed the vegetation was the most luxuriant I ever saw. The Palma Christi plants[1] around the door of the Makoba hut had leaves which when laid on the arm reached from the fingers end to the top of the shoulder, and crops of date trees were springing up from the seeds of the fruit eaten by the inhabitants, shewing much greater moisture of atmosphere. The country is quite flat and numerous anthills have become the stage on which trees grow. The ants seem to have first raised the ground above the level covered by the waters, and the reeds have floated to the mounds and vegetated. The intervening space is destitute of both trees and bushes and but covered with grass, so dense & strong it is difficult to force one's way. In some places it is 12 feet high and occasionally higher. There are numerous small paths running in different directions made by otters, others larger made by the elephant & hippopotamus, but these cannot be walked on for they sink in and leave large holes which do not appear in the water but one goes plump down about 18 inches when we expect to step no more than ten. The anthills are large and may be called mounds affording convenient places for surveying the country to both animals and men, but they are covered with such dense crops of vegetation I have frequently bent it down & walked over it without touching the ground, and when I reached the top I found myself only in a cup with the vegetation excluding the view in all directions.

We finished our provisions at the hut & then resolved to search farther East. On proceeding through two very deep branches we found an opening in the reed which from a

---

[1] 'The Castor-oil plant, *Ricinus communis*, having leaves of a hand-like shape' (*Shorter Oxford English Dictionary*).

mound we observed led to a broad sheet of water. We went back seven miles and brought the pontoon, and having drank a cup of coffee forced our pontoon through the reed. It was the river and about one hundred yards wide. We then paddled briskly along. A hippopotamus went off from beneath us with a splash, but feeling persuaded that they could not over-turn it, & if they dashed against it, it would only glide to one side, I instructed Connat to hold on to it whatever might happen. Several hippopotami fled before us and kept one ear above the water. Others snorted & blowed, but by holding along the river about 20 miles we came to Moremi's[1] just at sunset. Both sides of the river were covered with one wall of reed & scarcely an opening in it all, presenting the prospect of compelling us to spend the night among the reeds in our pontoon, and that just large enough to hold two persons. I began to wish we should get a good shot at a hippopotamus and enable us to spend Sunday with comfort on some island, but when we saw the pleasant sight of human habitations we pulled along vigorously in order to make a respectable entrance.

Great was the excitement produced by 'two men coming along the water on a bag'. It was, as they expressed it, as if we 'had fallen out of a cloud'.* All stood gazing in mute astonishment, but calling out to [them], 'Why do you stand there gazing, come here & help me to lift it out', some of them knew me and came, giving vent to their innocent won-derment in hearty laughs. The excitement produced by the adventure on the bag was the more intense because they have been accustomed to look upon their deep Chobe as a sure wall of defence against their enemies. But now that they had oc-cular demonstration of the capability of crossing it without their knowledge, they asked if the Boers had such instru-ments. The whole of the surrounding hamlets were summon-ed to see the pontoon.

* Others said I had come riding on a hippopotamus — 'Our forefathers who are dead never saw the like.' [D.L.]

---

[1] A Kololo headman whom D.L. had met in 1851, 'and who was now located on the island Mahonta (lat. 17° 58′ S., long. 24° 6′ E.)' (*Travels*, p. 177). Mahonta is not shown on modern maps, but Curson (*op. cit.*, p. 150) was told of a place, Mahundu, about 18 miles east of that mentioned by D.L.

They supplied us abundantly with provisions, and having remained over Sunday 1st May I returned with them on Monday the second in canoes in nearly a straight line, and found it only about 15 miles distance,[1] though in the way we had gone we had travelled about 100. With gratitude to God for his preservation. One leg lame. Connat quite knocked up, so that he walked next day with a staff. Shot two Lechwee.

Sunday 1st. We heard that the Mambari had come to Linyanti and that Sekeletu [refused(?)][2] to trade in slaves, that one party of them still remains at the Borotse, and they have a white man with them. Who can this be?[3] He has one horse & comes from the West.

Tues. 3d. Tried the different fords but found them totally impassable for waggons. The water dries up next month. I send off an express to Sekeletu to send down a number of canoes and take us all up with our goods to the town. Their respect for me is not diminished in the least. It is rather increased. This is of God. I thank him sincerely. They had heard that I was in the old path & immediately sent off people in that direction in search of us. They went Southwards and, hearing we had passed, Eastwards till they found the waggon spoor, and were at the waggon the day after I left. Another party saw us and seeing no one about the waggon was afraid to come. Great anger was manifested to this latter party for its cowardice, and they wished to punish the Bushmen for their desertion, but I had persuaded them from day to day to go on and fairly beat them out by constantly exposing them to the water. I do not wonder at their determination to leave us, for they imagined I should become angry with them when I found myself in inextricable difficulties. In our little bower we had a nest of a bird which builds of spider's web, thrusting it through leaves with its bill and lining it with hair.[4]

Wed. 4th May. Ponuane came this morning, having been sent down to see if we were here. He thinks the fords to the

---

[1] 'Not more than 10 miles' (*JRGS*, 1854, p. 292).

[2] In turning to a new page, D.L. inadvertently omitted one or more words. My conjecture is based upon what he wrote elsewhere: 'The Mambari found no market here' (*Letters*, vol. ii, p. 223).

[3] His name is given below (p. 127) as 'Porotle', i.e. Silva Porto.

[4] Cf. above, p. 119.

West ought to be examined. They are impassable. Is anxious that we go up to the town, which is in fact according with what I wish too. He informs me that the abdication of Mamochisane[1] was voluntary, and that all the different individuals are in the same position with respect to the young chief as they were to Sebituane. The favour manifested towards me is very great. Is it not an answer to the prayers of my friends at home? A water tortoise was brought and found to be excellent. Otters abound on the plains covered with water. The people in canoes hunt buffaloes in the water with great speed. They kill elephants easily when they are found in it. We wait in expectation of the canoes from Sekeletu.

Friday. Lobari[2] are a people who live in a hilly country far to the North. They have guns & clothing and grow sugar. Borotse grow sweet potatoes of two kinds.

The large water to which we approached when we made our way through the serrated edged grass is called Nyampetsi.[3] The grass is called Mokancha.[4]

Sat. Have been obliged to hunt three times this week. People are too weak to do it. After all it is hard work, and when I return tired I remember the toil which our friend Oswel endured on our account last year. He never spared himself when we needed meat, and the weather was much warmer than it is now. I shot 6 Lechwees and one Tsessebe,[5] and all the meat has been used. The Lechwee is much more tenacious of life than zebras or eilands. One shot right through the body went off as if untouched and lived more than an hour. Others shot right through went off altogether, and the people say unless a bone is broken he will make his escape.

It is much against the grain in me to go sneaking up to these lovely antelopes and point the murderous tube at their beautiful forms, but necessity has no law. I try to get a good shot and kill at once, and no animal escapes wounded without giving me much pain. If wounded severely they quit the

---

[1] In favour of her half-brother Sekeletu; cf. *Travels*. p. 179, and below, pp. 141.

[2] BaLovale; cf. above, p. 29.

[3] 'Niambezi' on Seiner's map (1909); now known as Liambezi Lake, approx. 17° 52′ S., 24° 12′ E.

[4] Not identified; possibly *Phragmites mauritianus*, 'swamp reed' (Curson, p. 137).

[5] *Damaliscus lunatus*, sassaby or bastard hartebeest (Tswana *tshêsêbê*).

herd and retire into the thickest jungle to die. One did so today. But if pursued all animals of the antelope kind rush to the water for protection. The Blacks of the river pursue them in the swamps in their canoes, manifesting great dexterity in the management of their canoes in the chase. They go as quick by punting with long poles as a horse canters, and few animals can escape their spears if the water is broad. They pursued Lechwees today while I was in the canoe and made the water fly from the gunwale of the canoe. A Rhinoceros usually utters a very piercing shriek when dying or when it gets a mortal wound. Antelopes often spring aloft in the same circumstances. Buffaloes are dangerous in consequence of a custom of lying down behind a bush close to their trail when wounded and waiting for their pursuer. In charging few horses could get away from them, and more natives are killed by them than by lions. The latter animals do not roar much in this country and are maneless.

Ponuane went of[f] this morning in order to hasten boats down. I offered to go up to the town with him, but he thought that Sekeletu would detain me by saying that I must rest myself, and perhaps he would detain me altogether, saying, let servants do the work of bringing the goods, Let us chiefs take our ease. He asked, supposing any accident should happen would they not be blamed? I replied that all knew my objects, and if I died no blame would be attached to them, except such as foolish people always would say. None of my friends would blame them.

The Banyenko repulsed Sebitoane's people three times. Their part of the river is full of rocks and rushes past with great velocity. They use small canoes and use their feet in managing them. We should come in contact with Mosilikatse if we went to the falls of Mosioatunya. I must try the Barotse first.

If a buffalo is wounded the herd expels it immediately, and if it is sick or old it is expelled too. Is this not to prevent the propagation of contagious diseases? Only the strongest animals propagate, for the weaker male is always expelled. At certain times the females congregate together. Female elephants always do so, and the males too. I have seen the frontal bone of the Rhinoceros broken by the horn of its rival.

Frontal sinus exposed. Elephants will kill a black Rhinoceros. It is his own stupidity which urges him to the conflict. A Borotse man here has the marks of an alligator's teeth on his thigh. When swimming in the river an alligator caught him and sunk to the bottom. When there, having the presence of mind to retain his assegai he cooly stabbed behind the shoulder. It immediately quit[t]ed its hold of his thigh and allowed him to rise to the surface.[1] Another man Seacona has the marks of the hippopotamus teeth on his thigh.

Mon. We remove to a spot quite on the bank of the deepest part of the Sansureh, as being more favourable for embarkation when the canoes come. The observations made for Longitude on Jupiter and the moon at the Moana tree[2] will do for Moŕemi's island, which is called Mahonto and is due North of us now. One river to the North is described as having water which smarts in the mouth.

We found a small variety of orange. It is about the size of a large marble. The leaf is different but the skin [and] smell are dicidedly citric or citronous. Shoñkodje.[3] If it pricks a person the wound is poisoned and excessively painful.

Tues. 10th May. Ponuane met Mahale coming down with canoes to take us and our goods up to the town and came back with him. It is cold now. A great deal of dew is deposited in the mornings, clouds called Mūe come up from the East, and the Hippopotamus comes out of the water and seems unable by scent to return ; they lie down in the forest and are sometimes killed having quite lost themselves. This most frequently arises from drizzling rains, Mayori.

We went over to the bank of the large river Sansureh and soon Mahale and Ponuane made their appearance with ten large canoes and upwards of seventy people. We immediately went out to hunt Lechwees to fill so many mouths. Got one only. Slaughter an ox. There are three large parties of Mambari—one remains at the Barotse, another at Linyanti, and a third has gone to the Bashukulompo to buy slaves. The white man who is with them expressed a desire to see me when I

---

[1] In *Travels*, pp. 254 f., D.L. describes this incident as having happened to one of his own men.

[2] Presumably the baobab mentioned above, p. 115 n.

[3] Presumably a vernacular name for the 'orange'; not identified.

came. He is called by the natives Porotle, and seems uncon-
nected with the slave-trading. If it had been Dr. Barth or
Overweg he would have written a note surely.[1]

Wed. 11th May. We placed all our goods in the Canoes
and went to the ford in the empty waggons. The water stood
8 inches deep in the waggons. We could not have crossed
without spoiling our goods. We sleep on the plain beyond
the long range of Palmyra trees. I have borne all the ex-
penses hitherto, and when slaughtering my good oxen usually
gave George the benefit of an exchange for his thoroughly
vicious ones, so that not only no expense is incurred by him
but he is a gainer by being[2] rid of vicious brutes the mere
refuse of the trader. He tried to persuade me today that I had
exchanged one of the very best oxen I have, instead of another good but not superior ox which I really did exchange.

Thursday 12 May. Reached the river with the goods.
George succeeded in talking me into the belief that his intentions were good, and as I am always willing to believe good
of people I am satisfied. It was well I mentioned it to him.

Cross River Chobe

Friday. Both goods and waggons were passed over the
river today. The spot of crossing is about 120 yards broad.
Six canoes were tied together and then the body of the waggon placed on them. 40 paddlers made them go at a fine rate.
There were upwards of 140 people helping, and those from
the chief were upwards of seventy of that number. The Barotse are exceedingly expert in the water. Their management
of the oxen in the water was quite a scene. The Bashubea got
the oxen into the river while the Barotse were still on the
other side, and they seemed afraid to go near them, but a few
Barotse came and soon guided the main body to the other
side. Coming for three which were refractory and obstinately
remained among the reed in spite of a shower of blows, they
sprang upon them, seizing them by the horns and nose in the
water, and by sheer force compelled the unwilling animals

---

[1] 'Porotle' was the Portuguese trader and explorer Silva Porto, whom D.L. subsequently met (cf. below, p. 188). Heinrich Barth (1821-65) and Adolf Overweg
were members of an expedition exploring the Western Sudan; at no time were they
anywhere near Barotseland, and Overweg had in fact died of fever in 1852.

[2] MS. has 'been', presumably a slip of the pen.

into the stream. They maintained their hold of them in the canoes and never quitted it till all were safe on the other shore. They sprang about in the water like alligators among buffaloes. If attacked by a hippopotamus they all sink to the bottom and the animal immediately loses sight of them, for he seems to seek for them on the surface only.

In the evening they enlivened the shore by a dance & song made for the occasion. The burden of the song was a fish made of pottery, sent by Miss Thompson[1] to the daughter of Sebitane. It was as follows :

> Re bonye lilo tsa likoloee,
> Re bonye lilo tsa batsamaee,
> Re bonye tlapee, re bonye tlapee,
> Re bonye tlapee ea likoloee.[2]

> We have seen the things of the waggons,
> We have seen the things of the travellers,
> We have seen the fish, we have seen the fish,
> We have seen the fish of the waggons.

We paid them 13 lbs of beads & five handkerchiefs, the latter given to those who had been most active. To each of the four underchiefs under whose direction everything had been done we gave a knife, an iron spoon, a tinder box, $\frac{1}{4}$ lb of powder & 20 bullets to shoot game for their numerous train on their way home, they being three days distant and their provisions expended. We gave them an ox, but not an atom of it remained in the morning. About $\frac{3}{4}$ lbs of beads to each of the underchiefs in addition. They seemed well pleased, and we had every reason to be so too.

Sat. 14 May. Inspanned, the first ever done on the North bank of the Chobe. We were told that no white man would be allowed to cross except myself. Though he offered a large

---

[1] Sister of the L.M.S. agent at Cape Town. Writing to him, D.L. says: 'The fish was an object of great attraction among the Barotse. Many disputes took place as to its genus, and, the scales being removed, whether it were roasted or only prepared for roasting. They made a little song about it' (Chamberlin, p. 190).

[2] In the modern orthography: 'Re bonye dilô tsa dikoloi, re bonye dilô tsa batsamai, re bonye tlhapi, re bonye tlhapi, re bonye tlhapi ya dikoloi'. The words are pure Tswana, and the translation correct.

price nothing would induce them to comply, they would even close up the opening in the reed made for us. The reeds of the Chobe are their defence against Matibele. I thank God for the favour with which he has made them regard me. Parota[1] seems to have come from the West coast. He refuses to buy slaves. The large party which went to the Bashuku-lompo [went] to purchase ivory & children. The people say that the path he has come is a good one, and that they think he has come to open it. We went only about three miles; in consequence of the bottoms of the little rivers being of very soft mud, we sunk deeply and broke a pole. Lat. on Sunday 17° 55', of banks of Chobe 17° 58'.

Sun. 15. Preach to about 60 people. They were very attentive. The fine evergreen tree called Mosikiri[2] yields a fruit from which oil an is extracted to anoint the head. Sekeletu resembles his father in some things, for he sent two bundles of corn, two of earth nuts, and two jars of honey to us as provisions. We have been liberally supplied by Moremi with corn, beans &c. Preached twice to the people here. It is only Divine power which can enlighten dark minds as these.

Monday 16th. Very heavy dews appear every morning, and not unfrequently the mist remains lazily spread over the landscape for an hour after sun rise. Therm. at sunrise 54°. Poisoning people by means of the water seems to have been practised by Jonke.[3] Many of Sebitoane's people were poisoned by drinking from a well which he had medicated for the purpose. The Matibele are as active in destroying people as ever. Pitsane[4] was nearly caught by them, but his gun prevented a small party which first saw him from attacking him.

We have about sixty people with us and they assist in every possible way. They wish to unload the waggons every time they become fast in these little rivers and carry the goods

---

[1] Silva Porto. D.L., not yet having met him, gives a Native version of his name (cf. 'Porotle', p. 127).

[2] *Trichilia emetica*, Cape mahogany.

[3] Hwange, chief of the BaNajwa (BaNanzwa) living S.E. of the Victoria Falls. His name is commemorated in the modern district and town of Wankie, Southern Rhodesia.

[4] A Kololo headman, subsequently leader of the men who went with D.L. to Luanda; often mentioned in the latter half of *Travels*.

over themselves. I have hunted all day for them with singular ill success. Only one small antelope called Mothoba[1] rewarded my toils. Saw a herd of wild dogs[2] as I galloped after a giraffe. They sprung back as I dashed through their midst. I went after them, but they shewed no disposition for a close acquaintance. The pheasants are laying eggs now. On the 12th I saw the eggs of the 'Pretty dear' partridge.[3] Cold seems to stimulate the procreative organs in Africa as much as heat does in England. We remain on the borders of a tsetse tract of country and will pass through it tomorrow night. Game is exceedingly abundant.

Tuesday 17. Remain over the day in order to pass through the Tsetse at night. Saw two black bucks, they abound here. They are called Ligalumo,[4] and are said to kneel down and strike with the horns backward. Got two zebras a tsessebe & Wildebeest. Our people will be filled for once. Passed through 8 hours of Mopane trees, the ground hard, a tsetse district, and crossed the Kalingo at its N.E. extremity. We had been travelling N.E. & now turn round to the S.W. We slept at the Palmyra trees where we rested and Mr O. cut long strings of goat's flesh and roasted them in our way to Sesheké.[5] We came to 5 lions through the night. It was clear moonlight and they only growled at the dogs.

Wedensday 18th. Pass on to the Bakalahari village where we eat Palmyra nuts last year and got a goat.[6] We are about 17° 40' now. The Chobe passes down to the ridge seen from Sansureh Eastward. Sansureh Long. will do for determ[in]-ing the North course of the river there. The rid[g]e seemed about 10 miles distant from Sansureh.

Thursday morning 19th. Leave the village of Setlagana and proceed on our old route towards the cattle post of Motoñka or Lebeola. We met a party going from the Batoka to Sekeletu with tribute of corn. They saw a party of Joanké's

---

[1] Lozi *mutobo,* reedbuck (*Redunca arundinum*).

[2] *Lycaon pictus,* the hunting dog.

[3] The Namaqua sandgrouse, *Pterocles namaqua.* Cumming (vol. i, pp. 145, 245 f.) mentions 'their soft, melodious cry of "pretty dear, pretty dear" '.

[4] I cannot trace this Native name. Elsewhere D.L. uses 'black buck' for the sable antelope, *Hippotragus niger*; cf. below, Appendix III.

[5] D.L.'s account of the first journey to Sesheke (cf. above, pp. 36 ff.) does not mention this incident.

[6] Cf. above, p. 37. 'Last year' should be 'two years ago'.

people who had come with clothing and beads to buy ivory. They seem to have been stirred up on both East and West coasts by our reports. They heard that the poor people of Mosilikatse on the small rivers which flow out of the Large Mosioatunya[1] are making canoes in order to attack Sekeletu. We hear many reports, but this being circumstantial may have some truth in it. They say four are made and the fifth is now being formed. The Mambari seem to drive on a brisk trade. If I can persuade the Makololo to engage in it they may soon have the market to themselves, and then we can surely use as much influence as [will] prevent the slave trade in the Batoka & Bashukulompo tribes of the North East.

The people seem to recieve ideas on Divine subjects slowly. They listen but never conclude that the truths must become embodied in active life.[2] They will wait till the chief becomes a Christian, and if he believes then they refuse to follow, as was the case among the Bakwains.[3] Procrastination seems as powerful an instrument of deception here as elsewhere.

Mpollo the chief's uncle[4] has great influence with his nephew. It is of prime importance in establishing a mission to get the good will of influential men and doctors. Though they may be very wicked men, kind words and politeness have great effect in modifying their opposition. It is not so gross and insulting, and sometimes they are reclaimed, but it is Divine influence alone which can touch the heart.

The chief wife of Sebituane has been taken by Mpollo as his right. Seipone is taken by Sekeletu. He wished to have Mariye too but she refused. He offered Mauñku to Mahale, but she said she would prefer Letloñkana. He then said to Mpollo, Mauñku must be your wife down here and she will

---

[1] The Zambesi (part of which is called 'R. of Mosi oa tunya' on Oswell's map; cf. above, p. 41).

[2] 'They listen, but never suppose that the truths must become embodied in actual life' (Blaikie, p. 142).

[3] Cf. below, p. 299.

[4] Mpololo, Sebetwane's younger brother. He became acting chief of the Ma-Kololo after Sekeletu's death in 1863, but ruled so harshly that the MaLozi rebelled, overthrew their conquerors, and restored the old dynasty (1864). He himself, wounded in fighting against them, 'ran and threw himself in the river, where he disappeared for ever' (Ellenberger, pp. 327 f.).

comply.[1] The ladies have more power over the disposal of themselves here than in the South. It is perhaps because the Basutu ladies are the aristocracy and highly valued. Mauñku is one of the Matibele.

Makoñkana is the name applied to the Lotus here. Those of the Sesheke are sweet, of the Chobe bitter. The grass has assumed its yellow wintry aspect. No frost yet, but very cold dews.

Thermometer in shade at Midday 86°.

If we can open up the Interior to the trade of the Coast, and persuade the Makololo to take the trade of this large section of country into their own hands, it will be an important step in the right direction. They will feel that the gospel is favourable to their advancement temporally at least, and we shall be independant of the Boers, who will do all they can to stop up the way between this and the South. Commissioners appointed by Government in the different sections [of] the slave producing territory would soon extinguish the iniquitous traffic.[2]

I would like to devote a portion [of] my life[3] to the discovery of a remedy for that terrible disease the African fever. I would go into the parts where it prevails most, and try to discover if the natives have a remedy for it. I must make many enquiries of the River people in this quarter.

What an unspeakable mercy it is to be permitted to engage in this most honourable and holy work. What an infinity of lots in the world are poor miserable and degraded compared with mine. I might have been a common soldier, a day labourer, a factory operative or mechanic instead of a missionary. If my faculties had been left to run riot or to waste as those of so many young men, I should now have been used up, a dotard as many of my school fellows are. I am respected by the natives. Their kind expressions sometimes make me

---

[1] Sekeletu took two of Sebetwane's widows, Mpololo 'got that chieftain's head-wife, or queen', and the majority 'were given to influential under-chiefs' (*Travels*, p. 185). Ellenberger (p. 322) includes Seipone and Mmanku is his list of Sebetwane's wives, but not Marije; she is, however, mentioned again below (p.238 ; cf. *Letters*, vol. ii, p. 183). Letlonkana I have not been able to identify.

[2] This suggestion was first made by Oswell (cf. above, p. 44).

[3] D.L. originally wrote, 'I would like to devote my life'; 'a portion' is an interlineation.

ashamed, and they are sincere. So much deference and favour manifested without any effort on my part to secure it come from the Author of every good gift. I acknowledge the mercies of the great God with devout & reverential gratitude.

We sleep at the Cattle Post of Sima.[1] Recieve a present of milk and corn.

From the hunting ground of black bucks to the Palmyra trees of the goats flesh   8 hours = 24 miles

To Setlagana's village	6	D°	= 18 —	
To Sima's cattle post	$5\frac{1}{2}$	D°	= 15 or 18	say
To hollow of the Likolobe	$3\frac{1}{2}$		10	64
To beyond Seloenda's	3		9	

hr

To Malebele's $2\frac{1}{2}$, to Korotse's $3\frac{1}{2}$ = 6 = 18 miles
Here we are about 16 miles from the Town.

Our train of attendants is 53, not including 10 or 12 more who are travelling the same way. The long line of dark forms winding along the plain with feathers in their heads is very pretty.

Friday 20th. The river of the Likolobe[2] has water in it. We passed through without difficulty as the bottom is sandy. The others were exceedingly difficult because of soft black mud into which we sank deeply.

Writing is to the natives here a profound mystery. There is nothing like it in the sphere of their knowledge. There is nothing with which we can compare it in order to give them an idea of it. They always look upon it as something super-natural, and expect the lokualo[3] to tell us things at a distance, or that we see in it things happening at a distance. It is as much beyond their ken as the things of Heaven are beyond ours. Machinery also cannot be explained to them, just as the unseen realities of the invisible world cannot be fully explained to us. 'We cannot comprehend' might be our language in many things as well as theirs for which we have fine sounding names meaning no more than insignia of our ignorance.

Frid. evening passed a black man's cattle post. He is named Siloenda and is probably a Morotse. He came after

---

[1] Not identified.
[2] Tswana *dikolobe*, wart-hogs, bush-pigs. No 'river' of that name is shown on maps consulted.
[3] Tswana *lokwalô*, book, letter, etc.; from *kwala*, to write.

us covered with perspiration and carrying a present of a large bowl of maize. We have everywhere recieved the greatest kindness and hospitality. Setlagana gave a present of milk, Ramocumisi milk & corn, Sima a large jar of excellent thick milk & a dish of corn, and now Seloenda adds maize. Moroa-motoñka[1] presented earth nuts. I do not make any sort of formal payment as it spoils their feelings of generosity but will manifest my thankful feelings to them all yet.

Saturday 21st May. We reach Korotse's post. Hear that the Mambari left immediately on hearing from Ponuane that I had crossed the river. We recieved handsome presents of milk from Letloñkana [and] Sebocoe, and mead & sweet reed from Malebele the doctor. The latter complained that he was leaner since the death of Sebituane. Their kindness is very great. If the Makololo have been selling slaves they may have wished the Mambari out of the way previous to my coming. I exercise no authority but that of love and kindness, so the Mambari need not have fled.

22d May Sunday. Lat. 18° 10′ South. At an outpost at which Korotse, Tlakatlaka and others dwell. Recieved a present of milk from the latter. How very much of the fundamentals, the elements of Divine knowledge, require to be communicated before an idea can be formed of the Christian system. We had upwards of one hundred this morning at service. The Makololo are nearly all slender men, and many of them complain of sickness. The River races are giants in comparison. Yet the former are their conquerors. All was probably owing to the energy of Sebituane, and he was selected as the instrument in the hand of Providence for opening these tribes to the influence of the gospel. If unhumbled these tribes are excessively impudent. Here Mosilikatse has humbled the Makololo too. They hence esteem the introduction of a new system as a great blessing.

On awaking this morning Lechwees were feeding close to the waggon and village in perfect confidence. It is a lovely sight to see the game so tame, but fire arms will soon dispel all this. The mornings are cold. At Twilight the therm.

---

[1] Morwa-Motonka, 'son of Motonka'; cf. above, p. 130, where D.L. mentions 'Motonka or Lebeola'. I have found no additional information about the other men named.

stands at 52°, but when the sun shoots his beams accross the atmosphere it sinks to 50°. The cold is always greatest just at sunrise. Do his beams act the part of a rod thrust into a chemical solution, the chrystals cluster round the disturbing element? Therm. pro[tecte]d at Midday 86°.

I will place no value on anything I have or may possess, except in relation to the kingdom of Christ. If anything will advance the interests of that kingdom, it shall be given away or kept only in reference to whether giving or keeping will most promote the glory[1] of him to whom I owe all my hopes in time and eternity. May the grace and strength sufficient to enable me to adhere faithfully to this resolution be imparted to me, so that in truth, not in name only, all my interests and those of my children may be identified with His cause.

I will try and remember always to approach God in secret with as much reverence in speech, posture and behaviour as in public. Help me Thou who knowest my frame and pitiest as a Father his children.

The Bayeiye say that their forefathers had the Bow, but it broke and they gave up the idea of independance and fighting.[2] They were in the habit of taking the children of their younger brothers and selling them for food or for a hoe. They point to the North East as the locality whence they sprung. Nearly all the tribes point in the same direction. We saw a man last Sunday who was shockingly burned by his son-in-law on the hip and elsewhere by holding a burning stick on it till even the bone was injured. His daughter had gone to some distance to beg pumpkins, and as it was believed that she had left her husband for good, and the father was accessory to her departure, the son-in-law had him held down and the torture inflicted. There are no bowels of compassion here.

All the black tribes have the idea that beauty and fairness are associated. The Basutu are much fairer than the river tribes & prize themselves accordingly. They seldom carry burdens. But in other respects all have the same ideas of comeliness with ourselves. Their remarks on first seeing

---

[1] '. . . it shall be given away or kept, only as by giving or keeping of it I shall most promote the glory' (Blaikie, p. 139).

[2] 'They have never been known to fight, and, indeed, have a tradition that their forefathers, in their first essays at war, made their bows of the Palma-Christi; and, when these broke, they gave up fighting altogether' (*Travels*, p. 64).

themselves in a looking glass are amusingly ludicrous. 'Is that me?', 'What ears I've got', 'What a big mouth', 'I have no chin at all', 'I would have been beautiful but for these high cheek bones', 'I am destroyed by these cheek bones', 'See how my head shoots up in the middle', 'My ears are like pumpkin leaves'—and laughing heartily all the while because the disparaging remarks are made by themselves. One man asked [for] the looking glass in the evening, and when I was lying as if asleep I observed him taking a long scrutinizing look and, after twisting his mouth in different directions, [he] remarked to himself, Kana ki mashue yañ![1] How very ugly I am!

The Basutus present that sickly appearance observed in all nations when becoming acclimatized. Very few of the women are stout and still fewer of the men.

The Bayeiye women are very fond of ornamenting the hair with large beads and shells. Three placed...thus [see facsimile below] is a favourite ornament.

observed - in all nations when becoming acclimatized. Very few of the women are stout and still fewer of the men.

The Bayeiye women are very fond of ornamenting the hair with large beads and shells. Three placed 3 or 4 & thus is a favourite ornament.

The wife of Sekeletu is here, she has borne him a son, His mother wished

The wife of Sekeletu is here.[2] She has borne him a son. His mother wished me to give him a name but I declined. She presented a large bowl of most delicious porridge made with honey. The meal being fine it was as good as a pudding.

---

[1] In the modern orthography, *Kana ke mashwe jang!*

[2] D.L. nowhere mentions her name. She was, however, not Sekeletu's only wife; cf. below, p. 144, 185.

IV

AT SEKELETU'S TOWN

Arrive at Sekeletu's Town

May 23d. Monday. Reached the town of Sekeletu.[1] He seems a soft good natured young man. His age may be 18. The town moved as if the population had been one man. All turned out to see the White man.[2] Many Lilliloos[3] greeted my ears, & kind welcomings. The elders said I had come to my child, and now that his father had come all hearts rejoiced. He expressed his own joy at seeing me and hoped I would give them rest and establish them. All whom we formerly knew welcomed me gladly. I met Mauñku by accident and she burst into tears. She having been a wife of Sebituane must have remembered vividly our former visit, and the reverse of her position now must have forced these tears from her eyes. What an amount of feeling and emotions there are in the world. How many interests are identified with the existence of one individual.

The Mambari fled as soon as they heard I had crossed the river. They went off at night to their own land without going towards the Borotse, their rendevous. Parota is a slave trader. He it is who heads the whole party. They said, when expostulated with for fleeing, that I would take all their goods from them, and when Mokanju replied that I did not use violence to any one, 'You are decieving us, he will attack us'. They were well armed. I wished to see them.

Kuenane proposed removal or rather hinted at the possibility of it. I told them my objects, and intend to enlarge tomorrow. War, with which they have been so familiar, is very unpalateable.

[1] 'We turned westwards towards Linyanti . . . where we arrived on the 23rd of May, 1853. This is the capital town of the Makololo' (*Travels*, p. 177).

[2] 'The whole population of Linyanti, numbering between six and seven thousand souls, turned out *en masse* to see the waggons in motion' (*Travels*, p. 178).

[3] The trilling sound (Tswana *tuduetsó*) that women make as a sign of enthusiasm or rejoicing, by rapidly and continuously vibrating the tongue sideways while screaming.

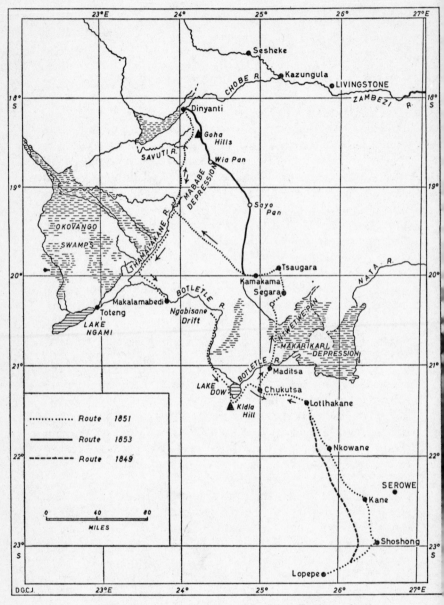

2. Livingstone's Routes in Northern Bechuanaland.

I presented the three goats, all that remains of a small stock of the improved breed which in obedience to the last request of Sebituane I had attempted to bring. The people & chief appeared highly pleased with them, and though disappointed that I had failed with the improved breed of sheep and a bull politely hoped that I would be more successful another time. The larger domestic fowls & cats pleased them mightily and was a sort of makeweight for the loss of the sheep and bull.[1] The maize we introduced as an improvement[2] was excellent the first season, but this last year having been one of drought the indiginous maize had borne it better and is much more palateable & soft than ours. Wheat did not grow, nor pumpkins nor any of the stone fruits, probably because planted in unfavourable situations, too wet or too dry. The seeds required some one acquainted with them to superintend. The model farm in the Niger expedition was a good idea if it had been fairly worked out.[3] All Africans except Bushmen are fond of agriculture and recieve seeds with great eagerness. Of eleven head of cattle left[4] only four remain alive, one ox is in good condition, two are very lean & never improve. Some of the number left were bitten by tsetse. We fear some of our cattle have been bitten by the insect now, though we never saw it in our route. It is a terrible scourge to a pastoral people.

The people on the plains to the West are an inoffensive race and would present no obstacle to an expedition were the tsetse not an insuperable one. Near the Borotse there is only one small strip of Tsetse country to hinder one

[1] In *Travels*, p. 191, D.L. writes: 'I had brought with me as presents an improved breed of goats, fowls, and a pair of cats. A superior bull was bought, also as a gift to Sekeletu, but I was compelled to leave it on account of its having become footsore'. He says further that he tried to bring the bull 'in performance of a promise made to Sebituane before he died'. But cf. above, p. 49, where he names Mphephe as the person to whom he promised the goats, etc.

[2] Cf. above, p. 49.

[3] In 1841 an expedition of three ships, sponsored by leading English philanthropists, had gone to the Niger delta in order to develop 'natural resources and legitimate trade' as a means of displacing the traffic in slaves. One of the methods planned was the establishment of a model farm. Shortly after arrival, however, almost all the members were stricken with malaria, which killed many of them, and the expedition was soon abandoned as a failure. Cf. C. P. Groves, *The Planting of Christianity in Africa*, vol. ii, 1954, pp. 4–12.

[4] Cf. above, p. 49: 'Leave 9 oxen & a calf'.

going Westward. Probably an opening could be found in it.

What is the reason that one animal is so much more easily killed than another? A Lechwee shot right through the body is almost sure to get away. If no bone is broken he manages to get off, while a zebra with a wound through the body soon drops dead. A Tsessebe too is very tenaceous of life. I shot one through the neck. He fell down, and when we went up to him my boy cut his throat deeply enough to bleed him thoroughly. He then started up and ran more than a mile, and had he not been brought to bay by a dog would have got clear off. I have seen a Rhinoceros while chewing the cud drop down stone dead from [a shot] through the stomach, while others shot through stomach and lungs go off as if little hurt. Probably that part to which at the instant of being pierced by the bullet the greatest amount of nervous influence is directed is the most fatal spot, the nervous shock being greatest. A giraffe has been known to drop down dead from being hunted by a good horse for two or three hundred yards, and an eiland when hunted a short distance is dispatched by a very small shot and in a spot not usually very fatal. If it were possible to ascertain the spot to which at the time of shooting the greatest amount of nervous influence was directed, we could dispatch animals with a less amount of suffering than usual.

Tuesday 24th. Sekeletu presented me with an ox as food, and an elephant's tusk by way of tumerisho.[1] As a mark of confidence I leave my ammunition in his hands. I give him half of it, and he requested me to ask anything I needed from him and he would gladly give it. I said I was still enjoying the pleasure of seeing him and would ask nothing yet. He sent about 50 people to cut reed and wall the waggons in for us. Mpollo came and told me that they had been much plagued by the Banyeñko, who gave in their adhesion to Sebituane and afterwards asserted their independance. They sent several embassies to Mpoa the chief, but he stoutly refuses submission.[2] Now, asked Mpollo, are we to endure

---

[1] *Tumedisó*, salutation, greeting.

[2] Cf. above, pp. 61, 125. 'Mpoa' (Imbua, called Limboa in *Travels*) was one of Santudu's sons. After the arrival of the MaKololo he and many other MaLozi had fled N.W. to the country of the BaNyengo, where they established an independent chiefdom. Cf. Jalla, *Litaba*, pp. 43, 60; *Travels*, pp. 485, 489, 497.

their scornful and murderous treatment of our people in silence? I suspect they must submit to it, and if peace could be established on any terms it would be a blessing. Better allow their independance than be beaten and forced to allow it.

I showed off George's stock of clothing and other goods to the best advantage, and then told them that having done so I left the rest to themselves and him. If we can succeed in making this an emporium of trade for the surrounding territory it will be a great blessing.

The Chief took me aside alone and requested me to sit down and talk with him of his position with respect to his sister Mamochisane. Sebituane's plan was to place her in the chieftainship, and that if she wished a husband to choose whom she might to sleep with her.[1] When her father died she wished to give up this system, for the wives of those husbands whom she invited to her had complained of her. She requested Sekeletu to reign and she would take a husband and live a private life. He was much averse to this and strongly advised her to reign. Mpollo took the same course as Mamochisane, but Sekeletu evidently reposed more trust in his sister than in any other. When I praised his father his eye brightened up and his countenance revealed by its smiles how highly he esteemed his father. He resolves still to communicate with her and shew her deference as his elder sister. He then pressed me to state what I wished to get from him. Anything in his town or out of it, if in his power, would be freely given. I declined anything at present but mentioned a canoe; as others of his people had them I wished to possess one of my own. The conversation produced an impression highly favourable to the young chief's tender affection for his father & sister.

Vines are shooting up at regular intervals in the courts of the chief. Saw Seipone. She too could not conceal tears on seeing me. One nice little child born to Sebituane after his death much resembles him and is called MaRobert.[2] This is the third Marobert I have seen.

[1] Cf. above, p. 29.

[2] After Mrs Livingstone, who in accordance with Tswana custom was generally known as Mma-Robert, 'mother of Robert' (her first child); cf. *Travels*, p. 126. The use of personal names to commemorate special events or visitors is described below, p. 125 f.

May 1853

Wedensday 25th. We heard today by a party of Leculat-hebe's people[1] that Pinaar's Griquas who went in for the purpose of discovery went past the Lake towards Libebe and are nearly all dead. They left 2 waggons in the field, and Lechulathebe sent men to bring down the only two people that remain alive in canoes to the town.[2] Thank God we have been spared this disaster. I do most unfeignedly praise & bless the author of all mercies for the abundant favour be-stowed on me in every step of my journey. My people are all recovered; although all have had Fever in a most severe form, all have been spared. I alone have escaped entirely.

My plan for the Makololo is that instead of forcing tribute from the different tribes which they have conquered, they would make it imperative for only a small tribute to be given in ivory, and the other products of the country to be bought at a fair price. Ivory for instance. Let it be known that every one who kills an elephant is entitled to one tusk, which may be sold to the trader here, and thus all the ivory will be at-tracted to one spot and the traders too will be attracted hither.[3] The Basutu will thus have a great and permanent influence in the country. They may then by means of the gospel be-come a permanent blessing to the tribes they have conquered. They are certainly not so degraded as the River tribes, and the Bible being already translated into their language less time will be needed for their evangelization than would be the case were we beginning with a new people and language. The plan of working on them and by them seems in accord-ance with that of Providence in bringing them into this coun-try and diffusing their language through this territory at the

[1] BaTawana, of whom Letsholathebe was chief.

[2] Chapman met those two men on 21 June, 1853, a little to the N.W. of Lake Dow. He describes them (vol. i, p. 142) as 'the remnant of a party who had gone in search of, and discovered, Lebebe. . . . Ten of their number had died of fever; their oxen had all been killed by the [tsetse] fly, and they were compelled to abandon their wagons 700 miles from this place. The two survivors had been cared for by the chief of the lake during their recovery'. Pienaar ('Pinaar') was presumably the party's leader.

[3] D.L.'s 'plan' was not adopted. In *Narrative*, p. 288, he records that in 1860 Sekeletu (still) claimed 'all the ivory of the country', and that some people thought this unjust, since both other Native chiefs and the Portuguese 'allowed the hunter one of the tusks'.

very time that the Fountain of Divine knowledge is rendered into Sitchuana.[1]

Mpollo informs me that there is a strong party against Sekeletu, and that Mamochisane is privy to it. He seems to believe that they ought to be killed. I tried to shew the great guilt of shedding human blood, and offered to be a mediator and peace maker between the parties. They shew the greatest deference to my opinions and sentiments. May God grant that I may be a healer of their factions and lead them to peace and good will. Domestic war would be disastrous to the tribe. My mission is that of peace and good will to all. By establishing a system of trade in the different quarters of the country the river tribes will be served, for at present they are entitled to nothing but their food, and not all that even. Sekeletu seems to love his sister, but she and Mpepe would not grieve though he were put out of the way.

26th Thursday. Mended some of the Makololo guns today. They are wretched stuff and have been wretchedly used. My tools having been taken off by the Boers I cannot work as I otherwise should. Sekeletu confirmed the statements of Mpollo, and added that Mamochisane hated Mpollo and would not listen to him. S. thinks she would listen to himself. I advised the use of every possible fair means before having recourse to bloodshed. Spoke of the value of human life and great guilt of shedding human blood. New doctrine to them. He is anxious to gain possession of gun medicine. All believe in its potency if they could only get it.[2] I proposed that it should be tried whether those who had never shot anything would by means of medicine shoot better than those who were accustomed to kill game with their guns. He has sent off to the Sesheke for ivory. All both old and young look upon us at present as their deliverers and bestow abundance

[1] Moffat had published a Tswana translation of the New Testament in 1840, and was now busy on the Old Testament, some books of which had also been published. He completed the whole work in 1857.

[2] Cf. *Travels*, p. 257: 'My men, having never had firearms in their hands before, found it so difficult to hold the musket steady at the flash of fire in the pan, that they naturally expected me to furnish them with "gun medicine", without which, it is almost universally believed, no one can shoot straight. Great expectations had been formed when I arrived among the Makololo on this subject.' In the same paragraph D.L. mentions that Sechele gave 'a large price for a very small bit' of sulphur, which was 'the remedy most admired'.

of fair names—Father, Lord, &c &c. But how long it may last no one can tell.

27th Friday. Some of the oxen are really bitten by Tsetse. They shew the usual symptoms of the terrible insect. Saw 20 hoes brought from the Manyeti[1] as tribute, and 23 large jars of honey and 14 bundles of corn. The chief divided them among his people, giving us four of the honey jars. They describe the country of the Barotse as exceedingly fertile. They reap four different kinds of grain in the year, and the women irrigate their gardens with their hoes.

28th Sat. Sekeletu asked many sensible questions about the system of Christianity in connection with putting away wives. They are always furnished with objections sooner than with true information.[2] I commended him for asking and will begin a course of instruction tomorrow. I mentioned my desire to see Parota, and he seems to have thought of going himself. There is a chain of tribes in the routes both towards Libebe and West of the Borotse. The river beyond the Borotse contains an immense series of water falls. Parota buys slaves, and the Mambari bought some here and elsewhere. It will be of importance to count the numbers. S. presented another tusk and a smaller one. I proposed to him to go on horseback. There is Tsetse in the way, but it can be gone through during the night.

Sunday. We had an audience of upwards of seven hundred both morning and afternoon. I explained after the service the nature of a book, and conveyed my meaning as well as it is possible to a people totally unacquainted with the use of letters. The chief fears the learning to read will change his heart and make him put away his wives. His age is nineteen. Much depends on his decision. May God influence his heart to decide aright.

Slaves seem of less value in the estimation of these people than oxen or tusks of elephants. The latter derive their value from the traders visits. The slave producing territory does not extend over more than ten degrees of Latitude.

The Hydrangeas grow to an immense size. Their flowers

---

[1] BaNyeti. They 'inhabit the south-eastern portion of the Barotse valley, and are found around the Gonye Falls' (F. S. Arnot, *Garenganze*, 2nd ed., 1889, p. 67 n.).

[2] '... sooner than with the information' (Blaikie, p. 140).

are however very poor. The people have actually made a garden for me at Linyanti,[1] but this year the produce is very poor in consequence of the drought. I have been invited to go and see it.

Monday 30th June.[2] First attack of indisposition except headac[h]e which I have had. It is a severe cold produced by the cold winds from the East which now prevail. Took Alt. & Lunar distances.

Tuesday 31st. By warm bath & warm drinks I am thank God recovered. A large party of Makalaka from Ramoshobotoane[3] has just arrived with tusks and maize for the chief. They are much more degraded in appearance than the Ba-

a kind of jingling sound . another
on the principle of the piano
having a board with iron rods stretched
over another rod. and a large calabash
attached to give sound
the third a single thread on a bow
with a calabash attached the
thread is struck by a stick

sutu. They have three kinds of musical instrument, one a rod with the seed shells of a kind of ......[4] strung upon it. The dry seeds rattle in the shells and the shake makes a kind of jingling sound. Another on the principle of the piano having a board with iron rods stretched over another rod, and a large

[1] Cf. above, p. 49.

[2] 'June' is an interlineation; it should read 'May'.

[3] Rra-Moshobotwane ('father of Moshobotwane'), chief of the BaToka at the Victoria Falls (*Narrative*, pp. 233, 248, etc.).

[4] Blank space in MS.

calabash attached by a cord to give sound. The third a single thread on a bow with a calabash attached. The thread is struck by a stick.[1]

The object of the musicians is to provoke the liberality of the chief. To beg or excite to give is the great object in view in most of their dances, praises, music &c &c. The antics of the three musicians were the most ungraceful I have ever seen. I was sorry to see any of our human family so utterly degraded, and when they followed me was glad to get them out of the way by a present or any other shift.

The principal man paid me a visit at the waggon and was exceedingly surprised by my hair, comparing it to that of a lion.[2] I cut off a little and handed it to him. The wonder he manifested shews that no white man ever visited his country, in his day at least. He seems about 40 years of age.

Ponuane informs me that the present cold prevents the fever. If it is warm in winter then the fever is very severe. This is the time in which the rivers are falling and the ajacent waters drying up. The proper name of fever is Letutumelo.[3]

The general name of Makalaka is applied by Basutus to all the black race on the rivers.[4] Those of Ramoshobotuane are Batoka. The Barotse are Baloiana.[5]

Wed. The chief presented 8 large and three small tusks this morning. I told them I would rather see them trading than giving them to me. They replied that they would yet trade with George, and that too as soon as he was well, but these they gave to their father, and they were just as any

[1] The instruments mentioned are, respectively, the hand-rattle, resonated xylophone, and musical bow. They (and some others) are described more fully by E. Holub, *Eine Culturskizze des Marutse-Mambunda-Reiches*, Vienna 1879, pp. 135–145.

[2] When among the BaLunda, in January 1854, 'By way of gaining their confidence, I showed them my hair, which is considered a curiosity in all this region. They said, "Is that hair? It is the mane of a lion, and not hair at all." Some thought that I had made a wig of lion's mane' (*Travels*, p. 274; cf. *ibid.*, p. 289).

[3] From Tswana *tutuma*, 'be in a feverish state' (Brown). Jalla (*Dictionary*, p. 127) translates *litutumelo* 'tremor, trembling, shaking, quivering'.

[4] Cf. *Travels*, pp. 186, 197. 'MaKalaka' is in fact the Tswana form of 'BaKalanga', the generic name borne by the Western division of Shona-speaking peoples; but as these were the first darker-skinned tribes encountered by the MaKololo when migrating north, the name may have become extended to others of the same complexion.

[5] More correctly, aLuyi or aLuyana, the original name of the people now called MaLozi (BaRotse); cf. Gluckman, 'The Lozi', p. 1.

other present. They asked after the gun medicine again, I suppose believing that now my heart would be warm enough to tell them anything, but I could not tell them a lie. I offered to shew Sekeletu how to shoot, and that was all the medicine known. I felt as if I should have been more pleased had George been amassing ivory than I. Yet this may be an indispensible step in the process towards opening the West. I must have funds, and here they come pouring in. It would be impossible to overlook His Providence who has touched their hearts. I have used no undue influence. Indeed I have used none directly for the purpose. Kindness shewn has been appreciated here, while much greater kindness shewn to tribes in the South has resulted in a belief that we missionaries must be fools. I do thank my God sincerely for his favour, and my hearty prayer is that he may continue it and make whatever use he pleases of me, and may he have mercy on this people.

Fever prevails most in the winter season, in the Intermittent form.

A party of Bayeiye from the River Tsow, or they pronounce it Chō, from the name of their chief,[1] came here today with tribute of corn. They maintain that the River of Libebe[2] comes from the same source as the Barotse R. and that the Chobe in its exceedingly tortuous course runs between them. It too must flow from somewhat the same source. The Lands ajacent to Sansureh and Linyanti were flooded this year by the Chobe, and the Sesheke was comparatively empty. It flooded all the way up to Libebe's.

The people danced the whole day. It was an exciting and savage scene, a hundred naked men all roaring at the top of their voices and making every variety of movement with arms heads and bodies. While the one foot is lifted high and a stamp on the ground given, a lesser stamp with [the] other follows. This seems the chief movement in common. The perspiration streamed off their bodies, and the louder the noise made, with but little regard to tune, the entertainment

---

[1] This river, now known as the Ngoga (cf. above, p. 26), is in *Travels* (pp. 67, 198) variously called Tzō, Chō, or Tsō. I have not found any other reference to a Yeei chief of that name. However, some of the BaYeei in Kabamokoni district call themselves 'VaDzo', and the MaMbukushu call all BaYeei 'MaJoo' (Schapera, field notes, 1940).

[2] The Okovango (cf. above, p. 48).

seemed to be the better. All was for an ox which the chief gave to be slaughtered. He was one of the most earnest per- formers in the company, but old grey-headed men joined in the dance, and a very few women also. The privelege of the latter seemed to be to enter into the middle of the ring and make certain movements in concert with the main body of dancers. They asked me what I thought of the dance. I remarked, 'It's very hard work, is it not?' They seemed pleased that I thought their work difficult though altogether unprofitable.[1]

Fever

Thursday 2d. A relapse shews that my indisposition par- takes of the nature of fever. The people inform me that the fever always begins so. A cold wind causes a shivering and then they draw near the fire, feeling though hot quite cold. They use means to restore the perspiration, and then recover. I invited them to try them on me. Sekeletu sent a doctor. He got some roots into a pot and made a kind of vapour bath. It did not assist. He then sought different kinds of plants and burned them. The hot ashes and smoke and vapour arising from these would have been a good auxiliary towards pro- ducing diaphoresis,[2] but I had used other means and per- spiration was re-established.

The cold winds passing over the swamps of the Chobe and Sesheke Eastward become loaded with watery vapour and probably malaria, and when one is exposed to it unprotected by warm clothing, or as among the natives with the skin anointed with fat, the perspiration is checked and fever en- sues. With[3] the closure of the pores in this case there is also a stoppage of some of the processes of the alimentary canal. Secretion seems to be restrained. The Bowels are constipated,

[1] At the foot of the page, which ends here, D.L. wrote: 'Continued after the extract from another journal'. The next seven pages (308–14 of Notebook I) con- tain a copy of 'Observations on Latitude and Longitude by Mr Maclear' (repro- duced below as Appendix II); then follows (p. 315) the 'memorandum' about 'rhinoceros birds' (see above, p. 117); and the next twenty-seven pages (316–42) contain the portion of the journal for 1848–9 printed below as Appendix I. The main narrative is resumed on p. 343 of the Notebook.

[2] 'I did not assist. He then sought different kinds of plants and burned them to hot ashes and smoke and vapour arising from these would have been a good auxili- ary towards producing diaphoresis' (Gelfand, p. 64).

[3] MS. has 'whith'.

and when this is the case for a few days the liver increases its efforts to free the blood of the noxious principles. An enormous quantity of bile is secreted.

The complaint exhibits itself variously in different individuals. In some the lungs are affected, in others the head, in others the loins, in others the nape of the neck, but pains along the spine are common in all cases and an immense heat of surface, the greatest amount being along the spine. In my case, which was the very mildest, differing little from a common cold, the heat in the axilla and heart scrobiculis cordis was 100°, at nape of the neck & spine 103°. Herpetic[1] eruptions round the mouth and nose frequently follow an attack.

A mild purgative with quinine seems the most effectual medicine. A violent purgative does not help. A mild purgative combined with quinine and the warm bath or pediluvium.[2] I have always observed that as soon as the slightest movement took place in the bowels the perspiration burst forth from the skin and the headache vanished. 3 grains of calomel, 3 of Quinine, 10 grs Rhubarb, 4 gr of Resin of Jalap mixed with a little spirit, is a good combination.[3]

Friday 3d. The chief presented another ox as food. It is the custom here and among all Caffre tribes to feed all strangers.

4th June Saturday. I presented a roll of brass wire, some flints and a box of percussion caps to the chief. He seemed anxious to get both rolls, those being all I had, by asking what I intended to do with them. I explained my intention of opening up a new path, and that the second roll was intended to purchase provisions. He replied, and where will the mehago or path food[4] be? This was as much as, I will take care you are abundantly provided for. I took the hint. It is always of importance to shew perfect confidence in their

[1] MS. has 'herpetetic'.

[2] 'A mild purgative with quinine seems the most effectual medicine. A violent purgative combined with quinine and the warm bath or ped chivium. I have always observed . . .' (Gelfand, p. 65).

[3] This may be the earliest recorded version of D.L.'s famous remedy for malaria. For later modifications (1860), cf. for example *The Matabele Mission*, ed. Wallis, pp. 90, 104; *Zambesi Expedition*, p. 393; Chamberlin, p. 272.

[4] Tswana *mhagô*, 'food for a journey' (Brown). 'Path food' is a literal translation of the Afrikaans equivalent, *padkos*.

honour. The expense excluding carriage is not great, and if the great end of my journey is thereby forwarded I shall be more than satisfied.

The fever is prevailing now. The winds feel very cold at night, and being loaded with vapour quickly draw off the heat from exposed bodies, though the leaves do not exhibit signs of frost.

Value of presents given to Sekeletu.[1]

<table>
<tr><td></td><td colspan="3"></td><td>100 lbs lead at Cape was £1.7.</td></tr>
<tr><td>Powder</td><td>£3.</td><td>2.</td><td>6</td></tr>
<tr><td>50 lbs brass wire</td><td>3.</td><td>3.</td><td></td></tr>
<tr><td>100 lbs lead from ...</td><td>2.</td><td>5.</td><td></td></tr>
<tr><td>25 lbs Tin</td><td>1.</td><td>11.</td><td>6</td></tr>
<tr><td>Percussion caps</td><td>2</td><td></td><td></td></tr>
<tr><td>Flints</td><td>1</td><td></td><td></td></tr>
<tr><td>A leaking pot</td><td></td><td>10</td><td></td></tr>
<tr><td>A frying pan</td><td></td><td>3.</td><td>6</td></tr>
<tr><td>A candlestick</td><td></td><td>2.</td><td>6</td></tr>
<tr><td>A powder horn</td><td></td><td>4.</td><td>6</td></tr>
<tr><td>an umbrellah</td><td></td><td>3.</td><td>6</td></tr>
<tr><td></td><td>16</td><td>6</td><td>0</td></tr>
<tr><td>P.</td><td>5</td><td></td><td></td></tr>
<tr><td>Tlo.</td><td>10</td><td>10</td><td></td></tr>
<tr><td></td><td>31</td><td>16</td><td>0</td></tr>
</table>

a Hat

Saturday. People of Lechulathebe arrive & report that the Boers are still troubling Sechele. Spoke to them about their chief selling children. He may now percieve his folly in inviting the Boers into his country by that traffic.[2]

Sunday 5th. The tongue becomes very sore and covered with apthae in this complaint. I could only speak to the people once today in consequence. There was profuse diu-

---

[1] In the list that follows, I cannot decipher the word after 'from' (in the third line), or explain the abbreviations 'P.' and 'Tlo.' D.L.'s first total (£16.6.0) should read £14.6.0.

[2] But in *Travels*, p. 31, D.L. says: 'never in any one case, within the memory of man, has a Bechuana chief sold any of his people, or a Bechuana man his child'.

resis in the commencement, slight headache, and great heat of stomach. Herpetic eruptions come out still round the mouth and nose. The complaint prevails extensively in the town. My people have relapses. George has been laid up for some days, considerable acidity of stomach & constipation of bowels.

People are here from Palleñ, S.W.[1] A large party. A stream of population is constantly visiting this [town].

Monday 6th. Two Mambari came here from Seseke. Their hair is plaited into three folds. They are very black. They say Parota does not buy slaves. He has a companion called Oboia.[2] Can it be Drs Barth and Overweg? It would be a happy meeting if it were these travellers. The words 'bon die', 'nabi' for 'navi',[3] shew that they are either French or Portuguese with whom these people have intercourse. They seem to believe that our waggon could go to their country. But four months would be required for the journey. They are understood by the Baponda and some of the Barotse. The country is flat and there are only two rivers to cross.

Tuesday 7th. One of the Makololo, Mantlanyane, having fled to Lechulathebe takes the liberty of going to the Bapalleñ and taking the tribute of elephants' tusks,[4] and then Lechulathebe advises Sekeletu formally to buy guns. This enrages the Makololo very much, and they threaten to kill those who flee from them and make use of their knowledge to their disadvantage. It is clearly a case of aggression on the part of Lechulathebe, and it is difficult to give advice in the matter.

8th Wed. The people are being collected to make a demonstration before the people of Leculathebe. Hope it may proceed no farther. There were about 200 yesterday and to-day there may be 400 all armed with shields. On such occasions any one, even an old man, who did not turn out was

---

[1] The modern Kabamokoni district of Ngamiland (cf. above, p. 26).

[2] Silva Porto, in his journal for 1853 (*Viagens*, Chap. V), mentions no companion of that or a similar name.

[3] Portuguese *bom dia*, good day, and possibly *navio*, ship.

[4] The BaTawana told me in 1940 that the land 'from Diyeei [the Chobe] to Kabamokoni' first came into their possession through Mantlhanyane, a Kololo immigrant from Dinyanti.

at once put to death by Sebituane and his carcase dragged forth to be devoured by vultures. He cared nothing for human life. Pity he did not live to know the value of the blood which cleanseth from all sin. Dances are got up daily and both old and young join in them.

In Bowdich's account of the Portuguese discoveries in Africa it is stated that Periera penetrated into the capital of the Molooas. Now this seems to refer to the Borotse, for their original name is Baloiana, and Seunturu the Moloiana was the only chief in all that country of any importance. All the other tribes were subject to him, and his sway was acknowledged from Mosioatunya to Bapallen & Libebe. He occupied the same place in the country that Sebituane did. The route laid down by Periera would lead exactly to his town, and the rivers Boa or Bui, Loanga, Loena, still farther confirm the conjecture that Seunturu is the chief he means. (Loena however flows west of his town.). His having been attacked by the chief Siñkautaba, the Chingamera (a Mashona chief) of the Portuguese, still farther corroborates this view.[1]

But one important link is wanting in the chain of evidence. There is not the vestige of a tradition in all that country of any white man ever having penetrated into the country previous to the visit of Mr Oswel and myself. This may be thought unimportant, but throughout Africa years are numbered only by important events having happened in each. Park says he is certain the year in which he travelled will be referred to as the year in which the white man passed.[2] And

---

[1] D.L. is mistaken. 'Moolooa' as used by T. E. Bowdich (*An Account of the Discoveries of the Portuguese in the Interior of Angola and Mozambique*, 1824, pp. 14 ff.), refers to the BaLunda of Katanga and neighbouring districts, who are called *Milua* (sing. *Mulua*) by the BaChokwe (cf. McCulloch, *The Southern Lunda*, 1951, p. 5); and on his map 'Moolooa' is shown far to the N.E. of Barotseland. Moreover, he makes none of the statements about Pereira that D.L. attributes to him, except (pp. 86 ff.) that in 1796 Pereira travelled to 'the territory of the Cazembe' (a Lunda chief). In *Travels*, p. 587, D.L. himself says merely, but more correctly, that 'Peirara' had visited Cazembe.

[2] 'The Mandingoes . . . distinguish each year by a particular name, founded on some remarkable occurrence which happened in that year . . . and I have no doubt that the year 1796, will in many places be distinguished by the name of *Tobaubo tambi sang*, "the year the white man passed;" as such an occurrence would naturally form an epoch in their traditional history' (Mungo Park, *Travels in the Interior Districts of Africa*, 1799, vol. i, pp. 274 f.). I am obliged to Mr. G. I. Jones for this reference.

in these parts the particular year of our arrival is dignified with the name 'the white men came', and a great number of children are named from the event. I have seen six MaRoberts (Mrs L's name), others are named Monare (Mr), others Jesus, others Setunya or gun, others Sepere or the horse, others Koloi or waggon.[1] Now so far from anything of the sort remaining as evidences of Pareira's visit, the Baloiana assert positively that no such visit ever took place. They say they must have heard of it. As Seunturu's own children are amongst the number, and some old men who say they must have heard of him had he come into their country at all, it is puzzling to realize Pareira's real route.[2]

The Barotse communicate readily with the Mambari. Indeed the Baponda, Barotse, Balojazi, Banyenko seem to speak the same language. Is this river a branch of the Zaire after all? The natives of the Borotse learn the Bunda language almost immediately.[3]

Journal of events &c in a
Journey in the country of Sebitane in 1853[4]

Demonstration

Town of Sekeletu 9th June 1853. 18° 17′ South.

The whole available force has been collected in order to make a demonstration before the Botaoana and thereby prevent them proceeding in their aggressions on the tribe and property of the Makololo. The numbers are about 500 ablebodied men. They are dressed out in all the finery they can command, and amused themselves by mock fighting &c for some time. They then adjourned to hear a declaration from the chief respecting the course he intended to pursue in future. The message sent by Lechulathebe evinces but little of

[1] *Monare* and *Sepere* are loan-words from Afrikaans 'meneer' (mister) and 'perd' (horse), and *Sethunya* is derived from Tswana *thunya*, to shoot.

[2] Starting from Tete, Manoel Gonsalvo Pereira crossed the Luangwa and Chambesi Rivers, and reached the court of Kazembe in the vicinity of Lake Mweru (*Northern Rhodesia Handbook*, 1951, p. 11).

[3] Notebook I ends with this paragraph. On the relationship of the languages named, cf. above, p. 30. 'Zaire' is an old name for the River Congo; 'Bunda' refers to the OviMbundu (cf. above, p. 37).

[4] D.L.'s heading on page 1 of Notebook II.

that wisdom for which Africans are famous. He directed the attention of Sekeletu to the Boers, while by means of one of his people he acts the part of the Boers in Sekeletu's district ; advises him to buy guns, while stealing the ivory with which alone guns can be bought ; begs servants from Sekeletu while it is known he sells them to the Boers, and takes every opportunity of enticing servants away from the Makololo.

Condition of Population

10th June Friday. The condition of the native population previous to contact with Europeans is one of constant coercion in so far as the public service is concerned. The condition in which the mass of society becomes patriotic is one of advancement in civilization. All public movements here are made under stern compulsion. Only a very few of the principal men would turn out to repel an invasion, the poorer classes would all succumb to the enemy. Even public demonstrations which are made at small trouble are yielded to by the body of the actors with an ill grace. They are forced to it. And every one who has the least illness—a thorn in the foot or hand, a pimple—always takes advantage of the circumstance to justify their remaining at home. How can it be otherwise? All property is vested in the chief. All expressions of loyalty and devotion are simply forms of begging. A man who rises up early and proclaims the praises of the chief with a loud voice soon gives up if no reward is given, and without shame mentions the want of pay [as] the reason why he desists. The entire system is one of selfishness. When Sechele was advised by the Boers to send away the women and children he refused,[1] answering his own people by asking who would fight if the women and children and cattle were not present. 'It is these alone which induces us Africans to fight'.

The great object of the Boguera[2] is to bind the bands so together that they must fight or be killed by their companions. If anyone fails in his duty he is insulted by his companions and used despitefully till he is known as one who has killed

[1] This is mentioned also in the official Boer report of the attack on Dimawê; cf. *Suid-Afrikaanse Argiefstukke, Transvaal No. 2 : 1851–1853* (ed. J. H. Breytenbach; Pretoria 1950), p. 365.

[2] Tswana *bogwêra*, the circumcision ceremonies preceding the formation of a new age-set of men; cf. *Travels*, pp. 146–9, and Schapera, *The Tswana*, pp. 38 f.

some one. When Mpololo brother of Sebituane failed in some duty to which he was detached, he approached where his brother and companions were drinking beer. When he lifted up a portion to his mouth Nokwane[1] tossed up the vessel to his face and spilled the beer over his whole person, this though 'Mpololo is brother to Sebituane. Mpololo mentioned this in the pico[2] a few days ago. When any dispute occurs they immediately refer to their exploits in war, and the greatest reproach that can be heaped on one is to call him a coward.

When we first came to Sechele he asked me to allow him to collect the people by means of the lash. I objected, and remarked that the service of Christ employed no means but those of persuasion. He looked at me with a look of pity. 'And do you really imagine that my people will ever believe unless I and my underchiefs compel them by the sambuck? Don't you know that I can do nothing with them without it?'[3] And so strongly is the idea of compulsion engrained in the native mind they look upon all entreaty and gentle treatment as indicative of weakness or desire to decieve, and it is only by a long course of conduct manifesting superior wisdom and power that they are at last undecieved.

There is a vast amount [of] wrongdoing and oppression, yet we must take into consideration the amount of pleasure which is actually enjoyed by all classes. There is seldom a very severe want of food of some sort or other in Sebituane's country. Fish may almost always be had, and then there is the inside of the date and Palmyra trees & tsitla or palmet. Great enjoyment seems to be experienced in the dance on all moonlight nights, and so much importance is attached to this by themselves the most insignificant village is careful to provide its own drum. Then though each man's property is covered by his hut there are a great many transactions which give enjoyment and zest to life, from the importance we are in the habit of attaching to our own little doings.

But on the other hand it must be acknowledged that their domestic affairs give them immense trouble. With all due

[1] A leading Kololo tribesman, mentioned again several times in later pages of the journal.

[2] *Pitsó*, a mass meeting of men for the discussion of tribal affairs; cf. Schapera, *op. cit.*, p. 53.

[3] Cf. *Travels*, p. 17. The 'sambuck' (sjambok) is a rhinoceros-hide whip.

respect for the sex we must confess that the women are a most unruly set. They are always running away, and the difficulties placed by their friends in the path to an amicable adjustment of differences require an immense amount of talk to overcome. The men say they would soon come into good condition were it not for the perpetual plagues inflicted on them by their fair(?) companions.[1] A woman who strikes her husband is compelled to come to the principal place of meeting in the centre of the town and carry him on her back home. The women however have some sort of right to bear themselves proudly, for they feed their husbands, raising all the corn, pumpkins &c. Yet it is very provoking for a husband who has five wives to come home hungry to find that they have struck, and all of them laughing and jeering at their crest fallen lord.

Sekeletu informed me of his intention to proceed to Sesheke and asked if I would go. I gladly consented, and proposed to go still farther, namely to the Borotse with Mpololo in order to get information from Parota. He does not like the idea of parting with me for any length of time. I hope he may consent. We hear that Wilson is coming.[2]

By the present position of society in these parts we are thrown back in imagination to the infancy of the world. Wherever an energetic chief arises we see another Nimrod, who by might raises himself to great power and wealth. His authority is absolute. His people are enterprising and brave, and to those who cannot see beneath the surface a kingdom seems established on as firm a basis as that of Romulus. His death is generally the signal for the breaking up of his tribe. His whole authority rested on brute force, and should his successor possess a milder nature his most devoted nobles become rebels and transfer their allegiance to some neighbouring chief.[3]

When societies of men such as these are brought into contact with superior civilization a state ensues which to superficial observers seems one of premature decay. The chiefs

[1] The query in parentheses is part of the MS.

[2] Wilson was at Lake Ngami in the middle of 1853, but there is no record of his having first visited the MaKololo. The report may have referred to James Chapman, who in August reached the Chobe with two companions (cf. below, p. 231).

[3] The substance of this paragraph is repeated briefly in *Narrative* (1865), p. 199.

lose much of their absolute power. The right of private individuals to hold property is recognized. The people become unwarlike. They may be thought indolent because they no longer follow their chief in crowds like a parcel of hungry hounds at his heels. They put some value on their exertions, and as they never possessed any of that devotion to the public welfare which induces a man to hazard everything for his country, it is not wonderful that they feel disinclined to yield that service which was previously the result of fear and compulsion or hunger. The listlessness which the great body of the people exhibited formerly becomes the peculiarity of the chiefs, the vigourous application they once manifested in the pursuit of their own objects becomes in a diluted form the property of the common people. And as there is no pressing necessity apparent to those whose wants are few they take the world easy. The few luxuries they know are supplied by the labour of the poor in Europe at a cheap rate. Each generation becomes more independant and civilized. Their wants are increased, and they gradually rise (query fall) to that state which we deem one of high civilization. This however [is] a very remote contingency, and one which it is probable will be accompanied with intellectual developement such as it is now vain to expect.

It is extremely difficult to explain to the people of this country the use of money or machinery, or of any of the sciences as sources of pure intellectual pleasure. If they can count as many as serve in all their simple transactions, which can almost always be effected on the fingers, what need is there for the rules of proportion &c? The art of writing is very curious, but of what use is it to those who can send all their messages viva voce and who have all their family and connections within five minutes walk of their own residence, and who have so little news to communicate that they begin their narration invariably with the formula, 'There are no news, We heard a few lies'[1]?

Saturday 11th. The attachment of the chief and people is likely to be a little inconvenient. He wishes me to go where he goes, but cannot bear the thought of my proceeding any-

[1] Cf. *Travels*, p. 151: 'If news is asked for, they commence with, "There is no news, I heard some lies only," and then tell all they know.'

where alone. He says he would be killed by solitude were I to go elsewhere. I have engaged Mpololo to take my side when it is proposed to go to the Borotse. A whole ox was cooked and devoured in a twinkling. Some did not get a taste. S. divided many of the goods obtained by trading with George in presents. I hope he may not forget to stimulate the other tribes to exertion by presents and that a trade will ultimately be established.

The general feeling between the two classes of native society is to keep the poor down. They are thoroughly despised, and every effort is made to keep them in the most abject condition. They wonder at my kind recognition of servants, and when a little present is sometimes given the master seems to think that he has a right not only to a present but a larger one, simply because he is master. They despise age too, and when an old man applies for eye medicine the young will point to his eyes with a laugh, as much as to say, what is the use of mending such organs? So long as an old chief lives the companions of his youth retain their influence, but when he is superseded by a younger man the companions are superseded too. Then there is a manifestation of sour feeling. The old rally the young on having done no exploits in the battle field—They eat oxen for which they never fought, they get young wives though not possess[ing] that bravery which deserves the fair. So long as the old maintained their ascendancy it was difficult for the young to get any but their cast off wives, and even among tribes which have been partially enlightened the old sticklers for use and wont appropriate all the good looking women of the tribe, and it is frequently difficult for a young man desirous of elevating himself in the social scale to get a passable wife at all. Where missionaries' wives reside this difficulty is less felt, for numbers are reared in knowledge and respectability, and though the parents are poor the daughters are eligible companions for young men who love civilization.

Among pure heathen tribes wives are subjects of constant contention, and nothing can exceed the perfect indifference with [which] transferences of wives are made. An elder brother getting a younger wife cooly hands over the elder to his younger brother, and not unfrequently same transference takes place between a Father and son.[1] Two sisters are often married by the same man, and not unfrequently, though it is disreputable, a mother and daughter are wives to the same person.[2] A sister by another wife is considered quite lawful, as in the case of Abraham.[3]

Any unusual phenomenon in the person of a child is noticed as a 'transgression' and not unfrequently punished with death. A child cutting the upper before the under incisors is put to death, and a woman bearing an albino is shunned by her husband. A woman came under our observation who clung to her albino child, a fine boy, for about five years, but at length yielded to the suggestions of her separated husband and put him to death. No notice was taken of it by the authorities.[4]

There is none of that feeling which exists so abundantly in England between the rich and poor. That constant stream of good offices and money which flows perennially in our native land from the higher to the lower classes of society does not exist in Heathen tribes. In those partially enlightened it exists in embryo only ; greater consideration is manifested to the lower classes and as a consequence they feel their own importance more. This latter feeling is especially obnoxious to those whose money elsewhere commands obsequious attention. They see in the upward tendencies of civilization only unmitigated evil, people becoming worse instead of better. They see and experience the truth of their opinions. Others can see in those opinions evidence of a very decided superficiality and shallowness in their powers of observation. In looking at both man and nature it is essentially necessary to retain our freshness of heart, a willingness to be pleased with

[1] In many Bantu tribes, a man may inherit his father's or elder brother's widow (cf. above, p. 131), but such 'transferences' during the husband's lifetime are unusual, unless he is impotent or (like Sechele, cf. above, p. 96) has first divorced the wife.

[2] Sororal polygyny is also widespread among the Bantu. Step-daughter marriage is prohibited by the BaTswana, but practised by OvaHerero and possibly others.

[3] Instances of marriage with a half-sister are known among BaTswana, BaVenda, and other Bantu peoples, but they are by no means common. For Abraham's marriage, cf. Genesis 20: 12.

[4] In *Travels*, pp. 576 f., D.L. says that the albino boy was killed at Mabotsa ('after I left the place'), and that children cutting their upper teeth first were 'always put to death' among the BaKaa and, 'I believe', also the BaKwena. Cf. Schapera, *Tswana Law and Custom*, p. 261.

goodness or beauty in any shape. The freshness of heart falls like dew on our spirits and gives zest to pleasures in trying to make the world better. It makes life always feel new, every new effort we make for the great end.

Sunday 12th. A good and very attentive audience. We introduce entirely new motives and were these not perfectly adapted for the human mind and heart by their Divine author we should have no success.

When lately recommending kindness and the stimulus of reward to those who should distinguish themselves in killing elephants and bringing in the ivory, Sekeletu asked if such a course 'would not induce his subjects to despise him'. I replied, they all despise the government by the lash at present and would prefer a milder rule.

Forty or fifty people sitting round the artificial horizon impart so much vibration to the mercury an accurate observation cannot be made. It must arise from the pulsation of their arteries imparting their quiver to the ground or air. Town of Sekeletu is 18° 17' South Latitude. Variation of the compass 21° West.

Proposal to visit Borotse

13th Monday. Sekeletu is very unwilling that I should proceed to Borotse without him. Offers to send for Parota, if I wish to see him. As he may imagine that having come down here entitles his nation to the entire trade of these parts I am unwilling he should come. Sekeletu intends to go himself. I have no objections to his going, but only to the delay. I suppose he wishes to have my influence to adjust differences there. We had a long discussion. I stated my objects freely and see I have many difficulties to overcome. Mpololo leaves tomorrow. Lechulathebe's people left very much frightened.

Took Obs. Lunar distances &c. Three sets of observations worked out give 1 hour 34m 56s, say 1h 35 = 23° 45' East Longitude. Our Waggon stand must have been on 24° East instead of 26°.[1]

The thermometer gradually falls during the night and is at its lowest point a little before sunrise. This morning, 14th,

[1] The observations made by D.L. at his 'waggon stand' of 1851 were defective because his sextant had been 'injured by a fall' (cf. *JRGS*, 1854, p. 306).

it stood at 48° unprotected in the waggon, a little after sunrise it was 52°.

14th. Sekeletu told me today that he would take cattle from the Bashukulompo because they had once or twice taken cattle from his father. I protested against it, but his ideas are entirely heathenish and he is probably anxious to distinguish himself in the only line in which from time immemorial distinction has been sought. I told him of the guilt shedding human blood brought on a man, and the uneasiness which filled the heart when, as they express it, 'the heart has drunk the blood of men'. Their consciences need enlightenment before this will be appreciated, for the Boers who know a little more than these people drink men's blood without compunction because they have black skins. No one can concieve the terrible depravity to which the children of Ham have sunk unless he has intimate knowledge of their language and customs, but to change their savage nature is the object of our mission and it will be accomplished by the power of God's spirit through the gospel. He is afraid of the portion of the tribe at Borotse, they are unwilling to obey him and refuse to give him the cattle which he had when there. I feel very anxious to proceed with my own objects, but obstacles are thrown in the way which I pray God to remove.

15th Wedensday. It is difficult to make these people believe that there is power in kindness. The rulers think that to be kind to their inferiors would cause them to be despised. Sekeletu says it is easy for me to talk of kindness, every one likes me, but he is hated by his rebellious nobles, and he fears them. A party came from the Sesheke with two Mambari, and another party from Borotse. The Tsetse is a great hindrance on every hand.

The people here seem determined to keep me to themselves. They send for Mpépe in my name and it may be to betray him. I must protest against this and if need be threaten to return. It is tantalizing to be kept just at the spot where we were last year, notwithstanding my having left wife and children for the very purpose of examining the country.

One of the Mambari gave me the bearings of his country from this town and the Borotse. From Sekeletu's town to

Kangombe's the Mambari chief[1] W.N.W. ($\frac{1}{2}$ N.W. & W.)[2] or 114° West of South point and the distance between one and two months. From the Borotse W. & by N. or 104° Westerly from S.P. From his town to the sea, which they call Kangola, is between one and two months, and the port seems to be Benguela, for he says Pangela, and knows the river Katumbela. His town seems situated on the Cobeele.[3] *And no tsetse exists in the path.*

The bearing of the Borotse from Sekeletu's town is 154° or N.N.W. That of Libebe 89° or nearly due West.

16th Thursday. The caterpillars are actively engaged in eating the leaves of the same tree which forms the food of the Ngoa.[4] The serpents are not dormant here. I saw one yesterday & another was killed lately at the waggons. The cold is not very intense, but the moisture in the atmosphere causes the sensation of a very great fall in the temperature. Colds are common among the [natives].[5] The Thermometer does not sink below 48°, and the vegetation is protected from injury by the general dampness. The pumpkin vines are the most easily affected by frost but they are not yet touched by it. The leaves of the grape vine and of the Ricinus are quite green and growing.

The chief has acceded to my request to proceed to Borotse and see the country. I told him my heart was sore because, having left my family to explore his land and if possible find a suitable location for a mission, I could not succeed because detained by him here. He says he will take me with him. He does not like to part with me at all. He is obliged to consult with those who gave their opinion against my leaving, but it is certain I am permitted to go. Thanks be to God for influencing their hearts.

---

[1] Kangombe is the official name borne by the chief of the Viye (Bihe) tribe of OviMbundu (cf. *Travels*, p. 218; V. L. Cameron, *Across Africa*, 1885, p. 442; G. M. Childs, *Umbundu Kinship and Character*, 1949, pp. 174, 225).

[2] The bearings placed in parentheses are an interlineation.

[3] The 'Cobeele' (Cubal) is a tributary of the Catumbela, which enters the sea between Benguela and Lobito; Cubal is also the name of a stream a little north of Lobito.

[4] The grubs of the 'poison beetle' feed on the leaves of *Commiphora dinteri* Engl. (cf. Schapera, *Khoisan Peoples*, p. 131).

[5] Word inadvertently omitted in turning to new page.

Thermometer at midday shews 80° in the shade and protected from draught, yet it is not disagreably warm. The evenings are generally close at 64°.

If the wind blows from the East the sensation of cold is very great.*

Took a set of Lunar Distances today and worked them out to 1h 35 4 or 23° 46' East Longitude.

The sets reduced to the apparent time of the mean distance as found by the Altitudes of the Sun were as follows :

Apparent Alt. of Sun's centre	16° 12' 1"
Apparent Alt. of Moon's centre	34° 59' 35"
Apparent Distance of ☉ & ☾'s centres	115° 53 26

Apparent time at station, worked out from the first four Altitudes of Sun increased to the time of the mean distance, 4 hours 9 minutes 57 s. Sun West, Moon East. 16th June 1853.

17th Frid. A kite's nest is reported at a cattle post. (Subsequently reported to have been a vulture or large Falcon.[1]) They are said to have migrated hence last month. I saw one somewhere since we crossed the river but forgot to note it. Swallows left last month, May, and return when the clouds begin to collect for rain.

Fever

The fever frequently affects the bowels, producing bloody stools and great pain. Laudanum & camphor eases this, but a weal extending half round the body under the ribs comes out. The people report the whole country as excessively sickly, and the appearance of the Makololo as contrasted with the aboriginal inhabitants fully confirms the assertion. The Makololo are all sickly looking & yellow with spare habits of body, while the Makalaka are stout and their frames are gigantic in proportion.[2] The latter are very black. As the Makololo have abundance of food and no work, conditions which elsewhere among Bechuanas always result in enormous obesity, the thinness of the Makololo must be ascribed to the un-

---

* A very cold south wind blows for three days occasionally. It becomes South East as we advance Northwards. Rains frequently fall for three days too (Why three days?). [D.L.]

---

[1] This sentence (my parentheses) was inserted at the head of the page.

[2] Cf. above, p. 47.

healthiness of the climate. And their whole country is of the same description. This for me is a serious view of affairs. Must I give them up, or expose my family to these pestiferous marshes? I desire to do what God wills, whatever that may be, and am pretty sure a long time will not elapse before I see some intimation of his will. I have never been brought to a standstill position yet. May God guide me, so that his glory may be promoted.

Sat. 18th. The East wind seems that which causes the fever. It produces the sensation of cold at 82° at midday. It is probably loaded with moisture from the Eastern marshes. Many people complain of illness. My own have had relapses. I have [had] three touches of it. There is invariably a stoppage of all the excretions, and if these are attended to and by mild measures recommence, the attack is over.

The people in this country have been in the habit of planting the Ricinus in their gardens and round their houses for the sake of the oil, which is used for anointing the body. It is even an article of barter, and is named 'Moni'.[1] The wild hemp, cannabis sativa, was introduced by the Makololo. It is now much used by all classes, and when about to attack an enemy they invariably smoke it in order to infuse courage into themselves. In the frenzy it produced none of the Makalaka could withstand them.[2]

Fabulous Opinions about Lion's Roar

The lions of this country seldom roar. The Bushmen seem to have taken this propensity out of them, for whenever a lion is known by them to frequent a certain locality they carefully trace him to his lair, and stalking carefully to within a yard of the sleeping animal insert an arrow armed with 'Ngoa behind his shoulder. At the instant of discharging the deadly weapon they utter a shout, which with the pain sets the coward off at full speed.

[1] *Ricinus communis* is called *mono* or *imono* by several tribes in N.W. Rhodesia (C. G. Trapnell and J. Clothier, *The Soils, Vegetation and Agricultural Systems of North Western Rhodesia*, Lusaka 1937, p. 79). Is D.L. suggesting that the name may be derived from 'money'?

[2] 'It causes a species of frenzy, and Sebituane's soldiers, on coming in sight of their enemies, sat down and smoked it, in order that they might make an effective onslaught' (*Travels*, p. 540).

The first person who ascribed noble qualities to the Lion seems to have been followed by the rest of mankind as sheep follow that one which has the bell, or as a string of geese does the leader. The Lion's roar is believed to be terrible. One writer (Cumming) on first hearing it knew the majestic sound at once.[1] Now the roar of the ostrich is so very like that of the Lion I never knew a European who could distinguish the one from the other, and though I have had during 12 years abundant opportunities of hearing both at all distances, I can only guess at which animal makes the sound. If it is made during the day I suspect it is an ostrich, if during the night a lion. The natives assert that there is a slight difference in the commencement of the sound which enables them to distinguish which animal it is, but there is none in the loudness depth or tone. Now whoever thought of speaking of the majestic roar of the 'silly bird'? Yet each has been roaring from time immemorial as loudly as the other, and neither makes such a majestic sound as a steam engine letting off its steam. Indeed, the snorting of the 'Iron horse' is better calculated to inspire awe than either lion or ostrich's roar. The possession of power is the reason why lion's roar seems awful and sublime, but let any one be placed in proximity with a carriage, with only half the chances of an attack which there is in viewing a lion or hearing it, and he will feel the sublimity of letting of[f] the steam to his finger ends.

Equally erroneous are the views held respecting his courage and generosity.[2] He rarely attacks animals during the day and even during moonlight nights he does not feel it safe to risk an encounter. If however it is dark and rainy and lions are in the vicinity, a traveller may expect his cattle to be dis-

---

[1] 'The night of the 19th [March 1845] was to me rather a memorable one, as being the first on which I had the satisfaction of hearing the deep-toned thunder of the lion's roar. Although there was no one near to inform me by what beast the haughty and impressive sounds which echoed through the wilderness were produced, I had little difficulty in divining. There was no mistake about it; and on hearing it I at once knew, as well as if accustomed to the sound from my infancy, that the appalling roar which was uttered within half a mile of me was no other than that of the mighty and terrible king of beasts' (Cumming, vol. i, p. 170). 'To talk of the majestic roar of the lion is mere majestic twaddle' (*Travels*, p. 141).

[2] D.L. possibly meant to write 'ferocity'. Cf. *Travels*, p. 139: 'Nothing that I ever learned of the lion would lead me to attribute to it either the ferocious or noble character ascribed to it elsewhere'.

turbed. But even then a very small circumstance is sufficient to move his fears. I have had lions coming up to within three yards of my oxen and refrain from springing on them simply because they lay still and were fastened to the waggon. A horse belonging to a gentleman of my acquaintance[1] broke away from [him] and was caught by the bridle on a bush. He stood in that position three days, and when found the ground all around was marked by the recent foot prints of lions, which were prevented from killing the horse by the fact of his being fastened [to] the bush. It is probable they suspected some strategem. I have seen them approach to within a short distance of the waggon and roar as loudly as possible in order to induce the oxen to start, and if they remained quiet no farther attempt was made, and his disappointment was expressed by retiring to a distance and uttering his roar of disgust.[2] The latter is that of the wolf or hyæna, which is sometimes that of strategem, most frequently that of disgust at being obliged to retire with an empty stomach. When endeavouring to entice little dogs near him he utters a kind of laughing sound. Sometimes it is an imitation of a jackall or other small animal. If no success attends his efforts it degenerates into the disappointed howl.

The scream or trumpeting of the Elephant is peculiarly piercing, and when seen charging the hunter and screaming it is really terrible, and one such charge has been enough to quash the aspirations of some mighty Nimrods for fame in elephant hunting.

It is only when in a state of desperation a lion will attack a man. When old & toothless & unable to kill game he breaks through the fear of man, but frequently not even the pains of knawing[3] hunger will induce him to attack the Lord of creation. A lioness in the Bahurutse country ate her own young though living in the vicinity of men.[4] When vegetable matter is seen in his droppings he is sure to be lying near in a state of exhaustion.

Facts about the People; their Deportment

19th Sunday. A good and attentive audience, but immediately after the service I went to see a sick man, and when I

---

[1] 'Captain Codrington' (*Travels*, p. 138).   [2] Cf. above, pp. 110, 112·
[3] So in MS.   [4] In *Travels*, p. 137, this one instance becomes 'well-authenticated cases'·

returned towards the Kotla[1] I found the chief had retired into
a hut to drink beer, and as the custom is about forty men were
standing outside singing to him, or in other words begging
beer by that means. A minister who has not seen as much
pioneer service as I have done would have been shocked to
see so little effect produced by an earnest discourse concerning the future Judgement, but time must be given to allow
the truth to sink into the dark mind and produce its effect.
The earth shall be filled with the knowledge of the glory of
the Lord. That is enough. We can afford to work in faith, for
Omnipotence is pledged to fulfill the promise. The great
moun[tain] will become a plain before the Almighty arm.
The poor Bushmen, the most degraded of all Adam's family,
shall see his glory, and the dwellers in the wilderness shall
bow before him. The obstacles to the coming of the Kingdom
are mighty, but come it will for all that.

> 'Then let us pray that come it may
> and come it will for a' that,
> That man and man the world o'er,
> shall brothers be for a' that.[2]'

The hard and cold unbelief which distinguished the last
century, and which is still aped by would-be philosophers in
the present, would sneer at our faith and call it superstition,
enthusiasm &c.; but were we believers in human progress
and no more, there must be a glorious future for our world.
Our dreams must come true, even though they are no more
than dreams. The world is rolling on to the golden age. The
inmates of our workhouses have more comforts than rich
chieftains in Africa have; they have soap, clean linen, glass
windows, and chimneys. Persons in very moderate circumstances put on finer clothes than Lords did in the time of
Queen Elizabeth. Fine cloth was not then known, and the
luxuries of tea & coffee and sugar & potatoes now relished
by all were equally unknown. Surgical operations are performed without pain, fire is obtained instantaneously, and it
is probable that before long we shall burn water instead of
coal. Intelligence is communicated instantaneously, and tra-

---

[1] *Kgotla*, council-place, place of public assembly.
[2] D.L. apparently cherished this passage from Robert Burns, which he quotes
again below (p. 210); cf. also *Letters*, vol. ii, p. 93.

vellers are conveyed on the ocean and on the land with a celerety which our forefathers could not comprehend and which Africans now consider fabulous.

Discoveries and inventions are cumulative. Another century must present a totally different aspect from the present. And when we view the state of the world and its advancing energies in the light afforded by childlike or call it childish faith, we see the earth filling with the knowledge of the glory of the Lord, aye all nations seeing his glory and bowing before him whose right it is to reign. Our work and its fruits are cumulative. We work towards another state of things. Future missionaries will be rewarded by conversions for every sermon. We are their pioneers and helpers. Let them not forget the watchmen of the night, we who worked when all was gloom and no evidence of success in the way of conversion cheered our path. They will doubtless have more light than we, but we served our master earnestly and proclaimed the same gospel as they will do.

Future missionaries will probably look on our attempts to stop rain making by asserting the impossibility of anyone making rain but God in another light than we do, for it is not impossible that power may be obtained over the clouds. An electrical machine attached to a kite will bring down rain from a cloud, and this may be so improved as to call down copious showers when needed. I have seen clouds stand over Kolobeng so thickly no portion of the sky could be seen, and so near it was astonishing that with the thunder rain did not fall. A machine would have been of inestimable benefit then. We discourage the rain doctor because in his work the people are led to give that honour to a knave which belongs to God only.

Temperature at sunrise 44° in waggon
an hour afterwards 56° Do
At Midday 74° Do

Windy and cloudy. If still and clear sky, 80° and upwards.

Many of the scenes exhibited by these savage tribes have become so familiar they excite no surprise. But were they seen by a writer possessing the descriptive power, clearer ideas of the actual state of savage nations would be conveyed to the European mind. On returning to the afternoon service

I found the chief and a band of about 40 young men engaged in dancing & roaring at the top of their voices. When I sat down one of the elder people who had visited Kolobeng[1] called on them to stop their play and come and hear my message. They did so, and while waiting for the rest of the people to assemble there were several disputes going on in their usual way. One man started up and called to another if it were not a fact that he had outrun the individual with whom he was engaged in dispute. Another asked, Where are your spear wounds? He shews one scar on his thigh & another on his back. 'O you ran away when you got that one'. 'No I did not'. Another party is in hot dispute on a similar subject; one gets up and imitates his actions in some engagement with the enemy, how he knocked one on the side of the head, and imitating the act of the other by clapping his hand to the spot a loud laugh follows. Another tells how he stabbed the enemy and imitates the death cry of the victim, a fine joke apparently from the hearty laugh exhibiting immense mouths, white teeth and glistening eyes. Another offers to try a race with his opposing companion and stakes an ox that he will win. Another calls out to a servant to go home and bring him snuff, and when some is brought to the chief, three or four hands are held out ready to grasp what remains after he has taken his pinch, which pinch is followed in every instance by a profuse flow of tears and that, they say, is the pleasure felt in taking tobacco. The pipe containing wild hemp is handed round and produces the loud half coughing, half shouting sound from the smokers. These with a loud hum from the entire company seated on the ground forms the picture untill all who intend to come have assembled, and Mapuleanyane the court herald[2] ceases shouting and calling the people to come & hear the word of God.

When I stand up all the women and children draw near, and having ordered silence I explain the plan of salvation, the goodness of God in sending his son to die, the confirmation of his mission by miracles, the last Judgement or future state,

---

[1] Cf. above, p. 3.

[2] '... an old man who occupied the post also in Sebituane's time' (*Travels*, p. 178); 'the old town-crier' (*Narrative*, p. 295); 'a man ... in constant attendance upon Sekeletu' (Roger Price, in *The Matabele Mission*, ed. Wallis, p. 144).

the evil of sin, God's commands respecting it, &c &c, always choosing one subject only for an address & taking care to make it short and plain and applicable to them. This address is listened to with great attention by the most of the audience. A short prayer concludes the service, all kneeling down and remaining so till told to rise. At first we have to enjoin on the women who have children to remain sitting, for when they kneel the[y] squeeze their children and a simultaneous skirl is set up by the whole troop of youngsters which makes the prayer inaudible.

After service a whole sheep roasted was set before the chief and his dancing companions. For it no doubt they danced. It was devoured in a twinkling. Not a few cases of snatching the morsel out of hands or catching the portion over which the lips of a neighbour could not close, and some few remorselessly swall[ow]ed all, a neighbour nudging them earnestly to tear off a bit for them. This however is not general. A person who gets only a mouthful shares it with his neighbour.

After consultation with his elders, who by the way usually give counsel in the very way the chief wants it, he informed me that he would himself take me to the Borotse, and he thus shews that those who counselled him lately not to go now counsel him to go. An immense preparation of boyaloa[1] is going on. He considerately asked what provisions I should prefer and what people. He has sent the boats round from the Chobe to the Sesheke, so we may expect to start in a few days.

Ants and Bees

Saw an Ants hill perched on a tree several days ago. It was about the size of a child's head and filled with myriads of the small black insect. Another kind plays an important part in this country. Every portion of a decayed tree is speedily reduced to dust by their means, and they are used as an article of food by the people of the country. On allowing a Bayeiye chief to taste some preserved apricots and asking if he had any such food in his country he said, 'Do you know lintlua?[2]

[1] *Bojalwa*, Native beer made of sorghum or maize.

[2] *Dintlhwa*, larvae of white ants (termites). The chief was Phalane (cf. above, p. 63), and the incident had occurred several years previously on the banks of the Botletle (cf. *Travels*, p. 464).

If you tasted them you would never desire better food, they satisfy the ap[p]etite perfectly'.

I saw too the hive of the very smallest bee I believe in the world. It is almost exactly the size of the small variety of black ants, and the cells of the comb are not $\frac{1}{16}$ of an inch in diameter. It was in a tree and the honey was eaten when I came up. The Mōka, another small bee not so large as a common house fly, abounds in some parts. Its hive is always in the ground. It has a sting but rarely uses it.[1]

There is a wonderful amount of economy manifested in the system of animated nature. The bounties which the vegetable kingdom so lavishly spreads out before the animal kingdom are recieved by multitudes of joyous beings, whose amazingly keen appetites render them eager and delighted partakers. Nothing capable of supporting life is lost. Every production on earth has some animal or insect capable by its appetites and powers of assimilation to turn it to account. The poisonous Konguane[2] which always accompanies the Camelthorn[3] probably affords as delicious a morsel to the little red insect which feeds on it as our peaches and apricots do to the beetles which flock to them in their season. Yet the same plant produces a burning sensation in the mouth of man and is a virulent poison. Even the droppings of larger animals are made subservient to the wants[4] of the insect tribes, and these again become auxilliary to man. The Scavenger beetle flies in crowds to what would otherwise be extremely offensive, and with great vigour rolls off pellets four or six times their own size in order to deposit it in the ground. This beetle not only manures the fields, but wherever it exists in numbers the villages are extremely clean. The useless excretions of one class of animals become sources of delight to another.

And then all these little creatures employed in gathering up the fragments that nothing may be lost seem so animated, so busy and so happy, ladies troubled with crusty husbands might effect a cure by leading them to the study of animated nature. There is a continual smile playing on the streams of

---

[1] Cf. above, p. 97.

[2] *Arthrosolen polycephala*, 'a yellow-flowered weed' (Miller, *Woody Plants*, p. 91).

[3] *Acacia giraffae*.

[4] Written in above the word 'support', which however was not deleted.

happy existence which everywhere meet the eye. Each race of animals contributes its quota of pleasure to the others. The invisible animalculae even are not forgotten, they turn to account those minutiae which escape the notice of their more gigantic bretheren. If we may form an opinion from the vivacity of their movements each one is in a state [of] as much enjoyment as innocents in a merry dance.

The ants seem to have all their movements by means of a power like that which resides in our involuntary muscles. They never tire. When the ground is heated to 130° Fahr., so hot the hand cannot be held on it, their movements are only the more active, and even during the night they seem never asleep. They form the soil, preforming the same work in hot countries which earth worms do in cold.

During the long droughts of this country few insects appear. The soil becomes like ashes and there are not many signs of life. But no sooner does a shower sufficient to saturate the soil fall than the prisoners all burst forth. The white and other ants swarm, filling the air in clouds and after a brief flight settling on some spot which if it suit them they immediately jerk off their wings and begin to burrow in the soil. The birds sing, pair, and build nests. Beetles centipedes and myriapods rush hither and thither. There is a perfect concert of music. The birds singing merrily have the chorus taken up and filled by the glad hum of insect youth. It is praise to him who is wonderful in counsel and excellent in working.

20th Monday. Busy preparations are going on. George is making a small tent for me which will be a great comfort in the wet dewy nights. As I must hunt again I look forward to some hard work. It is a sport to some. I wish I could so far enter into their spirit as to engage in it with pleasure. All the flesh for a large party must be the produce of my rifle. Sneyman is still too weak to hold a gun.

Sekeletu thinks my tea being agreable to his taste an evidence that my heart is pleasant towards him, and the traders' coffee being bad was evidence that their hearts were not kindly towards him.[1] The river Chobe is asserted to come from the Borotse by the Moenye,[2] and another river from the Nor West.

Borotse by the Moenye. and another river from the Nor We

[map sketch: Oneyenko, Borotse, sima, Seepo, Loiwa]

the Mambari come along that

The Mambari come along that of Libebe for some distance, then cross over to the Chobe, then along Moenye & accross the Moenye & Borotse.

One of the Mambari offered me his gun for some beads. They are Portuguese manufacture and so inferior the people in this quarter despise them, and when they are offered for sale not a single tusk is offered.

21st Tuesday. I worked out the observations for the Longitude of the Hill Ngwa or Dowga last night, and find it to be situated in East Longitude 25° 37'. This is confirmatory of my observations and work here, and it is now quite clear we were wrong in putting down the waggon stand as 26°.[3]

[1] 'Sekeletu, relishing the sweet coffee and biscuits, of which I then had a store, said, "he knew my heart loved him by finding his own heart warming to my food." He had been visited during my absence at the Cape by some traders and Griquas, and "their coffee did not taste half so nice as mine, because they loved his ivory and not himself." This was certainly an original mode of discerning character' (*Travels*, p. 207).

[2] Moenye (Mwenyi) is the name of a tribe living along the Luanginga River in Kalabo district, N.W. Barotseland; the Chobe, however, does not flow through that region, but much farther to the West.

[3] Cf. above, p. 160.

The observations were made 6½ miles south of the hill and were as follows :

14th April /53.

App. Alt. of Aldebaran   28° 31' 17"
Appt. Alt of Moons centre   31° 14' 46"
App. Dist Moon's centre from *   25° 15' 27"
    giving 1h 42m 28 = 25° 37' East.[1]

The progress of preparation goes on very slowly, and a period of inaction disagrees with me. I am perpetually threatened with fever, and must use remedies every few days. It is probable that the activity of hunting and travelling will drive it off. But what must be the state of a country in which malaria so fearfully prevails. Poor trodden down Africa, a nation scattered and peeled and not comforted. The prospect is dark and dreary, but God will guide and make all light. An East wind brings fever and knocks up those who are recovering. I must remain in these parts till I see some opening. Faint heart does not become a soldier of Jesus. At the same time I feel the prospects to be dark.

Field sports undoubtedly tend to render the whole character more hardy and resolute. They prove serviceable to the whole nation by preventing the growth of effeminacy. The petty appetites must be restrained, and this alone tends to brace the character, while the fatigue, adventure, & danger produce hardiness which cannot fail to be apparent when engaged in more serious pursuits. In this country hunting is a matter of necessity and serious dangers are encountered. I have had many narrow escapes myself and could relate hairbreadth escapes. That of a native is singular & will do. When stealthily crawling towards a Rhinoceros, he happened to turn his head and found a lion crawling up after him. He sprang up a tree and escaped.

Doctoring. Maps by Natives

22d Wedensday. The Doctors here uniformly throw the Litaola or bola[2] in cases of sickness, and different kinds of

---

[1] In *JRGS*, 1854, p. 302, and *Travels*, p. 684, D.L. says his position on 14 April was 'Ten miles S. of hill N'gwa (1st group)', and gives the bearings as 18° 38' S., 24° 26' E. Cf. also above, p. 110.

[2] Tswana *ditaola*, divining-bones generally; *bola*,' the small bones used in divining' (Brown), mostly astragalus bones of wild animals (cf. Schapera, *The Tswana*, p. 64).

oxen are selected according to the bone which makes the most prominent figure. The bones, about 20 in number, are selected from different coloured cattle. The animal selected is slaughtered and the blood sprinkled[1] over the sick person. They say it is in order that the Barimo[2] may take [the] ox instead of the man. It is a sacrifice.

Several Barotse gave me drawings of a number of rivers on the West of their large one. They begin with the Loeti and give seven beyond the Simah or Simaa.[3] Their drawing is as follows :

They have heard of the fabulous pigmies of the North and a fabulous animal called Kulué or Ngulue, which may be set down for the Unicorn as well as for any other.[4]

[1] Written in above the word 'thrown', which however was not deleted.

[2] Badimo, the spirits of deceased ancestors, to whom people pray and make offerings.

[3] D.L.'s 'Loeti' is the Lungwebungu (cf. Arnot, ed. Travels, p. 438), and 'the river Simáh, where a Thames steamer could ply at all times of the year' (Travels, p. 264) is the (Southern) Luete, 'Simaa' being in fact the name of a tribe living to its south on the Mulonga Plain (Senanga district, Barotseland).

[4] The 'fabulous pigmies' are presumably the Negrillos of Central Africa; the 'fabulous animal' I cannot trace.

They mention a large lake which is situated to the N.N.W. of this and called Nkalangé. It contains very large fishes, and is so broad when one wishes to cross he makes a fire and climbs a tree with a large torch, which perched on a pole he holds up as a signal. The people are called Lishwa & their chief's name is Mashi.[1] It is situated about ten days West or West South West[2] of the Borotse. People of this tribe have visited it.

Sibolamakoa is said to be only a reedy swamp, and not a lake.[3] It could not be reached in less than three months.

The prospects for these dark regions are not bright. The fever, the fever. One might risk his life in so good a cause, but if the first fell then others might esteem it a tempting of Providence to follow. It seems as if an attempt to conquer this terrible malady by investigating its causes and modes of cure by native and European practice would if successful prove a blessing to Africa. May God direct my steps.

Portuguese merchant Ferra arrives

Thursday 23d. A Portuguese traveller arrived from Linyanti having come all the way from St Philip de Benguela. He wishes to pass accross to Mozambique by way of the Bashukulompo. He speaks no language but his own. His name Signor Caetanao.[4] Does not come to trade but only to see the country. He carries no instruments. He came by Libebe and was six months in coming, but the way is very crooked.

24th Friday. This gentleman informs Sekeletu that he has come to see me and the articles I have, in order that when he returns to his own country he may get them and bring them

---

[1] D.L.'s informants seem to have been confused. Lishwa (Disho) was a chief of the MaMubukushu, nowadays living on the Okovango at and around Andara; they are reputedly an offshoot of the BaMashi, who inhabit the swampy bed of the Kwando (also called Mashi) River at approx. 15° 30′ S. to 16° 30′ S. (cf. A. St. H. Gibbons, *Africa from South to North through Marotseland*, 1904, vol. i, pp. 145, 272 f. and map). 'Nkalange' I cannot identify; the name suggests Ngalangi, a tribe of OviMbundu living at approx. 13° 30′ S., 16° E., but there is no 'large lake' in that region.

[2] 'and by South' deleted; 'South West' written in above.

[3] Cf. above, p. 44.

[4] Called 'Ferra' below; his name was in fact Caetano José Ferreira. In *Travels*, p. 180, D.L. describes him (anonymously) as a half-caste 'who resembled closely a real Portuguese'; he was, however, born in Barreiro, a suburb of Lisbon (Silva Porto, *Apontamentos* [1868], p. 25).

to him for nothing.[1] To me he says his object has been to go accross the country to Mosambique and then return by the Cape to St. Philip De Benguela. He speaks Portuguese only, and there was a contention between him and Port[o] about coming. If sent by Government he surely would possess instruments, but he has not even a common compass. Has my discovery of these parts awaked the suspicions of the slow Portuguese Government?

Sat. 25th. The enclosed colour[2] is that which is exceedingly admired by the dark tribes. This with bright or chrome yellow seem the best for the market.

One peculiarity of this climate is the production of an excessive craving for meat. The people seldom use salt, and the animal juices of the meat probably answers the same end in the œconomy as salt. They feel miserable if they get neither salt nor meat, and most of their medicines contain salt as an ingredient. Acting on the knowledge of this I made it a practice of supplying patients with a little salt instead of medicine, and found it remarkably efficacious in all forms of indigestion.[3] The craving for meat is one of the most exciting causes of wars. They all declare that they fight for the cattle. Milk though in an inferior degree answers the purposes of meat, and either the possession of cattle or guns by which supplies of game meat are obtained tend to diminish wars. The possession of fire arms prevents war in another way. The strong and the brave have no more chance than the weak & cautious. The old system is overturned and war is rendered more terrible. Great evils are however inflicted on the weak or on brave tribes which have not yet obtained possession of guns. In the course of 12 years only four cases of attack by one tribe on another have occurred since the introduction of fire arms, while the Boers in the same time have made no fewer than fourteen attacks & in each case carried off immense numbers of cattle.

Mr Ferra gives me his itinerary as 30 days from Bié to

---

[1] 'This man had no merchandise, and pretended to have come in order to inquire "what sort of goods were necessary for the market" ' (*Travels*, p. 180).

[2] A small piece of purple wool, slightly larger than a 6d. coin, was loosely inserted here between the pages.

[3] Cf. *Travels*, pp. 26 f., which, however, refer to the BaKwena, not the Ma-Kololo.

Benguela, and 600 miles from Bié to Sekeletu, as follows.[1]

He reports the way as impassable for waggons, and his people say there are a few tsetse in the Mambari country.

An ass or mule brought by Porto was bitten but did not die of the bite. He says they call the tsetse 'Kismangala'. The Governor General's name is Manjor.[2] The station of Bihe seems simply one of trade. Ferra is at one and Porto at another near. The intervening tribes are friendly. I have no doubt whatever but that they are both (Ferra & Porto) slave traders and both have their agents in the Bashukulompo country. F. returns tomorrow to await at some other spot the arrival of his agents. He probably finds that he can do nothing in his line here. Sekeletu says he will prevent the slave trade entirely in his whole country in another year. F. has 20

[1] Benguela and Bié (now called Silva Porto) are towns in Angola; Quibanda (Civanda) is the name of a tribe of OviMbundu living a little S.W. of Bailundu (Vila Teixeira da Silva); Cocema (Cuquema) is a tributary of the Cuanza, Kooshe (Cuchi) a tributary of the Okovango, and Quando (Cuando) the upper Chobe.

[2] Perhaps a corruption of the Portuguese title *majór*, 'major'; Serpa Pinto, for example, was known to the MaLozi as 'Manjolo' (cf. Jalla, *Litaba*, p. 75). The Governor-General of Angola, at that time, was Sérgio de Sousa, but the reference may be to Francisco José Coimbra, 'Major e Chefe' of Bié (cf. G. S. Dias (ed.), *Silva Pôrto e a Travessia do Continente Africano*, Lisbon 1938, pp. 41, 44).

slaves with him, he is carried by them in a swinging cot attached to a thick pole.[1] The natives despise this effeminacy.

Sunday 26th. A good and very attentive audience. Unfortunately an ox had just been slaughtered and was distributed just as the people collected. The furious roasting was going on and the entire ox would have been finished in half an hour had I had patience, but persuading them to let the meat alone I addressed them for a quarter of an hour, during which they were remarkably attentive. Mr Ferra and the mulatto[2] were present. They came to the waggon immediately after the morning service, but having shut up the sail in order to enjoy a short period of quiet I happened to be sitting within a few yards of them without knowing that they were present. I apologized for my apparent rudeness and they seemed satisfied.

Porto has sown beans without asking leave of any one. They beat their slaves perpetually, which affords a good contrast to our manners.

27th Mon. Mr Ferra leaves today. He is probably disappointed in his market. Having come here in the expectation of purchasing slaves he finds he cannot commence the traffic, and hence returns to some other tribe farther West in which he can be doing a little business while waiting for his agents who have gone to the Bashukulompo country. He says I should be welcome at Bié and in all the intervening country. No one would hinder me. He is from the farthest advanced Portuguese trading station, and this is farther than any slave trader ever advanced before. As the result of many enquiries I cannot avoid the conclusion that Pareira's journey was performed only on paper.[3]

The East wind brings the fever. As soon as it commences blowing I feel the fever begin, and George too. I have no appetite, and require every few days to employ means to restore

---

[1] 'He was carried in a hammock, slung between two poles' (*Travels*, p. 181).

[2] Probably Jorge José da Mota, one of Silva Porto's men, who had a camp at Dinyanti (cf. Silva Porto, *Viagens*, p. 124). D.L.'s use of the term 'mulatto' suggests that, at least at the time of writing, he did not consider 'Mr Ferra' (Ferreira) to be one (cf. above, p. 176).

[3] Cf. above, p. 152. In *JRGS*, 1854, p. 299, D.L. writes: 'The course of Pareira must be shifted northwards. He never visited the Barotse'. That, however, was obvious enough from the maps in Bowdich's book.

the skin to its proper state and work. I suspect Europeans could not live in this region. What is to become of its dense population? May God direct me.

We leave in order to visit the Borotse tomorrow, viz. Tuesday 28th. The vine leaves are frosted in some places and not in others, while many which have been cut down are shooting out vigourously.

V

VISIT TO THE BOROTSE

Leave for Borotse. Mpépe's death

Wed. 29th [June]. We remained over Tuesday and left to-day. Slept at Letloñkana's village, which is situated nearly due west of Maunku's village of last year.

Thursday 30th. We went to Shima's village and met Mpépe. A very slight circumstance is frequently sufficient to derange a well planned conspiracy. Mpépe had made arrangements with his people, who formed about $\frac{1}{3}$d of the tribe, to put Sekeletu to death as soon as they met. The signal agreed on was that if Sekeletu rose up to go away from the place where they might meet he would cut his tendo Achilles with a small axe which he carried.[1] If on the contrary he remained sitting in such a position as that Mpépe could seize him behind, his followers must stab him. The place of meeting was a small open hut in the Kotla, and it so happened that I went in first and sat down beside Mpépe. Sekeletu remained a few minutes outside and then entering sat down on my left, Mpé-pe being on my right. The conversation immediately turned on the oxen of Sekeletu which Mpépe refused to deliver up, and on the fact of Mamochisané being sick and unable to get an ox to slaughter by way of sacrifice. Mpépe admitted that he had kept back some of Sekeletu's oxen and remarked, Ma-mochisane is a dog, and 'eating is pleasant to every one'. The fact of my sitting between them seemed to derange Mpépe's plan. He laid down his axe and tried to engage me in conversation, but feeling indisposed for talk I simply answered his questions (I observed M's people all near their arms)[2] and then asked Sekeletu where we should sleep. He rose and took

[1] D.L. subsequently acquired and sent this axe to Moffat as a curio (cf. *Letters*, vol. ii, p. 237).

[2] This sentence (my parentheses) is an interlineation. Cf. *Travels*, p. 182: 'I knew nothing of the plot, but remarked that all Mpepe's men kept hold of their arms, even after we had sat down—a thing quite unusual in the presence of a chief.'

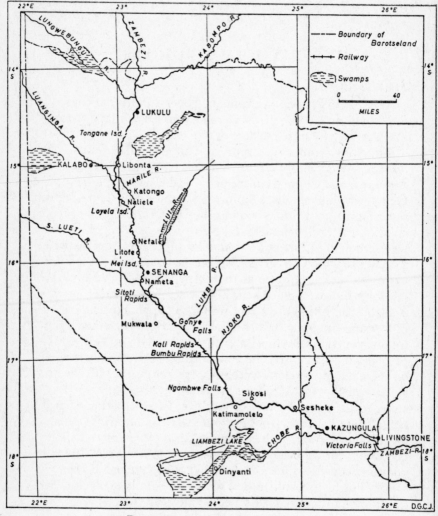

3. Barotseland and the Upper Zambesi.

me to the hut assigned to himself, remarking 'that is the servant who witholds the oxen given me by Sebituane'. I answered, 'but after you have talked over the matter together he will deliver them.' M. had brought a doctor with him who had the reputation of having killed Sebitané, and probably expected success by means of his charms.

During the night Mpépe's people revealed the whole conspiracy, and Sekeletu replied, if what you say you believe to be true you must kill him. I knew nothing of this nor did I suspect anything. When I rose in the morning I did not see any of Mpepe's people. He (M.) slaughtered a fine large ox in the evening and distributed the whole of the meat among his own people. I concluded he had gone on, as we had now resolved to return. I had fever and went away before Sekeletu. At midday I was informed that Mpepe's people had taken him out to the field, probably on pretence of talking over their conspiracy, and killed him. I was horrified, but when I heard the particulars of the conspiracy my mind revolted less.

They say his conduct has been extremely cruel, cutting off hands &c., and all wonder he did not kill me too rather than be hindered in his designs. Sebitane suspected him, for Sekeletu asserts that his father pointed to the house of Mpepe and said, 'If that house does not eat me it will eat you'.[1] Mpépe was unfortunately employed by Sebitane as a commander in several expeditions during the minority of Sekeletu, and always considered himself as having a better right to the chieftainship than Sekeletu. The latter was very much afraid to go to the Borotse on account of knowing Mpepe's hostility, and repeatedly said, 'I am taken to the Borotse by you'. I thought his presence and talk might win over the disaffected. He had resolved to sleep in the same hut with me for protection, but during our short tour he invariably yield[ed] up the hut appropriated to himself to me, sleeping outside himself. Had Mpepe come to the town Sekeletu would have slept at the waggons.

The cause of our speedy return was a report that a commando of Matibele had come accross the country to attack

---

[1] The 'house' was a specially-built hut in which Mphephe was believed to have been practising sorcery, 'by means of a number of Barotse doctors', against both Sebetwane and Sekeletu (*Travels*, p. 180).

the Makololo and were carrying two canoes in order to enable them to cross the Chobe. We heard the report on Wedensday but thought we had better proceed and we should obtain more certain information at Sesheke. On Thursday we met a party who had actually seen the commando, and thus all doubt as to which way we ought to go was removed.[1] Then Mpepe's tragic end followed. We returned with sad hearts to the waggon. This however is heathenism uncontaminated by contact with Christianity. Sebitane frequently put a man to death for not appearing when called to muster.[2]

Mpépe sent a man to us when we first came in sight, desiring Sekeletu to stand. S. answered, I am going to the cattle post near by, let him come. M. said it does not much matter, there will be none but servants with him who will say nothing. S. when he arrived went away to the field. M. enquired anxiously for him. He was thus disappointed three times in his purpose.

We passed a village of the people of Setōka.[3] The women care so little for appearances in front that a single fig leaf would be decency compared to their nondescript apron, and they stand looking at one with as little sense of shame as we do with our clothes on.

Mon. 4th July. Sekeletu seems disposed to celebrate his independance too. He is dressed out in his best. Several yards of gaudy coloured ribbon are wound round his body in different directions, and the Bola or divination says the drums of a certain man are to be beaten & a dance made before the man's own door.

The venereal disease abounds at the Borotse. It is called Manasa.[4] It was brought from the Bashukulompo.

6th Wedensday. Very cold winds from the East prevail and bring fever with them. I have had six attacks and have lost appetite and flesh. No more word of Matibele. It must have been a false report we heard.

7th Thursday. A great deal of food is devoured but in such a wasteful way but a small amount of comfort ensues. It is

[1] In *Travels*, p. 183, D.L. says that he and Sekeletu returned to Dinyanti because it was 'unadvisable' for them to go to Barotseland 'during the commotion which followed on Mpepe's death'.

[2] Cf. above, p. 151 f.   [3] BaToka.

[4] Lozi *manansa, mananza*, syphilis (Jalla, *Dictionary*).

gulped down. An ox is devoured in an hour. Immense quantities of porridge, beans, corn, beer &c. are quickly dispatched, yet much hunger is endured. As all the people were sick and nothing cooked for me, I asked the chief to send me some porridge in the evening. He has three wives here yet no one had cooked anything. He scolded them and sent some thick milk with an apology. They never cook regularly. The poorest decent person in Scotland has more real comfort than an African chief.

There is an exploration for witches going on. A man from the Barotse has two small calabashes filled with seed in his hand, with these he makes a jingling noise and utters a sort [of] song. When he works himself up into a frenzy he puts on a circlet of horse or gnu hair on his head. The dance proceeds fast and furious, and on whomsoever the circlet falls or strikes he is considered as given to witchcraft. A course of vigourous instruction alone would prove an antidote, and nothing else. The teacher's heart would often be grieved even during this by observing a persistence in their follies, but while able only to give occasional addresses I am forced to witness and protest almost in vain.

The Portuguese Mulatto came back with us from Sima's village. He has seven people with him, two of whom are very young, not ten years of age, yet all bear burdens and all must have walked accross an immense tract of country and will do so again on their return. Porto hearing of our coming has returned to the Borotse.[1]

8th Friday. A dance prolonged through the day testifies the chief's joy that his son has come home.[2] The witch doctor discovered nothing yesterday. People agree with me that such persons disturb the town, causing uneasiness in the minds of all. Therm. 66° at sunset (in the wind). It feels much colder. North wind prevails most.

9th Sat.   Water boils at 204°.

At Lake Ngami 207½.

10th Sunday. A good and attentive audience. In describ-

---

[1] But cf. below, p. 188.

[2] This may refer to the son recently born to Sekeletu (cf. above, p. 136), the implication being that mother and child had now emerged from the seclusion a woman customarily observes for several weeks after giving birth.

ing the god of this world a man remarked, that is Katwane,[1] the evil one who came first & decieved us. Dancing has been going on all day. They desisted at once when I went and called them, and came and listened attentively. An old greyheaded man is one of the most eager dancers. He says kia bapala,[2] he seeks pleasure.

11th Mon. Sun feels warm now. Therm. 80° in the waggon at midday. Preparing to go to Borotse again. Tribute of corn from the Bapalleñ & others.

Types of Humanity

There are undoubtedly prevailing types in the different races of man which serve to distinguish them from each other, but so far as I have had an opportunity of observing them systematic writers rarely hit on the proper one. Dr Prichard has been very happy in his selection of two Hottentot girls as types of that race, but the small noses, high cheek bones, colour, hair, shape of the head, would do for the Bushmen as well, and for those degraded Irish of whom he makes mention. He is not so happy in his Caffre.[3] A typical Malay would easily be found among that people, but not a true type of any black tribe I know. In M. Guyot's 'Earth and Man'[4] two plates are given for the purpose of shewing a gradual departure from the Caucasian type as we recede from the cradle of civilization. Now so far from these being typical of the respective races it is questionable if he would find a second example like any one of his specimens, except perhaps in the case of Capn Cook & the Caucasian. Among the black tribes I have seen people the very images of all the specimens given except the Malay, the Coroada Indian, the Terra del Fuegian,

[1] The BaTswana and other Sotho peoples believe that Kgatwane, a species of lizard, was the messenger responsible for the origin of death; cf. below, p. 190.

[2] *Kea bapala*, 'I am playing, I am amusing myself'.

[3] The reference is to J. C. Prichard, *Researches into the Physical History of Mankind*. Plates 4 and 5 of Vol. II (*Researches into the Physical Ethnography of the African Races*, 3rd ed., 1837) illustrate respectively 'female Hottentots' and 'a Koosah [Xhosa] Kafir', both from portraits by S. Daniell; and pp. 137–52 of Vol. III, Part I (*Researches into the Ethnography of Europe*, 1841) contain quotations from Strabo and other early writers as evidence that 'the ancient inhabitants of Ireland' were 'very barbarous'.

[4] Arnold Guyot, *The Earth and Man: Lectures on Comparative Physical Geography, in its Relation to the History of Mankind* (Boston 1849; translated from the French original).

& the Islander of Aleutia or Kotzebue. The Malay is utterly unlike the Malays of other lands. Indeed he is selected as typical of the Mexicans & other South Americans.[1]

It is only in the extremity of the varieties that much difference is seen. The ugliest seem to be selected for their very ugliness, but would it be fair to select the very ugliest varlet that could be selected amongst a crowd of the common rabble of England and compare him with the fairest Caucasian that might be found in the suite of an ambassador? I have often been struck by meeting countenances the facsimiles of renowned statesmen in everything except as to colour. One of Sekhomi's courtiers was the picture of M. Guizot.[2] Another amongst the Bamapela, could the ruddy colour of the original [have] been imparted, might have sat for the likeness of Professor Agassiz of Neufchatel.[3] It is not these exceptional cases which ought to be our guide. There is not another Joseph Makoniane[4] in Africa. And to obtain a typical face of any of the black races is, considering the immense variety of countenance which exists, what I fear will not be soon accomplished. For the purpose of comparison the portraits of chiefs ought to be taken, for they alone possess ease & competence equal to that which our poorer population enjoy. These have a most material influence on the features. The plates selected by M. Guyot if coloured dark find ready counterparts among the dark tribes. Even the Caucasian & Captain Cook may be found. By selecting the ugliest or the

[1] Plates V and VI of Guyot's book, which are 'intended to illustrate the law of the degeneration of the human type in leaving the central regions of Western Asia' (p. xi), contain 16 line drawings of facial types of different human races. Those mentioned by D.L. are: Plate V, No. 5 ('Portrait of Captain Cook'); Plate V, No. 1 ('A Circassian [not "Caucasian"] belonging to the suite of the Persian Ambassador'); Plate VI, No. 2 ('Malay, belonging to the group of the Koutousoff Smolensky'); Plate VI, No. 6 ('Coroado Indian, from the banks of the Rio Xipoto, one of the Rio Pomba, in tropical South America'); Plate VI, No. 7 ('An Inhabitant of Tierra del Fuego'); and Plate VI, No. 8 ('Inhabitant of the Aleutian Islands, after Choris; Voyage of Kotzebue'). The 'Malay' could readily be mistaken for Chinese, but is certainly not 'selected' by Guyot 'as typical of . . . South Americans'.

[2] François Pierre Guillaume Guizot (1787–1874), French statesman and historian.

[3] Jean Louis Rodolphe Agassiz (1807–73), naturalist and geologist.

[4] Plate V, No. 4, of Guyot's book is a portrait of 'Joshua [not Joseph] Makoniane, an old Bassouto warrior, a convert to Christianity'. Makoanyane Ntseke (baptized Joshua in 1840) was the trusted friend and commander-in-chief of the great Southern Sotho chief Moshesh. He is often mentioned in Ellenberger's *History of the Basuto*.

best looking of different races anything may be proved which the writer wishes.

Vertigo. Arrival of Senor Porto

12th Tuesday. Senor Porto[1] arrived here yesterday evening. (His full name is Antoneo Franscisco Ferreira Da Silva Porto.[2]) He says the river of Libébe is called Cobango by the Portuguese, and the Cobe Quando.[3] He enquires particularly after the courses of these rivers.

Last night I had several attacks of vertigo. They came on suddenly and ceased as instantaneously. I thought little of them, but today when looking up in order to observe the situation of the moon my head began to swim. Everything in the waggon seemed to rush to the left, and I fell heavily against the table and broke it. I had consciousness enough left to grasp the tent, this prevented me falling to the ground. I have felt several times since as if it were coming on in the severe form, but it has as yet kept to slight dizziness. It is probably the effect of exhaustion produced by the remedies used in Fever, and the subsequent want of appetite. It would be an easy death. But may God in mercy spare me and permit me to do a little for his glory in this heathen land. I feel it now when writing.

Wed. 13th. Troubled with vertigo. The arrival of Senor Porto will detain us a few days longer. I am not sorry for this, as I might fall off the horse, and this when all the muscles are relaxed is a serious fall. The whole weight is brought as if by a blow on certain parts, and the muscles there are not capable of imparting any elasticity by their tenseness. Slight headache on the right side of the head, and when a fit of giddiness passes the lower extremities become bathed in perspiration.

---

[1] António Francisco Ferreira da Silva (1817–90), who added 'Pôrto' to his surname in commemoration of his birth-place (Oporto), was the most distinguished Portuguese trader and explorer of his time in Angola and the regions farther East. Extracts from his journals, entitled *Viagens e Apontamentos de um Portuense em África*, were published in Lisbon in 1942. Chapter V (pp. 99–130) contain several references to D.L.'s visit to Barotseland in 1853.

[2] This sentence was added at the head of the page. Silva Porto says (*op. cit.*, pp. 124 f.) that at their first meeting he and D.L. exchanged slips of paper on which they had written their names.

[3] 'Cobango' is the Okovango, and 'Quando' (Cuando) the name given to the Chobe ('Cobe') in Angola.

A young woman died during the night in childbed. Unable to bring forth she was allowed [to] perish. I mentioned that had I known I might have assisted. They assist cattle, but thought it strange similar aid should be rendered to woman. Their husbands leave them. Their friends even desert them and the poor thing must do the best she can alone in a small hut got up for the purpose.[1]

Mr Porto gives his itinerary as 27 days to Bié and 105 thence to Ience[2] or here= 132 = 4 months and 12 days.

There is a space of only 30 miles between Sambo the source of the Rio Cuvo and the Cubango or Chobe.[3]

Thur. 14th. Took sets of Lunar observations on 13 and 14th. The results of 7 sets carefully worked out are 1h 35m or 23° 45′ East Longitude.[4]

Milk is said by Senor Porto to be liable to bring on an attack of fever if taken in the evening, but it may safely be used in the morning. He takes none in his coffee in the evenings. The remarks of the inhabitants of a country are always valuable, as being in general the records of experience.

Examined a small island near the town in order to make a small experimental farm on it. The cattle are to stand on it in order to enrich it for that purpose. Mr Porto reports the existance of a chain of Lakes as the sources of the Zambeeze river.[5] No one has seen them however. The country between this and Bié is one continued marsh ; they sometimes pass ten rivers all knee deep in one day. Fish abounds, and Crockodiles and Hippopotami in the larger rivers.

Benguela is very unhealthy. But Loando[6] is salubrious and is the capital of the Portuguese possessions in Western Africa. It is not much farther distant than Bié.

[1] 'The poor creatures are often placed in a little hut built for the purpose, and are left without any assistance whatever, and the numbers of umbilical herniae which are met with in consequence is very great' (*Travels*, p. 131). The description is accurate in that the woman is usually alone in her hut during labour; but, among BaTswana at least, her mother or some other elderly woman normally waits outside to give help if required, and keeps coming in to see if all is going well.

[2] Not identified; nothing resembling the word occurs in Silva Porto's book.

[3] Sambo, 12° 58′ S., 16° 10′ E., is in the district of Huambo, Angola, and the Rio Cuvo, which enters the sea close to Porto Amboim, rises in the Bié Plateau of the same district. D.L. wrote but subsequently deleted 'and' immediately after 'Sambo'.

[4] Cf. above, p. 160.

[5] This may be a reference to Lake Dilolo. Cf. *Travels*, p. 473.

[6] Luanda, 8° 50′ S., 13° 15′ E.

Still troubled with vertigo & headache.

15th Friday. Pitsané goes off tomorrow morning with the canoes for Seshéké. We shall leave on Tuesday or Wedensday.

Mr Porto remains till the rains commence. He says this is necessary because the dust goes up the nostrils and gives the fever. This disease takes the pluck out of one.

Hewn stones are said to exist in the Mashona mountains. They are probably the same as mentioned in Bowdich's work on the Portuguese discoveries in Angola and Mosambique.[1]

Sat. 16th. Gum copal abounds in the West. That seems the highest portion of this part of the continent, for the rivers descend all towards the East.

Sun. 17th. The audience as attentive as usual. Surely some seed sown will take root. Had a long conversation with several intelligent men afterwards on some of the leading truths of Revelation. They were much interested apparently as the account of sin coincided with their parable of the Cameleon and lizard.[2] Their sacrifices are prayers, deprecatory of the wrath of the Barimo, and the river tribes take a little water if sick and unsuccessful in hunting and placing it opposite the rising sun pray to Nyampi or God.[3] The Makololo say they are not inferior to them, inasmuch as they sacrifice oxen. Explained the nature of the institution of sacrifices. They say they have no word for 'mercy'.[4]

[1] 'At the present day, hewn stones may be traced in the mountain of Fura, which were formerly, it is said, piled upon each other with great art, and yet without lime.' Fura, described as a gold-bearing mountain near 'the village of Massapa', about fifty leagues from Tete (Bowdich, *op. cit.*, pp. 126 f.), is a Native name for Mt Darwin, in Darwin district, S. Rhodesia (F.W.T. Posselt, *Fact and Fiction*, Bulawayo 1935, p. 7).

[2] The Tswana version of this widespread Bantu myth is given as follows by D.L. (*Letters*, vol. i, p. 193): 'God sent a cameleon to say to men, "Though you die you do not vanish or become annihilated, you will return again." The cameleon being a slow walker was outstripped by the little black lizard sent by another, and the latter came first to man. The black lizard said to men, "One will come after me and tell you that when you die you will not perish but will return again. It is all a message of lies. When you die, you perish as an ox." When the cameleon came, men stopped his mouth by saying "O we know your message. It is all lies." '

[3] Cf. above, p. 175 ('barimo') and p. 47 ('Nyampi'). Gluckman says ('The Lozi', p. 76) that many MaLozi pray to Nyambe 'over dishes of water, each sunrise and sunset, at small altars at the edge of the village'.

[4] D.L. and his informants may have been at cross purposes; Biblical translators have usually managed to find suitable Tswana renderings (Brown's *Dictionary* gives four) for the concept of 'mercy'.

Monday 18th. Observed an occultation of Jupiter yesterday evening. It occurred at 5h 7m 7s watch time and by Alt.
of Sun taken about half an hour before.[1] True alt. ☉'s centre
13° 57′ 36″ at watch hour 4h 42m 45s. The watch error was
11m 25s fast for Mean time at station. This subtracted from
5h 7 . 7 makes the moment of occultation of the outer edge
of the planet to be 4 hr 55m 42s mean time, 17th July
1853.

19th Tuesday. Very strong Easterly winds prevail now.
They shake the old leaves off the trees and in the month following they sprout out afresh. The winds are cold to the sen-
sations though not lower than 65° at midday. Many people
complain of fever, discharges of blood. I am much troubled
with vertigo. The fever has prevented me going on with the
Dictionary.[2] I might have collected a thousand Borotse words
since I came here, but fever takes away the inclination to
work. I cannot go where I will either, for as a consequence of
favour they will not allow me to go where danger is appre-
hended, nor without a retinue of two hundred including the
chief and all the principal men. These consume on an average two oxen per diem besides large quantities of milk beer
and corn.

I wished to return by way of the mouth of the Chobe, but
there are too many Hippopotami there for this to be allowed
for an instant. The chief men request me not to allow Sekeletu to prolong his stay among the Borotse because their
hoeing time is near. If agriculture were a test of civilization
then these are not savages—but out and out savages they
undoubtedly are.

Offered them the use of my ivory[3] in case of need when
any white man came to trade. This pleased mightily. George
does not succeed well on account of not placing confidence in
them.

Manioc and Bananas grow on the Borotse river.

---

[1] The following words, originally following 'before', were deleted in the MS:
'viz. ☉'s L.L. 13° 45′ 50″.'

[2] On 24.ix.1853 D.L. wrote to Dr Tidman that attacks of fever and fits of vertigo
'induced me to give up collecting Borotse words and other materials for a Dictionary' (Chamberlin, p. 208).

[3] The tusks presented to D.L. by Sekeletu (cf. above, pp. 140, 144, 146).

Mr Porto say the Ganguelas[1] are very hostile, and large presents are paid them for a passage through their country. They cut off small parties of travellers, using guns, bows & arrows and short swords.

As Mr Porto knows the way and there are many English living at Loanda, the capital of Portuguese settlements in Western Africa, I think it is in accordance with the leadings of Providence that I attempt on the West Coast at Loanda rather than at Benguela, because the former is more healthy than the latter. The path however is full of small rivers and the country generally marshy, but it is fruitful and population is large. God has permitted me to be a pioneer in his cause. I feel deeply thankful and hope he may use me in the way which shall be best for Africa.

By easy stages Loanda may be reached in 148 days from Sekeletu's town. To Borotse 21

to Bié 83

to Loanda 44

148

20th Wed. Some of the Borotse pretend to possess the art of curing the bites of serpents. They tame them as the jugglers do in the East, and exhibit them to the terror of the other tribes, which believe these serpent charmers possess power to send serpents against any one whom they hate to destroy him. I saw one who took up a dead serpent and lacerated his arm with its fangs. It was probably innoxious.[2]

We leave tomorrow, viz. Thursday 21st.

Second Departure for Borotse

Left on Friday 22, slept at Tsatsa's, then 23 at Seriba.[3] A multitude following us, viz. 160, we were compelled to travel on Sunday 24th. They devoured on an average two oxen per

[1] A name 'used by the Portuguese to refer, because of their linguistic and cultural affinity, to a variable number of tribes in south-east Angola', including 'Luchazi, Luimbe, Mbunda, and sometimes Luena' (McCulloch, *The Southern Lunda*, p. 52).

[2] 'Some of the Bayeiye we met at Sebituane's ford pretended to be unaffected by the bite of serpents, and showed the feat of lacerating their arms with the teeth of such as are unfurnished with the poison-fangs' (*Travels*, p. 145). On the use of 'snake spirits' for malevolent purposes, cf. White, 'Witchcraft . . . among the Balovale Tribes', 1948, pp. 100 f.

[3] Not shown on D.L.'s (or later) maps; presumably small and unimportant villages.

day. We could not provide them with food. Yet though
of necessity I disliked the necessity, and wish all forms
of sin were as deeply hateful as that of Sabbath travelling
is. Persecuted most terribly by Tampans in Sekhosi's
village.

25th. Reached the Liambae or Borotse river. The former
is the better name as it means *the River*, and is called so to an
immense distance inland. The part we reached is called Katongo and the village Sekosi's. It is not a day distant from the
Town of Moriantsane on the Sesheke and is nearly due West,
for the Latitude is 17° 29', the Longitude by the watch 1° 49'
East of Sekeletu's town or 25° 35' E. Long.[1] By Lunars
24° 33', Sesheke 24° 58.

Detained till 30th by want of canoes, but leave on that date
with a fleet of 25. Sailed 30 miles West and by South, then
came to the bend and rapids. The canoes procured as tribute
on the river increased the number to 33. The paddlers all
standing present a pretty spectacle. One elderly man a doctor
called Litséke being in a small canoe heavily laden, the wind
overturned it and he unfortunately perished. The Borotse
paddlers were good swimmers and were much afraid of being
killed for allowing a Mokololo to be drowned, but the excuse
of the strength of the wind was satisfactory.[2] Our course was
Southerly of West during most of the day, Co.[3] West and by
South.

From Katongo towards Katima molelo[4] or 'I quenched the
fire'. 3½ hours brought us to the first islands and rapids.
Shoals of little fishes leaped out of the water in the confusion
produced by our vigourous paddlers, but turtle doves were
observed hatching their eggs in quiet about the roar of the
rapids and splashing of the canoes. The banks are covered
with trees down to the edge of the water, which send down
roots from their branches into the water as the Banian does to

[1] In *Travels*, p. 208, Sekhosi is identified as a Subia headman living at 17° 29' S.,
24° 33' E. ('about 25 miles W. of Sesheke', *ibid*., p. 684). On modern maps Sikosi
village is located at 17° 27' S., 24° 28' E.

[2] 'Had he been a man of more influence, they certainly would have suffered
death' (*Travels*, p. 212).

[3] This seems the most likely reading. Possibly an abbreviation for 'compass'?

[4] The modern village of this name (correctly translated by D.L.) is located at
17° 30' S., 24° 18' E.

the ground. Willows with catkins in full blow were seen along the shore. The day's sail was continued for five hours.

On the day following our course was N.N.W. and N.W. for six hours. The river becomes studded thickly with large islets of from $\frac{1}{4}$ to one mile in length & $\frac{1}{4}$ mile in breadth. The stream is broad and rapid, dark brown rocks jut out every where, and the expanse of rushing waters as seen occasionally between the densely wooded islands is from one to two miles in breadth. Sand martins are seen flitting about, they never leave the Liambae, and the foot marks of the Elephants along the shore shew that the numbers of that animal must be immense. Great numbers of Hippopotami also made their presence known by spouting and raising their heads in still eddies of the river.

Sleep on Monday Evening on the Island of Mambowe[1] after $6\frac{1}{4}$ hours N.W. & by N.

We passed the mouth of the river Njoko about ten minutes from our sleeping place.[2] It seemed about 30 yards wide.

The falls of Nambwe are from four to five feet in perpendicular height. Observed Alt of ⊙'s L.L. on 31st 108° 23' 10″, giving with Decn 18° 16' 8″ Lat. of 17° 17' 26 South.[3]

On Monday river less encumbered by islands, water deep, banks of calcareous tufa 100 feet high. Pass a beautiful island with a pretty name, Nuana Mei, 'child of the water',[4] the dense sylvan vegetation of which and the banks generally reaches to the water and the branches seem to recline on the bosom of the stream.

We reached the falls of the Bombwe and found them to be in 16° 56' Lat.[5]

$2\frac{1}{2}$ hours beyond Bombwe are the falls of Kalé.[6] On one occasion Sebitane lost some canoes here, and found that an elephant had been drowned in attempting to cross the river immediately above the falls.

[1] Mbowe Island, 16° 47' S., 23° 43' E. 'Monday' was 1 August.
[2] The Njoko joins the Zambesi from the North-East at 17° 7' 31″ S. (*Travels*, p. 684). The 'sleeping place' mentioned must have been that of 30 July, since D.L. passed Nambwe on the 31st (*loc. cit.*).
[3] In *Travels*, p. 684, the latitude is given as 17° 17' 16″ S. On modern maps, the 'Ngambwe Falls' are located at approx. 17° 14' S.
[4] Located on Ravenstein's map (1897) at approx. 17° S.
[5] 'Bumbu Rapids', 16° 55' S. on modern maps.
[6] Kali Rapids, 16° 49' 52″ S. (*Travels*, p. 684).

Falls of Gonye

Tuesday 2d August. Reach the Fall of Gonye.[1] The river has become narrowed by rocks to about 300 yards and in some parts less. The entire mass of its waters move along with considerable velocity. The rocks are of redish sandstone, stratified and having strata of an igneous rock intermingled. The sandstone is hardened. The banks are composed of low rocky hills about 200 feet high and still covered with beautiful trees of various form & hue. In some parts they are of a purple colour intermingled with dark green and bright orange.

This being the winter sailing is very pleasant. The rush of the water past our canoe seems equal to that observed in a steamer going at the rate of 12 miles an hour. I think I am within the mark if I state our rate of sailing to be seven miles or 8 an hour. The rowers are well formed for their work. Being Borotse they are accustomed to it from infancy, and the effect of their ancestors inhabiting a country flooded by the Liambae is seen in their largely developed chests, arms, and all the back muscles employed in the act of pulling. They pull vigourously the whole day without tiring, then pitch my little tent and cook without any grumbling. Sekeletu gave me the choice of all the canoes. I offered to go in any one he pointed out but he insisted on my making a choice. I chose one of the best, 34 feet by 20 inches. He took the largest, 40 feet long and 27 inches wide, and has 11 paddlers. I was assigned six of the best, and these being as many as the canoe admits of I can keep up to him. He waits at every difficult part till all have passed and sees all embarked before he steps in to his place. We have then a race to pass all the canoes in the fleet and come up to the next difficult part or midday resting place or sleeping place before any of the others.

Nearly midway between the Njoko and Gonye we passed the mouth of the river Lombe. It rushes down the side of a hill with great noise. The latitude may be 16° 50′ or 48′.[2]

---

[1] At 16° 38′ 50″ S., 23° 55′ E. (*Travels*, p. 684), 16° 40′ S., 23° 35′ E. (modern maps).

[2] Modern maps show the Lumbi joining the Zambesi from the N.E. at approx. 16° 43′ 30″ S.

Before reaching the landing place of Gonye we came to a high rock jutting out right to the middle of the river. This is called Semamoñko[1] and has caused the destruction of countless canoes & lives. One large canoe lay upon it and here Selbe[2] perished last year. From this rock the canoes are dragged or carried about one mile to the village of Mokwala, which is situated in Lat. 16° 38 46.[3] From Mer. Alt. ☉'s L.L. 2d Augst /53= 110° 40′ 30″.

The falls of Gonye are about ¼ mile South of the village. The Lat. of the falls is probably 16° 39′.

In the afternoon of Tuesday we went to see the falls, and to one who has been enduring the thirst of the desert the sight was exceedingly grand. Even the heathen who with Sekeletu accompanied us viewed the scene with awe. Tiho tsa Morimo lintsi yan ! ('How the works of God are !')[4] was the frequent exclamation. Others approached and washed their faces in the spray as a sort of charm, and others enquired what the rain was doing on the cloud of spray.

The falls are of a very peculiar shape. The whole of the water of the river is not precipitated over them. It is about a mile wide. On the Western side a portion of the water is separated from the main stream by an island, & passing round this it is precipitated in beautiful cascades at some distance 300 yards below the falls. On the Eastern side the same phenomenon occurs, and we waded through 150 yards of rapid stream rushing on to minor falls about the same distance down. The falls proper are situated in the middle of the stream ; and from the island above referred to, which is covered with a mass of sylvan vegetation with the beautiful feathery date palm resting against an azure sky, the mighty mass of water rushes unbroken over a ledge of rock about 40 feet high and 150 yards in length. At the Eastern end it becomes broken, the ledge having been broken so as to allow the water to rush down in a sloping direction, but here it is met at a distance of about 20 feet by the mass of rock on

[1] 'Manauko Rock' on Ravenstein's map (1897).
[2] Not identified.
[3] In *Travels*, p. 498, Mokwala is described as 'the head-man' at Gonye. The modern village of Mukwala, evidently named after him, is at approx. 16° 37′ S., 23° 33′ E.
[4] *Tirô tsa Modimo di ntse jang*, 'how (wonderful) are the works of God'.

which we stood. It falls as the natives said into a pot, and the tremendous violence of the collision produces the cloud of spray on which a rainbow reclined. Two Banyeti Hippopotamus hunters too eager in the pursuit of a wounded animal approached too near, and Hippopotamus and hunters all perished in the water, which confined below to about 150 yards of river rushes away with frightful velocity. The mass of water appears white with the seething. The roughness which appears in the centre of a rapid stream here becomes a ridge of about two feet in perpendicular height.

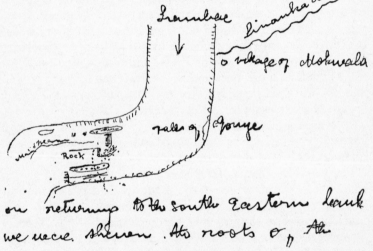

On returning to the South Eastern bank, we were shewn the roots of the Sekutsane[1] in the garden of a man called Linañka, who of old fled from the Borotse and led out the water of the river for irrigation. There is a small river by Mokwala's village called by his name.[2] No poet ever sung the praises of this beautiful scenery or of the strange scenes which have been enacted on its banks. What a great want is that of writing. I think possession of letters is a surer criterion of civilization than agriculture or government or laws. The scenery

---

[1] *Sekhutsane* (Lozi *sikuswani*) is the Livingstone or finger potato (*Coleus esculentus*). In *JRGS*, 1854, p. 295, D.L. says that he dug out 'some yams' from this garden; in *Travels*, p. 213, he refers to them as 'an inferior kind of potato (*Sisinyáne*)'.

[2] Not marked on modern maps. GSGS 2871 Rhodesia (May 1919) shows an 'unsurveyed' stream, the Lunanka, joining the Zambesi at Sioma.

around infinitely surpasses that of Scotland, notwithstanding all that poets have said and sung about it.

Saw the swallow which migrates from Kuruman on 2d August. The sand martins never leave the Liambae.

The whole of Wedensday was spent in carrying our fleet of canoes over land.

On Thursday we embarked again. River more than a mile broad. Pass along among several islands, one called Anandanga, another Mofomba. Pass confluence of River Linañka, seemed 40 yards wide. On the islet Malombe a singing bird attracted notice by the loudness and sweetness of its notes. Inga, rested. Island Moamba and Namakau or Wasi. All these islands are covered with sylvan vegetation and are very beautiful.[1] At a distance they seem like masses of vegetation resting on the bosom of the water. Tsetse lighted on us though at some distance from the banks. The ajacent country is well adapted for residence. It is fruitful and well wooded with a great variety of large trees, very many of which are evergreen, and all are distinguished by leafiness. Many are fruitbearing and edible. The islands are from one mile to 4 miles long and many of them broad enough to turn the stream. The bottom is rocky and the bends of the river are straight. Passed mouth of the small salt river Seepo in the afternoon. At a distance it seemed 10 yards wide. The river is a magnificent one. It is narrowed among the low hills through which it has forced a passage. These are generally not more than 2 or 300 feet high.

Borotse Country commences

At the confluence of the Seepo commences the Western ridge. Setoto rapids are near the confluence. The banks now became clayey and we left the tsetse country. Late in the evening we passed the mouth of the Simah River, and after a hard day's pull in which the paddlers never shewed one symptom of fatigue we arrived at Nameta village.[2]

[1] Of the islands named, Ravenstein's map (1897) shows Anandanga (approx. 16° 35' S.), Inga (16° 24' S.), and Moamba (16° 22' S.). On modern maps, Mwamba (Moamba) is located at approx. 16° 29' S., and none of the others is marked.

[2] The 'Simah R.' is the Southern Luete (cf. above, p. 175). The Seepo, shown on D.L.'s map as a small stream joining the Zambesi from the West, does not appear on other maps consulted. The Sitoti ('Setoto') rapids are at approx. 16° 21' S. Nameta is located by D.L. (*Travels*, p. 684) at 16° 12' S., approximately where the modern village of Mubita is.

In the evening one of our people broke a portion off a dead tree and found that a kind of down with which it was covered entered the pores of his skin and prevented sleep by the great irritation it produced. The Borotse were well acquainted with it and told us it was never touched by them.

We passed the Loi[1] last night.

We left Nameta on Friday morning and soon came to the River Masongo on our right. It is large and comes from a great distance N.N.E.[2]

Saw first kite returned from Migration on 6th August. They are much later at Kuruman.

As we passed along great numbers of sandmartins sat by their nests on the banks prinning and sunning themselves. Some flew out of their holes. We passed the Oyama river. It too is large and comes from the N. and by E.[3] Owing to a head wind our progress was slow. Great numbers of the ibis religiosa were met with, also spoonbills, scizzor bills, and a hawk sort of kingfisher. It has the manners of the hawk with those of the kingfisher, is about the same size, light blue colour, and is perpetually on the wing. The scizzor bill hunts at night chiefly. The dark ibis, a kind of adjutant the feathers of which resemble those of the ostrich, and a great variety of water birds, enlivened the scene.

The banks now are low and sandy, the bends of the river much more curved. A species of grass 12 feet high and at the bottom one inch in diameter with a fringe of reed.

We rested at midday on the island Mei or 'water', and found it 16° 0′ 42″ Lat.[4] Soon after starting again we came to Litofe island and town. This was one of Sebitane's stations. It is in 15° 55 from Mer. Alt. ☉ L.L. 114° 16′ on 5th Aug.[5]

Large numbers of sweet potatoes and a white variety of potato, tasteless. The red is called Nkolu, the white Moyela.

---

[1] The Lui River joins the Zambesi from the N.E. at 16° 19′ S., below the Luete.

[2] Neither D.L.'s maps, nor others consulted, show such a river in this vicinity.

[3] Although marked on D.L.'s map, this river is not named on modern maps. It may, however, be the small stream (shown on GSGS 2465, sheet SE 34) which joins the Zambesi immediately above Senanga, 16° 6′ S.

[4] In *Travels*, p. 684 (cf. *JRGS*, 1854, p. 302) the latitude is given as 16° 0′ 32″ S.

[5] The date was followed by the words, 'Decn. 16° 58′ 16″', subsequently deleted by D.L. Litufa, called Itufa by Jalla (*Litaba*, p. 51), is listed above (p. 22) as one of Sebetwane's chief towns. It is named Litofeltu on GSGS 2871 Rhodesia (4th ed., 1942).

Also the Moanja or Cassava.[1] Immense pots of porridge were prepared, and (10)[2] ten oxen slaughtered. Then commenced the dismal dance of the warriors, which consists in various motions of the body head an[d] arms, and a consentaneous stamping of the ground with one foot alternately. The chorus is one continued roar, and each one thinks he excels in proportion to his power of roaring. This music or more properly roaring has been my lullaby almost every night since we left. A dance is often set up immediately after a service.

Leave Litofe and pass through a country abounding in inhabitants and food. Visited several villages. 94° Fahr. in shade. Six villages visited. Remain at Nefale[3] for the night. 4 oxen.

In our progress we saw very little to interest one. One group of dark evergreen trees, five Palmyras and one Boabob, alone shewed themselves on the dead level. Groups of cattle feeding on the coarse but succulent grass of the flats. An alligator now and then slipping off its basking place as we approached. The villages and cattle stations appearing as walls of high reed, which indeed forms the only enclosure.

Two men executed

In the afternoon of Monday we stopped [at] a large village the headman of which was the father of Mpépe. I went up to it entirely unprepared by any hint which had fallen for the horrid scene there transacted. We sat down and then followed an ominous silence. When we had remained a few minutes Sekeletu enquired for Raunkwe (father of Mpépe). He then told him why he had put his son to death. No answer was returned. Mothibe[4] then rose and said, it being well known what the will of Sebitane was in reference to the chieftainship, and the decision of Mamochisane not to rule equally so, and Mpépe setting up claims to the rule as evinced in the erection of a large house at the chief town, it seemed strange that his father had not reproved him; but neither he nor the other head man of the place [had] done so; he thought it strange, but would not enlarge on the subject. Sekeletu started up and said, 'let the chief men of this town stand'. The two men were

---

[1] *Manihot utilissima* (Lozi *mwanja*). [2] Added in margin.
[3] Nifale, 15° 46′ S., 23° 11′ E. (GSGS 2871 Rhodesia).
[4] Sekeletu's father-in-law (cf. below, p. 213).

instantly seized. Men had by previous arrangement been stationed round the fated individuals, and they were led forth with a man on each side and one behind each with a battle axe in hand to execution. They were led slowly to the river, there hewn down and their bodies deposited by means of a canoe in the middle of the river to be the food of alligators. When seized by preconcerted signal several were on the outside of the circle with light spears in order to intercept if flight were attempted. This was not needed for the men, both upwards of fifty, were paralysed with terror.

We all started to our feet, but I saw in an instant that nothing could be done to save them. The whole of the under-chiefs were with the executioners, in order to ensure the certain operation of their own previously laid plan of ridding themselves of those whom they hated, and whom Sekeletu both hated and feared. I was exceedingly grieved and shocked, and the more so as Mothibe fired his gun, and in the confusion of the moment some may have thought I did it. I immediately left the scene, and in two hours from the time of our stopping we were again on our way.

I am still very sorry that this tragedy was acted while I was present, and shewed it in explanations to both chief and others.[1] I am sorry to be mixed up with scenes of blood at all, but who will stop the stream of human blood which has flowed for ages in these dark places if we with our great instrument the gospel do not? Raunkwe had been privy to his son's ambitious schemes and had encouraged him. It was known too that he would not forgive Sekeletu for his death. The other head man had proposed to Mamochisane to put Sekeletu to death and reign alone,[2] but her sisterly affection would not permit her to give her assent. She preferred resigning the chieftainship into his hands and marry[ing] as a private person. She left their town and went to live at that of Masekeletu. The headman deprived her of many of her cattle and it cost him his life.

[1] The MS. actually reads: 'I am still very sorry that this was tragedy was acted while I was present and shewed this it in explanations to both chief and others'; 'shewed this' are the last words of a page.

[2] 'When we came to the town of Mpepe's father, as he and another man had counselled Mamochisane to put Sekeletu to death and marry Mpepe, the two were led forth and tossed into the river' (*Travels*, p. 215).

We proceeded and reached the village of Masekeletu[1] on Monday evening the 8th.

Mamochisane

9th. Visited Mamochisane in the morning.[2] She is a sickly looking slender woman of the nervous temperament. Had never seen a white man before and was much amused with my hair. She seems a good mother, whatever sort of chief she may have made, for when sitting with us she sent to see if her child were awake and it being still asleep remained some minutes longer, and as soon as informed that it was awake hurried off much more quickly than ladies usually do in this country.

She seems to have resigned the chieftainship gracefully and sincerely. Her father wished her to rule, and when stating her wish to retire into private life and marry she said she had been induced to rule only by her father. She here burst into tears, and when Sekeletu asked her still to continue as heretofore she asked if he could be a husband to her. Her father had told her if she wished a husband to take whom of her people she liked, but when she did so the women's tongues could not be restrained, they abused her for using their husbands, she therefore wished to have her own husband. And the whole long discussion of three days duration ended by one whom she had appointed standing up in the assembly and saying 'I have married her'.[3]

Naliele. Santuru

We left on Wednesday, our fleet increased to upwards of fifty canoes, and after about 2 hours sail reached Naliele,[4] the chief town of the Makololo and that which was the capital of Seunturu of the Borotse. It is the only one deserving to be

---

[1] 'Opposite the island of Loyela' (*Travels*, p. 224). Mma-Sekeletu (cf. above, p. 29) was Sekeletu's mother.

[2] She was then living at the 'south end' of Loyela island, lat. 15° 27′ 30″ S. (*Travels*, p. 685).

[3] Cf. above, p. 141. But after the overthrow of the MaKololo, she was 'taken to wife' by the new Lozi king Sipopa (Lotanku), who thereby 'gained considerable prestige, even among his own people' (Mackenzie, p. 244). She died in Barotseland in 1888 (Coillard, p. 367).

[4] Located by D.L. at 15° 24′ 17″ S., 23° 5′ 54″ E. (*Travels*, p. 685). Not shown on modern maps.

called a town and yet it is not large. It does not contain 1000 inhabitants. The reason why all the people in this valley are in small villages is the annual inundation of the whole country between the ridges, except the very small spots actually covered by the houses. It comes so near to a complete submersion of the country the people have nowhere to resort for the calls of nature but the canoes. The whole of the cattle are removed to the country ajacent to the ridges, and but for the difficulty of removing the goods to and from the ridge the whole population would remove thither too. The gardens are situated there, also a large population of Banyeti or carpenters and smiths.

Seunturu was a chief of superior intelligence. Was a great hunter and delighted in taming the young of wild animals. He had a tame hippopotamus and several Machwee,[1] and loved his people much. The Mambari visited him of old and offered to buy children, but he gave them large presents of cattle and told them he loved his people too much to think of selling them. He employed all his people for several years in building the mounds on which his towns stood. His principal town stood on a mound which has been all washed away by the river except a few square yards. It might have stood long enough had he taken the precaution to fill up a narrow channel which separates an island above the town from the main stream. Had the channel been filled up the island would have given the river a sweep to the opposite shore instead of right to the now vanished site of his town. His large boat[2] was destroyed by the conquerors. His people foolishly attempted to stop the Makololo in their flight before the Matibele. They came peaceably requesting protection, and when assaulted were rendered desperate by being place[d] between two fires. Seunturu was spared by Sebitane and died of fever afterwards.[3]

---

[1] Plural of *lechwee* (*Kobus leche*). In *Travels*, p. 217, where some additional details are given about Santudu's menagerie, D.L. says that he had 'two young hippopotami', one of which was, while 'reclining in the sun', speared by 'a stranger . . . on the supposition that it was wild'.

[2] Cf. above, p. 32.

[3] The traditional version is that Santudu (Mulambwa) died before the Kololo conquest, which was indeed facilitated by a dispute among his sons for the succession to his chieftainship (Jalla, *Litaba*, pp. 39, 41).

We can now obtain a better view of the country. The ridges on the right and left are country covered by trees and having no tsetse. The[y] run about N.N.E. and N.N.W., and at their greatest distance from each other seem to be about 20 or 30 miles apart. The intervening oblong dead level is that which is annually inundated. It is a Lake then, and probably was one at an antient date previous to the river forcing a passage through the hills of Gonye. There is a tradition of its overflowing on one occasion towards the East and killing all the inhabitants. It then burst through its present channel. Is this a tradition of the flood? In proportion to the ignorance of the people is the event of the destruction of the world by water placed near or in distant ages. If they have nothing but tradition the event is described as recent, if they have the knowledge of letters then it is placed at an antient date.

The valley is covered with a coarse but succulent kind of grass and patches of reed. It is intersected on all hands by watercourse branches from the main stream which form numerous islands. They are formed by eddies and currents. The main river carries off immense quantities of the alluvial soil of its banks—large portions frequently broke off as we went along—and its work is visible as far down as the Sesheke in fragments of clay mixed with the white sand from which Sesheke derives its name. At least fifty yards of the embankment of Seunturu's town has been swept off in the course of ten years. The outer edge of the site of the town is now at least that distance out in the middle of the river. The perpendicular height of the mound is between ten and twelve feet above low water mark. The rest of the country is all lower than this. Only a few trees are seen, and seven of these were transplanted from the ridge by Seunturu's mother.

The latitude is 15° 24, and Long. 23° East[1] as calculated from Ap. Alt. ☉'s centre 29° 4' 37", Ap. Alt. ☾'s centre 40° 23' 30". Ap. Dist. ☉ & ☾'s centres 109° 39' 29", on 13th August at ap. time 3h 39m 20s.

Senor Porto visits Naliele

12th. Senor Porto came from the part called Katongo

---

[1] For the corrected version, calculated by Maclear from D.L.'s observations, cf. above, p. 202 n. 4.

where for the present his residence is fixed.[1] He kindly brought a present of bread and vegetables which he has planted there. He had a large company of slaves with him and some half blood Portuguese. He had sent a company with letters to Quilimane but they were turned back by a chief called Kabonda or Kambonga.[2] They had passed the Maninche, named by them the Loenga.[3] The part on which he has fixed his residence is called Katongo, but that is a frequent name,[4] and it is on the ridge Eastwards of Naliele. There were two capitals. The Loi or Lui one is the present residence of Mpololo.[5] It is pretty evident from this gentleman's account that no Portuguese communication was ever made from coast to coast.

The people who live on the ridges frequently steal children from ajacent tribes in order to sell them for clothing to the Mambari. I have seen young girls brought as tribute to Sekeletu twice. They were divided among his people just as other tribute is. They are called children afterwards.

Mr Porto has all his principal people at the same table with himself. This must be thought of in our line. Sekhutsane is the potatoes.[6] The country ajacent to this is covered with the dense mat of grass usually seen in the Borotse. It is so deep when laid down one sinks and finds difficulty in walking without lifting the feet perpendicularly.

14th August Sunday. Had a very large audience, most of whom had never heard aught of the word of God before. They were remarkably attentive, as usually is the case on the first occasion. No one can concieve the state in which they live. Their ideas are all earthly, and it is with great difficulty they can be brought to detach their ideas from sensual objects. They are all smeared with fat and seem to feel comfortable

---

[1] D.L. subsequently visited this place (see below, p. 226). He gives its latitude as 15° 16′ 33″ S. (*Travels*, p. 220), which suggests that it was at or near the site of Mongu, long. 23° 8′ E.

[2] Cf. below, p. 207. Quelimane, 17° 53′ S., 36° 51′ E., is a coastal town in Moçambique (Portuguese East Africa).

[3] Cf. above, p. 43.   [4] Cf. above, p. 193.

[5] Traditionally the MaLozi had, and still have, two capitals; the king lived in the northern one, and his sister, the 'princess chief', in the southern. Every successive king, before the Kololo conquest, established his own capital, which was the tribal headquarters. (Cf. Gluckman, 'The Lozi', pp. 23 f.) Mpololo's residence was at Naliele, which Silva Porto (*Viagens*, pp. 103, 105) calls 'the capital of the Lui country', i.e. of Barotseland proper.   [6] Cf. above, p. 197.

only when shining by means of grease. All their clothing is soaked in fat, hence mine is soon soiled. And to sit among them from day to day, and listen to their roaring music or loud coughing when smoking wild hemp or the Cannabis Sativa, is enough to give one a disgust to heathenism for ever. If not gorged full of meat and beer[1] they are grumbling, and when their stomachs are satisfied then commences the noise termed singing. Bad as this is it has more life and jollity in it than the miserable Hee Hae of the Southern Bechuanas. That is the most dismal of all doleful sounds.

There is nearly at all times an indescribable confusion in all their movements. The younger ones of same age with the chief crowd around him on all occasions, and when he comes to the fire there is quite a press to secure seats in the circle round it. He always selects my fire, and when taking food all are looking on and very often all talking at the same time. Their discourse directed on every side is wonderfully well heard. Frequent scoldings take place between parties, but though most abusive epithets are employed no one strikes, and the usual resort is had recourse to of abusing the valour of each other. Large pots of porridge are brought and there occurs a perfect squab[b]le over them, every one pulling and tearing, and frequent admonitions are given to take care and not break the pot. When meat is discussed the same confusion exists. They divide it however with great impartiality, dealing it about to all though the portions are very small. If a piece is sent to a person at a little distance off in the circle, the person who hands it from the donor usually takes a good mouthful off it in passing it, and when the portion is small in one's hand it is not unusual to see a neighbour snatch it out of the mouth of the person who is consigning it to his own stomach. It is all done in good nature, and abundance of laughing and scolding intermingled. The scolding is nearly all performed in the same words. They are easily remembered, even the whole vocabulary of abuse in daily use.

This is the capital town of Seunturu. He had another and smaller town at a short distance from this called Cashiko.[2] He

[1] MS. has 'bear'.

[2] Kasiku (Jalla, *Litaba*, p. 35); not shown on modern maps. In *Travels*, p. 685, D.L. calls Santudu's 'old town' Linangelo (cf. below, p. 212 n. 1).

began to reign there when young and employed it afterwards as a hunting station, but when become powerful and afflicted by a complaint in the eyes he removed to Naliele and built the site of the town.

Senor Porto came here on the 12th on a visit.[1] He had been exactly the same time in the way as we were, not having been detained anywhere as we were. He kindly presented 2 dutch cheeses, cabbages grown at Katongo, bread and preserved pears. He had 10 people with him. Departs from this part in October. A party of his people was sent towards Mosambique but they were plundered of the clothing they carried by Kangomba or Sinangombe, a Batonga chief living among the mountains. Sinamane & Boe are other Batonga chiefs in that quarter. Kobo is a Letibele or Caffre chief.[2]

The Portuguese seem anxious to open up a communication with their East African possessions over land because the current setting North from the Cape of Good Hope prevents them reaching that port[3] in less than 80 days. Mr Porto wishes to send an exploring party overland to the Cape, and thence to Quilimaine. He seems to have recieved a respectable education for mercantile purposes, but our communications are sadly cramped for want of words. He knows no English, and I scarcely more Portuguese. Chevalier Du Prat's recommendation has had a good influence thus far.[4] Senor Porto is certainly inclined to be hospitable, and is so far

---

[1] Silva Porto states (*Viagens*, p. 127) that he got back to Kotongo on 4 August, and visited D.L. and Sekeletu at Naliele on the 5th, having heard that they had arrived there on the 2nd. D.L.'s dates seem to be more reliable; for example, his arrival at Dinyanti is referred to by Silva Porto under 'March 1' (*op. cit.*, p. 118), when he was in fact nearing Kamakama (see above, p. 102). There is also internal evidence that Silva Porto's journal, as published, contains later additions; thus, in Chapter V ('1853'), he refers (p. 111) to the death of Sekeletu, the accession of Mpololo, and the revolt of the MaLozi, all of which happened in 1863–4.

[2] Silva Porto mentions the failure of the caravan he had sent to Moçambique in March, but gives no further details (*Viagens*, pp. 118, 127, 128). Of the chiefs named, Sinamane is described in *Narrative* (p. 315) as 'the ablest and most energetic of the Batoka chiefs we have met'; he lived on Chilomba island in the Zambesi, near the confluence of the Sebungwe. 'Kangomba or Sinangombe', previously called 'Kabonda or Kambonga' (cf. above, p. 205), may be Sinakoba, a Tonga chief living in Gwembe district. Boe and Kobo I have not identified.

[3] Presumably Moçambique.

[4] Silva Porto mentions that D.L. showed him Duprat's 'circular' at Dinyanti, 'which we read and then handed back to him, telling him that all our help was at his disposal' (*Viagens*, p. 125).

as I can judge very enterprising. There is probably a premium in prospect of which he says nothing.

Observed an occultation of Jupiter last night, viz. 13 August 53. The last glimpse of outer edge of the planet as it disappeared behind the dark limb of the moon was observed at the watch hour 13h 18m 36s. The watch at 4h 7. 39 of same day shewed no error. It[s] rate was 30" gain per day, but at 3 o'clock there was no error.

The strong spathe which grows in such abundance on the Zouga and of which the nets are made is formed into a curious cap by some of the tribes on the West.[1] When blackened it looks exactly like horse hair and might be exported for stuffing mattrasses chairs &c. It grows singly and I have

[facsimile of manuscript handwriting:]

which the nets are made is formed into a curious cap by some of the tribes on the West. When blackened it looks exactly like horse hair and might be exported for stuffing mattresses chairs &c.

It grows singly and I have seen it in flower It is very widely distributed in the country.

The people called Cassaquare exist

seen it in flower. It is very widely distributed in the country.

The people called Cassaquare[2] exist in great numbers in the West and present all the characters of the Bushmen. They

---

[1] Cf. *Travels*, p. 274, where D.L. says that the BaLunda sometimes make 'wigs' from the fibre of 'ife' (*Sanseviera angolensis*), which they dye black and twist 'so as to resemble a mass of their own wool' (*sc.* hair).

[2] Possibly the !O !Ku ('forest people'), a tribe of Bushmen known to their Bantu neighbours as 'BaSukuwera' (cf. Schapera, *Khoisan Peoples*, p. 34).

are just as wild and fond of shooting with poisoned arrows in Lat. 14° as on the borders of the Cape Colony. Their language presents the same peculiarities.

Endeavouring to have our Sunday services as calm and peaceful as possible I thought I had succeeded pretty well today. There was only a miserable attempt at dancing, and the audience about one thousand. When I was about to commence, a man caught a boy about 6 years of age who was passing accross the square with his mother, and after shouting out at the top of his voice in praise of the son of Sebitane said, I thank you, and led off the boy, whose heart seemed bursting with agony, to his own house. I asked Sekeletu if the boy were really captured, and when he replied in the affirmative I called the man to me and asked Sekeletu to give the man to me, as I wished to purchase a new jacket with him. The man laughed at first, but when I persisted he began to think it serious and said, surely the son of Sebituane won't part with an old servant? I answered he was old and useless, whereas the boy was young and would make a good soldier. I think by the remarks made all saw that I regarded the act as odious. He afterwards told Sekeletu he was afraid I would kill him.[1]

Immediately after the service a party of Bakisi came with two drums. Two of the principal actors were dressed as grotesquely as possible. Every part of the body was covered and the face deformed with a kind of snout. One had breasts like a woman, the other something like the male attire, with bells which in his strange contortions made a jingling sound. The people collected again, and some said these are the gods of this river. Bechuanas who had never witnessed heathen orgies like these were horrified.[2]

A large bundle of spears were next brought in. They had belonged to a party of Borotse who, annoyed by a Mokololo, had resolved to flee to Seunturu's son Masike who now lives

---

[1] This incident is not mentioned in *Travels*.

[2] These masked dances, known as *makishi*, are characteristic of the BaLovale and allied peoples, among whom they are held in connection with initiation and funeral ceremonies. The dancers, termed *akishi* ('ancestral spirits'), 'usually wear fibre costumes, covering the whole body, and have distinctive head-dresses, often very elaborate' (White, *Material Culture of the Lunda-Lovale Peoples*, 1948, p. 13; *idem*, 'A Note on the Makishi', *N. Rhod. J.*, No. IV, December 1951, pp. 67–70).

on the Liambae far up.[1] They were met by a party of Makololo in their flight and fought for liberty, but all who could be caught were put to death, and these were the spears which had belonged to them. The perpetual internal capturing and sale of children seems to call as much for the Christianization of Africa as the external slave trade.

15th Aug.[2] Mon. Enduring the dismal dance and roar of the Makololo. The cattle of Mpépe are expected to be distributed, and each one who approaches the chief calls out, 'Give cattle, O chief'. The good time is coming for all that,
    When man and man the world o'er,
    shall brothers be for all that.
There is no want of food in this fertile valley. It yields abundantly Caffre corn of great size and beautiful whiteness, Pumpkins, melons, beans, Maize, and earth nuts, Moanja or Manioc, Sweet potato and another kind of potato called Sekhutsane, Sugar cane, and the Banana farther North.

The cattle too resemble in size those of the Cape Colony, and though liable to be cut off in large numbers by epidemics, if the calves are left the[y] propagate so quickly it is pronounced a good land for cattle. If an ox is seen to be sick it is immediately slaughtered in order, as an Irishman would say, to save its life. The Borotse when removed from this valley mourn after it as the Israelites did after Egypt. At Nariele the valley is at least 40 miles wide.

There still lives an old man called Lebompo, who was a companion of Seunturu from childhood and asserts that no white man ever visited the capital Loi. Pereira must have fabricated his journey.[3] Senor Porto is the first Portuguese who has seen the Liambae or Zambesi in the Interior of the continent.

Wedensday. Mpepe's designs have become abundantly evident in his appropriation of the cattle of Sebitane to himself. They have turned out in large numbers from his own,

---

[1] 'Masike' (Imasiku) was in fact the son of Santudu's son Mubukwanu. Like several other members of the Lozi royal family, he had fled north after the Kololo conquest and established a small kingdom of his own, at Lukwakwa, near the confluence of the Zambesi and Kabompo. He was killed by the MaMbunda in 1859. Cf. Jalla, *Litaba*, pp. 43, 65 f. There are many references to him in *Travels*, Chaps. XIV, XV, XXIV, XXV.

[2] MS. has '14th'.   [3] Cf. above, pp. 152, 153.

and others have been found secreted among the cattle of his servants. He intended if he failed in killing Sekeletu to remove this portion of the tribe to the Batoka country. We are detained at Naliele settling the affair of the cattle. When that is finished we shall proceed to Katongo on a visit to Senor Porto.

Twenty six oxen have been slaughtered in two days, yet many complain of not having tasted meat. They are distributed chiefly among those strangers who have come in large numbers to visit the chief. All dancing and praising are, it is every day more evident, just other terms for the most abject begging.

18th Thursday. Resolve to leave tomorrow morning for Libonta. The work of the chief here seems endless, and he has not the tact of going through with [it] quickly. His father had an excellent head for business, and would not allow any one to accompany him who appeared more anxious to eat than work. Dancing and roaring songs seem more to Sekeletu's taste than business.

The water of the Liambae moves at the rate of one hundred yards in one hundred seconds of time.[1] It is now at its lowest. It probably moves faster when the river is swollen.

$$1000 \text{ yards in}$$

About four miles $\quad 60\overline{)1000(} \text{ seconds}$
per hour $\qquad\qquad 16.40$

$$\frac{4}{64}$$

Libonta

21st. At Libonta, Lat. 14° 58′.[2]

We left Naliele on Friday 19th, and at midday took an Altitude at a tree which marks the site of the town of one of Santuru's wives. It is called Linangelo, and the whole of the

---

[1] 'The current of the Leeambye is rapid; 100 yards in 60 seconds of time, or between 4 and 5 miles an hour' (*JRGS*, 1854, p. 297; cf. *Travels*, p. 221).

[2] Elsewhere given by D.L. as 14° 59′ S. (*JRGS*, 1854, p. 302; *Travels*, pp. 221, 685). GSGS 2871 Rhodesia (1919) locates it at the same latitude, and long. 22° 58′ E. Modern maps show 'Libunda' at 14° 47′ S., 23° 3′ E., on the opposite (Eastern) bank of the Zambesi, which suggests that the village has been moved.

site is washed away by the river except about four yards.[1] As this too has taken place with the chief town of Santuru, at Naliele, the river must be wearing away towards the East. The present town of Naliele was merely the storehouses for corn of Santuru. The capital he occupied when young and with[out] power is called Lilonda,[2] and is nearly due East of Linangelo and about 10 miles from the river.

The river Makomo[3] was passed on Friday, and the point from which the branch Mareele diverges off forms a very large Island.

We visited the large villages of Rapulanyane or Pulane,[4] Mpololo &c, and slept at a village of Mothibe. I discovered that Sekeletu had furnished me with a herald, who whenever we approached a village began to roar out at the top of his voice, 'Do we not see a great Lord? Here comes a Lord. Let every one come and salute the father of Sekeletu. Whoever has corn or milk let him bring it'. These heralds are useful, inasmuch as their duties include providing abundance of fuel for the Kotla fire, keeping that place clear of bones & filth, and [acting as] public sextons for those who may be respectable yet die while their male friends may be absent, and dragging forth to the vultures the deceased poor, as well as issuing public proclamations and sounding the praises of the chief and others whom he may delight to honour. Their emoluments are the heads and necks of all the oxen slaughtered by the chief and a choice of two of the large bundles of corn, nuts &c &c, of every party of tribute which comes to the town.

I proposed to our herald that he should divide the praises between me and the people who liberally supplied us with milk and porridge, but he stuck to his instructions from the

[1] 'Linangelo, old town of Santuru (site nearly swallowed up), Lat. 15° 18' 40" S.' (*JRGS*, 1854, p. 302; *Travels*. p. 685); '. . . the site swallowed up by the river except a few square yards. It is nearly the same latitude as the first capital of Santuru, and on this account I took the latitude' (*JRGS*, 1854, p. 305).

[2] Cf. below, p. 224: '. . . Lilonda, the capital which Santuru occupied when still young and without influence'. But in *Travels*, p. 219, Lilonda is called 'his more recent capital'. The apparent contradiction is explained by Jalla's statement (*Litaba*, pp. 36, 39) that Santudu first ruled at Lilundu (Lilonda), on becoming king established his capital at Namuso (Naliele), and afterwards returned to Lilundu, where he died and was buried.

[3] Luanginga. 'Makomo' (Makoma) is the name of a tribe living on its banks (cf. Jalla, *Litaba*, p. 30), in Kalabo district.

[4] Probably Pulane Bogatsu, a kinsman of Sekeletu (cf. below, p. 236).

chief, and when we reached a large village such as Libonta, possessing a herald of its own, there was a perfect storm of roaring, the one trying to outvie the other and secure the heads to himself. As my man compelled me to accept of his honours I invariably gave the heads to the locum tenens, presenting at the same time my 'barker' with a pot of milk or beer, which has a wonderful effect on them all. One may have as much food served out to him regularly as he is able to eat, but the actual possession of a quantity most of which he must distribute to his companions is much more agreable.

On Sat. visited the village of Mothibe, father-in-law of Sekeletu. I have always found that the man who begs much is niggardly. There is a great sameness in the banks of the river. They are alternately composed of dark coloured mud, ferruginous sand and pure sand in layers of every variety of form and inclination. Some were even twisted as if pressed on by a huge boulder rolling along. They are scarc[e]ly ever more than four feet high above the present level (the lowest) of the water.

A great number of excellent fish were procured by our boatmen from their friends the Borotse who were fishing with nets in a branch of the river. They seemed to take them very unceremoniously from their owners, who in scorn called after them, 'though you had taken the whole of them we shall catch more before midday than we can carry'. They were taking them out of the nets as fast as they could kill them by knocking them on the head. There were [some] like very large perches but much finer. A fish having large conical teeth which appear when the mouth is shut frequently falls a victim to the fish hawk, which seizes it in its talons as he is following his prey in shallow water. He is about 18 inches long and beautifully striped. We frequently saw them half devoured lying on the banks.

In the Evening we came to a very large herd of Hippopotami which were perfectly unconscious of danger. I shot one for our people. The flesh is excellent, resembling the finest pork. The teeth are finely adapted for tearing off and cutting the water plants on which he feeds. He has not the appearance usually given in pictures. The teeth are not visible when at rest, and even when feeding they do not come beyond the lips. He is a dangerous animal at night, but danger is in a measure avoided by winding along the banks by day and taking the middle of the river by night. He is always in the middle of the river or in deep still pools far from the banks by day, but at night he approaches the shores in order to feed and a canoe approaching him in his walk appears to him an attack. He strikes it with feet and breaks it to shivers, and generally makes off. A few old gentlemen who have become crusty take to canoe breaking, and one shot by Mr Oswel was afterwards ascertained to be the individual which destroyed an immense number of canoes. They are probably males driven into solitude by stronger competitors and then become disgusted with every one. When an attack is made on a canoe by an animal bent on destroying the people in [it], the Borotse invariably glide down to the bottom. He seeks men on the surface only. I have seen the scars of horrid wounds inflicted by his teeth.

Certain of the Banyeti are Hippopotamus fishermen hereditarily, and display astonishing presence of mind in the chase. Their canoes are very small, but they keep their equilibrium most admirably and go with great speed.

Reach Libonta and spend Sunday 21st. Lat. 14° 58′. The island is larger than any one we have seen in the Borotse country. Sekeletu sent a man after me post haste with the request that I should return to him, as the people to whom I was about to proceed did not like him and he feared for my safety. I replied these were antient words, which I did not like to hear, and I refused to return because I was bent on introducing the new system by which all tribes would have intercourse without danger. I had never killed any one, and therefore nobody would think it worth while to kill me. We left this day Monday.

22d. Visited several small villages of fishermen. The women usually brought a little present in their hands when coming to salute and see the white man. I should like to acquire the Borotse language, for they can hold converse in it with Mambari and nearly all other tribes in this region. We reached the large village of Mambowe, the main body of which tribe live in the North.[1] This party live by hunting

---

[1] Chiefly in the region where the Lungwebungu and Kabompo join the Zambesi. In *Travels*, p. 490, they are mentioned as subjects of Imasiku (cf. above, p. 210).

Hippopotami. The headman brought a large bundle of its dried flesh to us as a present. He went with us in order to shew us the river. Trees make their appearance now in clusters. The banks are about 20 feet high. The country here is probably not so long submerged as[1] in the Borotse proper. In the distance from our sleeping place, the island Matende,[2] may be seen a dense cluster of Palmyras. Date trees abound, and a tree from the fruit of which snuff boxes are by being scooped formed. It is edible. Also sycamores covered with their fig-like fruit. The Moporotla is now of a beautiful bright green, the leaves being fresh & young, and with its clusters of huge pods presents a splendid spectacle. Its pods are frequently upwards of 20 inches long, and the fruit stalk twice that length. The country literally teems with game of all sorts. A pretty little brown antelope called Poku is probably unknown.[3]

Hundreds of the holes made by a small swallow-like bird which migrates Southwards and subsists on beetles are seen at different parts of the banks. They seem to hatch in society. The holes are like those of the sandmartin, and the birds disturbed by our passing flew over our heads in hundreds. It seems to have one feather in the centre of the tail much longer than the others. Also a very large and beautiful kingfisher. It seemed larger than a dove.

Fever

On 19th I walked accross the island of Mpollo, and as I had taken off my stockings to wade through patches of water which we came to in our path I washed my feet in the river and walked to the canoe to procure some medicine for a sick man. I think I may have had my feet in the cold river water about 7 minutes. I was soon seized with my seventh attack of fever. I became cold & shivered, and during the whole night was in a raging fever with pain in the bowels but none in the head. Next morning discharges of blood and scybalae, though the bowels had previously been regular. A dead pain in lower

[1] MS. has 'is'.
[2] On Gibbons's map (1904), 'Matende' is shown as a small stream joining the Zambesi from the N.W. at about 14° 45′ S.
[3] Cf. above, p. 37.

part of bowels towards left. After discharges of blood & tenesmus for three days I am becoming better. Great thirst alone remains, & that chiefly by night. I drink cold water freely, and have never interfered with the discharges of blood among the natives, believing them to be efforts of nature to remove peccant matter. From my own feelings I imagine the parts chiefly affected were the portion of the intestines in which Pierrian glands[1] are situated. I forget the name but have frequently seen them enlarged and containing pus in fever subjects in Glasgow. If I had proper food and could take meals regularly I should not be so liable to attacks of this complaint. As it is at present, thick milk and porridge eaten when one can get them constitute my diet, and a very unsuitable one, for the former eaten in the evening is almost sure to bring on an attack.

Tuesday evening 23d. We heard the first lion's roar for a long time, but wherever game exists the lion lives.

The river presents very much the same appearance as at Sesheke. The banks are about 20 feet high, and in many parts thickets extend down to the water's edge. Vines were intertwined in some parts, and Molopo, the tree which inflicts a pricking to the skin.[2] Other beautiful evergreens were seen. The grass is finer than in the Borotse country, but still the country is subject to inundation. A ridge appears tonight about six miles off on the right bank. The island Tongane in 14° 38' contains a small village of Mambowe, and tonight we sleep at the confluence of the Senyenki, a river which comes from the Mambowe country in the N.E.[3] Great numbers of game. 81 buffaloes defiled slowly before our camp this evening. I shot an eiland for our people this evening. They are roasting and boiling and drying it on sticks over the fire, and are in good spirits. The river has a great deal of Easting beyond Libonta. The headmen of two villages have come along with us. One of them pointed out the site of his father's town. He said the old ones were all killed by Makololo. 'Killing is very bad'.

[1] A name at one time used for the superficial glands in the groin nowadays known as 'inguinal glands'. (For this information I am indebted to Dr M. Allanson.)

[2] Not identified; cf. above, p. 199.

[3] D.L.'s map suggests that the Senyenki may be the stream joining the Zambesi from the East at Lukulu.

Robbery by Mambowe

Wedensday. On leaving our sleeping place we found the river very much obstructed by large sand banks. Among these it presents a less noble appearance than when flowing majestically between banks covered with forest down to the water's edge. We soon reached such scenery. A great many willows grow along the banks, interspersed with other trees one of which is very much like the mangrove. Another tree which yields a fruit which when scooped out constitutes the snuff boxes of the Makololo and is exceedingly admired by the Southern Bechuanas. A considerable number of a kind of acacia with thorns appear also, with often times along the bank below it a fringe of reed.

As we proceeded on our course we came upon a party of fishermen who were engaged in hunting hippopotami. We called upon them not to run away and they seemed inclined to come accross the river to us. But my informant of the Makololo sins of yesterday got into a canoe and commenced a continual call of, Come and see Monare,[1] at the same time paddling towards them with all his might. This aroused their suspicions and they returned to the shore and fled, leaving everything they possessed behind them in their canoes. We called to our own people to let the property alone & come back, but the wind was high and the breadth of the river & more than all their own greediness prevented them hearing. This was very annoying, and as it was done while my name [was] mixed up in the affair, as soon as our own people came we searched them and collected all the spears knives skins oars &c. in a heap on a sand bank in the middle of the river. My informer had been very active and secured a large booty and a canoe which he impudently brought to the island. He seemed in high glee, but we hauled up the canoe and I said to him, 'Now as you were not [told][2] by any one to steal and your conduct is the very sort of thing which makes people attack innocent visitors, as soon as I see an attacking party I shall shoot you as our greatest enemy. Your bullet is here in the left hand barrel. You complain of the Makololo, and won't yourself be restrained from their deeds.' He saw he was in a dangerous posi-

[1] From Afrikaans 'meneer' (Dutch 'mynheer'), 'a term of respect often employed in South Africa when a minister or the Gospel is addressed or spoken of' (Pettman, p. 331).　　[2] Word inadvertently omitted in turning to new page.

tion, and looked very much downcast till midday, when he made an approach to reconciliation, and after a little more lecture of a less savage nature the breach was made up. Too soon I fear, for another of his party secreted a canoe and property, whither we could not discover. They then began to lag behind instead of as usual keep their places in front of the other canoes.[1]

On leaving the thieving place we came right over a hippopotamus which had been wounded by the fishermen. The front of the canoe appearing over it made it utter a low grunting sound beneath the water. The canoe was quickly backed, and we went round somewhat to avoid so dangerous an animal to the light craft in which we were.

Before midday we reach[ed] a high perpendicular bank of about 60 feet on the right. It seemed Marly sandstone, and it gives the river its turn to the West. Our course has been never much more North than N.E. or N.E. & by N. since we left Libonta, but here it takes more Northing and a little Westing even. We stood at Midday to take an observation on an island called Kowrie. The part on which the horizon was place[d] was of mud, dried in the sun. A slough prevented our party of 18 from dispersing as usual among the trees around. I enjoined silence but, as I have often seen before, a considerable party sitting on the ground conveys so much vibration to the quicksilver a good observation cannot be made. Their arterial pulsations seem to effect it. If in a village we must always ajourn outside for observations, but if several walk about near the crowd which always proceed to see the strange water & put their fingers in it, the quicksilver vibrates. This indifferent observation Double Alt. 128° 38 ☉ L.L. gave 14° 20. 17 as Latitude.[2]

---

[1] This incident is described much more briefly in *Travels*, p. 222.

[2] Cf. above, p. 160 In *JRGS*, 1854, p. 302, D.L. gives the latitude of 'Cowrie Island' as 14° 20′ 5″ S., with the following comment (p. 305): 'The bank on which we landed to make the observations was of soft mud encircled by a slough, which prevented the boatmen from dispersing over the island as usual. Though they sat quietly near me, the presence of a number of men caused a vibration in the mercury. This circumstance, and its being too near noon to go elsewhere, made the observations less certain than the others. The confluence of the Loeti . . . being almost 2 miles N. of the island, makes me regret the circumstances, for I had no other opportunity for observing so near the Loeti. I suppose the confluence of the Loeti with the main stream may be set down at lat. 14° 18′ or 14° 19′.' 'Cowrie Island' is not shown on any recent map consulted, but the junction of the 'Loeti' (Lungwebungu) with the Zambesi is generally marked at approx. 14° 19′ S., the figure given by D.L. in *JRGS*, 1854, p. 302 (cf. *Travels*, p. 685).

Confluence of the Loeti

About 2′ bearing or one hour in the canoe we reached the confluence of the river Loeti. The bottom of both rivers is now rocky, and immediately beyond the junction southwards several stones jut out of the stream. The waters of the Loeti are slightly tinged as if a small quantity of mud were suspended. The difference of colour between it and the dark Liambae is very distinct in the small rapids above referred to, for the water in rushing over the stones is lifted so as to become apparent to one standing at the Loeti. It seemed between 200 and 250 yards wide. Yet with a large body of water the Liambae beyond did not seem greatly altered in breadth. Later in the evening however it was narrowed between high banks to about 300 yards. It is then deep and rapid and still a noble river. The Loeti as painted by those who have[1] been some distance up it comes from Lobale, which is N.W. or N.W. & by W. from the confluence. Lobale is probably that region through which Senor Porto travels in which he has often to cross ten rivers in one day.[2]

On reaching an island a little beyond, one of the Mambowe asserted that the branch which winds round it was the Leeba.[3] As this was contrary to information previously recieved I refused to turn, telling him he was decieving. On telling my own people to move on I saw some of them had been in the plot, and we soon found out that it was an island.

Confluence of the Leeba or Lonta

In the Evening we slept on an island where vines were in full leaf and quite untouched by frost. A great herd of Hippop[otami][4] kept up a continual bellowing before us for a considerable time, and after about one ¼ hour's[5] sail in the morning of Thursday 25 August we came to the confluence of the Leeba. The Liambae is here called Kabompo,[6] and the

---

[1] MS. has 'whave', possibly under the influence of the preceding 'who'.

[2] Cf. above, p. 189.   [3] The Zambesi, above the confluence of the Kabompo.

[4] D.L. wrote 'Hippop-', but did not complete the word when starting the next line.

[5] The '¼' is a marginal addition; probably 'and' should be inserted immediately before it.

[6] As noted above (p. 41), D.L. regarded the Kabompo as the main stream of the Zambesi, and the 'Lonta' or 'Leeba' as a tributary.

Borotse who fled from Sebitane live up it. The Liambae takes its former course here. The first reach is E.N.E. or N.E. & by E. The Leeba is about 100 yards [wide], with a high ridge not flooded on its Western bank. The Liambae (200 or 300) is excessively rapid when flooded and coloured redish.

As this is the point on which I determined my investigation should cease in this direction I wait only till 12 oclock for an Observation for Altitude and will then return. Took 4 sets of Lunars this morning. Gave a present to all our paddlers, so we all return pleased, and I most sincerely thank God who has helped and protected me thus far.

Thursday Evening. We returned to the great bend from the West, the scene of our thieving operations. When we came thither we found our Mambowe friends waiting for us. They had returned by night and secured all the booty, and of course stoutly denied having any knowledge of what had become of either it or the canoes. We landed and examined the foot prints. We measured them, and both by measurement and putting the foot in them we found them to be no other than those of our friends. One foot wanted two toes. The tallying of this good criterion confounded some of them, others continued to vociferate innocence. The novelty of the expedient greatly amused our own people.[1] I feel sorry for the poor men who have thus lost their all, & as there is no intercourse there can be no reparation. These fueds carried on between tribes keeps up perpetual irritation. Children are often captured. This is the region afflicted with the evils resulting from the slave trade. Mpépé had planned to go with his portion of his tribe with S[ilva] P[orto]. The chief feature in his character seems to have been inordinate conciet. He was a very little man. This is one of the characteristics of such.

The Tsetse and Elephants appear for the first time from Nameta at this bend. When I saw the insect I felt our object to establish a large mission could not be effected in this quarter and I could almost have turned, but the River Londa or Leeba goes to Londa and a quick water conveyance may yet be established from the West by its means. The part called Katongo on the East of Naliele is perhaps the best of

[1] This piece of detective work is not mentioned in *Travels*.

very indifferent localities in the country.[1] We must submit to malaria and trust in God for the rest. It is easy to trust in Providence when there is no danger.

There is an immense amount of insensible perspiration going on while on the river.* I drink great quantities of water by day and always wake during the night to swill and quench my parched tongue. Those who anoint are not so much troubled, and if I wear clothing which fits loosely the thirst is greater.

There is an undiscovered antelope in these parts, also an animal [which] from its discription and horns I conci[e]ve to be the Indian bison. It is named in Serotse Liombikala. Large horns like an ox. Gondi, short horns—burrows. Bumé or Boomy, one horned animal, probably a variety of Rhinoceros.[2]

Friday 26th. Sleep at Mambowe village. Passed large herds of different kinds of antelopes. About one hundred Eilands and amazingly tame. A large one had been killed by lions and afterwards dragged into the water by alligators. A pretty brown antelope called Poku abounds.

By Mer. Alt. of ☉, L.L. on Thursday 25 August 1853 = 129° 38' 10, I find the Latitude of the confluence to be 14° 11' 3". 2 Sets shew Long. to be 23° 40' & 23° 41' E.[3] We stood on the right or southern bank of the Liambae. It is about 30 yards high and formed of clay. There was nothing conspicuous to mark the spot, but the confluence of the Lonta or Leeba itself is of sufficient notoriety for a Geographical point. Written on 25th.

---

* The fluids of the body seem to partake of some ration of the current from the river in exhalation. [D.L.]

---

[1] The modern administrative centre of Mongu is situated there.

[2] 'My boatman informed me that he had seen an animal, with long wide spreading horns like an ox, called *liombikalela*—perhaps the modern bison; also another animal, which does not live in the water, but snorts like a hippopotamus, and is like that animal in size—it has a horn, and may be the Asiatic rhinoceros. And we passed some holes of a third animal, which burrows from the river inland, has short horns, and feeds only by night. I did not notice the burrows at the time of passing, but I give you the report as I got it' (*JRGS*, 1854, p. 300). Jalla (*Dictionary*) defines *liombekalala* as '(fabulous) aquatic cow'. *Gondi* and *bumé* I cannot trace; but on the fly-leaf of his 1853–6 *Journal* D.L. noted: 'Mbume, light coloured animal, hornless (Tolo?); Ngondi, burrowing antelope, horns 8 inches long'.

[3] This sentence was added at the head of the page. In *JRGS*, 1854, p. 302, and *Travels*, p. 685, the junction is said to be at 14° 10' 52" S., 23 °35' 40" E. Modern maps have the same latitude, but longitude 23° 11' E.

VI

RETURN TO LINYANTI

Return to Libonta

26th [August]. It is much more pleasant to sail down than up the river. The sun beats fiercely on the front of our persons when going North, but on our backs on returning. The alligators abound in this river and are very fierce. Every now and then we see them gliding into the water from the banks on which they love to bask during the day. They retire as soon as we appear in sight. Their nature leads them to shew skulking habits. They swim with great speed when prey is in prospect. Leap quite out of the water like a fish when seizing an antelope drinking. They are more savage and destructive in some rivers than in others, and the people declare they are more fierce in one part of a river than in another.

A beautiful plant shaped like a fern and another resembling a small cabbage grow in the water. Their roots are suspended in the water but quite unfixed to the ground.

Sat. Returned to Libonta and found two men bitten by a lion. One of them had his thigh bone quite broken. The animal was wounded in several places yet managed to do much mischief.[1] We passed on to Mothibe's villages and will spend Sunday here.

Mothibe informs me that Sekeletu put another man to death after we left Naliele, because on some former occasion he had said to him that he was not the son of Sebitane.[2] 'He did not wish me to become great', was a sufficient reason in the chief's mind for destroying the poor man. He is surrounded by evil bloody minded counsellors and most of the tribe lament it. Mothibe though partaker in the other deeds of blood seemed greatly shocked, and insisted much on the necessity of a protest to the chief against this evil course,

---

[1] This incident is described in *Travels* on pp. 249 f., dated '17th December'.
[2] Cf. above, p. 29.

which is sure to alienate the tribe from him. I shewed him the evil in another point of view, viz. in prospect of the judgement when Sekeletu, his counsellors and victims would stand naked before the dreadful tribunal of the Almighty before whom all are alike. We had a long conversation on many subjects of revelation, and on Sunday morning another after the service, which was well attended, and I pray and hope that some of the good seed may take root and bring forth fruit to God's Glory.

The people have an unconvincible belief that all we do is by means of medicine. The book must be nosicoe or drunk for,[1] medicine of the book must be taken or it will never be understood. There is not convincing them to the contrary. 'If as we tell you it is good news, God's message, his counsel, his last words of advice to his [son?][2] which he wishes all his people, all the world, to hear & obey, do you think it would be sent with a medicine which we his servants deny the possession of?' 'Ah, but what is ivory for, what do the traders give such large prices for but that they may make book and gun medicine with them?'

Mothibe presented a large ox as provisions. S[ilva] P[orto] has gone Eastward, he has obtained information from Kaiñko[3] that he may proceed to the coast through his country. He is very desirous of going to Mosambique. Probably a reward is offered by the Portuguese Govt for the discovery of a way accross the country.[4] I shall visit his establishment & then go to the waggon and prepare for the Western journey. The prospects in this part are very dark in this bloody land.

The more intimately I become a[c]quainted with barbarians the more disgusting does heathenism become. It is inconc[i]evably vile. They are always boasting of their fierceness, yet dare not visit another tribe for fear of being killed. They never visit anywhere but for the purposes of plunder and oppression. They never go anywhere but with a club or spear in hand. It is lamentable to see those who might be

1 From Tswana *nosa*, 'give water to, cause to drink'.

2 Word omitted in starting new page.

3 Kaingu, an Ila chief living on the Kafue River at Itumbi, Namwala district.

4 Cf. above, p. 208. In *JRGS*, 1857, p. 373, D.L. says that a reward had been offered of 'one million of reis (about 142 *l.*), and an honorary captaincy in the Portuguese army'.

children of God, dwelling in peace & love, so utterly the children of the Devil, dwelling in fear and continual irritation They bestow honours and flattering titles on me in confusing profusion. All from the least to the greatest call me Father, Lord, &c, and bestow food without any recompence, out of pure kindness. They need a healer. May God enable me to be such to them.

Therm. 90° in shade at Noon. The coldest night we have had in this country has not caused the mercury to fall below 40°. Water boils at 203° at Mambowe village.

Santuru's Altar

Monday 28th. Left Mothibe's village and after 4 hours' sail rested at noon at the point where the Marile branches off Easterly from main stream. By Mer. Alt. ☉ U.L. 131° 20′ 30″, it is in 15° 15′ 54″ or in round numbers 15° 16′.[1] The country does not contain any large towns, but as far as the eye can reach it is dotted over with villages and cattle stations. It is a land of plenty, milk and corn besides other grains and roots in great abundance.

We visited Lilonda the capital which Santuru occupied when still young and without influence in it.[2] A mound was pointed out as that formed by Santuru for a man who fled from the Batoka after they had cut off his hands. He gave him cattle and sustained him. After sitting a few minutes on the site of his capital and admiring the trees, all of which he transplanted hither, I told them my object in visiting the country. One rose up and requested me to follow. Leading me to the other end of the mound he pointed out a large log formed thus[3] by art. In front of it were some pieces of iron curiously fashioned thus[3] &c representing spears axes hoes &c &c in miniature and of very neat workmanship. One appendage very nicely wrought and resembling a basket hilt of a broad sword but the holes in [it] more regular I could not concieve the use of, unless to burn incence. They said, these

[1] 'We came down a branch of the Leeambye called Marile, which departs from the main river in lat. 15° 15′ 43″ S., and is a fine deep stream about sixty yards wide; it makes the whole of the country around Naliele an island' (*Travels*, p. 223). Modern maps show the Marile branching off at 15° 7′ S. and rejoining the main channel at 15° 28′ S.

[2] Cf. above, p. 212.　　　　　　　　　　　　　　　　[3] See facsimile, p. 225.

end of the morni... he pointed out a large log formed thus Y by art in front of it were ... some pieces of ... curiously fashioned thus ... representing spears axes hoes. ... in miniature and ... very neat workmanship one appendage very nicely wrought and resembling a basket built of a broad ... but the holes in more regular

are the things on which Santuru presented offerings to the Barimo (gods or dead ones). I asked if I might take the basket-looking instrument with me to shew my friends. 'O no', was the reply, 'their owner won't allow it'. 'Who won't allow it?' 'Santuru refuses. They stand here just as he left them'. This seems to point clearly [to] their belief in future existence.[1] They said also, If you would wait you would see the 'cow of God', it is never milked.[2]

The remark of my chief boatman Moshauana,[3] who was in attendance to tie up the instruments when I had finished making an observation for Altitude at the confluence of the Lonta and Kabompo, shews the same faith. There was a Halo of about 20° in diameter round the sun. I remarked to him after taking the observation, with the view of eliciting his opinion on the weather from the increased watery vapour in the atmosphere which such phenomena indicate, 'Does that

[1] Cf. *Travels*, p. 219: 'The Barotse also showed some relics of their chief, which evinced a greater amount of the religious feeling than I had ever known displayed among Bechuanas'.

[2] I have found no other reference to this animal, except that Jalla (*Dictionary*, p. 96) translates *komu ya Nyambe* (lit., 'cow of God') as 'kind of winged insect'.

[3] One of the men who subsequently accompanied D.L. to Luanda and back (cf. *Travels*, p. 251, etc.). Together with some other 'chiefs', he was killed *c.*1888 by the Lozi king Lewanika on a charge of conspiracy (Coillard, p. 362).

Halo not foretell rain?' 'No', was his ready reply, 'The Barimo have called a Peecho, don't you see they have placed
the Lord in their centre?'[1]

After giving the people of Lilonda, who are all Borotse,
some information as to the proper mode of worship, and praying with them in our simple inexpensive form,[2] I left and
proceeded to a village in the same latitude as Naliele. The
Marile is winding and from 40 to 50 yards broad.

Katongo. Arabs

31st of August. Wed.

Went to Katongo yesterday and returned to Marile today.
It is 6 miles distant, and the ridge is at least 200 feet high. It
is covered with trees, many of them evergreen. A fine view is
obtained of the Borotse flat, which seems to extend to the
horizon. It must look well when covered with water as a Lake.
Senor Porto has erected a stockade and two houses of the
style in use by Kangombe. A flagstaff is placed in front for
the display of the Portuguese flag, and I suspect for the purpose of proclaiming the sovreignty of Portugal over these
realms.[3] He has a very large company of Mambari with him.
They are arranged under the sons of different Portuguese
traders and of half blood—Urbano, George, Peidro, Rapezo
&c. Each has his own establishment, and they appear
civilized in comparison with the Mambari, all of whom are
naked with the exception of a piece of cloth wound round the
loins. They have their wives with them. As Sekeletu has gone
on to his mother's I left apricot and peach seeds with Urbano
for S.P. to plant in his stockade for future use. They may
muster 200 capable of using firearms. They treated us very
kindly, insisting on my sleeping in S.P.'s bed, which as I had
an attack of Intermittent proved very acceptable. On re-

[1] In *Travels*, pp. 219 f., this incident is also cited 'as showing a more vivid per-
ception of the existence of spiritual beings, and greater proneness to worship, than
among the Bechuanas'. 'Peecho' (*pitsó*) is a mass meeting of men for the discussion of
tribal affairs.

[2] '. . . and praying with them in the simple form which needs no offering from
the worshipper except that of the heart' (*Travels*, p. 219).

[3] 'A stockade was erected at Katongo, and a flag-staff for the Portuguese banner'
(*JRGS*, 1854, p. 294); the stockade is also mentioned in *Travels*, p. 181, but not the
flag. Silva Porto says that D.L. spoke of having seen the flag, to which he replied,
'it had been our daily custom, since 1841, to hoist the Portuguese flag wherever we
happened to be' (*Viagens*, pp. 127 f.; free translation).

turning today we saw one of the Mambari digging up moles
or mice in the field for food. They are not overfed.[1] A chain
full of slaves had one wretchedly lean woman with her little
child in it—seemed perishing of hunger.

The following is the writing[2] of Nyafman ben Chombo

her little child in A - *seemed perishing of*
hunger. the following is the writing of

يَا حِبْنَا الْمُؤْمِنَ أَزْ تَكْرُمْ مَا نَكْرَمُ مُ حَدَّزْنَا الْجَرِيرَ

أَو مَنِّى يَكْلَى يَا كَلَى بْ سَ حَفَظَهُ اللهُ وَ أَمْدَهُ وَ

حَجَّ عُثْمَانَ رَضَنَا مَنُوبَ سَرَلُودَ حَبَّحٍ جُوعٍ فَهَكَلَامَ

١٢٩٢

Nyafman ben Chombo. Shirarze
Rya syde bo Sultana of Imame of
Muscat

[1] '[The Mambari] showed also their habits in their own country by digging up
and eating, even here where large game abounds, the mice and moles which infest
the country' (*Travels*, p. 218).

[2] 'We met Arabs from Zanguebar, subjects of the Imaum of Muscat. One of them
wrote readily in my note book, from right to left' (28.ix.1853 Frédoux, in *Letters*,
vol. ii, p. 225). I am greatly indebted to Mr E. Kedourie for the following note on
the Arabic text: 'The writing seems to be that of a not very literate East African
hand. The inscription seems to be merely complimentary. The first line is quite
clear, a formula which the writer seems to have mastered, but the second and subsequent lines are blurred and their characters misshapen, and they seem to contain
grammatical mistakes. In view of this, a number of interpretations are possible, and
I have chosen the reading which seemed the most consistent with the text as a whole
and the most probable. Even then, the last few words, which seem to be a date, have
defied reading.' Mr Kedourie suggests this translation (emphasizing that 'a number
of readings are, inevitably, guesswork'): 'O dear one who loveth us and who art
noble, exceedingly noble, the noble one whom we hold dear; Livingstone(?), may
God and his Agent [Prophet] (?) give him help; Abi 'Uthman bena Chubu (or ben
Achubu?) sent it(?) on. . . . (presumably the date)'.

Shiraze Rya Syde bo Sultana of Imame of Muscat. His companion [is] Alem Minokombo Rya Syde bo Sultane Imame of Mascat.

On reaching the village where our canoes lay we found two Arabs from Zanguebar had arrived. They are of the party of Syde Bon Habib ben Salem Lafifi,[1] Rya Syde bo Sultana ben Imame Muscat. They came last year or that previous, and having seen Ponuane's expedition went Westward to Bie & Benguela, and are now intending to go Westward again to obtain goods on Porto's account, which when they have disposed of among the Bashukulompo they will return to their home in Zanguebar. Baloze,[2] English at Zanguebar. They seem to pass and repass accross the country. They came of old and the Barotse compelled their chief to refuse them access into the country because, said they, 'the country is spoiled by children being sold'. The people of Londa came down the river and brought cloth for cattle and were much liked by Santuru.

Matiavo is chief [of] Londa. Cazembe is his son & inferior.[3] They point N.N.W. to Londa.

The slave trade seems pushed into the very centre of the continent from both sides. It must be profitable.

The two Arabs paid me a friendly visit this evening. Our communication is carried on with the assistance [of] guessing, and both being anxious to understand each other we manage wonderfully by words and signs. An ox left for our use was to be slaughtered as soon as it arrived. They came to take leave at midday, but remembering they were probably hungry I told them to wait for a portion. This they gladly consented to

[1] D.L. met this man at Naliele on 12 December 1853 (*Journal 1853–6*), and often again subsequently (cf. *Travels*, pp. 501–8 *passim*; *Zambesi Expedition*, pp. 258, 261, 394, etc.; *Last Journals*, vol. i, pp. 335, 357, etc.). He was a wealthy slave-dealer. 'Rya Syde' etc. apparently means 'subject of Said-bin-Sultan, Imam of Muscat' [and Sultan of Zanzibar] 1806–56 (R. Coupland, *East Africa and its Invaders*, Oxford 1938, pp. 108 etc.).

[2] A Swahili word meaning 'consul, political agent' (F. Johnson, *Standard Swahili-English Dictionary*, 1939, p. 26).

[3] Mwata ('Chief') Yamvo, also known in the literature as Matiavo, Mwanti-yanvwa, etc., is the official name assumed by every successive ruler of the northern BaLunda in Katanga. Kazembe is similarly the name borne by the ruler of the eastern BaLunda (Luapula valley). His chiefdom is an offshoot of Mwata Yamvo's, to whom he consequently refers as 'my father', though the original Kazembe was apparently of alien stock. (Information from Dr I. Cunnison).

do. And knowing their dislike to eating anything slaughtered by Makololo, I shot it and told them to slaughter for themselves a fore and hind leg.[1] A kind word or deed is never lost, and they are each of great importance in the missionary field. They came to shew their respect and endeavoured to communicate all the information they thought interesting. They say that the Leeambae proceeds near to Londa, whose very powerful chief is called Matiavo, and his son Cazembe. He lives on the banks of the Tanganyeka, which from its tides, large waves and sailing boats seems to be a Lake. The Leeambae is nothing compared to it. They say the Londa comes out of the Cassavi.[2]

The Rio Voma, a small river, falls into the sea at Zanguebar, and the Zimbati is like the Leeambae in size.[3] The home of these men is in Zangebar, but they have been accross the country to Loanda and Benguela, and give the same account as others of the intervening country and numbers of English

[1] 'As they had scruples about eating an animal not blooded in their own way, I . . . gave them two legs of an animal slaughtered by themselves' (*Travels*, p. 223).

[2] Kazembe's people live S.E. of Lake Mweru, not Tanganyika. 'Cassavi' is the Kasai, which rises in the same watershed as the 'Londa' (Zambesi), but flows in the opposite direction.

[3] 'Voma' may be the Wami, flowing into the Zanzibar Channel between Sadani and Bagamoyo; 'Zimbati' I cannot identify.

at Loanda & Benguela. (Arabs give Kainko 8 days, Katanga 30 days, Cazembe 30 days, Orore 30 (Terente), Zanguebar sequenta (70)?)[1] They knew the names of the prophets, of David Abraham Ismael Isa[2] &c. But, added they, Mohamed was the greatest of them all. I admired their fearless praise of their prophet. Cazembe and Matiavo his father are not Mahometans. Spoke of the Portuguese as filthy, ĝgram,[3] 'They eat pigs'.

They came in the morning and convoyed me towards the canoes. We reached the town of Mamochisane in the afternoon. Sekeletu said he had been waiting for me, and for me only. He produced a pot of meat and two of beer as refreshment, and told me he had given orders to Liseban[4] to shew me the garden appropriated to the purpose I wished of experiment.[5] As we did not pass Naliele I did not see it. Among the positively asserted news was the arrival of Mrs L and Mr Oswel at the waggons.[6]

We leave tomorrow morning 2d September and will pass Litofe.

Litofe. Sesheke

Friday. Reached Litofe early, and departed on Saturday morning at 20 to 7 a.m. After one hour's stoppage in the morning we had a hard pull from Seori sa Mei[7] to Gonye, which we reached at 20 past 6 P.M. Thus in about $10\frac{1}{2}$ hours we passed through 44 miles of Latitude, or with the Long. at least 50 miles = about 5 miles per hour.[8]

[1] The sentence placed in parentheses was added at the head of the page. Kainko and Cazembe are the names of chiefs (cf. pp. 223, 228), Katanga is the region east of the Upper Kasai (Belgian Congo), and 'Orore' (Rori) is (according to Doke, *Bantu*, p. 53) another name for the WaSangu, a tribe living in Mbeya district (Southern Highlands of Tanganyika). 'Terente' and 'sequenta' are presumably the Portuguese numerals 'trinta' and 'setenta'.   [2] The Arabic form of 'Jesus'.

[3] Probably Swahili *haramu* (from Arabic *haram*), 'forbidden, unlawful, prohibited' (Johnson, *Dictionary*, p. 128). Cf. *Travels*, pp. 223 f.

[4] One of the principal Kololo headmen of Naliele (*Journal 1853-6*); called Lisibani by Jalla (*Litaba*, p. 56).   [5] Cf. above, p. 189.

[6] Like several other reports mentioned in the journal, it was incorrect; cf. below, p. 231.   [7] Mei island (cf. above, p. 199); Tswana *seodi*, island, peninsula.

[8] 'We went 44 miles of Latitude in one day of $10\frac{1}{2}$ hours, and taking into account the windings of the river, and our course being what sailors term a $2\frac{1}{2}$ point one, the actual distance must have been upwards of 50 geographical miles' (Chamberlin, p. 202).

Plagued by an intermittent. The evaporation from the surface of the body during the day is excessive and after the cold stage is over a fire burns within which cannot be quenched by frequent libations of water.

Will leave Gonye on Monday 5th September. Sleep at isd. Sanjamba.[1]

6 at Sekosi's, Lat. 17° 29′ 26″, Long. 24° 33′.

7 at Sesheke, Lat. 17° 31′ 38″, Long. 24 58′.[2]

10th. Remain at Sesheke waiting for Moriantsane. Traders have arrived from the South at Moremi's.[3] I am glad of the detention. The intermittent weakens so, I have been lying useless all the time and only now, Sunday morning, had power to move. Had an audience of about 500.

We came down the river rapidly. From Litofe to Sesheke in four days. We arrived here while a case of stealing from the Mambari was being investigated. The chief thief would probably have been killed, but I suggested payment of a fine. He had nothing, and his master had to pay for him. He went to seek a boy for the purpose, but I preferred to pay for him rather than allow a youth to go into slavery. Many were pleased with my resolution and the Mambari were satisfied. What I gave was of more value than the missing goods.[4]

Mpepe's character & intrigues

It is now evident that I cannot without risk go up to the Borotse with the horse, for the Tsetse bites by night. During the great rains he goes to breed and does not bite. This is not unpleasant news for me, for I had become disgusted with the

[1] Not shown on maps consulted.

[2] In *Travels*, the latitude of Sekhosi's is given as 17° 29′ 13″ S. (p. 208), and the longitude of Sesheke as 25° 13′ E. (p. 684, from observations made on 31 August 1855).

[3] James Chapman (1831–72, author of *Travels in the Interior of South Africa*, 2 vols., 1868), Francis Thompson (killed by Native rebels in Griqualand West, 1878), and Donald Campbell (son of a Grahamstown physician), had reached Moremi's village late in August (Chapman, vol. i, p. 164; for Thompson and Campbell, cf. *Matabele Thompson: his Autobiography*, ed. Nancy Rouillard, revised ed., 1953, pp. 17 ff., 127 ff.).

[4] This incident is described somewhat differently in *Travels*, pp. 234 f., where D.L. says also: 'The case was referred to me, and I solved the difficulty by paying for the loss myself, and sentencing the thief to work out an equivalent with his hoe in a garden. This system was immediately introduced, and thieves are now sentenced to raise an amount of corn proportioned to their offences.'

slave merchant's party when I saw the chains &c, and more than all became more fully acquainted with the intrigues carried on by Mpepe. Frequent and long conferences were carried on in Senor Porto's house, the only persons present being Mpépe Sandillah and Senor Porto himself.[1] All Sekeletu's ivory was handed over to Porto by Mpépe. Oxen in great numbers were furnished for his table, and with the full authority of Mpépe he went through all the Banyeti villages buying up slaves and ivory, to the great detriment of the lawful chief and spoliation of the villages, for when it was said, Mpepe orders you all to sell children, the poor people were in some cases compelled to obey in order not to displease him. In others a man who disliked his wife sold her and child into slavery. It is very probable, though Porto will say nothing of it here, that Mpepe has given off the lands of Katongo to the Portuguese. Hence the Portuguese flagstaff and stockade. They furnished Mpepe with a small cannon,[2] and had he succeeded in destroying Sekeletu their arms would have been employed in bringing all the Makololo into subjection and establishing the slave trade on a firm footing in this region.

When I mentioned to Porto that Mpepe was killed he said, 'Yes I know he spoke a great deal against Sekeletu'. Up at the Borotse, when he had got time to think on the great loss he had sustained, he ventured to speak of him in very favourable terms, 'A very brave man, very liberal'.[3] Among Bechuanas I never met with a specimen of conciet equal to his. He was a very little man. Sebitane asked his father to send him to his (S.) town to look after his cattle, as he was now getting old and unable to do so himself. The little man took it for granted that with the care of the cattle he must be destined to be the future chief, and took possession of the cattle more as his own than Sebitane's. The chief could scarcely get a good ox to slaughter, and at last in irritation said, if you treat my son

[1] Silva Porto relates that Mphephe sought his aid in a scheme to secede from Sekeletu and establish an independent kingdom in the country of the BaIla; he claims, however, to have decided against taking part (*Viagens*, pp. 118 f.). D.L.'s reference to 'Sandillah' (cf. above, p. 83) is a curious slip of the pen; elsewhere he wrote, 'Long interviews were held in which were the slave merchant, Mpepe, and a Mambari interpreter' (*Letters*, vol. ii, p. 219). The interpreter's name was Joaquim Mariano (Silva Porto, *op. cit.*, p. 108).

[2] '. . . a large blunderbuss to be mounted as a cannon' (*Travels*, p. 216).

[3] Silva Porto does not mention discussing Mphephe's death with D.L.

so he will kill you, I did not give you the chieftainship when I gave you charge of the cattle. Mpepe then commenced to work by means of enchantments, and built a house for the express purpose of slaughtering oxen therein and, as Sebitane thought, bewitching him. In reference to this house Sebitane said to Sekeletu, 'if that house does not eat me it will eat you'.[1] He was extremely anxious to obtain a name for bravery, but when he went against Masiko he saw an appearance of resistance and returned without striking a blow. The only engagement in which he ever appeared was at Sekota and there it was a flying enemy.

When Mr Oswel and I met him[2] he said, 'Why go to Sesheke when I have come; though you don't see Sesheke you see me'!!! and again when I met him where he was killed[3] he said, 'Where are you going?' 'To the Borotse'. 'But I have come and you will find nothing there but a ruin', viz. When I the great Mpepe left there was nothing & nobody worth seeing in all the Borotse country.

These Intrigues make me quite dislike the idea of travelling in company with slave merchants. I shall try and proceed by my own route Westward, and where ever I find a people it will not be my fault if they are unwilling to recieve me again. A few sweet words spoken from the heart have a wonderful effect. A short route back would be through Londa and down the Leeba or Londa.

The Makololo would have starved the party of Porto out of the country forthwith, but I persuaded them not to do so at present as it might be prejudicial to me in the west.[4] He will not be allowed to take up his residence so easily at Katongo again.

The crowding together from all quarters of slave merchants to the Bashukulompo country shews it must be a very profitable trade. The Zanguebar Arabs pass accross the country in order to get supplies of goods and probably in order to dispose of their slaves most profitably, for there is much less risk in shipping from West African ports than from the East.

---

[1] Cf. above, p. 183. [2] Cf. above, p. 45. [3] Cf. above, p. 181.

[4] 'They thought of attacking them by starvation. As the chief sufferers in case of such an attack would have been the poor slaves chained in gangs, I interceded for them. . . .' (*Travels*, p. 216).

The oceanic current carries a ship accross to Brazil in 25 days.

The internal evils of Africa make the slave trade appear a small evil in comparison. A number of women and girls were brought in today from a tribe living ajacent to Mosilikatse. Their husbands were engaged in making canoes for the Matibele, and it is believed that an attack on the Makololo by their means is contemplated. It was considered good policy to break up these canoes and capture the wives and children of these men, and they were accordingly distributed among the people of Sekeletu. The canoe makers themselves are between two fires, if they obey one chief they displease the other. Such captures are of constant occurrence throughout the whole country. No country needs the gospel more than Africa, and no people are so completely in the dark as to the effects of missions on savage tribes than the Colonists of South Africa, more especially the Eastern portion of them.

19th. We remained over 8th, 9th, 10* & 11th at Sesheke waiting for Moriantsané. He came on Sunday evening, and we started on Monday morning. I walked for two days and then the horses which had been sent for came up. Recieved letters when I reached the waggons on 16th by Mrss Thompson and Chapman, who left immediately without my seeing them.[1] Weather very hot indeed, close and cloudy. When rains begin I intend going West. Clouds prevented my taking Lunars at Sesheke, but the Lat. from two observations was 17° 31' 36". It is about 25 miles East of Sekhosi's.

Sunday. A large audience as usual, but not so attentive as could be desired. Kuruman people amazed at the indifference and indecorum. Their own fathers plagued the missionaries much more. These however are it must be confessed terrible savages. A garden is hoed for me.

* Theft from the Mambari would have been punished by death but I recommended fining instead. The chief man went to bring a fine but it was a boy who was brought at the time. He had no idea of anything else. I then gave as much property as the man had stolen and redeemed him.[2] [D.L.]

---

[1] Chapman relates (vol. i, pp. 179 f.) that on 1 October, 'receiving a letter from Dr. Livingstone, from which it appeared that Poonoani [Ponwane] had informed Sekeletu that we had already left, I determined on paying the former a hasty visit.' While on the way, he learned that his oxen and horses had been bitten by tsetse. 'This disastrous intelligence' made him change his plans, 'and we immediately put about to return towards the lake [Ngami]'.   [2] Cf. above, p. 231.

21st Wedensday. A party of Batauana came yesterday. Damaras visited Lechulathebe, and white traders are reported as trying to go to Libébe again. A very thick haze covers the horizon and last [night] there [was] thunder and lightning in the North. The haze is so thick nothing of the sun can be seen mornings and evenings when it is 8 or 10 degrees from the horizon.

The Damaras are precursors of two white men, very probably Anderson and another.[1] The aggressions of Lechulathebe irritate the Makololo. They have captured people from Bapalleñ and again try and direct the attention of the Makololo to the Boers & the proposal to remove to Kueba hills.[2]

24th. A return of cold by a south wind yesterday. Sekeletu promises to supply cattle for those which are bitten by the Tsetse. The path Westward is very difficult in consequence of the tsetse prevailing so generally in the district West of this.

25th Sunday. A quiet audience today. The seed being sown, the least of all seeds now, but it will grow a mighty tree. It is as it were a small stone cut out of a mountain, but it will fill the whole earth. He that believeth shall not make haste. Surely if God can bear with hardened impenitent sinners for 30, 40 or 50 years, waiting to be gracious, we may take it for granted that his is the best way. He could destroy his enemies, but he waits to be gracious. To become irritated with their stubborness and hardness of heart is ungodlike.

27. Witnessed the sickening spectacle of a number of spears brought in from a Batoka village which was situated between Mosilikatse and the Makololo. They were forced nearer the Matibele and then killed by Makololo because they had gone nearer. About 20 captives, women and children, were brought and distributed among the people here. Poor creatures, their lot is hard in this life and they have no hope for the future. Satan is a hard master.

---

[1] Charles John Andersson (1827–67), author of *Lake Ngami* (1856) and several other works, was the first European to reach the Lake from the West (July 1853). He had no white companions, though at the Lake he found the trader J. H. Wilson, who had come by the usual route across the Kalahari.

[2] Kgwebe Hills, S.E. of Lake Ngami (cf. above, p. 20). The 'proposal to remove' there may refer to Sebetwane's idea of settling closer to Europeans (cf. above, p. 26 and also p. 137).

28th Wed. Mothibe and Mamire[1] came to the waggon about midday, and shortly afterwards Sekeletu. The conversation led to the policy which by their counsels the chief is following. I gave a full & frank statement of what I concieve to be the truth as to the murdering &c which has been transacted within the last few months. They attempted to defend some parts of his conduct but failed, and at last joined in condemning the shedding of blood. Then a long discussion ensued on the gospel. They persist in believing that medicines or charms must be used in order to cause a reception of the gospel, and after prolonging the discussion in the true palaver style untill night we part with a promise to renew it on the morrow. I offered to commence teaching to read and the offer was accepted.

1st October Sat. Mothibe and Mamire came and continued the whole day at the Alphabet.[2] In the evening they and fo[u]r or five others knew the Alphabet perfectly. They have again spent a day on it and continue to make gratifying progress.

Nokwane's illness

Nokwane[3] is very ill—not expected to live. He sees the image of Mpepe before his eyes continually and, says he, it is Mpepe who is killing him. The power of conscience. Some circumstances have been mentioned by Mothibe which make it probable that the murder of Mpepe was premeditated. Nokwane was the first who caught him.[4] Explained to Mothibe the nature of the stain which murder leaves. Will go & see Nokwane tomorrow.

[1] Mamidi Bogatsu, senior half-brother of Pulane (cf. above, p. 212). D.L. says in *Travels*, p. 513, that he 'had married the mother of Sekeletu', but in *Narrative*, p. 272, calls him Sekeletu's 'uncle'. According to Jalla, he was Sekeletu's maternal uncle (*malume*), and when his nephew died in 1863 (allegedly because bewitched by him) he tried to usurp the chieftainship; he was, however, defeated in battle by Mpololo and fled to Letsholathebe, by whom he was put to death (*Litaba*, pp. 63 f.). The BaTawana told me in 1940 that he and several other Kololo refugees were killed for conspiring to murder Letsholathebe.

[2] 'Sekeletu's father-in-law and step-father were appointed to learn to read, in order that their experience may serve as a beacon to others' (24.ix.1853 Tidman, in Chamberlin, p. 204).

[3] Cf. above, p. 155.

[4] Cf. *Travels*, p. 182. This conflicts with the version given above (p. 183), according to which Mphephe was killed by his own people at Sekeletu's command.

People engaged in killing Elephants. Hear from & reply to Wilson.[1] Anderson reaches the Lake.

Busy writing letters to Roy Geog. of London and Paris, Lieut. Colonel Steele, Maclear, Mrs L. 3 (8), Charles 2, Thompson, Revd Moffat, Oswel, Paris Geo. Soc., Fredoux, Holmes, Hoffmeyr, Watt, Parents, Mary 3, Dr Tidman, & brother John, Dupratt.[2] To Steele about my perplexities & request advice to meet me at Loanda.

6th October. Send off my parcel with a bag of seeds.[3] Elephants abound. People trying to kill them.

7th Friday. The belief in the bewitching powers of the Borotse seems to affect Nokwane, and his friends all look on the case as hopeless.[4] To catch one charmed by them is, as they express it, like catching a serpent. The power of conscience is not recognized by them. Sent off a packet of letters this morning. The heat is oppressive, 103° in the shade in the afternoon and 90° at 10 o'clock at night. Mosquitoes commenced.

Borotse Boatman's song

The Borotse Boatman[5] made a ditty on our passage up to

---

[1] The letters were concerned chiefly with some remarks D.L. had published about Europeans trading with Natives. Their content is described briefly in *Letters*, vol. ii, p. 239.

[2] Cf. above for Steele (p. 68), Maclear (p. 81), Thompson (p. 87), Moffat (p. 18), Oswell (p. 7), Frédoux (p. 96), Watt (p. 69), Tidman (p. 87), Duprat (p. 81). 'Mrs L.' and 'Mary' presumably both refer to D.L.'s wife, and 'brother John' was her brother John Smith Moffat (1835–1918), then a theological student at Cheshunt College, Herts. The other persons named, apart from D.L.'s parents, were his younger brother Charles (1821–73), a clergyman in the United States but subsequently a member of the Zambesi expedition; Captain Gideon Skull Holmes, U.S. consul at Cape Town, through whom D.L.'s letters to Charles were sent; and Mr Hofmeyr, also of Cape Town, from whom D.L. had rented a house when there in 1852 (cf. *Letters*, vol. ii, p. 168).

The letters to D.L.'s parents, Robert Moffat, and Frédoux, are published in *Letters*. vol. ii, pp. 214–29; those to Thompson, Tidman, and Frédoux, in Chamberlin, pp. 198–212; that to the Paris Geographical Society in *Bulletin de la Société de Géographie*, IVe Sér., May 1854, pp. 367–72; and extracts from those to Tidman, Steele, Maclear, and the Royal Geographical Society, in *JRGS*, vol. 24, 1854, pp. 291–306.

[3] 'I think this goes by Walwich [Walvis] Bay. If the packet should reach you by this route, a small bag of seeds for the Botanic garden [at Cape Town] accompanies it. They were collected on the way here' (11.x.1853 Thompson, in Chamberlin, p. 214). The 'parcel', etc., were taken south by Chapman.

[4] Nokwane died of 'his strange disease' before D.L.'s return from Luanda in 1855 (*Travels*, p. 503).   [5] Presumably Mashawana (cf. above, p. 225).

the Kabompo. The chief feature in it beside the incidents of the voyage was the chorus Leeambye. It may be Englished thus :

> We sailed along the Leeambye,
> The Leeambye, the Leeambye.
> Close by the banks away we hie,
> And fear to wash in Leeambye :
> Its alligators are so sly,
> Always hungry & seldom shy.
> The Leeambye, the Leeambye ;
> We went intent to do no harm,
> Yet never slept without alarm.
> Angry river ! you made us sigh ;
> You treat us ill, O Leeambye !
> We reached a confluence of brothers,
> The Leeba and Loeti rivers.
> Billowy wavy river ! Nobody knows,
> Whence it comes, or whither it goes.
> We sat the red Kabompo by,
> And saw above us in the sky,
> Barimo sit in grand Peecho,
> But what about I do not know.
> If they were angry, so was I,
> And that with thee, O Leeambye.[1]

8th. The punishment of choking or strangulation has been of frequent occurrence among the Makololo. Women have been called into the Kotla and the sentence forthwith executed. The bodies are dragged off immediately to be the food of vultures.

A song bird enlivens us in the mornings with its full note of 'O pretty po, pretty po' &c.

9th Sunday. Surely the good seed will find a reception in some hearts. They have need of it, for they have no comforter in their afflictions. Moriye has had a sore heart ever

---

[1] The following is all that D.L. cared to publish of this 'ditty' (*Travels*, pp. 523 f.):
'The words of the canoe-song are—
   "The Leeambye! Nobody knows,
   Whence it comes and whither it goes." '

since Sebituane died, and now it preys on her spirits and causes her to dream & think perpetually of those who are dead. Mokanju dreamed of the Barimo perpetually, some wished to kill him, others not, and Nokwané is seized with a strange affection, all his muscles creep & portions of each contract continually. At midday all the muscles of his body & limbs contract & relax so as to cause him to cry out and appear to be in the act of catching people. He sees Barimo too. A large dose of laudanum & camphor gave him a sleep and caused profuse perspiration. He cannot vomit. If he does it will have a good effect on his imagination. It is the power of conscience.

Dialogue shewing rain maker's arguments

12th Wedensday. Hot winds prevail now, they are loaded with dust. The atmosphere seems thick, and towards the horizon of a colour as if mixed with smoke. The sun sets in this thick haze quite red and he gives no rays below $10°$ or $15°$. The wind ceases in the evenings but begins about 6 or 7 o'clock in the morning and blows very strongly all day. Rain is much longed for and certainly this is the most unpleasant time of the year. Dances quite exhaust the performers in a few hours. The following contains some of the arguments which I have heard used among the Bakwains.[1]

Missionary (coming to a rain doctor who has a great number [of] bulbs, roots, plants, and pots & powders about him). Hail, Father! What are you doing with so many medicines?

Rain Doctor. I thank you, my son. I am charming the rain. We are killed by the Sun.

M. You can make rain then.

R.D. We need rain. Without it we have no milk, the cattle having no grass. We cannot get roots in the field either if the stalks are not brought to the surface by rain. Without it the women would hoe the gardens in vain, we should get no corn. We should perish if we had no rain.

M. As to the benefits of the rain you and I are of one mind, but I believe no one can make rain but God.

[1] The published version of this famous dialogue (*Travels*, pp. 23–25) is both shorter and also differs in many details from that given above. Still another version is found on pp. 78–81 of a notebook in the Livingstone Memorial, Blantyre.

R.D. You water your garden by means of the river, but we who use no irrigation must make rain or we should get no corn. We have done it from time immemorial, and we know it is better to apply rain to the whole plant, than a little river water applied only to its root. You do according to the customs of your forefathers, and so do we. You don't need rain but we should die without it.

M. As to the benefits & good influences of the rain, and superiority over irrigation, we are perfectly agreed. That which I dispute is that your medicines have any influence on the rain whatever. God alone can make it.

R.D. I know that perfectly. God alone can make rain, my medicines don't make it. But he has given us the knowledge of certain plants and trees by which we pray to him to make rain for us. We charm the clouds, & He makes the rain for us.

M. But God has told us that there is only one way by which we can pray to him acceptably, viz. by Jesus Christ.

R.D. Truly. And he has told us differently. God has been very good to both white and black. To the white he has given the knowledge of guns, gunpowder, horses, and many other things which we know nothing about. He has given you wisdom too. We see it. To us blacks he has not been so liberal, but he has given us the knowledge of some things too, and the most important is that of certain trees and plants which we use to make rain. We have the knowledge of rain making, you have it not. Now we don't despise those things God has given you, though we are ignorant of them. Nor should you despise what he has given us, though you do not know nor understand them.

M. When did God give you the knowledge of rain making?

R.D. In the beginning, of old. When we first opened our eyes in the world, we found our fathers working with these medicines, they were taught them by their fathers, & so from the beginning, and we now do as they told us to do. We follow in their trail.

M. But God has given us his book, and that gives us correct information as to what he did. Our origin is the same, and in the book which never forgets we have what God revealed to our common ancestors, and he tells us that he has appointed seed time and harvest, summer and winter, and that he gives rain from heaven and fruitful seasons. And this he does to the good and the evil alike, and I think he would give you rain without any medicines. I don't despise your knowledge, I only believe you are mistaken, and should like you to make a trial. God will give us rain if we get it at all.

R.D. No he won't. He might to you white people, but not to us blacks to whom he has given the knowledge of his plants. He has no heart to us.

M. Have you ever tried?

R.D. How could we? We should starve. The town would become scattered. And whoever thought of trying starvation? We cannot buy corn as you do. We must grow it, and it is rain which causes it to spring up and yield.

M. But your medicines so frequently fail, and you never use them except at New & full moon, or when you see the clouds collecting.

R.D. Truly. And so it is with all medicines. We administer medicines to sick people and so do you, though people often die. If God does not please to heal, the patient dies. And so it is with the rain. We do not fail, but God refuses to give us rain. We have always made rain, it's our custom from of old.

M. I think you are wrong about the medicines. We apply them to animate, you to inanimate things. You often make a great smoke, and it never reaches the clouds which you say you are charming.

R.D. We apply medicines to every thing, and if you wish us to throw aside our medicines why do you retain your own?

M. I apply them to living beings, and see and know their effects. You make smoke and cause all the women of the town to pass through it. They feel no effect. You sprinkle all with medicines, no effect is visible, but effects are always visible from my medicines. I can foretell their effects. Can you tell us when we shall have rain?

[*R.D.*] There are defects in all medicines, but I see plainly you don't want rain. We do, and cannot do without it. If you make rain for us I shall let it alone.

M. I do wish rain most heartily, and I think your work tends to drive away rain & displease God. He wishes us to feel our dependance on Him alone, and though you say you pray to him all the women in the town believe that you make the rain. They call it your rain, & praise you for it instead of God.

R.D. Well, if you wish rain and pray to God for it, why does it not come? You fail as well as we.

M. We pray for it but do not make it. We leave it to his good pleasure to give or withhold it. You say you pray to him, but you believe you make it independant of him.

R. And so we do. We make it, and if people—witches— did not hinder us by their witchcraft you would soon see it.

[*M.*] Well, as you can make it will you make rain for me during the dry season, or on all the gardens now and not on mine? Or will you appoint any day within a fortnight in which it will rain?

(If he accedes to any of these propositions he is easily exposed. But as of old the King was generally the chief priest too, so here the chief is generally the principal rain maker. And a very large [field] is hoed by all the women in the town as the price of rain from the chief, and collections of corn are made by the chief *for the rain makers* as soon as the harvest is brought in, the lion's share of which remains in his possession.[1] Then he is loudly praised when the rain falls, but daily importuned if it fails. His relatives are also bothered, & hints are given of transferring allegiance to other chiefs if rain is withheld. The more ignorant of the population are retained in their allegiance by believing in the rain making of the chief, & the principal men gain popularity by presents of oxen to the rain maker. The great droughts, accompanied by hot winds, render the people languid and dissatisfied, and some employment is necessary. This is found in numerous expedients for gaining time which the rain doctor knows so well how to invent.)

M. Let us try our medicines. I shall foretell the effects of mine on any person or animal. Will you now cause the clouds to assemble?

---

[1] Among the BaTswana the chief is indeed 'generally the principal rainmaker'. But the field cultivated for him is not so much 'the price of rain' as the means by which he regulates the cycle of agricultural activities, all of which must be initiated there, and the corn furnished by the harvest tribute is used mainly to feed people visiting him and to relieve those in want. Cf. Schapera, *Native Land Tenure in the Bechuanaland Protectorate*, 1943, pp. 155-7, 196-8.

R.D. I need one medicine for it which I will send for first.

M. If you really believed you could make rain, command the clouds, you would not be unwilling to try. I can never get you to make a trial. You wait till you see the clouds coming, then commence your incantations, so that no one can percieve whether your medicines have any effect. I think they have no effect.

R.D. No effect! Magala makapā.[1] Whose rain was that which fell lately but mine? And by whom did the people eat corn for so many years? Who caught the clouds for them but me?

M. The rain was given by God, & would have fallen had you let your medicines alone.

R.D. Of course, and it is so with all medicines, people get well though they use no medicines. But I see you don't want rain, and your talk is just like that of all who talk on subjects they do not understand. Perhaps you are talking, perhaps not. To me you appear to be perfectly silent.

M. Remain well, my friend.

R.D. Depart pleasantly, Father.[2]

The argument may be continued for days together, and the only effect produced on their minds is a conviction that we do not want them to have rain. They sometimes become angry, but apol[o]gize by saying, it is our stomachs make us speak so, if we had rain we should feel very differently. If the corn is withering they become very anxious and vigilant, and woe to the person who ventures to bring a branch of any tree, an elephant's tusk, or any forbidden article into the town in broad daylight then.[3]

[1] Tswana *magalamakapaa*, an exclamation of surprise.

[2] The last two sentences are translations of formulae conventionally used when people part: *Sala sentle*, 'remain well', and *Tsamaya sentle*, 'go well (or pleasantly)'.

[3] Taboos such as those mentioned are still observed in many Tswana tribes during the early part of the cultivating season, in order to prevent 'the spoiling of the year', i.e. failure of the crops. Anybody found violating them is liable to punishment. Cf. Schapera, *op. cit.*, pp. 186 f., 263 f.

VII

NOTES ON WILD ANIMALS ETC.

Taste for the Beautiful

13th [October] Thursday. Missionaries ought to cultivate a taste for the beautiful. We are necessarily compelled to contemplate much moral impurity and degradation. We are so often doomed to disappointment, we are apt to become either callous or melancholy. Or if preserved from these, the constant strain on the sensibilities is likely to injure the bodily health. On this account it seems necessary to cultivate that faculty for the gratification of which God has made such universal provision. See the green Earth and blue sky, the lofty mountain & verdant valley, the glorious orbs of day and night & the starry canopy with all their celestial splendour, the graceful flowers so chaste in form & perfect in colouring. The various forms of animated life present, to him whose heart is at peace with God through the blood of his son, an indescribable charm. He sees in the calm beauties of nature such abundant provision for the welfare of humanity & animated existence, there appears on the quiet repose of earth's scenery the benignant smile of a father's love. The sciences exhibit such wonderful intelligence and design in all their various ramifications, some time ought to be devoted to them before engaging in missionary work. The heart may often be cheered by observing the operation of an ever present intelligence, and we may feel that we are leaning on his bosom while living in a world clothed in beauty and robed with the glorious perfections of its maker & preserver. We must feel that there is a Governor among the nations who will bring all his plans with respect to our human family to a glorious consummation. He who stays his mind on his ever present, ever energetic God will 'not fret himself because of evil doers'. 'He that believeth shall not make haste'.

Facts about Elephants

14th Friday. A large elephant passed close to the waggon

this morning. The people have begun to shoot them, and very soon none will appear in this part of the country. They retire before the gun sooner than any other animal. He alone deserves to be named the 'King of the Forest'. He retires before no animal but man, and all others flee from him in dread. If not compelled by scarcity of water to remain in one locality the large game forsake his feeding ground. No other animal dares to dispute his sway. A black rhinoceros, in the stupid rashness for which he is famed, was observed by the Bakwains once to give battle to the King of beasts and was instantly crushed to the ground and killed. His amazing strength is seen in the devastations among trees where he has been feeding. Tall Mimosa trees from one to two feet in diameter are strewed around, having been twisted down in order to allow his feeding on the extreme branches. When exasperated he rushes through thickets, making thorn and other trees of twenty feet high bend under his feet as so many bulrushes. The trees spring up again and no opening is left by which the huntsmen may pursue him. Palmyras sixty feet high are shaken, moved hither & thither with the greatest apparent ease in order to dislodge the fruit, which he picks up from the ground and eats.

The height of the African elephant is from ten to twelve feet. The female is about nine feet, or one foot taller than a large Indian male. But there is a small variety in Africa too which does not rise above eight feet (Makongkwané).[1]

The colour is brownish black. Some seem grey, or the colour of road dust in England. The skin is spongy, and bare. A very few extremely coarse hairs exist about his head and end of the tail. Those in the latter situation resemble pieces of whalebone more than hair.

A near approximation to the size of an animal whose footprints are met with may be found by measuring that of the forefoot. Twice its circumference is the height of the elephant.[2] And the deeper the marks of the cracks in the sole of his foot, the older he may be considered, and the heavier the ivory he carries.

[1] *Lekolonkwane* (plur, *makolonkwane*), 'a species of small elephant' (Brown). Not recognized by taxonomists.

[2] This rule, D.L. says in *Travels*, p. 563, 'is applicable only to full-grown animals'.

The African differs from the Indian elephant chiefly in the greater height, size of the ear, & different arrangement of the enamel of the molar teeth. The average height of the African is I have already remarked 12 feet, while the average of Indian Elephants stand 8 feet high. The highest Indian Elephant ever known was 10 feet. The external ear of the African species (male) measures from $4\frac{1}{2}$ to $5\frac{1}{2}$ feet in diameter, while that of the Indian is from 18 inches to two feet. The enamel of the African elephant runs in wavy lines, while that of the Indian exists in ovals or what are termed oblate spheroids.

The food of the Elephant is very much varied, and in noting his extensive bill of fare we remark many very nutritious articles. His food exists in such abundance in the country he never touches the grass on which he is obliged to feed in England. He probably takes it as men do sawdust in bread. He devours different aquatic plants and roots abounding in starch, such as the tsitla, Lotus, Reeds & stalks of corn, maize, Water melons, pumpkins in the gardens and wild melons in the fields, different kinds of Mimosa and acacia trees containing much gum in their fibres. The woody parts pass along the alimentary canal undigested, but all the gummy matter is probably digested. Among gum yielding trees on which he feeds we know the Mōka,[1] Mahata, Mohotlo (camel thorn), Mokhi, Mongana (wait a bit thorn), Moselesele (a low thorn bush whose straight thorns cut like knives, he digs the roots of these), Mokhoba, Moshu. These are either Mimosa or Acacia. Other gum yielding trees are Mopane, Monato, Mokabi, Mochweeré, Morala. Of trees which yield saccharine juices we know the Mohonono, Moretloa and grape vine. Of tubers and bulbs he has a considerable variety. Some yield gelatine & some water & astringent tannic matter. Mokotlané, Moraroane, Khané, Sekanamé, Lerushua, Motlalagari, Sekopané, Likongkota, Sibité, Sehouhatsa, Mokaikai, Mositsane (used for tanning), Segwhere, Likokwe, Mositatlou, Mosimama, Mocaca (bitter), Tlakushubé, Tetele, monokané.

Furnished with these the male can bear the want of water

[1] For identifications of the trees and other plants named here, and in similar lists later in the chapter, see below, Appendix IV.

for several days, but females with calves require to visit the water almost daily. In respect to the habitats of the African and Indian species, the former feeds far from fountains while the latter is almost always found in the vicinity of rivers and never far from water. When however he does come to the water he seems to have great enjoyment. He throws the water over his body with his proboscis and screams with delight. If the banks are not muddy he takes to the water readily and swims strongly. The whole body is submerged except the proboscis, top of the head, and ridge of the back. If a herd is driven into a muddy hollow they are so much at a loss from sinking in the mire they will stand till the whole are shot. When annoyed by pitfalls near the water he comes to it only by night, and when morning dawns he has regained his feeding ground 15 or 20 miles distant.

Even in his wild state he is remarkable for his sagacity. In parts where a range of pit falls are dug so as quite to fill up the space down to the water except walls about 2 feet broad between them, the leading elephant in the herd will pass down along this wall or partition, opening all the pitfalls on each side of his route. And when driven into a kind of trap (in India) for catching & taming them, a male has been observed to seize a female and push her before him as a sort of feeler of the ground, he all the while preventing her from turning to either side by keeping her between his tusks. The African elephant has never been tamed at this end of the continent, but in the wild state opens pitfalls and helps a companion out who may have fallen into one of them.

When wishing to descend the steep bank of a river each animal sits down on his haunches and, keeping his forelegs stiffly extended before him, he glides down a declivity so steep that a man could not walk down it.

Herds of opposite sexes are rarely or never seen together. Young males associate with females till their sexual distinctions become apparent. They are then expelled from the female herd, and seeing they are probably forty or fifty years old they are well able to shift for themselves. A few males follow the herd of females when in 'must', and the latter probably drop out towards them. Dicitur, coitum a nonnullo vidisse.

The female is supposed to go three years with young, but the supposition is founded on the fact alone that they have occasionally brought forth after three years' captivity. In a tame state, when their chief food is grass and so different from that which they delight in, they are sterile. When born it is, in proportion to the size it afterwards attains, the least of all calves. It is not so large as the calf of a common cow. Many full grown dogs are larger. As it imitates the movements of its ponderous progenitors the little red thing presents a most grotesque appearance.

The female shews much less affection for her young than any other large animal. She deserts it instantly on being pursued, while the Rhinoceros always keeps hers in front. Indeed, after shooting the latter animal it is known whether the wound will be immediately fatal or not, by the position she assumes with respect to her calf. If she places herself behind it the bullet has not pierced a very vital part. If she starts off before it she will probably not run more than one hundred yards before she drops dead. While the female elephant does not seem to care much though her calf is speared by her side, she however lifts it out of pitfalls. Her teats are situated on her breasts in front. The milk is a thin whey-looking liquid possessing a pleasant taste.

Elephants attain to maturity about the age of fifty and live between 200 & 300 years.

The largest Indian Elephant seldom carries a tusk 80 lbs in weight. But an African was shot by Mr Oswel at Kiria,[1] River Zouga, with a tusk weighing 106 lbs. The two tusks were 205 lbs. Another was shot by the same gentleman on the Limpopo, one tusk of which weighed 101 lbs. These weights have we believe never been exceeded except in one instance (136).[2] Many animals of both sexes are tuskless.[3] Others have broken off the ends of the tusk by using them to wrench up the roots of trees. The digging for bulbs is performed by the forefoot.

In hunting elephants bullets hardened with Tin, Zinc or

[1] Kidia Hill, 21° 26′ S., 23° 47′ E.

[2] In *Travels*, D.L. gives examples of larger tusks from Angola (pp. 438 f.), and says also that the size increases 'as we approach the equator' (p. 564).

[3] 'We met an elephant on the Kalomo which had no tusks. This is as rare a thing in Africa, as it is to find them with tusks in Ceylon' (*Travels*, p. 545).

best of all type metal, must be used. Soft bullets or a gun which does not drive hard only irritate, for they never injure beyond the external muscular covering. One hardened bullet will go to the heart of a female but from four to six at a distance of 30 paces are required for a male.

The female is more irritable than the male, charges furiously when first wounded and runs faster, but seldom repeats the charge. She is soon disheartened if she cannot get away from the huntsman. It is different with the male. He seldom charges when first attacked, but renews the chase again and again. If he charges or is chased and fatigued, a considerable portion of the vital power seems expended [and] he is more easily killed. If he stands still and husbands his strength, as it were, he may remain so for two hours, although he has recieved a wound which would have proved mortal forthwith had he charged.

His pace in charging is equal to that of a horse at full gallop, and his screaming is then terrific. It resembles the word Furreep and is peculiarly piercing. He can sustain this for about 150 yards only & is then exhausted. The Bushmen take advantage of this fact, for when he charges they glide off at right angles to his course and, keeping up with him, as soon as they observe that he is looking beyond them they rush in and stab him with their spears. When preparing to charge he curls up his trunk as a butterfly does, spreads out his ears, & sometimes retires a few paces, or puts his head to a considerable tree & glancing past then breaks it right off before him as if to intimidate his tormentor. Two shots in the face at this time are said to prevent a charge, or a whistle behind or barking of dogs in the same position will either prevent a charge or arrest him in it. The Bushmen use the whistle, and some sportsmen dogs. In the latter case no danger is incurred, he pays no attention to man if dogs are barking about him. It is with regret one sees this noble animal, chief of the ways of God, so venerable from his great age, so often cut down.

His paces are a slow and quick walk, the hind legs bending forward like the knees. Though apparently walking he passes over the ground very quickly. In running this walk is only increased in quickness. A slight indentation of the toes enables the native to see by his foot prints whether the animal has been running or walking.

The flesh is excellent, particularly the part of the proboscis on the face, and [the] forefoot. He has usually a large quantity of fine white fat.

Sat. 15th. Hear that George's servant[1] has been using freedoms with the wife of Mahale. The consequences will be serious. This man was once a pet with a missionary, he thought of making him a teacher, but he has become a nuisance (escaped punishment on my account).

No one ought to deal in hints. If I have anything to say to a neighbour, I ought to say it boldly. If a person gives me a hint I ought to take no notice of it. It is lending countenance to a bad custom to let any one know that his hint is taken and has caused the annoyance he intended, and if one is given to take hints he often imagines he is hinted at when the speaker has no thought of him. I have never given a hint so far as I remember to any living soul, and never recieve a hint intended to annoy (& to these alone I refer) except by mistake or when off my gaurd.

16th Sunday. The attendance is always good and generally very attentive. Chief has the mumps. It is not an uncommon complaint here. Nokwane is improved by large opiates. Mr Thompson has left Moremi's village.[2] Mahale's wife said to him, If I am guilty you will become sick. This is believed evidence that she has medicines of the Banyeti by which she can inflict death. The weaker parties in this land are always believed to [have] the power of revenging themselves by means of enchantments. This makes their masters less overbearing and cruel. Some imagine they change themselves into lions & attack the cattle of those who may offend them.

Swallows

17th. Saw a small flock of white bellied swallows pass the waggon in the evening going in a straight line South East.

[1] Identified in *Letters*, vol. ii, p. 232, as Oepeng (cf. above, p. 105), a convert of William Ashton at Kuruman.

[2] Chapman states (vol. i, p. 182) that he and Thompson left Dinyanti together on 10 October, 'halted for a day near Moreymi's village', and started again for Lake Ngami on the 13th.

On the morning of the 18th when going to the town saw a pair of the brown bellied sitting on a bush.

I saw the first house swallows on the 19th September last year at Kuruman, and the first Kite a few days afterwards. Mr Moffat observed the swallows a week before. He has seen the Kites on the mountains in winter. I saw the first kite on the 6th July at Naliele. The sandmartins seem to remain at the Orange river too, for I saw some there in August 1852, or in winter.

18. The first shower fell last night, being accompanied with loud thunder. George's servant's conduct has almost produced a fatal effect on Mahali. His wife used the words of an incantation, and he was seized with well marked symptoms of inflammation of the bowels. He had been complaining a little previously, and the incantation proved a[n] exciting cause. He had great coldness of the extremities, countenance pinched, lancinating pains over the whole abdomen so sharp they made him shrink involuntarily, pain on pressure & tenderness of surface, pulse small hard & jerking, and when his bowels were moved the dejections were bloody. A copious bleeding softened the pulse, causing a profuse perspiration and immediate and decided relief. I note the symptoms because of the effects which seem induced by mental emotion on the body.[1]

People were sent Westwards in order to ascertain if any path free of Tsetse could be found. They report that the whole country to the N.W. is infested by the insect and that certain small strips of country are free, but these are never continuous so as to admit of a path being formed. I am shut up to the Borotse and will therefore go thither and then proceed Westward.

White ants working vigorously drawing straws to their holes. This is a precursor of rain.

19th. Moriantsane's arrival. Watch on the 12 & 13 Nov. for shooting stars. 20th Eclipse. A fair and lovely world this certainly is. It is robed in beauty and radiant with the perfections of its blessed Author.

African miseries & barbarism
20th. Having gone to the town as usual today, saw a

[1] Mahale's illness, and the attendant circumstances, are not mentioned in *Travels*.

251

woman and two boys brought into the Kotla for distribution. When taken the woman must have been stripped of all her clothing, for she had only a little piece of a sort of gunney bag on, 2 inches broad. Her child was about a year old. The party from which she was brought fled to the quarter of Kaiñko, & being followed up were killed & these three brought here. They probably fled from oppression and now are killed & dispersed. O miserable Africa! How much need there is for the gospel in thy Interior.

The chief invited me into the house, and Moriantsané, being there, began to describe the defenceless position of some Batoka tribes, who being alarmed by a discharge of fire arms by the party of Syde bon Habib ben Salem Lefifi fled and left the oxen & cattle at once. He advised strongly an expedition there. I told them that now they had the warning voice of God they were no longer in the position they formerly occupied, that the rod of God could reach them, mentioned the instance of Matibele, driven from them by disease and death, and protested against the shedding of human blood. The subject would not have been introduced before me but for the ignorance of Moriantsane. He tried to justify himself by the word 'sela', or picking up anything lost.[1] I left them abruptly & will repeat my warning again.

In the evening Mamire, Kuenane, & Kumele[2] came and commended my having spoken out so faithfully, strongly advising me at all times to protest against wickedness in his (the chief's) elders who counsel bloodshed. Kuenané is hagard & lean, has been ill, probably remorse preys on his mind. The chief himself made an apology for himself by throwing all the blame on Moriantsané, 'it was he who suggested evil'. I had directed my remarks chiefly to him, and Sekeletu took advantage of this by saying, 'the affair was between you men having beards, Letlari[3] may transgress your law but not I.' The counsellors said I was in the place of Sebituane, his father, and if I did not freely reprove my son they would suppose I did not abhor evil.

[1] Brown (*Dictionary*, p. 277) translates *sêla* as 'pick up one by one . . . with the fingers'.

[2] Not identified.

[3] The context suggests that this was the personal name of 'Morantsiane' (cf. above, p. 39).

Barbarism or savageism is the effect of ages of debasement & vice. And agriculture, fishery, hunting, manufactures as of iron, brass &c, or the nomadic life, afford no criterion whereby to judge of the civilization of a people. Neither of these pursuits raises certain tribes in this land from the lowest forms of barbarism, as evinced in perfect nudity of the men and mere pretence at covering the private parts in women. They possess neither courage, patriotism, natural affection, honour, nor honesty. They have no stimulus for any mental improvement. Most of their thoughts are concentrated on eating & drinking, smoking wild hemp and snuffing tobacco. Yet Idiocy is very rare among them. I have only seen two cases of partial idiocy in twelve years. Insanity is very rare. I have seen three cases in the same period of time and these were put to death because of cursing[1] or trying to kill their chiefs.[2] Deformity too is very rare, and the vis medicatrix works much more actively than in white men. Homoeopathic globules never produced a single symptom or alleviated one in a native. Their diet is not regular enough for a change therein to have any alteration in the feelings as a result.

The idea of transgression ('tlola', pass over) has contributed to the lowest forms of barbarism. If a man is bitten by a zebra or Alligator, in some tribes, he is forthwith expelled & forced to take up his residence with Bakalihari or Bushmen, and descends to their state.[3] Others have been driven thither by Matibele. Albinoes are shunned or killed. A child which cuts its upper front teeth first is also put to death in some tribes, and so are twins.[4] The natural man presents few points of loveliness.

When a woman becomes old she is thrown aside as nobody, and becomes a servant to a daughter. It not unfrequently happens that she becomes a wet nurse too. The child-

[1] 'because of cunning' (Gelfand, p. 68).

[2] These cases are not mentioned in *Travels*, where D.L. says merely, 'I have observed . . . very few cases of idiocy, and I believe that continued insanity is rare' (p. 409).

[3] In *Travels*, p. 255, D.L. says that the usages described, about which he gives fuller details, are observed by the BaNgwato and BaKwena, and 'scarcely exist' among the MaKololo. 'These curious relics of the animal-worship of former times', as he calls them (*loc. cit.*), are part of the totemic ritual common to all Tswana tribes, though the sanctions he mentions are no longer enforced; cf. Schapera, *Tswana Law and Custom*, pp. 6 f.   [4] Cf. above, p. 159.

ren are applied to the breast, and milk flows of a colour and consistence nearly like that of the daughter. I have seen two instances in which the grandmothers had not suckled any child since the parent of the grandchild was weaned, and yet the entire nourishment of this grandchild was drawn from her breasts.[1]

21st Friday. The floods of the Chobe take place in June or July, those of the Borotse country in .....[2]

Notes about Ants

The Ants perform a most important part in the economy of this country in forming the soil and speedily conveying dead vegetable matter underground. The white ant[3] is almost constantly at work on dead branches, stalks of plants, or droppings of animals. They cover them first with a coat of earth. It serves as a covered way or gallery for their future operations, protecting them from the rays of the sun, from wind and the ravages of birds. Underneath this gallery they work, and generally all that remains after their operations on a piece of wood or other vegetable matter is [a] thin shield of earth of the exact shape of the article now in the vaults below. When decayed wood is scarce they not unfrequently clothe living trees with their galleries and labour assiduously in removing the dead outer bark. The parts which have been or are still the abode of Colonies of Ants are raised some feet in perpendicular height above the dead level of the country between the rivers, and are the spots chosen for gardens.

The first shower of the season brings forth swarms of these white ants furnished with wings & exceedingly fat. They fly one or two hundred yards or less, and alighting bend back their wings and break them off with the after part of their bodies & legs. The wings appear as if hooked on, for if drawn backwards a portion of flesh comes with them, but if bent forwards towards the insect's head in the same manner as it does itself they break clean off. They instantly betake themselves to burrowing in the ground to form a new colony. All

[1] Fuller details are given in *Travels*, p. 126. The instances mentioned were observed among southern BaTswana.

[2] Blank space left for the date. The Barotseland floods start in December, and reach their height in February and March (Gluckman, 'The Lozi', p. 8).

[3] Termite.

manner of insect-loving birds and fowls crowd on them in these seasons, and the natives too make what they esteem a delicious meal by picking them up in quantities.

The rains are so often delayed in this country they must possess the power of preserving their wings entire though so easily broken off afterwards.

The large black ants go on marauding expeditions against them. The army is usually about from 3 to 6 inches broad and about 6 feet in length. They make a chirping or hissing noise, and from the manner in which they run about when disturbed in their march seem ready for all the exploits of a 'brutal soldiery'. In a short time they may be seen returning, each with a white ant in his mandibles. The captive catches hold on all the blades of grass along the route, but the black is the stronger one, and the prisoner can scarcely retard the progress of his victor beyond the space requisite for a vigorous tug.

They are used for food in this country and not as slaves, no evidence of their workmanship being evident in the establishments of the black gentlemen. Indeed I saw one army in a cold damp morning which had removed the legs of the white ants that they might be the more easily carried. And another on a warm day seemed to have stung all their captives and probably injected the same substance as the Mason bee or Dauber does into the caterpillar which it deposits for the food of its young. They were in a state [of] anaesthoesia from formic acid, I think, and did not attempt to escape though liberated.

The evidence however on which I ground my belief that they are not employed as slaves is except in these two instances of a negative character. The forays took place frequently before my house at Kolobeng, and a large anthill made by the white ants was completely destroyed in consequence of my having built the house out of [it]. The colony seemed dispersed, and it was against the dispersed & scattered villages that the forays were directed. No appearance of work performed by the captives was ever visible above ground. None of my operations ever led me to open a black ants' establishment, so that I can only assert respecting the two facts mentioned above, that it is not probable they are made slaves of in this country as the blacks are reported to do with their miserable white bretheren elsewhere. Some ants have stings, and if the juices or fluids near that organ are taste[d] the presence of a concentrated acid is recognized. This is the formic acid, and that probably which the antients used in somewhat the same way we now employ Chloroform.

Ants exist in great variety in this country. I can now recall to recollection no fewer than fifteen varieties, and it is probable an Entomologist would detect several others.[1]

I. A jet black ant. A full inch long. Slow & deliberate in all its movements. Emits an offensive effluvia when irritated or alarmed. (Leshonya)[2]

II. White Ant, $\frac{1}{2}$ an inch long, yellowish head & light coloured body, builds Anthills from 10 to 12 feet high, feeds on vegetables, decayed wood &c.

III. Black with a tint of grey, $\frac{1}{2}$ an inch long, goes on marauding expeditions against the white ant; food animal matter.

IV. Shining black, shorter and thicker in the body than No. III. Has a sting which if pressed emits a yellow sour liquid. Some of them have purple heads. Goes on marauding expeditions too. Seen in great numbers after rain. Devours insects & all kinds of animal food.

V. Thin body of Brownish red colour. Transparent. Nearly $\frac{1}{4}$ inch long. Eats sweet or saccharine matters only. No sting.

VI. Black body and drab belly. The latter is carried erect. Seen in the hollows of decayed wood, which it probably eats.

VII. Greyish black, with a sting. Eats animal food.

VIII. Brownish red. Thin body scarcely $\frac{1}{4}$ inch long. Bites or stings sharply.

IX. Two very small varieties, $\frac{1}{8}$ inch, black, animal food.

X. Like No IX, but body thicker, after part of body triangular, seen on bark of trees, harmless.

XI. Black, $\frac{1}{4}$ inch long, very quick in its movements on the hot soil.

[1] This classification is not given in *Travels*.   [2] Cf. above, p. 76.

XII. Black entirely, stands high on his legs, carries his belly erect.

XIII. Head & body dull red, belly black & triangular, $\frac{1}{16}$ [inch] long, vegetable food.

XIV. Head & body dull red, belly glossy drab with hair, $\frac{1}{4}$ inch long.

XV. A sort of tiger ant, dark with drab spots or drab with black spots. $\frac{3}{4}$ inch long, destroys larvae of other insects as the dauber, sting $\frac{1}{4}$ inch long.

Ant lions very numerous. New insect. Eats ants.

[handwritten:] black with hair 1/4 inch long.

[handwritten:] — A sort of Tiger ant. dark with drab spots or drab with black spots 3/4 inch long — destroys larvae of other insects as the dauber — sting 1/4 inch long.

[handwritten:] lions very numerous) New insect / eats ants —

[handwritten:] to in general possess no enmity to each — one walks over another without shewing

Ants in general possess no enmity to each other. One walks over another without shewing any symptoms of having come into contact with a member of another clan, but if a dead body is stumbled upon it is instantly taken possession of either by the members of its own community or of another. White ants are seized by all the carnivorous ants without ceremony, but several are required in the case of the smaller ants to master one. At certain seasons either by night or by day the white ants rush out and collect pieces of grass or straw with great activity. It frequently foretells a change of weather by this means.[1]

[1] Cf. above, p. 251.

22d Saturday. Some of the chief men again expressed their thankfulness to me for opposing the project of Moriantsane for a foray against the Batoka. They feel that I am right and said in addition, To you alone we look as one that will intercede for us. Each one is in dread of his neighbour, and when the death of any one is resolved on there is no one to stand in the gap.

Sunday 23d. It is desirable in general to erect a place of public worship as soon as possible. Reverence and decorum are much more easily induced by meeting in a house than meeting in a place where the people are accustomed to meet only for play or noisy dispute and the transaction of all public business, as hearing causes and dispensing justice &c. But this erection cannot at present take place here. They are upon improving in their deportment but it is still far from what it ought to be, and high winds disturb by drifting sand into our faces and drowning the voice. We had fewer people today than usual in consequence of most of the women having gone to the gardens. Rains are expected, but they are long in coming. Great cloudiness and haziness seem to portend the early commencement of the much longed for blessing.

As erroneous notions of what conduces to the health of the body tend to corporeal weakness, so error generally tends to produce mental weakness. Sin is dementia. It is stark folly, for the very violation of God's laws tends to the degradation of the offender. Slavery for instance working upwards corrupts the children. We cannot degrade the lower stratum of society without lowering ourselves.

Monday 24th. A poor girl in a state of destitution lay near my path to the town. She was wretchedly lean. I told her to go to the waggon and I gave her some food. She was quite naked. George gave her a piece of cloth for the loins. She came several times and I spoke to her owner about her. He complained of want of food himself, but being a rich man I thought it was only talk. The wretched girl came to the waggon again & again. I gave her food several times, but my own people being in want drove her away. On asking her owner yesterday where she was, he said she had gone into the field and probably died there of absolute starvation.[1] Poor

---

[1] This incident is described, with some variations in detail, in *Travels*, p. 511 (entry dated 1 October 1855).

wretch, this is the fate of many in this benighted land. They wander forth and become the prey of hyaenas.

I attempted again to introduce a system of kindness into the dealings of the Makololo and conquered tribes, by proposing again to Sekeletu to obtain beads and present them to such of them as bring tribute in ivory. If they only make a commencement, the system in other things will follow. Sekeletu and his counsellors highly approved the suggestion, but the practice is not so easily put into operation. They quote attempts of Sebituane in the same line which were unsuccessful. He gave oxen, but they rewarded his kindness by bringing the Matibele upon him.

Moriantsane came and apologized for his talk and hoped I would not keep up any bad feeling. I replied all I said against their ways was on their account & for their benefit alone.

Facts about the Rhinoceros

Mistakes have been made respecting the species of Rhinoceros in Africa by observing the same species at different stages of its growth and giving individuals different names as the natives do, though these are only meant by the latter to express differences in the length or appearances of the horns. To me all the African Rhinoceros I have yet seen amount to two species only, each species having two varieties, the only characteristic of which is the length and direction of the horn s.[1]

They are :
  species⎫ R. Mohohoo
    I. ⎭ the White Rhinoceros, or large long headed, grass feeding one.
  1. A variety called Kuabaoba, exactly the same as the other except that its horn is long & straight. He is found in company with the other and is in no respect different in feeding habits &c.

[1] Cf. above, p. 62, and *Travels*, p. 612. Cumming likewise writes (1850): 'Of the rhinoceros there are four varieties in South Africa, distinguished by the Bechuanas by the names of the borèlé, or black rhinoceros, the keitloa, or two-horned black rhinoceros, the muchocho, or common white rhinoceros, and the kobaoba, or long-horned white rhinoceros' (vol. i, p. 215 n.). Modern taxonomists recognize two species: black rhinoceros (*Diceros bicornis*) and white rhinoceros (*Diceros simus*).

species⎱ R. Boreelé or Black Rhinoceros, short headed,
II. ⎰   feeding on trees & bushes.
2. variety Boreelenyane, or little black short-horned animal feeding on trees & bushes. Habitat on rocky
hills.

The Keitloa is the full grown black Rhinoceros or Boreele.[1]
When the horns are full grown, the front & second horn are
of the same length. The grain of the horn is finer than in the
other species. The Boreelenyane[2] is a short snubnosed little
animal. The colour of all Rhinoceros is the same ashey grey.
It is probable that he who gave the names white & black saw
the latter in a black soil, and when they have rolled themselves in dark mud they look black enough.

Rhinoceros is the next in point of size to the Elephant.
The Mohohoo or white longheaded long horned animal is of
an ashey grey colour & about 5 feet 6 in. high. Extreme
height does not exceed six feet. The horns are placed on the
lower part of the forehead. The longest is slightly bent backwards or upright recurvated, the short one a cone flattened
from side to side. The large one is from 3 feet 3 inches &
under, & 10 inches in diameter at the base and tapering to
a point. It is so firmly fixed to the frontal bone it is frequently
necessary to remove that with the horn.

The horn of the Kuaboaba is slightly bent downwards or
straight. When seen running the horn seems to stand quite
horizontal. The point is generally abraded or worn off in consequence of the horn touching the ground when the animal
is feeding. He can see better than the Mohohoo whose horn
is bent up towards his forehead, because the horn does not
interfere with the line of vision. A horn has been seen of 3 ft
10 inches in length, and another a foot longer, but these are
extreme cases. The short horn behind the other is from 10 to
15 inches long. A Boreelé was seen with his horn bent in the
same manner as the Kuaboaba, and antelopes frequently
exhibit variations in the shape of their horns.

The Kuaboaba is found in particular localities only & is

---

[1] Roberts (*Mammals of South Africa*, p. 241) gives *kgêtlwa* ('keitloa') as a Tswana
name for the white rhinoceros (together with *mogohu* and *kôbaôba*). Most other
writers agree with Cumming and D.L.

[2] *Bodilenyane,* dimin. of *bodile* ('boreele').

scarce in all. The White Rhinoceros is partially gregarious, being met with occasionally in groups of five or seven. They feed on coarse long grass and have no incisor teeth. He deposits his droppings in particular spots, always excavating the centre of his heap when he comes to it. The undigested grass appears in them, and a kind of solaneum generally springs up from the part. It is the most inoffensive of all the large animals. Elephants sometimes assault a village at night, overturning the huts and killing inhabitants, or enter gardens and when the women attempt to drive them off follow and kill them. But a Mohohoo never molests any one. The males occasionally break in the frontal sinuses of each other in their affairs of gallantry, but that is a private affair between themselves. He is a placid good natured fellow and almost always fat. He may often be seen sauntering along the banks of rivulets in the afternoon, after having spent the heat of the day in some shady bower. His sight is deficient but his hearing is acute, and if unaccompanied by a friendly bird called 'Kala'[1] (Crotophaga ani or Buphagi (beefeaters)) he is easily approached from under the wind. The bird by flapping with its wings and screaming gives him warning of the approach of danger. As his flesh is usually loaded with fat, and a single bullet behind the shoulder slanting upwards a little in its direction is sufficient to kill it stone dead, it soon becomes extinct after the introduction of fire arms into a country. His skin is from an inch to an inch & a half in thickness.

His trail is known by a distinct impression of three toes, the outer one producing an ovoid mark on the sand. The foot is much larger than that of the Boreele, and wherever it is seen it is the cheering sign of proximity to water. He cannot bear deprivation of water for any length of time. Delights to roll in the mire and then rub himself against an anthill or tree. He feeds during the evening & night, and stands or lies under a shady tree by day. He utters a hoarse grunt when pleased and frequently tears up the ground with his hind feet, throwing out the legs behind & rubbing them hard on the ground as a dog does when apparently cleaning his toes, and then ploughs up the ground or a bush with his horn. He seems to do it in the joyous consciousness of strength. Dogs

---

[1] Cf. above, p. 119. The words placed in parentheses are an interlineation.

after stretching their legs so usually take a spring away as if in joy. But some have thought that a similar phenomenon in the Rhinoceros indicates 'ungovernable rage'. Horned cattle make the same use of their horns. The least approach to rage I have seen is when he ploughs the ground on coming to the droppings of the black Rhinoceros or when driven off by man.

He is not affected with any disease except worms in the intestines. These are of different kinds—flat, round, and thread, but each variety very large. Worms are often seen in the eyes.[1] All Rhinoceros when alarmed rush off with a loud puffing noise.

The female shews much affection for her young, always taking the danger side or keeping the calf in front in escaping unless mortally wounded. She then loses the maternal feeling and rushes past it.[2] This is a sure sign that she will soon expire. In the agonies of death they often utter a peculiarly piercing shriek, and tears flow, making one regret that the progress of civilization and the necessities of human stomachs have doomed these ponderous masses of animal life to destruction. The calf follows the dam till nearly full grown. They are not many years in reaching maturity, and not so long lived as elephants. They are supposed to go ten months with young & bring forth one, sometimes two, at a birth.

The chief food is grass, but to this they add the tender shoots of some trees. Such are the Monokane & Mokabe (gum yielding) & Morupaphiri (a short thorn), Moguana (sweet), Mosilabele (bitter), & Morolane (a solaneum narcotic). The grasses of which he is most fond[3] are called Mosegashule & Tlokwane.

II. species. Boreelé or Keitloa. He is known by being of less size than the Mohohu, & his head & snout are much shorter. His horns are shorter and finer in the grain but of the same shape as the other. When running the nose is so held that the horns are nearly erect or perpendicularly to his nose. His tail is held nearly so too. He is much less timid than the Mohohoo, and often turns savagely on the hunter. His sight not being acute he charges the smoke of the gun or a bush or tree in the direction of the sound. If the hunter remain per-

---

[1] Cf. above, p. 74.   [2] Cf. above, p. 248.   [3] MS. has 'found'.

fectly still he often takes him for the stump of a tree and charges close past him. He is both stupid and savage, often attacking and killing both persons and cattle without any provocation. My waggon has been twice assaulted by this animal,[1] but in one case he charged past me when wounded and saw the waggon only. If he sees any unwonted object approach, as a man on horseback, he cocks up his nose in the air, snorts, and makes movements from side to side as if he meant to charge, but generally goes away. If wounded he becomes very angry, and will kill a buffalo or other animal which he may meet with. He seems a crusty fellow on the whole, and never has an ounce of fat on his flesh. The flesh however is not unpleasant. His ill temper induces him sometimes to insult the quiet Mohohoo male, with a fatal result to one of the parties. But both instantly retire before the Elephant. The Buffalo retires from both Rhinoceros.

The same remarks are applicable to the variety Boreelenyane. Of the propriety of calling it such indeed I have some doubts. The points of difference are, the Boreelenyane is a small very snub nosed scabby looking thing, the horn is 8 or 10 inches long while [that of] the Keitloa is from 18 inches to two feet in length, and the two horns are of nearly equal length. Its habitat is on rocky hills. But neither of them are attached to particular runs as the Mohohoo. His droppings, met every where, contain much indigested wood. Their food and temperament are the same and may be described under one head.

The low thorny Acacia tortuosa or wait a bit thorn is a favourite article of food. He commences to graze early in the afternoon. May be met with anywhere, having no particular run, so is more dangerous than other animals, for he frequently rushes out on a traveller who is unconscious of his proximity. The acacias or Mimosas on which he feeds are Moshu, Maoka (Acacia nilotica), Mōka (gum yielding), Mopura chukuru & Moretloa (sugar & gelatine yielding). He digs one tuber called Kelerisa. It has been attempted to rear them, but hitherto unsuccessfully. Their food ought to be assimilated to that on which they thrive in a wild state.

She goes ten months with young. Never brings forth more

[1] For one such 'assault', cf. below, p. 303.

than one at a birth. Shews much affection for her calf, fighting bravely with the hyaenas for it, but her sight is so defective and her movements so awkward it is not unfrequently killed by both them and lions. It is seldom a Boreelé is seen without the marks of the Hyaena's teeth on his ears, the wounds having been recieved in his youth. The calf when born is about the size of an ordinary sized bull dog, but stands low on his legs and is then of a dark red colour.

Their paces are a slow walk, quick trot in which he turns his head a little from side to side, & a heavy ackward but very swift gallop.

Tuesday 25th. Droughts seem to prevail here as well as to the Southward. There is very little corn here in consequence of one last year. There is so much moisture in the country generally, and so many trees, it is remarkable that rains do not prevail more. The average heat by day is 98°, of the evenings 90; in the mornings it has fallen as low as 80°. The ground is very much heated, yet the grass and trees spring forth vigorously.

Plasterer

Several of that most useful insect the 'Dauber', or as I would name it the Plasterer,[1] have been working in my waggon for some months. They build the cells for their young with great assiduity, going four or five times in succession to a little heap thrown up by the white ants, and selecting a load of the earth which is most recently thrown up and of course contains the most moisture. They quickly transform it into soft plaster by moisture drawn from their stomachs, and flying with the bolus about the size of a pea to the part where operations are being carried on form the walls of their cells neatly with their mandibles. They seem to have a stock of water for about 4 or 5 pellets, and then fly away to the water for more. Their economy in the use of water is seen in their selecting the moist portion of the White ant's heap. The air being so dry, all that which this insect throws up in the manner of moles is instantly dried except the point of the

---

[1] '. . . a hymenopterous insect called the *plasterer* (*Pelopœus Eckloni*), which in its habits resembles somewhat the mason-bee' (*Travels*, p. 538).

heap. This is invariably selected and by this means visits to the water are less frequent.

The form of the cells is oblong like that of the body of the full-grown young. And though when plastered in as firmly as a vault in a burial ground the larva is not much larger than a pin's head, the remaining space is filled with caterpillars or spiders all in a state of anasthoesia from the Chloroform which the plasterer has injected with his sting. The young insect lives and grows on these, and the supply is just about sufficient for his wants till his body fills the cell. Some are then of a beautiful bright green colour and much less in size than the parent, who is of a jet black. He does not therefore make the cell from the measurement of his own body. Yet all cells of the black plasterer are of the same size. These insects sometimes sting, but having never interfered with those in the waggon they seem to keep on the best terms with me. If I sit directly in front of their cells, they fly gently in front untill they observe an opening & then glide quietly past. The natives call the collection of cells 'The house of God'.[1] Is this idea derived from Egypt? I think I have seen the Plasterer in Hieroglyphics.

(Though white ants work on the rock in dry weather, their operations are all carried on with moist clay. They seem capable of procuring supplies of moisture from the air.)

The plasterer is very useful in the destruction of spiders and caterpillars. When bringing one of the latter it is frequently as much as it can carry, and when compelled to make certain curves in order to reach the cells he often alights with his burden to rest. At other times the industrious architect, instead of abandoning a load far beyond his powers, uses both wings and legs to drag his prey along the ground, the caterpillar all the while lying perfectly motionless & stretched out to its full length. Another kind of these insects burrows in the ground untill it forms a cell, deposits its egg or larva and stock of caterpillars, and then closes the aperture so neatly no one could detect its presence. This is an elegant thin insect about an inch in length. The Plasterer is reported sometimes

---

[1] In Southern Sotho, *ntlo-ea-balimo* (lit., 'house of the ancestor gods') is used for 'nest of white ants, nest built of clay by certain insects' (Mabille and Dieterlen, *Dictionary*, 1950 ed., p. 408).

to deposit its egg in the eye of persons or animals, causing violent inflammation of the organ. Is the male light green? All the plasterers I have seen seem to be females, and are jet black.

Notes about Giraffe

The Giraffe or Tutlua[1] forms a striking and beautiful feature in our landscapes, but the aspect of calmness and repose, the freshness of vegetable life, & the delicious climate of the morning are seldom realized in connection with the stately forms of these lordly animals after firearms are introduced. At present I am permitted to view verdant lawns with graceful antelopes, zebras, gnus, majestic elephants and gigantic giraffes feeding undismayed except by the near approach of man. The movements of this last animal is when undisturbed in such keeping with the solemn stillness of the wilderness, they are liable to be mistaken for the naked stumps of decayed trees.

The male attains a height of 18 feet and the proportions seem to be 6 feet of leg
$$\left.\begin{array}{l} 6 \text{ D}^o \text{ of body} \\ 6 \text{ D}^o \text{ of neck \& head} \end{array}\right\} 18 \text{ feet}$$
The female is a few feet lower or from 14 to 16 feet high. Both are of a dun colour with dark brown spots, the female being a little lighter than the other. They are generally met with in herds of from seven to twenty in number, frequenting parts in which mimosas and acacias abound. The very long pliable tongue enables it to gather into its mouth the leaves and young shoots of these with great facility, though from the thorniness of some it is difficult to see how it can manage. The thorns are like fish hooks bent back on themselves and very sharp & strong. Yet he thrives on them, and the flesh of the female is usually fat, tender and good. They require but little water. A traveller might perish by thirst where they subsist in comfort on the sap contained in these leaves. It subsists for months together without water, and when it does attempt to drink he is obliged to throw his legs asunder in a most ungainly manner before his head can reach the water.

[1] Tswana *thutlwa*. Little of the information given in this section was published in *Travels*.

The great height to which the eye is raised enables him to keep a look out as if from a mast head. Hence it is very difficult of approach, and the idea of the lion coming up to this magnificent animal, and spring[ing] at such a distance as to raise himself in the curve to a height of twelve feet, is fabulous. It has never been seen; pictures of it are purely imaginary. And we have positive evidence of him failing to reach the backs of oxen, eilands and buffaloes not half the height.[1]

His paces are a peculiar kind of walk and trot in which he bends his neck & body forwards and backwards in a see saw manner. His speed is not great. He can be turned easily by a good horse. If pressed hard he attemp[t]s a gallop, but this never lasts more than one hundred yards and he then comes to a dead halt. He has been known at this stage to drop down stone dead from excitement and nervous shock. The males have occasional disputes, conducted by striking their heads and necks together in a manner far from handsome. Their contests sometimes end in the death of one. Though furnished with horns about 8 inches long & covered with the common integument of the forehead, they do not use them for goring. They being flat at the end and covered with a bunch of hair would not answer the purpose of horns in general. They can kick from behind and stamp with the forefeet with tremendous power, but with respect to all other animals they are perfectly harmless.

The hoof is cleft and the trail seems that of a gigantic ox. Their droppings consist of oblong pellets about an inch in diameter and $1\frac{1}{2}$ inches long. They resemble exactly those of the eiland. Indeed the pellet form is peculiar to the whole antelope genus. By what contrivance in the smaller intestines are they cut so systematically to the same length?

The cow giraffe goes the same time with young as the domestic cattle. Brings forth one, rarely two at a birth. The 'times when the hinds do calve' are so well known to the people of this country, they have named certain months after this manner: Pallane (lit., little pallah), the month in which

---

[1] 'They have sprung on some occasions on to the hindquarters of a horse, but no one has ever seen them on the withers of a giraffe. They do not mount on the hindquarters of an eland even, but try to tear him down with their claws' (*Travels*, p. 139).

the pallahs calve[1]; and it is believed to occur so regularly that any dispute as to which month it is is settled by any one who may have seen these antelopes with their young. Another month is known as that in which the males of certain animals are expelled from the female herds.[2]

The giraffe grazes on	(wait a bit)	= Mongana
		= Motlopi
		Morulane
	camel thorn	= Mahotlo
	hooked thorn	Mokalo
		Mochweere
	thorney acacia	Moshu
		Mokoba
		Mokabi
		Mopane
	Palmyra	= Mokolane
		Moretloa

Some idea of the numbers of Giraffe in this country may be formed when it is stated that in a peculiar season for drought ninety-six were seen in one day.

Eiland or Pohoo

After the Giraffe stands the Eiland or Pohoo[3] for size and beauty. The Dutch have named it eiland or Elk, not from any resemblance to that Antelope, but simply from their own habit of naming everything new by something else of which they possess some idea. Rivers are named Sand river, Reed river, or Brack river by the dozen in a country where nearly every river contains sand or reed or is of brackish taste. Hence some parts having exclusively Dutch names are as easily distinguished as the Owens and Joneses in a Welsh Regiment.

This beautiful animal, the largest of all the Antelopes, has straight upright horns, each horn having a ridge about $\frac{1}{2}$ an

[1] Phalane is the Tswana name for October.

[2] Probably Pôane or Pôwana, the month (September) of 'young bulls', who then 'begin to fight and kill one another' (Schapera, field notes).

[3] Tswana *phofu* (*Taurotragus oryx*). Relatively little of the information in this section appears in *Travels*.

inch high & one broad running spirally round upwards and outwards from the base to about two thirds of its length ; the remainder is smooth and runs to a sharp point in the female and an obtuse one in the male. In the former case they are used in defending the young, in the latter they are employed chiefly to settle the point which seems to be the law in all cases, that the stronger animals alone shall propagate the race. The horns of the male are two feet long & 10 inches in circumference, of the female three feet but more slender. The head is formed after the graceful antelope kind with a thick tuft of hair (brown) on the forehead.

The colour is, of the male a light grey, of the female a yellowish grey. At the Borotse country they have bands of white about $\frac{1}{2}$ an inch broad encircling the body, and a dark brown band round the upper part of the forearm, which in a herd gives them the appearance somewhat of a regiment with their knee pans on.[1] In other parts of the country the white bands appear only in the calves when very young. The body of a full grown male is equal in size to a very large ox, but the legs are more slender. Its dewlap is very deep, and it stands upwards of six feet high. The hoof and trail resembles that of oxen of large size, but that of the female is smaller and a little compressed from side to side.

He lives in the most desert places, often far from water, and can thrive though deprived of this fluid for many months. He can extract moisture sufficient for his wants from the succulent leaves on which he feeds, but he does not disdain to take a sip if he passes its vicinity. In great droughts however, when all vegetation [is] desiccated, he too must come to the rivers and drink statedly. Their leaness in these cases shews they must have suffered considerably before resorting to water. They are endowed with amazingly acute organs of vision. They are scarcely ever stalked even by natives, but want of fleetness renders them an easy prey to a man on horseback. The males especially take on immense quantities of fat, and when pursued all the fat bulls are left behind by the herd, covered with foam. Their pace is now a slow walk, but they

---

[1] Cf. *Travels*, p. 210. This variety, 'differing from the typical southern form in having distinct stripes in adults', is now known as *Taurotragus oryx livingstonei* (Roberts, *Mammals*, p. 307; cf. Ellerman *et al.*, p. 210).

obstinately refuse to go down the wind even in these circumstances, and will attempt to gore the horse of the rider who attempts to turn them. Their paces are an easy trot or quick gallop, the latter never except when pursued.

It is found in very large herds where firearms are scarce. The cow brings forth one at a birth, and shews as much affection for her calf as the domestic animal does. One shot near Sesheke had the marks of a lion's claws on her hind quarters in four long scratches on each side. The lion had probably caught her calf, and made an attempt on the dam when attempting to rescue her young. The udder was as large as a common cow's and so distended with beautiful white milk it ran in copious streams after its death. A native looking at the beautiful [animal] and its rich supply of milk remarked in their usual irreverent way, 'Jesus did not know how to bestow, He ought to have given us these instead of cattle'.[1] It is a pity they are not domesticated in England. The flesh is excellent.

(To ascertain the weight of an animal by its dimensions, the grazier's rule,

Multiply the square of the girth by the length and by 24. Divide the product by 100. If the dimensions are given in feet, the weight will be in stones. The girth to be taken behind the shoulder blade, and the length from the foremost corner of the blade bone to the hindmost point of the rump. Ex[ample]. Let the girth be 8 feet and length 6 feet.

$$
\begin{array}{r}
8 \\
8 \\
\hline
64 \\
24 \\
\hline
256 \\
128 \\
\hline
1536 \\
6 \\
\hline
9216 \quad = 92 \text{ stones}
\end{array}
$$

---

[1] This incident is described in *Travels*, p. 210, with the amendment 'five long deep scratches'. The 'native', named there, was Lebeola (cf. above, p. 36).

Eiland killed at Maguaila[1] 1st Nov /51 6ft. 3 in. height. 9 ft. 4. length of body. 6 ft 6 in girth Neck 4 ft

$$
\begin{array}{r}
6 \\
6.6 \\
\hline
39 \\
5 \\
\hline
195 \\
24 \\
\hline
780 \\
390 \\
\hline
4680 \quad = 46 \text{ stones}
\end{array}
$$

Young Bull. From top of withers to middle of breast bone $41 \times 2 = 82$. Length of body 5 ft 2

$$
\begin{array}{r}
7 \\
7 \\
\hline
49 \\
245 \\
24 \\
\hline
980 \\
480 \\
\hline
5780 \quad = 57 \text{ or } 59 \text{ stones.)}
\end{array}
$$

They love bitter plants. The bowels sometimes taste of them. Of trees having succulent leaves he feeds on

	Monyelenyele
Hooked thorn	Mokhalo
	Morula
	Morala
	Monuana
	Mopane
	Monokane
	Mohata

---

[1] Not identified. At the time mentioned, D.L. was in the territory of the Ba-Ngwato.

Camel thorn	Mohotlo
	Mokabi
	Moretloa
	Moguana
	Moreaboku
	Mosilabele
	Monato

Absence of Beauty in Native Women

26th Octr Wedensday. I have not yet met with a beautiful woman among the black people, & I have seen many thousands in a great variety of tribes. I have seen a few who might be called passable, but none at all to be compared to what one may meet with among English servant girls. Some beauties are said to be found among the Caffres,[1] but among the people I have seen I cannot concieve of any European being so far captivated with them as to covet criminal intercourse.[2] The whole of my experience goes towards proving that civilization alone produces beauty, and exposure to the weather & other vicissitudes tends [to] the production of deformity and ugliness.

A lion entered the town last night, but did no harm except frightening a little girl by chasing her into the compound. He then went to a cattle post and killed two head of cattle, fed heartily, and retired into dense reed where it is impossible for the people to follow him. If it had been moonlight he would not have ventured so far.

Mahale says he knows the Makololo, and though they speak fair now they will certainly follow their old system as soon as my back is turned. It is only fear of displeasing me which prevents them following Moriantsané's advice, and that though now quiet he has not spoken in vain. They would care nothing for George. M. says it is their custom, and if any one objects they immediately set him down as a coward, saying, 'if you are such a coward, remain at home, we shall go

---

[1] As used in South Africa, this term generally applies to the AmaXhosa and other coastal tribes, in contrast with the BaSotho and BaTswana of the interior plateau.

[2] '... I cannot conceive of any European being captivated with them. The whole of my experience...' (Blaikie, p. 148).

and "sella", or pick up what we can', and none of the chief
men can resist the temptation.

Some of the chief men see the difference of our eating and
their ravenous gulping, and would like to imitate. They say
their way crams the teeth full, for every one is trying who can
get meat fastest into his stomach.

Hornets

There is a nest of hornets near the table under the lee of
the waggon, at which I write. These insects make their collection of cells very nearly like that of our yellow wasps at
home when they build on a tree. They increase amazingly
quick in a fruit garden and destroy much fruit by eating holes
into the ripest grapes peaches &c &c. They are then perfectly harmless unless one approaches their nest. The maternal storgee (στοργη) is so strong they dash with the greatest
fury at the face of any one who approaches it, and they inflict
a most intense pain by their sting. They not unfrequently
follow an intruder a distance of twenty yards, and any one
who has felt their sting once requires no greater hint than
their buzz to induce a precipitate flight. But away from their
nests they may be approached with perfect impunity, and a
garden may be cleared of them by snipping them through
with a pair of scizzors while sipping the nectar of flowers.
Though legs & wings are cut off on these occasions they
never attempt to use their sting, though when near the nest
it is instantly resorted to. The flowers of orange trees produce
a kind of intoxication in them of which they are very fond.
They lie in a dormant state in thatch during winter.

In writing the foregoing, the chief & his young companions came to learn to read. They acquired the alphabet, and
went to the town with a copy intending to continue reading it
there. They were much delighted with the pictures of the
magic lantern[1] and begged me to come again with them this
evening, and explain them. The two last nights brought such
a concourse of women and the pictures so loosened their

[1] Cf. *Travels*, pp. 230, 278, and especially 298 f., where D.L. says that the lantern
had been brought from England by Mungo Murray, who accompanied him and
Oswell to Lake Ngami in 1849.

tongues it was only occasionally I could get in a word of explanation. Tonight they propose to make Mapulanyane stand with a switch and keep them off, but I object, and hope milder measures will be effectual in preserving the peace. May the Holy spirit plant some of the good seed sown & make it fruitful.

Notes about Buffaloes

The African is quite a distinct variety from the Indian Buffalo. He has the base of the horns prolonged over his forehead except a small sulcus of about an inch wide in the middle. This mass of horn seems intended to protect the brain in the contests of the bulls which are necessary for deciding which shall propagate the breed. In all gregarious animals the strongest is retained for that purpose, while the weak or old retire. The old gentlemen driven into a state of celibacy become very crusty and dangerous. They not unfrequently on observing a man approach kneel behind a bush and suddenly spring out on the unsuspecting victim. The natives in these cases squat down prone on the ground & hold by the roots of the grass. He cannot then, without turning his head half way round nearly, insert the point of the horn under the body so as to toss them. His horns are so bent as to prevent this, though when a person is upright he would instantly be gored. Two of my people were attacked in this way by a couple of buffaloes without the least provocation. After trying to turn them over they pommeled the poor fellows with their foreheads and feet, then left them badly bruised internally, but they both recovered. They sent home for an emetic to enable them to vomit the blood which they felt internally and both recovered.[1]

The colour of the male is black and blackish brown, the latter is the colour of the cow. The size & shape are that of large clumsy oxen. Height 16 hands or 5 feet four inches. The hoof is that of the ox but a little compressed from side to side. His hide is hard and tough and the hair coarse & thinly planted.

He feeds chiefly by night and stands under shady trees by

[1] This incident, which occurred in 1846, is not mentioned in *Travels*, but cf. *Letters*, vol. i, p. 179.

day, chewing the cud. If a few lie down others stand to keep a look out. They begin to graze about an hour before sunset & towards the water. They delight in the succulent grasses which grow in moist parts and the same kinds of grasses on which oxen thrive best. These grasses are called Mosegash-ule, Motloa and Tlokwané. The herb Tépe (or Bret). They feed on bushes too as Moretloa, Moguana, Mahatla, Mono-kané, Morulane, Monato, Morulega, Moshukubyané, Mo-rupaphiri.

These constitute such a large portion of their food, at some seasons the flesh has a strong odour of them. Even the marrow in the bones partakes of the flavour. Domestic cattle take a mouthful of most of these plants in passing, and they are found to thrive best in a country where they may be had. The herds lead them in a different direction every day in order to give them an opportunity of selecting their fare. They cannot remain long without water and come to it every night. No danger will deter them.

When rains descend in any spot after a long drought, all the game crowds away from the never failing streams to which they have been compelled to resort, and spread out on the new grass & fresh springing herbs. The fresh pasture & abundance of rain water makes them lose flesh immediately, but they prefer the new fare to the more substantial but withered pasture of the former year. They are believed to be guided to these spots of verdure by seeing the clouds collect in the distance, but I think it is more probable they are led by the sense of smell. The natives in support of their view mention that the game frequently goes away towards a collection of clouds expecting to find rain had fallen, but are obliged to return by thirst to the perennial fountains. Rains are very partial in this country, so the animals may have learned something by experience.

The pace of the buffalo is a very heavy looking canter in escaping, but this is increased to a very quick gallop in charging. Erecting his tail in the air he plunges forward at a pace which few horses could escape. Few of the natives ever manage to get out of his way in these circumstances. He is exceedingly dangerous when wounded. He runs in the direction from which the spear has come, or if he tries to escape he doubles on his trail and, coming back some distance abreast of it, kneels down behind a bush or in a rut waiting patiently for his pursuer. Many more natives are wounded or killed by buffaloes than by lions. They are very tenacious of life. Their ribs are broad & overlap each other $\frac{3}{4}$ of an inch. A lion is no match for a bull. Mr Oswel & Captain Vardon were eyewitnesses of a buffalo resisting the attempts of three lions to pull it down, though it had itself recieved a deadly wound behind the shoulder.[1] It is doubtful if a cow buffalo even is ever killed by a single lion. More than one are required to kill a giraffe, though that has no such effective weapons as the buffalo's horns.

27th. Intermittent again yesterday evening; action of the heart violent during the sweating stage. The rains still withheld, though it seems to have rained all about us. It is very cloudy. Thermometer last night 82 at $\frac{1}{2}$ past eleven.

Socialism among the Makololo

There are perpetual contentions about wives. A wife of Lebeola, for whom he gave 30 head of cattle, being scolded ran off to Mokhari her brother.[2] Lebeola went after her, but seeing Mokhari come out of her hut retired without saying anything. Mokhari retained all the cattle. After she has borne Mokhari a child,[3] she is taken from Mokhari by Mamire. Mokhari makes a loud complaint at this, and is answered by, Why, Lebeola did not cry when you took her from him.

On one occasion Sebitoane caused the herald to proclaim, Whatever woman wishes to marry, let her marry whom she will. Many exchanged their husbands. Lebeola found Kuenane's wife by his side that evening. Next morning Sebitoane proclaimed, Now let there be no more marrying, each woman must remain with the husband she has chosen. He hoped

---

[1] An extract from Vardon's journal, describing the incident more fully, is given in *Travels*, p. 139 n.

[2] Probably Mokgari Mosimolodi, a Tawana headman who had been taken captive by Sebetwane. After Sekeletu's death he returned to his own tribe with one of the latter's widows, Mma-Sellwane, who was subsequently married by Letsholathebe (Schapera, field notes, 1940).

[3] If Mokgari were merely her half-brother, such a union would not necessarily have been considered incestuous (cf. above, p. 159).

thereby to prevent the frequent exchanges and runnings away. Lebeola says Kuenane takes other people's wives constantly. 'If he visits one, and is told to sleep with one of our wives as a piece of hospitality, he is sure to wheedle her away with him.' They nearly realize the socialist's idea without any pretensions to philosophy. It is wonderful that Socialism should ever be thought of by any one having the least pretension to manhood. On explaining our state in relation to love as the chief ingredient in marriage, its perpetuity &c, Lebeola remarked 'You understand how to marry, but *we are not men*'.[1]

Porto stealing

In the afternoon Sekeletu came to tell me about the doings of Senor Porto when leaving the Borotse. He caught two men and a woman and bound them among his gangs of slaves. But when he came to Naliele he found Mpollo and a company of Makololo drawn up with shields and spears ready to recieve him. Mpololo asked why he had bound these people. Porto replied he had only taken tribute from his ally, viz. Mpépe. 'Then', replied Mpololo, 'you had better take all these too', pointing to his company, '& I shall tell Sekeletu you have taken all his men'. Porto then delivered up the captives and was allowed to cross the river. The Mambari not of his company protested against this theft as not their but Senor Porto's act entirely. It is well he did something to shew his real character to the Makololo and enable them to decide whether slavers are the proper sort of visitors.[2]

Scavenger Beetles

The Scavenger beetle now makes its appearance here. It is one of the most useful of insects. Endowed with amazingly acute scent, no sooner do animal droppings or ordure reach the ground than these insects percieve it, though they may be several hundred paces distant, and fly with wonderful precision to the very spot. Each insect breaks off a portion four or five times its own size and, rolling it round, it trundles it

[1] These 'socialist' practices, and Sebetwane's proclamation, are not mentioned in *Travels*.

[2] This incident is not mentioned in *Travels*.

along as boys do a snowball, but instead of facing it the head and forelegs are on the ground behind while the body is placed against it and the hind legs roll it. It is as if the Unicorn in the Royal arms were turned upside down against the shield. Sometimes two strive for the same bolus, & they may then be seen, one in front, the other behind, rolling with all their might, apparently ignorant of each other's presence. They bury this mass by excavating below and throwing the earth out round the sides. An Egg is deposited therein, and a large grub comes out of it and finds nutriment in the ball till full grown. The ratel[1] and Kotoko[2] dig them up and prey on them. The latter little animal holds the grub neatly in its paws while eating, and always begins at the head. A Bechuana village without the scavenger beetle is as filthy as Rome and other Italian cities are, but where they abound the village is clean & without smell, though the habits of 'people are identical. The Pope ought to domesticate them in his dominions.

Kokong[3] or Wildebeeste

This is the most grotesque antelope in Africa. He is much more fierce in his appearance than a lion, yet the most easily alarmed of all animals. He takes to flight immediately on the appearance of danger, and by his vigilance and speed manages to hold his ground longer against fire arms than any other animal except the ostrich. His face is very long & aquiline, & it is lengthened in appearance by a large mane and beard.

The body resembles that of a slim active pony. The limbs and feet are those of the antelope tribe. His colour is an iron grey, which seems black in the distance. He seldom stands with his broadside to danger but faces it whether man or beast bravely. Hence it is difficult to distinguish a front view, at the distance of a mile or so, of his slim figure enlarged above at the chest & head from the human form. They possess keen and long sight, and like all antelopes give a loud snort if apprehensive of danger. He prefers open flats destitute of trees, if much hunted, to the shady spots and better

---

[1] *Mellivora capensis*, the honey badger.   [2] Tswana *kotoko*, a species of meerkat.
[3] Tswana *kgokong*, blue wildebeest (*Connochaetes taurinus*).

grass to which he resorts when he feels more secure. And if one carries a gun in approaching him, he takes good care to give the stranger a wide range. He prances, bounds and whisks his tail round and round in a most fantastic way in leaving the danger behind, & they frequently increase a very swift gallop by chasing each other as if in play along their course. If one has no weapon he may approach much closer. They very soon learn the different ranges of musket bullet & old bow & arrow and act accordingly.

They invariably follow a leader, and a large male brings up the rear. He keeps a little behind the rest and stops frequently to survey the danger. If the leader, generally a female, is shot they (all antelopes) are much at a loss. I have seen them stand in a state of bewilderment after that event. For what peculiarity is she selected? I saw one (a leader of zebras) which had many marks of a lion's teeth on her, and suspect this encounter had rendered her more vigilant afterwards.[1] Probably this superior vigilance induced the others to follow her, for whenever one antelope sees another running away he immediately apprehends danger and runs too. Certain birds as pheasants in rising utter a loud scream, this is sufficient to set off all the game within hearing. And an ostrich will start off the whole of the game on a large plain though he is running he scarcely knows why.

The canter and gallop of the Kokong when once seen can never be forgotten. The movements of certain other animals are also easily distinguished. The Zebra for instance is totally distinct in his movements from the Kokong or Kama[2] or Tsessebe or gemsbuck. Indeed, familiarity with the different appearances of different animals at great distances, their differences of movements, and the peculiar physionomy of the country, explains the opinion held by many that uncivilized people have better eyesight than Europeans. When my eye was quite untutored in these matters I was astonished to find the Hottentots pointing out animals in the distance which I could with difficulty detect with a spy glass. But by careful observation I learned that what they confidently pointed out

---

[1] In *Travels*, p. 547, D.L. says this was a young mare shot by himself, 'which at some former time had been bitten on the hind leg by a carnivorous animal'.

[2] Tswana *kgama*, hartebeest (*Alcelaphus buselaphus*).

as animals, and which I now know readily to recognize, have not the appearances which I expected them at first to have. And though I have no remarkable superiority of vision beyond [that] of my fellow countrymen, I excel many of the natives in the distances at which I can recognize objects. Both myself and Mrs L. have frequently pointed out game to our servants which [they] could with difficulty or not at all see by their eyes.

But the sense of hearing, to which I have not given the same attention, still appears to me to be surpassed by that of the Bushmen. I believe however from all I have observed that Europeans subjected to the same education, viz. brought up as Bushmen, would see and hear and smell as acutely as they do. And many of our gentlemen of the higher ranks even trained as Bushmen are would outrun the fleetest of the fleet. Civilization has not tended to degrade them from what their forefathers the barons bold were. They are elevated both physically and morally.[1] The only superiority I have been able to detect in the natural man is greater activity in the reparative powers of the body, when wounded or reduced by disease, and in woman less danger in parturition.

There are two varieties of the Kokong, one that described above, and another with a white brush to his tail and having his horns bent down toward his eyes, then bent on themselves forwards and upwards. He is a little larger than the Kokong and darker. He is called the white tailed wildebeeste or Poruma.[2] Their flesh is good tasted but very dry, they seldom take on any fat. They feed almost entirely on grass, and cannot live long without water. He is one of the animals which indicate the proximity of that most precious element.

Fascination by fire as of serpents

28th Friday. Serpents are said to possess the power of fascinating birds by their eyes. I have never been a witness of this singular phenomenon. But fire seems to possess the same fascination over different kinds of insects and toads.[3] I have

---

[1] 'I believe that with half their training Englishmen would beat the Bushmen. Our present form of civilization does not necessarily produce effeminacy, though it unquestionably increases the beauty, courage, and physical powers of the race' (*Travels*, p. 166).

[2] Tswana *pudumб*, black wildebeest (*Connochaetes gnou*). [3] Cf. above, p. 114.

repeatedly seen toads and beetles make the greatest haste into the fire, and never cease their efforts to get into the very reddest part till their limbs by roasting were useless. They never shrink nor quiver back on first touching the live coals, nor cease their efforts in a forward direction while life lasts. The black Rhinoceros is attracted by the fire too, but his conduct seems to indicate that he looks on it as an enemy. He points to it, advancing with slow measured steps in the manner of a bully, then makes a rush through it, and has sometimes killed those who were sleeping by it.

Serpents rarely bite wantonly. They are usually in fear of being hurt themselves before they inflict pain on others. If the tail is trodden on they bite instantly, or if they are so situated as to see no way of escape. In huts they emit an offensive smell if alarmed, which is often sufficient to alarm the inmates. In cases of bites all natives apply suction and an emetic. Few die under this treatment unless bitten by the Mokhoapa, a black snake or a little yellow.[1] A large quantity of bile is always discharged, the liver having instantly become more active as a depurating organ as soon as the poison entered the blood. In cases of persons struck by lightning too the emetic causes large discharge of bile.

A fine rain today presenting all the appearance of being a three days' one. The last shower was instantly evaporated, but this will shew its effects in cooling the atmosphere and causing plants to spring. I shall soon be able to go Westward. The conduct of this slave merchant has made me decide on going towards Londa or Sinyama.[2] The former is near the Leeba, the latter near the Loeti. There are no persons here who can give a good account of it, those who have visited these parts being all at the Borotse. It would be unwise to follow on the trail of Porto, because those tribes to whom he shews his airs will look upon me as belonging to the same clan.

The conduct of the people whom we have brought from Kuruman shews that no amount of preaching or instruction

[1] 'Basilisk' deleted after 'yellow'. *Mokôpa* is the Tswana name for the mamba (*Dendrastis angusticeps*), one of the most deadly snakes in South Africa.

[2] Chinyama, a Lunda chief living in Balovale district.

will ensure real piety. George's servant was proved by witnesses to have been guilty of criminal connection with Mahale's wife while I was absent at the Borotse and the husband was down the Chobe with the traders.[1] In one instance he was proved to have acted in the most beastly manner in broad day light![2] And I overheard one of my people this morning objecting loudly against people going to their gardens, because their doing so would drive away the rain.[3] The old superstitions cannot be driven out of their minds by faith implanted by preaching. They have not vanished in either England or Scotland yet after the lapse of centuries of preaching.

Kuruman, the entire population of which amounted in 1853 to 638 souls, enjoys and has enjoyed the labours of at least two missionaries—4 sermons, 2 prayer meetings, Infant schools, Adult schools, sewing schools, classes, books &c &c. And the amount of visible success is very gratifying. A remarkable change indeed from the former state of these people. Yet the dregs of heathenism still cleave fast to the minds of the majority. They have settled deep down into their souls, and one century will not be sufficient to elevate them to the rank of Christians in Britain.

The double influence of the spirit of commerce and the gospel of Christ has given an impulse to the circulation of men, ideas and commodities over the face of the earth,[4] and the discovery of the gold regions has given enhanced rapidity to commerce in other countries and the diffusion of knowledge. But what for Africa? God will do something else for it. Something just as wonderful and unexpected as the discovery of gold.

Sat. 29th. Sowed on a small island by the town American Maize, Apricot stones, walnuts, beans, onions, carrots, parsneps, Beet Root, melons & watermelons, Tea & coffee. On 31st wheat, melons, pumpkins & dates.

---

[1] 'We had been a fortnight or three weeks on the Chobé when Poonoani and Mahali arrived' (Chapman, vol. i, p. 177).   [2] Cf. *Letters*, vol. ii, p. 232.

[3] In most Tswana tribes people may not start work in their gardens until the chief has proclaimed the new cultivating season open. Violation of this rule was formerly believed to affect the rainfall adversely. Cf. Schapera, *Land Tenure*, pp. 185-7.

[4] 'The double influence of the spirit of commerce and the gospel of Christ has given an impulse to the civilisation of men. The circulation of ideas and commodities...' (Blaikie, p. 148).

Sunday. Heavy and almost constant rain. The Atmosphere is cooling. The Temp. this morning 66°. I have not seen it so low for a long time. It was 82° in the evening of Friday though rain had fallen, 80° yesterday morning though it felt cold. The white and other ants swarmed after the first shower.

Had an intermittent last night. It has assumed the tertian type. Only one service, being hindered all morning by rain.

Mon. 31st. Insect youth burst forth into merry existence. Rhinoceros beetle flies at night producing a deep booming sounding, fire flies glance through the gloom by night, and all the birds are vocal by day. The country is very beautiful, the air is balmy as an English May.

Tuesday 1st Novr. Therm. morning 76°.

Wed. 2d. Sowed a small patch of rice in a moist part by way of experiment. People seem to know it, for they call it Seboyoiyo.[1]

Habit

Habit is a blessing, for we are enabled to bear many disagreeables by means of this property of the mind without inconvenience. When I first came into the country I was much annoyed during the hottest period of the day by the piercing chirr of the Seereneené, a large sort of cricket.[2] There is not the slightest variation in its note & that note is continuous, being produced by a sort of vibration of the wings and body, & as sharp as the shrillest scream of the Boatswain's whistle. Now however there may be scores of them all about, piping away with all their might, and unless I direct my attention to them I do not even hear them. Various insects too crawl about and on the parts on which one sits. These at first create very uneasy feelings, but after a time, as they are quite harmless, one is not annoyed by their presence. The meat of Zebras smells much like that of the horse, but by habit it comes to be regarded as about the best in the country.

Buceros Hydrocorax or Khoroe

The Khoroe, Buceros Hydrocorax,[3] presents us with a

---

[1] But in 1865 D.L. wrote: 'wheat, rice, and yams they have never seen' (*Narrative*, p. 278). 'Seboyoiyo' I cannot identify.

[2] Not identified.   [3] Red-billed hornbill; cf. above, p. 109.

picture of conjugal devotion in the male which I suspect is unequalled by any bird of the feminine gender. The nest is situated in the hollow of a tree, the result of a branch having decayed laterally or from the side inwards and downwards. This being scooped out to a convenient size, the opening is plastered up till space is left for her body only to enter. She continues to plaster afterwards with her droppings and those of her young till there is only a small slit left, about 3 inches long & $\frac{1}{2}$ an inch wide. She soon begins to lay her eggs, and in hatching them strips off all the feathers from her body. The cock feeds both her & her offspring, and so well does he perform this task she becomes enormously fat and is much prized as a dainty morsel by the natives in consequence, while her devoted slave of a husband is quite emaciated. Indeed, it frequently happens that the fall of temperature consequent on rains benumbs him, and he perishes in the midst of his exertions for the lady in the straw.

When the young are nearly full fledged she emerges, and well she may, she has been upstairs about 3 months. I have never been a spectator of one emerging from her confinement, but watched one for ten weeks and saw no indication of her quitting her comforts. The first time a nest was pointed out to me I broke it open in order to satisfy myself that a bird was really within. She was unfortunately killed. But passing the same spot about eight days afterward, I found that the widower had like most inordinately disconsolate husbands taken unto himself another wife and she was plastered in and all right. The process of wooing must have been short. There were few difficulties on the lady's part probably in view of such a comfortable settlement.

There are two varieties, viz. that mentioned above and another with a horny protuberance on his bill which has given rise to the name Buceros Rhinoceros. They are omnivorous, and are generally seen feeding on the ground. They eat the seeds of nux vomica, and so do the natives the pulp between the seeds, which is very pleasant to the taste & not unwholesome.

Facts about birds' nests

The little bird which builds the cotton nest is called Ton-

tobané by Bechuanas.[1] It is the smallest bird I have seen in
Africa, yet builds a nest which is quite a wonder of labour
and skill. The materials are a very short stapled kind of cotton and spider's web. The latter is much more tough than the
same material seen in England, and when formed of many
folds or strands, as the main stay or suspendor of the web is,
it resembles strong yellow silk sufficient to knock a light
straw hat off the head. The little architect works these materials untill it resembles felt. The spider's web seems to be the
connecting material in the fabric, yet it is marvellous how so
small a bird can so construct it as that it can be torn asunder
by man only with a very strong effort. It is furnished with a
tubular opening about 2 inches long and $\frac{3}{4}$ inch in diameter.
Immediately below the end of the tube is a semilunar hollow
having a neatly rounded lip of the same form. The natives say
this is used as a sleeping place or Kotla for the male bird while
the hen is hatching. This idea is taken from their own practice of sleeping in the kotla, or place of meeting for the men,
while their wives are confined. The Chief's Kotla is equivalent to the 'gate' in old testament times. It is more probably
formed in order to afford a firm standing place for the parent
birds while employed in opening and shutting the end of the
tube, which is left rough and thin in order to be the more
easily compressed. Its lips are always brought together when
they go in search of food, and the hole being so small and
yielding it would be impossible for them to open it and fly
into it from the wing. Other birds having nests with tubular
entrances make them wide and strong so that they can dash
into them from the wing. This little bird has hers thin &
flexible in order by shutting it to exclude the cold from her
most diminutive brood, and consequently requires a stand on
which to alight.

I am not quite certain that this is the true explanation, but
I have observed that the hole is alway[s] shut by being compressed from side to side when the lady is out, and open when
she is 'at home'. If the end of the tube is brought into the

---

[1] Identified by Roberts (*Birds*, p. 349) as the black-chested prinia, *Prinia flavi-
cans*, though D.L.'s description of the nest suggests the penduline tit, *Anthoscopus
minutus* (Roberts, p. 281). Brown (*Dictionary*, p. 324) translates *tontobane* 'a small
bird of the tomtit species'.

hollow it readily retains its place there, and the nest presents the appearance of an oval ball, but this I never saw as an effort of the birds themselves. When broken into by hawks or owls, it is usually by an opening made from above, they don't seem to understand that the tube is the opening.

The bird is less in size than our English wren, not nearly so active, has a short bill, the breast is canary coloured, back dark grey, lays two or three eggs spotted pale red. It does not seem to fear man much, only removing to the other side of a thick branch on his approach. It seems very affectionate towards its tiny offspring, and its nest is so constructed as to preserve them effectually from the vicissitudes of weather which would soon prove fatal to them.

Birds shew considerable intelligence in the construction of their nests. The oriole strips off all the leaves from the branch to which hers is attached, either to prevent dropping of rain from these or give her a clear view if a serpent should approach. Some of these are constructed over pools and are never used for incubation. They are semicircular in shape and have an opening corresponding to each point at which the circle is cut off. The space between is used as a shelter in time of rain & by night. She sits secure, able to escape at both ends. Her tail is not long enough to present any obstacle to

inculcation. They are semicircular in shape and have an opening corresponding to each point at which the circle is cut off. The space between is used as a shelter in time of rain & by night. She sits secure, able to escape at both ends. Her tail is not long enough to present any obstacle to her turning round. When these nests are constructed in the Bakwain

her turning round. When these nests are constructed in the Bakwain or Bakalihari country, where but little rain falls, they are made thin and light, but I have seen them in parts of the Colony, where rains are abundant, about four times the size & weight of the Bakalihari nests. She sometimes resolves to breed in them, and then patches up one of the openings and increases the thickness of the whole nest. It is lined with feathers too. The new and old materials are easily distinguished, the new being bright yellow, the old dark brown. The straw is very neatly woven together, the openings shewing a great amount of skill. It is not uncommon to see a male bird working most assiduously on a nest for days together, and then his wife begins in the most absurd manner and deliberately pulls it all to pieces. Whether it is the result of some private 'tift' between themselves, or some defect she has seen in its construction, or whether she is not a usurper destroying in order to afford materials for her own husband to work with, I am unable to discover. I never had time to observe for any considerable period, and they being gregarious it would be difficult to distinguish different individuals.

The swallows very often build tubes to their nests. I have seen some of these 8 inches long, and occasionally I have seen two tubes from the same nest, viz. the one on one side & the other on the other. I was on one occasion the cause of double tubes to a nest. It was built under the eaves of a low thatched house into which I frequently entered after the nest was finished. The opening of the tube faced me and was just my height as I approached the door, and after being alarmed two or three times & obliged to escape by first flying towards me the birds broke open the after part of the nest and built another tube in the opposite direction.

Another, observed at Motito, had built the tube straight, but some Hornets (Morothuane),[1] which are excessively pugnacious when near their young, had erected their nest exactly in front of the orifice of the nest. It is probable that matters went on amicably while the hornets were few, but when they increased the swallows were obliged for the sake of peace to build an addition to the tube and make it bent on itself so that the door looked away from the hornets.

[1] Tswana *moruthwane*, 'a hornet, a wasp' (Brown).

Thursday 3d. The natural effects of the murders perpetrated at the Borotse begin to shew themselves. Nokwane was attended by a doctor, who now reports that when engaged in this he was requested to allow him to die by certain of the chief men here, because, said they, he killed our chief Mpepe. This upsets the chief's sense of security. He came to inform me of it and seemed very uneasy. I let him know that this was the natural effect of the murdering he had been led to, and that he had thereby laden himself & his child with blood-guiltiness.

Insects

In the hottest season of the year shelter under a deep umbrageous tree called Motsikiri[1] is peculiarly pleasant. At noon the birds retire into the thickest shades to sleep. The large game take the only repose they seem to enjoy. The Elephants stand in a sort of stupour, giving their immense ears occasionally a lazy flap, & may be approached quite close if care is taken to break no branch, but treading on a very small twig is sufficient by its snapping to arouse them. The buffaloes, Rhinoceros, &c are all lying except the sentinels. The wary gnu, zebra, Pallahs, &c &c are all lying down, and are more ready to run off to a great distance if disturbed than either in the mornings or evenings. A hare roused from her lair at this time becomes bewildered by the noontide glare, and by watching into what tuft of corn she next rushed for shelter I several times caught them in my garden at Kolobeng by falling down upon them, seizing them by the neck and body.

Yet though it is the period of repose for most animals, not so of the insects. When neither birds nor beasts give forth a sound, there is a louder hum in the air than in the morning, a peculiar stifled sound issuing from every bush & tree, from the air under the trees and from beneath the soil. Myriads of ants both above & beneath. They work under thin covered galleries, knawing with unwearied mandibles the decayed vegetable matter. Other insects in thousands and of every form & hue sing merrily their monotonous songs,

---

[1] *Trichilia emetica*; described by Miller (*Woody Plants*, p. 40) as 'large umbrageous tree'.

others glance hither & thither & in every variety of course in the sunbeams. The attrition of millions of active wings, the nibbling of millions of never wearying jaws, and the whirr of myriads of organs of song, make one feel as if moving in the midst of a vast sea of organic life & enjoyment. All nature seems to breathe forth a song of mirth, and proclaims that God has clothed this fair world with a vast mantle of happy existence.

At this time after the rain all the labourers who by the intense heat were forced to work beneath the arid & dusty soil burst forth like merry schoolboys. The pleasant evenings are also seasons of enjoyment. The firefly glances in the surrounding gloom. It is scarcely possible to write with a candle now, so many different Coleopteri, gryllae, wingy ants, moths, crickets, crowd around and over the paper [and] one's face and body. The candle is full of them, and an immense red spider which gets its prey by running quickly about and seizing it creates alarm to one sitting on the ground. It is including the legs about $1\frac{1}{2}$ inch in length. It is named Selalee[1] and is perfectly harmless.

There is a little round jet black beetle armed with a sting. With this exception, and an ugly long black fellow, all the beetles are quite harmless. One with a pretty white band round its body like that on ships has the power of squirting out an extremely acrid fluid on any one who may presume to handle it. Its name is Sirotekamelo (don't micturate in the milk vessel).[2] The fluid is never ejected on other animals except in self defence. It is so acrid it will blister the skin of the hand, and it has caused the complete loss of an eye.

A curious insect may be seen where ants abound. It resembles a caterpillar of about one inch long & one eighth of an inch broad, covered with tufts of dark brown hair and possessing a pair of forceps at its tail end. I have seen it with one half of its body, viz. the head half, under ground, and the forceps end erect above. To this is given a quivering motion

[1] Tswana *selaledi*, 'tarantula spider' (Brown).

[2] *Serotêlakgamêlô*, 'a species of large black beetle with yellow marks' (Brown). They belong to the genus *anthia*, and 'must be handled with care, since they can eject a stream of formic acid from the anal orifice to a quite considerable distance' (G. Arnold, in *The Victoria Falls*, ed. J. D. Clark, Lusaka 1952, p. 108). D.L.'s translation of the name is correct.

in order to attract the ants, and as soon as one comes within the sphere of the forceps they instantly seize it and convey it to the edge of the hole in which the upper portion of the body is inserted, and down it goes at once to the head.[1] How does the insect see how to guide the forceps, the head and I suppose eyes being below ground?

Preparation for Departure

3d, evening. I intend to leave about the middle of next week with this country's people entirely. The Kuruman people return, for which I am very thankful. They are a nuisance, the very offscourings of that station.[2] Sekeletu promises me four pack oxen instead of one which I asked. They are at the Borotse, and I am induced to forgo the use of the horse by the fact of tsetse existing between this and the Borotse, which would almost certainly prove fatal to it. I therefore go by water, and having asked the favour of one pack ox Sekeletu kindly places all he has there at my service. He presents too the large canoe in which he went to the Borotse to me for my use, and will give a Mokololo man as a companion. All of the principal men agree in believing that Londa is a better way [than] the route by which Porto goes. I deposit my goods in Sekeletu's house for safety.

5th Saturday. Busy making preparations for the journey. I take the magic lantern and pontoon, Beads to pay my way, 20 lbs of coffee, three or fo[u]r of tea, biscuits, ammunition, books and bedding, a small gypsey tent, and sextant.[3] I send off by George a bill of £30 dated 14 Decr/52 to Mr Moffat to pay the people I have brought in and now send back. Wrote Mr Rutherfoord[4] about George & the waggon, and gave him (George) a share of my stock of food.

Mapuleanyane dreamed of a wife whom he had in former years, she scolded him and said may his house perish. He came to Lebeole and requested that his wife, who is a relative

---

[1] Cf. above, p. 105.

[2] 'Our servants were the worst possible specimens of those who imbibe the vices without the virtues of Europeans' (*Travels*, p. 120). Their shortcomings are detailed in *Letters*, vol. ii, pp. 231-4, 236-7, 238-9, 240-2.

[3] A more extensive list is given in *Travels*, pp. 230 f.

[4] Howson Edward Rutherfoord, a prosperous Cape Town merchant who had backed George's trading venture; cf. *Travels*, p. 120.

of the departed consort who keeps up her scolding propensities in the other world, [should] anoint[1] his face with oil and charm him. If one person treads on another he puts his finger to the person's heart and crown of the head to charm away any evil effects of the tread.

6th Sunday. Large audience. Kuruman people don't attend. If it is a fashion to be church-going many are drawn into its observance, but placed in other circumstances the true character comes out. This is the case with many Scotchmen. May God so imbue my mind with the spirit of Christianity that in all circumstances I may shew my christian character.

Had a long conversation with Mothibe, chiefly on a charm for defending the town or for gun medicine. They think I know it but will not impart the secret to them. I used every form of expression I could think of to undecieve him, but to little purpose. Their belief in medicine which will enable them to shoot well is very strong, and simple trust in an unseen Saviour to defend them against such enemies as the Matibele is too simple for them. I asked if a little charcoal sewed up in a bag were a more feasible god[2] than he who made all things, and told them that one day they would laugh heartily at their own follies in bothering me so much for gun medicine. A man who has never had to do with a raw heathen tribe has yet to learn the missionary A.B.C.

Mokhele's journey down the Sesheke

Mokhele[3] from Sesheke informs me that he was sent by Sebituane down the river a long way. The[y] went to the junction of the Bashukulompo river with the Zambesi. That river recieves another from Sebolamokoea. There is no Lake in these parts. They were two months going East and other two in returning. They had often to wade through extensive swamps up to the middle in water. Yet there are high mountains there. They met the party of Rya Syde &c, or as they

---

[1] MS. has 'to anoint'.

[2] 'a more feasible protector' (Blaikie, p. 151).

[3] Mentioned in *Narrative* (pp. 271, 276) as 'headman of the new town' of Sesheke, in succession to the executed Morantsiane (cf. above, p. 39). Still alive in 1885, when he travelled with Coillard, who calls him (p. 177) 'one of those venerable pagans that one loves to know'.

name him Tsaeri, and returned with him. These had been only seven days from their home. It is only six or seven days from Sesheke to the Bashukulompo river, and one could go down it to the Zambesi without any hindrance from water falls. The Bashukulompo river is very far from the Borotse but near Sesheke. There is a small river on the south side of the Zambesi navigable by canoes.

[handwritten reproduction of the above passage]

Notes about Ostriches

There are no ostriches on the lands which are annually flooded, probably because the food in which they delight does not grow on swampy ground. They seem to have been destined to inhabit arid plains such as the great Kalihari desert, for they are provided with feathers the loose pile of which affords a good shade from the sultry sun without increasing the heat. The black colour rather assists in lowering the temperature by radiation. They very rarely seek the shade of trees. Their food consists of the hard pods of Mositsane, Morulane and Mhatulancoe, & to assist the digestion of these a large number of small stones are swallowed. An instance occurred of an ostrich choking itself by attempting to swallow a wild melon.[1]

[1] 'He picks up also some small bulbs, and occasionally a wild melon to afford moisture, for one was found with a melon which had choked him by sticking in his throat' (*Travels*, p. 155).

They are polygamous, and sometimes two hen birds lay in the one nest. Forty nine eggs have been observed in one such nest. A single bird lays about a score of eggs, and the nest is merely a little of the soil scooped out from the space occupied by the eggs. There are usually a few smaller eggs lying about the nest which are never sat upon. What the object of these supernumeraries may be it is difficult to say. She is very particular about her nest eggs, & the Bushmen sometimes keep her laying some time by the daily abstraction of an egg. In approaching the nest they are careful to come up the wind, and they employ a long stick to take out the egg from the nest, lest the least scent should escape their bodies to the remaining eggs. They say a single foot print near the outer edge of the nest is quite enough to make her forsake it altogether. But though so very jealous of intrusion after she has made her nest, she is very careless before this period. She commences laying long before she thinks it necessary to make a nest, and then drops her eggs wherever she may happen to be. I have lighted on them thus thrown away frequently. Indeed, so commonly are they found at the season which precedes incubation that herds look out for them and Jackalls are reported to eat numbers of them. When the birds begin to make nests they are no longer seen. The Bechuanas have a distinct name for these foundlings and those which the parent intends to rear.[1]

They are very wary birds, possessing acute and long sight. They maintain their ground long after the introduction of fire arms. This they are enabled to do by their great speed and selection of level plains for their habitat. They are very foolish, often commence running without any apparent reason and often run to the danger instead of avoiding it. Sportsmen detest them, for they commence running and often set all the game in sight in motion ; and I have heard them called 'horrid fools' and other harsher names than that of the 'silly bird' of Job.[2] When the young come out they are covered with coarse down, and when alarmed squat down flat by the nearest bunch

[1] 'An ostrich egg not found in the nest' is called *lesetlha* (Brown; cf. *Travels*, p. 154); an ordinary ostrich egg is *letsae* (Brown).
[2] 'Because God hath deprived her of wisdom, neither hath he imparted to her understanding' (Job 39: 17).

of grass, the parent bird in the mean time pretending to lameness in the manner of lapwings in order to draw off the attention from the young. The eggs possess great vitality. I have kept a newly laid egg for three months in a cool place, and then find that a young bird had been in process of formation and still alive.[1] The eggs, especially the white of them, possess a strong disagreable flavour. There are few stomachs which will manage a single egg. The flesh of the bird itself when in good condition is not unpleasant. The colour of the male is jet black, that of the hen a dark brownish grey. Both have beautiful white feathers in the wings & tail. Those in the male are finest. They are sometimes killed by the lion, but can give a most effective kick. Dogs are killed by a single stroke of the foot. Their roar is almost exactly that of the Lion.

Though capable of going long without water, in seasons of intense drought when all their food is thoroughly desiccated they too must come to the rivers to drink. Many are then killed in pitfalls.

Eve of Departure

Mon. 7th. Arranged with George to take the driver out to Kuruman. He has but little regard to truth, and tried to force three months' additional pay from me by lies.[2] I feel sorry for him. I have only 21 oxen remaining, have lost six by tsetse.

Tuesday 8th. It is probable that the Leeambye, Maninche, Makoma, Loeti, Kabompo and Leeba are all branches leaving and returning again to one river in passing through a level country. The following is an outline of these rivers as given by Kolombota,[3] who has travelled among them. [Sketch]

Our intentions are to go up the Leeba till we reach the falls, then send back the canoe and proceed in the country beyond as we best can. Matiamba is far beyond, but the Cassantse[4] (probably Cassange) live on the west of the river.

[1] 'One kept in a room during more than three months, in a temperature about 60°, when broken was found to have a partially developed live chick in it' (Travels, p. 155).

[2] This apparently refers to Snyman (cf. above, p. 107, and Letters, vol. ii, p. 241).

[3] Probably 'Kolimbota', subsequently one of the party that set out with D.L. for Luanda, though he deserted en route; cf. Travels, pp. 268, 296, 483 f., etc.

[4] A tribe of BaNgala living between the Cuango and Lui Rivers, Angola. 'Matiamba' is Mwata Yamvo (cf. above, p. 228).

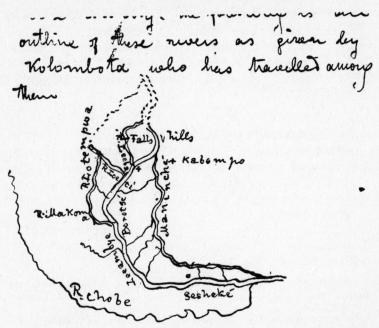

outline of these rivers as given by Kolombota who has travelled among them

May God in mercy permit me to do something for the cause of Christ in these dark places of the earth. May he accept my children for his service and sanctify them for it. My blessing on my wife. May God comfort her. If my watch comes back after I am cut off, it belongs to Agnes. If my sextant, it is Robert's. The Paris medal to Thomas. Double barreled gun to Zouga.[1] Be a father to the fatherless, and a husband to the widow for Jesus' sake.

9th. I deposit my waggon and goods in charge of Sekeletu and will leave tomorrow morning. This volume I leave in his charge too.[2] We embark on the Chobe. He has furnished an ox to be slaughtered as provisions when we start. May God bless this people and grant me success in opening up their country to the sympathy and succour of Christians.

10th. Detained today by the preparation of two Makololo

[1] The nickname of D.L.'s son Oswell, who was born on the banks of that river (cf. above, p. 68, and *Letters*, vol. ii, p. 143). The watch and sextant are briefly described in *Travels*, p. 231; the 'Paris medal' was the large silver medal awarded to D.L. in 1852 by the Geographical Society of Paris for the discovery of Lake Ngami (cf. *Letters*, vol. ii, p. 222).

[2] Cf. *Travels*, p. 229, and Introduction, p. x.

who go with me. I have two of the principal Borotse men. The party will be upwards of a dozen.[1] Seven oxen are provided as food for the journey, 4 pack oxen, and presents of beads oxen and fat for the chiefs of Londa who sent clothing to Sebituane for similar gifts. We leave tomorrow morning.

In the event of my being cut off in the midst of my efforts to open up the Interior of the Continent to the sympathies of enlightened & civilized Christians of other lands, I beg those into whose hands this may fall, to convey it so that it may reach my family. I leave for the North West next week.

David Livingston[2]

Linyanti
3d Novr 1853.

[1] It consisted in fact of D.L. and twenty-seven Natives, of whom two were Ma-Kololo, the others being 'Barotse, Batoka, Bashubia, and two of the Ambonda' (*Travels*, p. 228).

[2] This passage was written on the page facing the front end paper of Notebook II.

Appendix I

FRAGMENTS OF KOLOBENG JOURNAL
1848–9

The Portion of a Journal lost in the distruction
of Kolobeng by the Boers of Pretorius.[1]

May 10th 1848. Several deaths in the circle of our acquaintance—Pilanie,[2] Paulus[3] &c. No effect produced by attempts to improve these events. The spirit must breathe on the dry bones. All our expectations for success are in his blowing on them and quickening them. Rakhobe[4] promises to send his son to learn.

May 20th. Medicines applied to an ox in order that if enemy is in the field it may refuse to leave the pen, or if the enemy has come to the town it may refuse to come home.[5] Spoke to chief of the evil of trusting in medicine instead of in God. Confessed he was alarmed at the idea of offending Him. Was unaware that he could shew disrespect to the Divinity by working with them. All Bechuana medicines are of the same nature, all are believed to operate as charms or spells. There is no contending with God. Felt afraid to dispute on the subject. He would give up all medicine if I only told him to do so. I was gratified to see symptoms of tender conscience. May God enlighten him.

12th June. Thatching house. Put in a plate of lead in wall. That house is an evidence that I tried to introduce Christ's gospel into that country.

---

[1] D.L.'s heading (Notebook I, p. 316).

[2] Chief since c.1825 of the BaKgatla-bagaKgafêla, inhabiting the district named after him Pilansberg (Western Transvaal).

[3] Not identified.

[4] Not identified; possibly Rakubu Senna, one of Sechele's household stewards.

[5] Similar usages are still observed to protect cattle from disease, theft, straying, etc. Cf. Schapera, 'Herding Rites of the Bechuanaland BaKxatla', *American Anthropologist*, vol. 36, 1934, pp. 561–84.

10th July. Entered new house on 4th currt. A great mercy. Hope it will be more a house of prayer than any we have yet inhabited.[1] Recieve invitation from Dr Campbell to contribute to British Banner.[2] Seems a call to usefullness, for several points required to be brought prominently forward— Progression in Missionary work, Eastern tribes &c.

Sunday 6th August. Sechele remained as a spectator at the celebration of the Lord's supper, and when we retired he asked me how he ought to act in reference to his superfluous wives, as he greatly desired to conform to the will of Christ, be baptized, and observe his ordinance. Advised him to do according to what he saw written in God's book, but to treat them gently, for they had sinned in ignorance and if driven away harshly might be lost eternally.[3]

Monday 7th. A day of great commotion in the town. All seemed to be in perplexity. Complete cessation of work. Women all remained at home, although on every other lawful day they are seen going to the gardens in crowds. The men seemed downcast and dismayed. A large meeting in the Khotla. Many spoke fiercely, so much so as to surprise the chief himself. Next morning he resolved to call the people together generally and explain his conduct, and say if they wished to kill him to do so immediately. I went to see Makhari.[4] Poor thing, she was melted in tears, could not speak but with a choking voice. Offered me back her book, 'as she must now go where there is no word of God'. Wished that they could have remained in the town that they too might be saved, but Makhari has no relations. She was much loved and worthy of it. We shall not cease to pray that she may be saved.

---

[1] D.L. had previously lived at Mabotsa (1843–5) and Chonwane (1845–7).

[2] A nonconformist weekly published in London; founded (1848) and edited by John Campbell (1794–1867). The issues of 4 July and 14 November, 1849, contain articles by D.L. (signed 'A Surgeon') on 'The Peace Makers of the Interior of South Africa', criticizing the Native policy of the Transvaal Boers.

[3] Sechele then had five wives. On becoming a Christian he divorced all eccept Mma-Sebele (cf. p. 89), 'and sent them to their parents with an intimation that he had no fault to find with them, but that in parting with them he wished to follow the will of God' (*Travels*, p. 18).

[4] Mmakgari. First married to the Ngwaketse chief Sebego, she had eloped with Sechele after a visit he paid to her husband (Schapera, field notes, 1938; cf. Methuen, 1848, p. 217). Her ancestry has not been recorded.

Mokokoñ[1] said, while the tears chased each other down her cheeks, she would serve MaRobert or any one, but she could not leave us & her child.

Motsipi and Maokañeñ[2] rather angry than otherwise. They have no children.

10th. Makhari left this morning, did not take her books. May the Lord look upon her.

Pico[3] held at night in order to intimidate Sechele. Ramiko[4] said he too would put away his wives. The proposition put to Sechele was that the wives should be allowed to remain in their houses though he did not live with them.

Hear of the Griquas in the Desert at a stand for want of rains.[5]

15th. Sechele says the immemorial custom of the people in this country has been to imitate their chiefs. If he is fond of oxen all the men live at the cattle posts, if fond of hunting all rear dogs and hunt with him. But the Bible, though they see he likes it, and it is his own, not the teacher's or Paul's or Mebaloe's, yet not one follows him in learning it.

Maokañeñ came to church on Sunday.

1st September. Much opposition, but none manifested to us as individuals. Some however say, 'It was a pity the lion did not kill me at Mabotsa'.[6] They curse the chief with very bitter curses, and these come from the mouths of those whom Sechele would formerly have destroyed for a single disrespectful word. The truth will by the aid of the spirit of God ultimately prevail.

Sechele kept on probation for two months and then ad-

[1] Mokgokong, daughter of the Ngwato chief Kgari (c.1817–28), and mother of Sechele's children Bantshang (a girl), Kgari, and Mokgwaosele.

[2] Motshipi was the daughter of Sechele's paternal great-uncle Mmatlhi; Maokaneng may be another name for Modiagape, whose people (the BagaSeletlo) were immigrants of alien stock.

[3] *Pitsó*, a tribal assembly (cf. p. 155).

[4] Rra-Mhiko ('father of Mhiko'), alias Segakisa; head of Difetlhamolelo ward, and Sechele's chief henchman.

[5] This refers to a large party of hunters and traders trying to reach Lake Ngami. They did not succeed. (Cf. *JRGS*, 1850, p. 138).

[6] A reference to the famous incident in February 1844, when D.L. was injured by a wounded lion (cf. *Travels*, pp. 11 f., and *Letters*, vol. i, pp. 90 f., 93). Mabotsa, 25° 19′ S., 25° 46′ E., was his first mission station, among the BaKgatla-baMmanaana under Mosielele.

mitted. He had spoken to Paul about what God had done for his soul, and on the subject of prayer, before he opened his mind to me.

Sechele was baptized on the first Sabbath of October. Many shed tears of sorrow to see him 'so far left to himself'. Others wonder[e]d that it was only water, and not the brains of men. 'It seemed water only', said another—'this beats the last affair altogether' (putting wives away). Discovered in the evening that a horridly Satanic idea had long been promulgated among the people generally 'that the Lord's supper was a scene of impurity'.[1] It ought to be open to all. But for the propensity to laugh at everything solemn it would be publicly observed.

Finishing smithy. Waggon gone to Bamangwato.

October 22d. Smithy finished. Begin to cut corn. Setefano[2] was baptized on first Sabbath of October.

Novr. No rains. Much discussion on rain making. A rain doctor brought from Bamapela dismissed with an advice and reproof from Sechele. He rewarded him too & sent him off.

People intensely set on rain making fooleries. The most insignificant persons in the tribe talk with great insolence to Sechele. No one doubts his ability to make it. Old men come to me and entreat me to allow the chief to make rain. If I only do so all will come to meeting, and all will pray to God together. The people say the missionary too has medicines. 'Why does he use medicines if he does not believe in their power? He does not know ours, as we do not know his. God has given white men many things which he has not given to black men—guns, waggons, &c—and he has given black men many things which are not given to white men. The knowledge of trees which can make rain is one of these, and to ask us to give up rain making is the same as if we were to ask him to give up his waggon. And it is easy for him to give

[1] 'You can form but an imperfect idea of the forms of delusion Satan employs among this people. He has taught them that the ordinance of baptism is the administration of dead men's brains, & the Lord's supper a scene of impurity' (xi.1848 Drummond; cf. *Travels*, p. 18).

[2] Stephen, the baptismal name of Tumagole, Sechele's second son by Mma-Sebele. 'He mentioned his intention of calling his youngest child Setefano, in allusion to himself as wishing to be (like him) the first follower of Jesus in this country' (2.ix.1848 Moffat, in *Letters*, vol. i, p. 256).

up rain-making, for he has food got by irrigation, but we have none, and we cannot even get milk or roots without rain'. 'It is God alone who makes rain'. 'Of course, we know that, and never entertained any other idea, but it is God who cures diseases too. Whoever heard of one who could cure when death came? We pray to God by means of the medicines which he has given to us. We don't make the rain, he does'.[1]

Long for rains. Everything languishes during the intense heat, and successive droughts having only occurred since the gospel came to the Bakwains I fear the effect will be detrimental. There is abundance of rain all around us. Mosielele remarked that he had abundance of rain though he had no regard for God or the gospel, and yet we who have our chief at our head in attachment to the Word recieve not a drop. Has Satan power over the course of the winds & clouds? Feel afraid he will obtain an advantage over us, but must be resigned entirely to the Divine Will.

Novr 27. Rain making the great controversy. They say, 'We are very angry, we don't like you to speak on the subject. It is our bellies make us angry. We want rain, and if you argue about the means we think you don't want it and our throats make us angry'. O Devil, Prince of the power of the air, art thou hindering us? Greater is he who is for us than all who can be against us.

Intend to proceed with Paul to Mokhatla's.[2] He feels much pleased with the prospect of forming a new station. May God almighty bless the poor unworthy effort. Mebaloe's house being finished will leave more time for such efforts. Preparing woodwork for Paul's house.

People assert most positively that of old, before they ever heard of white men, they were in the daily habit of speaking of God and referring certain events to his will. All who possess intelligence speak in the same strain.

Decr 10th. At Mabé's[3] on our way to Mokhatla's in order

[1] This paragraph is evidently an early draft of the famous 'dialogue', an expanded version of which appears above (pp. 239–43).

[2] Mokgatlê, chief c.1835–89 of the BaFokeng in Rustenburg district, W. Transvaal. He had visited Chonwane in 1846, 'and expressed satisfaction with the idea of obtaining Paul as his teacher' (17.iii.1847 Tidman, in Chamberlin, p. 97).

[3] Chief c. 1820–69 of the BaTlhako at Mabeskraal, Pilansberg district.

to settle Paul there. May He who has the hearts of all men in his hand open [and] prosper[1] our way for us.

14th. Passed on by invitation to Hendrick Potgeiter the commandant. Wished me to shew him where the 25° Lat was. My instruments being at home I could not comply.[2] Buurman, who is very much like a Jesuit, shewed violent opposition to the English. Speaks high Dutch. I don't well understand him.[3] He seems to talk at me. Potgeither opposed to building school on the ground that that would be taking possession of their land for Govt in defiance of their right of conquest. Endeavoured to explain but ineffectually. He threatens to attack the tribe and drive it to the Limpopo if I offer to build. Told him if he hindered the gospel the blood of these people would be required at his hand. He became much excited at this. Found the Boer living at Mokhatla's friendly.[4] Resolve to proceed with the work.

Sunday 17th. Heard that Dr Robertson of Swellendam & Mr Faure of Stellenbosch had come to Kruger's to the Boers.[5] Resolve to go thither in order to engage their influence on our side. Dr R. very friendly. Boers very violently opposed. Potgeiter and Kruger promise to use all their influence on our side at a meeting to be held next month, and as they are sure of a majority on our side they will write me. They entreat me not to go on now in spite of those who are opposed, but rather return home, and they will at the meeting secure a vote of free permission to teach the people whenever I choose. I replied that I had permission from Christ and in his command sufficient authority and needed no other; but, replied they, if you go on now it will be like doing in spite of those who are

---

[1] Interlineation after 'open'.

[2] Andries Hendrik Potgieter (1792–1852) was Chief Commandant of the Boers in the Northern Transvaal. His wish to ascertain the whereabouts of Latitude 25° S. may have been due to the fact that the jurisdiction of courts in the Cape Colony did not extend farther north; cf. *Letters*, vol. ii, p. 12.

[3] Hendrick Theodorus Bührmann, a schoolmaster who sometimes acted as Potgieter's secretary, was a recent immigrant from Holland (hence his speaking 'high Dutch' instead of the nascent Afrikaans of the Boers). D.L. at one time mistakenly thought him 'a Jesuit missionary' (cf. *Letters*, vol. ii, p. 9).

[4] His name was Johannes Lodevicus Pretorius; cf. *Letters*, vol. i, p. 236.

[5] Revs. William Robertson (1822–79) and Philip Edward Faure (1811–82) were visiting the Transvaal Boers on behalf of the Dutch Reformed Church in the Cape Colony. Gerrit Johannes Kruger, Commandant of Magaliesberg district, lived at Hekpoort, about 30 miles E.S.E. of Rustenburg.

violently opposed to missionaries. At their entreaty I resolved to allow the building to stand for [the] present and went in the direction of Mamogale,[1] which is beyond Kruger's; but when bidding the clergy, Kruger & Potgeiter farewell they persuaded me not to go to Mamogale's at present, as they intended to attack him. I sent word to Mamogale of their intentions and took the road back.

Went to Pilanie's.[2] Had large attentive audiences at two villages. Could not get them to discuss the subject. Reach Mabé's on Tuesday. When on the way home, Paul & I looked for a ford in a dry river.[3] Found we had got a she black Rhinoceros between us and the waggon, which was only 20 yards off. She had calved during the night—a little red beast like a dog. She charged the waggon, split a spoke and a feloe with her horn, and then left. Paul & I jumped into a rut as the guns were in the waggon.[4]

Soon after our arrival at Kolobeng, we heard that Potgeiter had written to our Committee demanding my immediate recal, and that I should never be allowed to come into the country again, and intimating that if the Comm. did not remove me, the Boers would. They complained that I had given Sechele a cannon. This was the 'permission on a vote by the whole' which they promised me. They alluded to Khake's affair too, and concluded with the enormous fib that I had run away from them. The missionaries were perplexed by the epistle.[5]

[1] Chief c.1835–84 of the BaKwena-baMogopa in Rustenburg district.

[2] Pilane had recently died (cf. above, p. 297); his tribe was now ruled by his son Kgamanyane (cf. *Letters*, vol. ii, p. 12).

[3] 'Went to Pilanies. Had large attentive audiences at two villages when on the way home. Paul and I looked for a ford in a dry river.' (Blaikie, p. 92).

[4] This incident seems in fact to have occurred not now, but during an earlier trip to the Transvaal (cf. *Letters*, vol. i, pp. 235 f.).

[5] For Potgieter's 'epistle', cf. *Letters*, vol. ii, pp. 22 ff., and *Travels*, p. 38. In *Travels*, pp. 44 f., D.L. mistakenly says that his conversation with Potgieter (above, p. 302) was subsequent to its despatch. 'Khake's affair' was an attack made by Sechele in 1846 upon his uncle Kgakgê, successor of Bubi (cf. p. 99); Potgieter accused D.L. of violating an earlier promise by not warning the Boers that Sechele was on the war-path. He complained also that D.L., when invited at Hekpoort to answer various charges brought against him, had 'hastily fled without daring to greet anybody'. D.L. greatly resented this imputation of cowardice, maintaining that he left openly after making the proper farewells (cf. *Letters*, vol. ii, pp. 23 f.).

1849—Lake discovered

March 7. Mrs L. delivered of a son, Thomas Steele[1]—quick recovery. May God accept & save him.

Symptoms of pregnancy observed in Mokokoñ. Enquired of Sechele. Confessed he had been twice with her during Sentuhe's visit about beginning of January 1849. Wished to put her away, but where she is to go is always the difficulty. It is thought Sekhomi would kill her if she went there, as she is the rightful chief of the Bamangwato.[2] He shews much sorrow for his sin. Cut him off for a season. Isaac[3] too is cut off, for adultery. Boers and Satan seem determined to have me out of the country. Mrs L. leaves for Kuruman on the 15 April, 1849. She is to be accompanied by Mebaloe and family.

Resolved to visit the Lake Botletle,[4] but an express from Mr Oswel delays me till he comes.

People arrive from the Lake on 1st May.[5] Waiting for Mr Oswel.

3 May. Bakaa reach the Kolobeng. They have been driven from their own country by Sekhomi and have come to live here.[6] May they find a blessing.

1st June. Left Kolobeng for the Lake. Found water at Serotle[7] by digging down to a hard stratum of sand, about

---

[1] Named after (Sir) Thomas Steele (p. 68); cf. *Letters*, vol. ii, p. 33.

[2] Her mother having been Kgari's chief wife, Mokgokong was Sekgoma's senior half-sister. But as a woman she was barred from the succession; and despite the fear reported by D.L. she did later go to live at Shoshong (with her second husband, Moitoi). Her full brother Macheng, long held captive by the MaTebele, was brought back in 1857 by Moffat. Since he was the true heir, Sekgoma resigned in his favour. He ruled so badly that he was soon afterwards driven away, and Sekgoma became chief again.

[3] Son of the Native evangelist Paul, and Cumming's interpreter in 1845. Cf. *Letters*, vol. i, pp. 154 f.; vol. ii, pp. 27 f., 29.

[4] Cf. *Travels*, p. 62: 'The river Zouga was often spoken of by the same name as the lake [Ngami], viz. Noka ea Batletli ("river of the Batletli")'. Nowadays the Zouga is usually called Botletle. The 'Batletli' (BaTeti) live along its lower reaches.

[4] This was a party of seven men sent by Letsholathebe, inviting D.L. to visit him. Cf. *Travels*, p. 53; *Letters*, vol. ii, p. 50.

[6] The BaKaa, an offshoot of the BaRolong, had settled in the Shoshong hills early in the 18th century. They were found there *c.*1780 by the BaNgwato, also coming from the south, with whom they lived on friendly terms until Sekgoma, having acquired firearms, began to oppress them. Cf. *Letters*, vol. ii, pp. 25, 35; Schapera, 'Notes on the History of the Kaa', *African Studies*, vol. 4, 1945, pp. 115 f.

[7] Approx. 22° 42′ S., 25° 47′ E. (GSGS 2871 Transvaal).

five feet from the surface. If this is perforated the water disappears. The Bakalahari insert a reed into the wet sand which lies above this stratum, having a bunch of grass tied round the lower end. The sand is firmly rammed down around it. A little water is thrown around it in order to assist in the formation of a vacuum below. The mouth applied to the free end easily draws up abundance of water, which is guided by means of a straw from the mouth into their ostrich egg shells. Went our way North and providentialy found rain water 50 miles beyond at Mathuluane. Thence to Magana,[1] and then down the Mokokoñ dry river. A poor woman setting traps for small game was caught and shewed us Nchokotsa, a salt pan 20 miles in circumference.

4th July. Rode to river Zouga at Tsarologa's place.[2] People all come armed. Sekhomi had sent men all the way ahead of us to drive off the Bakalahari, so that we should not find water and be compelled to return. The River people were told that we had come to attack them. The man who performed this service became sick on the river & died. Saw people catching fish. Pelicans on the water.

Rode past Tsapoé's and Pampa's.[3] Spent Sunday at Bushman village, where Mr Oswel killed an Elephant, one of the tusks of which weighed 107 lbs.[4]

Elephants abound in immense numbers.

Saw Pate & Moiñ.[5] Spoke to people of both on the word of God, Jesus & the Resurrection. Women did not venture near. Moshen's next.[6]

Then Palane[7] with a fleet of canoes—had been down the river in order to kill hippopotami by means of harpoons and strong ropes. River about 60 yards wide, current 3 miles an hour.

[1] Mangana Vlei (cf. above, p. 100).

[2] Not identified; possibly the 'village of Bakurutse' mentioned in *Travels*, p. 63.

[3] Phampa, called 'Pompey' by some travellers, was a Khurutshe headman living a few miles south of Tsapo (cf. above, p. 7), to whom he was subordinate.

[4] The elephant was shot at Kidia Hill (cf. above, p. 248).

[5] Pati was a Teti chieftain living at approx. 21° 10′ S., 24° 43′ E. (GSGS 2871 Transvaal). Moeng I cannot identify.

[6] Masenyo was a Khurutshe headman living at approx. 21° 8′ S., 24° 36′ E. (GSGS 2871 Transvaal).

[7] Phalane lived at or near Makalamabedi (p. 20); he was therefore some distance from home when D.L. met him.

16 July. Left waggons at Ñabisane, all proceeding in Mr Oswel's small waggon. Reach Lake on 1st August. Lat. at Palmyra tree N.E. end of it Lat. S. 20° 20'.

Lechulathebe is a poor young fellow, the chief of the Bataoana. I tried to go to Sebitoane's, but he prevented me by ordering the Bakoba to refuse me a passage accross the river.[1]

Water of Zouga pure soft & clear ; has an oily feel in washing, but becomes harder as we descend.

Saw the Tamunakle. Is this not a highway into the Interior? A glorious prospect. Feel a great liking to the Bakhoba. Sent a message to Sebituane by Samuñana[2] & Palane.

Fruit bearing trees discovered—Palmyra, Mokucoñ, Motsouri, Moporotla.[3] The last bears a fruit 20 inches long and three in diameter.

Reached Kolobeng 16th October.

Visited by Mr Freeman[4] & Mr Moffat on last days of 1849 and beginning of 1850. Visit very agreable. A triennial deputation would have a good effect on all the missions.

Aspect of mission very discouraging in consequence of the ungodly conduct of Paul's family,[5] but we do not see it duty to drive the family away or suspend him.

The . . . . . . hen[6] retires into the hollow of a tree and is plastered up with the exception of a very small slit about 4 inches long & ½ an inch broad. She denudes her body of feathers to form a nest, hatches her eggs and does not come out untill the young are fledged. During the period of confinement she becomes quite fat and is a dainty morsel for Bechuanas, while the male is worn to a skeleton by constantly

---

[1] Letsholathebe's obstruction of D.L. is described in *Travels*, p. 69, as due to his fear that once the way was open Sebetwane would be able to acquire firearms from traders.

[2] Semonganga, headman of a Yeei village at approx. 20° 13' S., 23° 55' E. (TSGS 1539 Kalahari).

[3] Respectively, *Hyphaene ventricosa; Diospyros mespiliformis* (Tswana *mokotsong*); *Garcinia livingstonei* (Tswana *motsaodi*); and *Kigelia pinnata*, the 'sausage tree'.

[4] Joseph John Freeman (1794–1851), Home Secretary of the London Missionary Society, had been sent by the Directors to inspect the Society's mission stations in South Africa and Mauritius. His visit to Kolobeng is described in his book, *A Tour in South Africa*, 1851, pp. 279–92.

[5] It consisted in 'excessive impurity' and use of 'enchantments' (12.x.1852 Thompson, in Chamberlin, p. 182).

[6] D.L. left a blank space for the name, which he gives elsewhere (above, p. 283) as 'khoroe', the red-billed hornbill.

catering for her, and not unfrequently on the fall of temperature consequent to the occurrence of rain he falls a victim to his conjugal attentions. Saw one in December. Took her out. In about 10 days after, the male had provided another mate and she was plastered in as the other. Period of confinement said to be from 4 to 5 months.

Mr Freeman said if our Society abandoned the Hottentots they would sink again into their former state, for neither Dutch Church nor Wesleyans care for them. But are our stations to be kept up for ever because others will not do their duty? Perpetual tutelage and everlasting leading strings would enfeeble angels. Mr F. admitted that the Colonial system produced decrepitude. The fact of our continuing the system is a good salve for the consciences of those who do nothing. 'O they are cared for already'. But who cares for the millions beyond?[1]

An extract from a Journal the greater part of which was lost in the plunder of my house by the Independant Boers in September 1853.[2]

[1] Cf. above, p. 93.
[2] D.L.'s memory (or pen) was at fault; the correct date is 1852 (cf. above, p. 85).

Appendix II

OBSERVATIONS ON LATITUDE AND LONGITUDE BY MR MACLEAR[1]

In the Nautical Almanach, pages 551–564, a list of Occultations, viz. the elements for computing the occultations that will be visible from some point or other of the earth during the year, are given.

One observed Occultation will give a better determination of the Longitude than 50 Lunars. The instruments wanted are, a telescope, sextant and watch—the former to observe the instant of disappearance of the star behind the Moon's limb, the latter to find the true time in the ordinary way.

Thus, Observe an Altitude for time, viz. for the watch's error,

 Observe the Occultation,

 Observe an altitude for the watch error.

The difference between the first and last watch error furnishes the rate of the watch to correct the time by observation of the occultation.

The Column 'Limiting Parallels' indicates the Occultations which may be visible in a given parallel.

Thus, page 564 Decr 18, χ^4 Orionis will be visible somewhere between the parallels of Latitude 47° North and 9° South but nowhere on the outside of these Parallels.

It is useless to attempt to observe an occultation at the moon's bright limb with a small telescope, but a common spyglass will do for a star of the 5th Magnitude when the immersion and emersion happen at the moon's dark limb. They are best seen when the moon is young, or near the change. Within seven days of the change (before or after) the outline of the dark Limb is usually visible to the naked eye, and the limb can be watched approaching the star. When they seem to be nearly in contact, the spyglass should be rested on the waggon or some other support, and the star

[1] Notebook I, pp. 308–14.

308

kept in view, the observer being seated. The moment of disappearance, which happens with the celerity of lightning, is so quick that it may be estimated by a practical observer to the tenth part of a second. At that moment the distance at the eye between the star and moon's centre is of course the moon's semidiameter. Therefore an occultation furnishes a lunar distance, but measured with a degree of precision which no instrument (as a sextant) could furnish.

The calculations are somewhat difficult to persons unpracticed in Astronomical computations, therefore should be turned over to a regular calculator.

Two instants of time are wanted, viz. an instant of time at the station, and the corresponding instant at Greenwich. The instant at the station is found from an altitude of the sun or a star. The corresponding instant at Greenwich is found by the position of the moon, either observed at the moment of taking the Altitude or by reducing the one to the other by means of a watch.

The instruments required are one or more sextants and a watch.

If there is only one observer, the order of observing should be such as to cause the several means to approach the same moment—thus,

Altitude of the Sun or Star to be observed with the moon.
Altitude of the Moon.
Distance of the Moon's bright limb from the sun or star

$$ * - (\qquad * - \math>D $$

Altitude of the Moon.
Altitude of the Sun or Star.
Noting the time of each observation by *the watch*.

If there are three observers, and the Sun or Star measured from the Moon is in a good position for obtaining the time viz. as near due East or West as possible, the watch is not wanted, provided with the day *the nearest hour* of the day is entered with the observations.

A near estimate of the Longitude may be obtained by observing the Altitudes *only* of the sun or star and the moon's defined limb. Thus, if there is only one observer and the watch,

Altitude of the Sun or Star
Altitude of the Moon
Altitude of the Sun or Star.

If two observers, both Altitudes can be taken at the same instant, and the watch is not wanted, only note the day of the month as usual, and the nearest estimated hour of the day. Also whether both objects are on the same side, or one to the East and the other to the West of the Meridian, and stating also which is East and which is West.

In all cases the Latitude requires to be observed. Jupiter and Saturn are easily distinguished, & though not so good as the sun or a star for comparison with the Moon or for the Latitude, yet if well observed and all circumstances registered, so that the motion of the planet may be allowed for, they will afford a near approximation.

As a first approximation to the index error of a sextant, any distant tree stick or stone may be selected and both images of it be made to coincide, viz. the one to overlap the other. Then if 0° on the Vernier is to the left of 0° on the limb, viz. if the 0° on the Vernier is on the arch side of 0° in the arch, or 'On' in sea language, the difference is to be subtracted from any angle measured by the instrument. In short, the point on the limb corresponding to 0° of the Vernier is the starting point of the angle to be measured.

Bringing both images of a star or planet exactly into *one* is still more accurate. The Sun's disc is rather too large, still if brought so that only one disc is visible, in other words that one exactly overlaps the other, the corresponding point on the limb or arch will be the starting point, and the difference between that point and the 0° of the limb will be the index error, to be subtracted if 'On' or added if 'Off'.

A much more accurate method is to make the Sun's limbs just touch. The centres are then separated by an angle equal to the Sun's semidiameter, viz. by twice the semidiameter. The reading having been noted, the opposite limbs are to be brought into conduct, and the reading noted. Half the difference of the two readings is the index error to be applied as before mentioned.

Copied on Zouga 15 June 1850.

Appendix III

NATIVE NAMES OF ANIMALS, ETC.[1]

Stride of ostrich when walking leizurely is 2 feet one or 2 inches.

$$\begin{array}{r} 30 \\ 4 \\ \hline 120 \\ 6 \\ \hline 720 \\ 60 \\ \hline \end{array}$$

30 strides in 15 seconds of time

120 in one minute

6 average length of stride 6 ft.

$$1760)43200(\ 25 \text{ miles an hour}$$
$$\underline{3520}$$
$$8000$$
$$8800$$

I have lost a note of the length of stride when at full speed, and if it were as I think 12 feet that would give about 50 miles per hour.

Height of the Batoka calf, 22 inches.

Enquire after following plants &c :[2]
The Kukama or Gemsbuck digs Mokhopa and eats Likongkota or Letlōpō (a medicine for bowels[3]), Tlakushube.
Khoodoo eats Mohotlo, Mogonono, Setlasinyana (a low bush), Mokaikai, Mokabi, Morulana, Mokalo, Mōka.
Ostrich : (stones?), Morulane, Mositsane, Mhatulancoe.
Pute :[4] Kanné, Mashu, Bolatsi ; drinks in winter only.
Puruhuru[5] drinks in winter only, feeds on grass & bulbs.
K'okama :[6] grass, & Letlopo.

---

[1] Miscellaneous jottings in Notebook II, pp. 349–54, 357, and two end leaves.
[2] For identifications of the plants, see Appendix IV.
[3] Interlineation above the words 'Likongkota or Letlōpō'.
[4] Tswana *phuti*, grey duiker (*Sylvicapra grimmia*).
[5] Tswana *phuduhudu*, steenbok (*Raphicerus campestris*).
[6] Apparently an alternative for *kukama*, gemsbok (cf. Shortridge, p. 560).

Motlogo, 'Mhala : what are they ?[1]

Little unknown animals :[2]
Sarikwe
Sehalamolokwane
Makotokwe [plural of *kotôkwe*, 'a grey ground squirrel with short tail ; a species of meercat' (Brown)]
Leselemotlaka [*Lesêlamotlhaka*, 'a small animal living in reeds, destructive to fowls' (Brown)]
   Khanu [*Kgano* : slender mongoose, *Herpestes sanguineus*]
   Setlora [*Setlhora* : bush squirrel, *Paraxerus cepapi*]
   Khamoe e mitlua, is red like Tsipa [Called 'Khanametla' by Chapman, vol. ii, p. 337, who describes it as a reed-dwelling animal somewhat resembling the otter. For Tsipa, see below, p. 313]
   Shageshagé
   Pheho [*Phifo* : Selous' meerkat, *Paracynictis selousi*]
   Letototo [*Letôtôtô* : banded mongoose, *Mungos mungo*]
   Chiakaka
   Siakatsie
   Kwaga, like Motlose [For Motlose, cf. below, p. 315]
   Tukwe [*Thukhwi* : aardwolf, *Proteles cristatus*]
   Sebalabolokuane, like Tsipa [*Sebalammolokwane* : black-footed cat, *Felis nigripes*]
   Motsikitsiki [*Tsikitsiki* : rock dormouse, *Graphiurus platyops*]
   Motibicuana
   Motselekutega

Small animals :
   Armadilla, kaga [*Kgaga* : Cape pangolin (scaly anteater), *Manis temmincki*]

---

[1] Neither word occurs in Brown's *Dictionary*.

[2] In this and the following lists of animals, I have wherever possible included in brackets after each name the modern Tswana spelling, the common English name, and the scientific identification. For the last I have relied initially upon G. C. Shortridge, *The Mammals of South-West Africa*, 2 vols., 1934, and A. Roberts, *The Mammals of South Africa*, 1951, both of which give Native names of the animals described; but for the scientific names themselves I have preferred to follow J. R. Ellerman, T. C. S. Morrison-Scott, and R. W. Hayman, *Southern African Mammals 1758 to 1951: a Reclassification* (British Museum. 1953). Lack of annotation means that I have been unable to identify the animal as named by D.L.

Takaru, anteater (large) [*Thakadu* : antbear, *Orycteropus afer*]

Pela, hyrax [*Pela* : dassie, hyrax, *Procavia capensis*]

Tlolo, rabbit [*Tlhôlô* : red hare, *Pronolagus spp.*]

Mutla, hare [*Mmutla* : Southern bush or scrub hare, *Lepus europaeus*]

Tsipo, jerboa [*Tshipo* : spring hare, *Pedetes capensis*]

Tsipa, spotted ocelot [*Tshipa* : spotted genet, *Genetta spp.*]

Page, wild cat [*Phagê* : African wild cat, *Felis libyca*]

Ntlolane= Tsipo [*Ntlole* : spring hare ; cf. *Tshipo*]

Sekatemosima, squirrel [*Sekate*, 'a species of ground squirrel' ; *mosima*, 'an animal's hole in the ground' (Brown)]

Mesha, meercat [Plur. of *mosha* : yellow mongoose, *Cynictis penicillata*]

Lenyebi, otter [*Lenyebi* : Spotted-necked otter, *Lutra maculicollis* ; Cape clawless otter, *Aonyx capensis*]

Noku, porcupine [*Noku* : Cape porcupine, *Hystrix africaeaustralis*]

Setlong, hedgehog [*Setlhong* : Cape hedgehog, *Erinaceus frontalis*]

Macuane, ratel [*Matšhwane* : ratel or honey badger, *Mellivora capensis*]

Nakeri, polecat [*Nakedi* : striped polecat, *Ictonyx striatus*]

Khabu, monkey [*Kgabo* : vervet monkey, *Cercopithecus aethiops*]

Cuene, baboon [*Tshwene* : chacma baboon, *Papio ursinus*]

Mohole, sloth(?) [*Mogwêlê* : bushbaby or night-ape, *Galago senegalensis*]

Serunya, mole [*Serunyi, serunya* : used for moles generally]

Pachydermata :

Elephants, Tlou or Tlow [*Tlou* : African elephant, *Loxodonta africana*]

Rhinoceros, Chookuru [*Tshukudu* : rhinoceros (generic)]

Hippopotamus, Kooboo [*Kubu* : hippopotamus, *Hippopotamus amphibius*]

Wild Hog, Kolobe [*Kolobe* : wart hog, *Phacochoerus aethiopicus* ; bush-pig, *Potamochoerus porcus*]

Antelopes :

Giraffe, Tootlooa [*Thutlwa* : giraffe, *Giraffa camelopardalis*]

Eiland, Pohoo [*Phofu* : eland, *Taurotragus oryx*]

Kukama=gemsbok [*Kukama* : gemsbok, *Oryx gazella*]

Kualata=Tagetsi, bastard gemsbuck [*Kwalata, Thagetsi* : roan antelope, *Hippotragus equinus*[1]]

Kaama, haartebeeste [*Kgama* : hartebeest, *Alcelaphus buselaphus*]

Tsessebe, Bastard D⁰. [*Tshêsêbê* : sassaby, tsesseby, *Damaliscus lunatus*]

Nonne=Noonyana, roan antelope[2] [*Nônê* : blesbok, *Damaliscus dorcas*]

Kokong, wildebeeste [*Kgokong* : blue wildebeest or brindled gnu, *Connochaetes taurinus*]

Pallah, roibuck [*Phala* : impala, *Aepyceros melampus*]

Tsépe, springbuck [*Tshêphê* : springbok, *Antidorcas marsupialis*]

Phute, duiker [*Phuti* : grey duiker, *Sylvicapra grimmia*]

Puruhuru, steinbuck [*Phuduhudu* : steenbok, *Raphicerus campestris*]

Potokuane, black buck or antient oryx [*Potokwane* : sable antelope, *Hippotragus niger*]

Lehele [*Lehele* : mountain reedbuck, *Redunca fulvorufula*]

Lekabayane, klipspringer [*Mokabawane* : klipspringer, *Oreotragus oreotragus*]

Tsama, Angus' antelope [(?) : inyala, *Tragelaphus angasi*]

Lechwee [*Letšhwe* : lechwe waterbuck, *Kobus leche*]

Nakong [*Nakong* : marshbuck, sitatunga, *Tragelaphus spekei*]

Tolo, khoodoo [*Thôlô* : kudu, *Tragelaphus strepsiceros*]

Mochose=Putega, water buck

Letumaga, D⁰. or modern oryx [*Letumuga, motumuga* : waterbuck, *Kobus ellipsiprymnus*]

Poku [*Poku* : puku, *Kobus vardoni*]

Buffalo, narri [*Nare* : African buffalo, *Syncerus caffer*]

---

[1] *Kwalata* is also used for sable antelope; the identification given is based upon the names *thagetsi* and 'bastard gemsbuck' (Afrikaans *bastergemsbok*).

[2] D.L. is probably mistaken; the usual Tswana names for 'roan antelope' are *kunkuru* and *kwalata*.

Seroolemotlokwe, bushbuck [*Serôlôbotlhôkô* : bushbuck, *Tragelaphus scriptus*]

Teeanyane [*Tianyane* : oribi, *Ourebia ourebi*]

Puruma, witquas wildebeeste [*Pudumô* : black wildebeest or whitetailed gnu, *Connochaetes gnou*]

Twane, lynx or roikat [*Thwane* : caracal lynx, *Felis caracal*]

Pukuye, silver jackall [*Phokojê* : Cape fox or silver jackal, *Vulpes chama* ; black-backed jackal, *Canis mesomelas*]

Motlose, dark jackall [*Motlhose* : bat-eared fox, Delalande's fox, *Otocyon megalotis*]

Tau, lion [*Tau* : lion, *Panthera leo*]

Nkgwe, cheeta [*Nkwê* : leopard, *Panthera pardus*]

Letlotse, hunting cheeta [*Letlotse* : cheetah, *Acinonyx jubatus*]

Pheeree, hyaena : dark or spotted, & light-coloured = e encu. Letlongkana, Tamagana, & Serooroome. [*Phiri* : hyena (generic) ; *e ntsho*, black (adjective) ; *Letlonkana* : brown hyena, *Hyaena brunnea* ; *Thamagana* : spotted hyena, *Crocuta crocuta* ; *Serurume* = (?)]

Tware, spotted cat (large) [*Tadi* : serval, *Felis serval*]

Letlaleroa, or wild dog [*Letlhalerwa* : hunting dog, *Lycaon pictus*]

[Animals killed]
 Zebras 3
 Mocosa 2 ['*Mocosa*, a reed buck' (Brown)]
 Tagetse 1 [*Thagetsi*, roan antelope]
 Machwee 5 [Plur. of lechwee]
 Eilands 1, 1
 By Sneyman[1] 17 head
 Elephants 3
 Buffaloes 1, 1 = 35
 Oxen 5, 1, 1

[Vegetables and fruits]
 Moyelo} sweet potato
 Nkolu }
 Moanja } manioc
 Mpahisa}

---

[1] The name is crossed out in the MS.

Mobola[1]

Sekhutsane⎱
Eāya   ⎰ batata or potato

Moshuati, sugar

Birds on the river in large numbers :

The Chenalopex or Egyptian goose, eating lotus; the Oidemia or scoters, with large tumour on bill; Anser albifrons; Clangula histrionica—wee, wee, wee; and among the Lamellirostres the spoonbill. Sterna or Terns, flying like swallows and plunging for their food. Rhynchops or skimmers or scizzor bills. Fish hawk. King fishers, 3 varieties, white bird. Balearic crane or Numidian crane. Adjutant— white breast & slate-coloured back. Pretty little black bird with yellow bill, red legs.

Swallows return October, Motseganoñ depart.

Ñuanatsele, when the mushrooms grow; Palane, trees sprout.[2]

Swallows reported to leave in May & return again in October.

LeKoñka, corn of Borotse.

[1] *Parinari mobola.*

[2] *Motsheganong, Ngwanatsele,* and *Phalane,* are the Tswana names for May, November, and October, respectively.

Appendix IV

NATIVE NAMES OF PLANTS[1]

Bolatsi   *Kalanchoe rotundifolia*

Kanné
Kelerisa
Khane

Lerushua   Lerishô, lerushô, 'a species of large edible bulb' (Brown)

Letlōpō
Likokwe
Likongkota

Mahata   Plur. of Mohata, q.v.

Mahatla   Mafatlha, plur of mhatlha [mofatlha], *Tarchonanthus camphoratus*

Mahotlo   Plur. of Mohotlo, q.v.

Mashu   Plur. of Moshu, q.v.

Mhatulancoe   Mhatlhwantse, *Lachnopylis heterotricha*

Mocaca   Motšatša, *Adenia glauca*

Mochweeré   Motswiri, *Combretum imberbe*

Mogonono   *Terminalia sericea*

Moguana   Mogwana, *Grewia cordata, G. grisea, G. occidentalis*, etc.

Mohata   *Lonchocarpus capassa*

Mohonono   *See* Mogonono

---

[1] The plants listed here are those mentioned in the text (Chapter VII and Appendix III) as being eaten by certain animals. The left-hand column gives (in alphabetical order) the name as recorded by D.L.; the right-hand column gives the modern Tswana spelling (where it differs from D.L.'s), and the scientific name of the plant (according to O. B. Miller, *The Woody Plants of the Bechuanaland Protectorate*, 1952) or other identification (according to Brown's *Secwana Dictionary*). No entry in that column implies that I have not been able to find the relevant information.

317

Mohotlo	Mogôtlhô, *Acacia giraffae*
Mōka	Mooka, *Acacia karroo*
Mokabe, Mokabi	Mokabi, *Combretum transvaalense*
Mokaikai	*Bergia decumbens*
Mokalo, Mokhalo	Mokgalo, *Zizyphus mucronata, Z. abyssinica, Z. zeyheriana*
Mokhi	*Acacia gerrardi*
Mokhoba, Mokoba	Mokôba, *Acacia burkei*
Mokhopa	
Mokolane	*Hyphaene ventricosa*
Mokotlane	
Monato	*Burkea africana*
Mongana	*Acacia detinens*
Monokane	Monokwane, *Heeria salicina, H. paniculata*
Monuana	Monwane, *Byrsocarpus orientalis*
Monyelenyele	*Ochna pulchra, O. pretoriensis*
Mopane	Mophane, *Colophospermum mopane*
Mopura-chukuru	Mophuratshukudu, 'a tree which grows in black ground' (Brown)
Morala	*Gardenia spathulifolia*
Moraroane	Moralwane, *Secamone viminale*
Moreaboku	
Moretloa	Moretlwa, *Grewia flava*
Morolane	Morolana, *Solanum panduraeforme*
Morula	*Sclerocarya caffra*
Morulana, Morulane	Morulana, 'a shrub the root of which is pounded and used for sores' (Brown)
Morulega	
Morupaphiri	*Rhus commiphoroides*
Mosegashule	Mosegaseolo, 'a very strong species of grass used for thatching' (Brown)
Moselesele	Mosêlêsêlê, *Dichrostachys glomerata*
Moshu	Mošu, *Acacia litakunensis, A. spirocarpa, A. arabica*
Moshukubyane	Mošukubyane, *Lippia asperifolia*
Mosilabele	*Rhus lancea*
Mosimama	*Senecio laxiflorus*
Mositatlou	Mositlatlou, *Mundulea sericea*

Mositsane	*Elephantorrhiza elephantina, E. burkei*
Motlalagari	
Motloa	Motlhwa, *Cynodon dactylon*
Motlopi	*Boscia albitrunca*
Seghwere	Segwêrê, 'bulb' (Brown)
Sehouhatsa	
Sekaname	*Urginea burkei*
Sekopane	
Setlasinyana	
Sibite	Sebete, *Cassia obovata*
Tépe	Thepe, *Amarantus paniculatus*
Tetele	
Tlakushube	
Tlokwane	

LIST OF REFERENCES

A. Manuscript Sources

Letters from D. L. to W. C. Oswell, 15.xi.1851 (in Rhodes-Livingstone Museum, Livingstone); W. Thompson, 12.x.1852 (in L.M.S. archives, London); A. Tidman, 12.xii.1852 (in L.M.S. archives).

Livingstone's Journal, 1853–6 (owned by Dr H. F. Wilson, St Fillans, Perthshire).

B. Books and Articles

(In general, only works cited more than once are listed here, unless they refer specifically to Livingstone or the regions in which he travelled. Biographical dictionaries and other standard reference works have been omitted.)

ARNOT, F. S. *Garenganze, or Seven Years' Pioneer Mission Work in Central Africa.* 2nd ed., London, 1889.

See LIVINGSTONE, *Missionary Travels.*

BLAIKIE, W. G. *The Personal Life of David Livingstone.* London, 1880; 2nd ed., 1881.

BLEEK, DOROTHEA F. *A Bushman Dictionary.* New Haven, Conn., 1956.

BREUTZ, P. L. *The Tribes of Marico District.* Pretoria, 1953.

The Tribes of Mafeking District. Pretoria, 1955.

BROWN, J. T. *Secwana Dictionary.* Tiger Kloof, 1931.

CAMPBELL, R. J. *Livingstone,* London, 1929.

CHAMBERLIN, D. (ed.). *Some Letters from Livingstone 1840–1872.* London, 1940.

CHAPMAN, J. *Travels in the Interior of South Africa.* 2 vols. London, 1868.

COILLARD, F. *Sur le Haut-Zambèze: Voyages et Travaux de Mission.* Paris, 1899.

CUMMING, R. G. *Five Years of a Hunter's Life in the Far Interior of South Africa.* 2 vols. London, 1850.

CURSON, H. H. Notes on Eastern Caprivi Strip. *S. Afr. Journal of Science,* vol. 43, 1947, pp. 124–57.

DEBENHAM, F. *The Way to Ilala: David Livingstone's Pilgrimage.* London, 1955.

DIAS, G. S. (ed.). *Silva Pôrto e a Travessia do Continente Africano.* Lisbon, 1938.

DOKE, C. M. *Bantu: Modern Grammatical, Phonetical, and Lexicographical Studies.* London, 1945.

DOLMAN, A. *In the Footsteps of Livingstone.* Edited by John Irving. London, 1924.

ELLENBERGER, D. F. *History of the Basuto, Ancient and Modern.* London, 1912.

ELLERMAN, J. R., MORRISON-SCOTT, T. P. S., and HAYMAN, R. W. *Southern African Mammals 1758 to 1951: a reclassification.* London (British Museum), 1953.

[FAULKNER, D. E., and EPSTEIN, H.] *The Indigenous Cattle of the British Dependent Territories in Africa.* London, 1957 (Colonial Advisory Council of Agriculture, Publication No. 5).

FREEMAN, J. J. *A Tour in South Africa.* London, 1851.

GELFAND, M. *Livingstone the Doctor, his Life and Travels.* Oxford, 1957.

GIBBONS, A. ST H. *Africa from South to North through Marotseland.* 2 vols. London, 1904.

GLUCKMAN, M. The Lozi of Barotseland in North-Western Rhodesia. *Seven Tribes of British Central Africa,* ed. E. Colson and M. Gluckman (London, 1951), pp. 1–93.

HODSON, A. W. *Trekking the Great Thirst.* London, 1912.

HOLUB, E. *Eine Culturskizze des Marutse-Mambunda-Reiches.* Vienna, 1879.

JALLA, A. *Litaba za Sicaba za Ma-Lozi.* 3rd ed. Sefula (N. Rhodesia), 1934.
Dictionary of the Lozi Language. Vol. I: Lozi-English. 2nd ed. London, 1936.

KIRBY, P. R. (ed.). *The Diary of Dr Andrew Smith, 1834–1836.* 2 vols. Cape Town, 1939, 1940.

LESTRADE, G. P. Traditional Literature. *The Bantu-Speaking Tribes of South Africa,* ed. I. Schapera (London, 1937), pp. 291–308.

LEYLAND, J. *Adventures in the Far Interior of South Africa.* London, 1866.

LIVINGSTONE, D. Expedition to the South African Lake Ngami; extracts of letters. *J. R. Geogr. Soc.,* vol. 20, 1850, pp. 138–142.

Second Visit to the South African Lake Ngami; extract of a letter. *J. R. Geogr. Soc.*, vol. 21, 1851, pp. 18–24.

Latest explorations into Central Africa beyond Lake Ngami. *J. R. Geogr. Soc.*, vol. 22, 1852, pp. 163–74.

Explorations into the Interior of South Africa. *J. R. Geogr. Soc.*, vol. 24, 1854, pp. 291–306.

Explorations into the Interior of Africa. *J. R. Geogr. Soc.*, vols. 25, 1855, pp. 218–37; 26, 1856, pp. 78–84; 27, 1857, pp. 349–87.

Missionary Travels and Researches in South Africa. London, 1857; new ed., with notes by F. S. ARNOT, 1899.

See CHAMBERLIN, MONK, SCHAPERA, WALLER, WALLIS (eds.).

LIVINGSTONE, D. and C. *Narrative of an Expedition to the Zambesi and its Tributaries.* London, 1865.

MABILLE, A., and DIETERLEN, H. *Southern Sotho-English Dictionary.* Revised by R. A. Paroz. Morija (Basutoland), 1950.

MCCULLOCH, MERRAN. *The Southern Lunda and Related Peoples.* London, 1951.

MACKENZIE, J. *Ten Years North of the Orange River.* Edinburgh, 1871.

MARAIS, J. S. *The Cape Coloured People 1652–1937.* London, 1939.

METHUEN, H. H. *Life in the Wilderness; or, Wanderings in South Africa.* 2nd ed. London, 1848.

MILLER, O. B. *The Woody Plants of the Bechuanaland Protectorate.* Kirstenbosch, 1952; reprinted from *Journal of South African Botany*, vol. 18.

MOFFAT, R. See SCHAPERA, WALLIS (eds.).

MONK, W. (ed.). *Dr Livingstone's Cambridge Lectures.* Cambridge, 1858.

NETTELTON, G. E. History of the Ngamiland Tribes up to 1926. *Bantu Studies*, vol. 8, 1934, pp. 343–60.

OSWELL, W. C. Expedition to the South African Lake Ngami; extract of a letter. *J. R. Geogr. Soc.*, vol. 20, 1850, pp. 143–51.

With Livingstone in South Africa [and other South African reminiscences]. *Big Game Shooting*, ed. C. Phillipps-Wolley (2 vols., London, 1894), vol. I, pp. 26–153.

OSWELL, W. E. *William Cotton Oswell, Hunter and Explorer.* 2 vols. London, 1900.

PASSARGE, S. *Die Kalahari.* Berlin, 1904.

PETTMAN, C. *Africanderisms: a glossary of South African colloquial words and phrases.* London, 1913.

ROBERTS, A. *The Mammals of South Africa.* Johannesburg, 1951.

The Birds of South Africa. Revised by S. R. McLachlan and R. Liversidge. Cape Town, 1957.

ROUILLARD, NANCY (ed.). *Matabele Thompson, his autobiography.* Revised ed. Johannesburg, 1953.

SCHAPERA, I. *The Khoisan Peoples of South Africa: Bushmen and Hottentots.* London, 1930.

A Handbook of Tswana Law and Custom. London, 1938 (2nd ed., 1955).

Short History of the BaNgwaketse. *African Studies,* vol. I, 1942, pp. 1–26.

Native Land Tenure in the Bechuanaland Protectorate. Lovedale, 1943.

The Ethnic Composition of Tswana Tribes. London, 1952.

The Tswana. London, 1953.

SCHAPERA, I., and VAN DER MERWE, D. F. *Notes on the Noun-Classes of some Bantu Languages of Ngamiland.* Cape Town, 1942.

SCHAPERA, I. (ed.). *Ditirafalô tsa Merafe ya BaTswana.* Lovedale, 1940.

Apprenticeship at Kuruman: being the journals and letters of Robert and Mary Moffat 1820–1828. London, 1951.

David Livingstone: Family Letters 1841–1856. 2 vols. London, 1959.

SCHULTZE, L. *Aus Namaland und Kalahari.* Jena, 1907.

SEAVER, G. *David Livingstone: his Life and Letters.* London, 1957.

SHORTRIDGE, G. C. *The Mammals of South West Africa.* 2 vols, London, 1934.

SILVA PORTO. A. F. F. DA. Apontamentos sobre a Obra do Ex.mo Sr. D. José de Lacerda 'Exame das Viagens do Dr David Livingstone'. 1868. [Published as a pamphlet entitled *Silva Porto e Livingstone.* Lisbon, 1891.]

Viagens e Apontamentos de um Portuense em África. Lisbon, 1942. See DIAS, G. S. (ed.).

SMITH, A. See KIRBY, P. R. (ed.).

SMITH, E. W. *Great Lion of Bechuanaland: the Life and Times of Roger Price, Missionary.* London, 1957. (Appendix A, pp. 367–410: 'Sebetwane and the MaKololo'.)

SMITH, E. W., and DALE, A. M. *The Ila-Speaking Peoples of Northern Rhodesia.* 2 vols. London, 1920.

SMITH, E. W. (ed.). *African Ideas of God.* London, 1950.

STREITWOLF, H. *Der Caprivizipfel.* Berlin, 1911.

TABLER, E. C. The Life of Frederick J. Green. *Africana Notes and News,* vol. 11, 1954, pp. 35–42.

Historic route from the lower Botletle River to the Chobe River. *Africana Notes and News,* vol. 12, 1956, pp. 35–43.

THEAL, G. M. *History of South Africa,* vols. VI and VII. London, 1915, 1916.

TURNER, V. W. *The Lozi Peoples of North-Western Rhodesia.* London, 1952.

WALLER, H. (ed.). *The Last Journals of David Livingstone, in Central Africa, from 1865 to his death.* 2 vols. London, 1874.

WALLIS, J. P. R. (ed.). *The Matabele Journals of Robert Moffat 1829–1860.* 2 vols. London, 1945.

The Matabele Mission: a selection from the correspondence of John and Emily Moffat, David Livingstone, and others, 1858–1878. London, 1945.

The Zambesi Expedition of David Livingstone 1858–1863. 2 vols. London, 1956.

WELLINGTON, J. H. *Southern Africa, a geographical study.* 2 vols. Cambridge, 1955.

WHITE, C. M. N. Witchcraft, divination and magic among the Balovale tribes. *Africa,* vol. 18, 1948, pp. 81–104.

The Balovale peoples and their historical background. Rhodes-Livingstone Journal, No. 8, 1949, pp. 26–41.

WOOKEY, A. J. *Dicò tsa Secwana.* 3rd ed. Tiger Kloof, 1929.

C. Maps.

By 'modern maps' is meant chiefly the relevant sheets of: (*a*) South Africa 1:500,000, Topographical edition (Pretoria: Trigonometrical Survey Office) and (*b*) Africa 1:1,000,000 Nos. 2465, 4646, 4648 (Geographical Section, General Staff), together with (*c*) World Aeronautical Chart ICAO 1:1,000,000, sheets 3177, 3178, 3274, 3275, 3300, 3301 (Pretoria: Trignometrical Survey Office).

References to those of earlier date are as follows:

Gibbons 1904: See GIBBONS in (B) above.

GSGS 2871: Africa 1:2,000,000, Rhodesia (1919), Transvaal (1924).

Passarge, 1904: See PASSARGE in (B) above.

Ravenstein, 1897: E. G. RAVENSTEIN, 'Map of part of the Kingdom of the Marutse', *Geogr. Journal,* vol. 9, 1897.

Seiner, 1909: maps in F. SEINER, Ergebnisse einer Bereisung des Gebiets zwischen Okawango und Sambesi, *Mitteilungen aus dem deutschen Schutzgebietes*, vol. 22, 1909.

TSGS 1539: Africa 1:1,000,000, sheet 120, Kalahari. (Topographical Section, General Staff, 1905.)

D. *Abbreviations used in Footnotes*

JRGS, 1850 [etc.]	Livingstone's articles in *J. R. Geogr. Soc.*, 1850 [etc.]
Letters	*David Livingstone: Family Letters*, ed. I. Schapera
Narrative	*Narrative of an Expedition to the Zambesi*, by D. and C. Livingstone
Oswell	*William Cotton Oswell*, by W. E. Oswell
Travels	*Missionary Travels and Researches*, by D. Livingstone
Zambesi Expedition	*The Zambesi Expedition of David Livingstone*, ed. J. P. R. Wallis

INDEX

Aesop, quoted, 5
Agassiz, J. L. R., 187
Albert, Prince-Consort, 29
Alcohol, views about use, 92–3. Cf.
Wine
Alheit, C., missionary, 84
ALuyi, 30. Cf. BaRotse
Andersson, C. J., 235; reaches L.
Ngami, 237
Animals, xix, 37, 65, 73, 114, 121,
125–6, 130; diseases, 74–5, 125;
Native names of, 312–15; tenacity
of life when wounded, 124, 140.
Cf. Buffaloes, bull-frog, cattle,
crocodiles, eland, elephants, giraffe,
hippopotamus, hunting, lechwe,
lions, marshbuck, puku, rhino-
ceros, sable antelope, wild dogs,
wildebeest, zebra
Ant-hills, 36, 121, 170, 254
Anthrax, 74
Ant-lion, 105, 257, 289–90
Ants, 79, 170, 172, 251, 254–6, 257,
265, 283; eaten by Natives,
170–1; species, 76, 256–7
Arab traders, visit Barotseland, 228–
230, 233
Arend, Joseph, hunter, 68
Arrowsmith, J., cartographer, xviii
Astronomical observations, xviii, 11,
12, 15, 34–5, 40, 54, 80, 99, 107,
109, 110, 126, 145, 160, 163,
173–4, 189, 191, 194, 196, 199,
204, 208, 218, 220, 221, 224,
225, 234. Cf. Latitudes, Maclear

BaBimpe, dental evulsions, 49
BaBindele, servants of Portuguese, 31

BaBirikwe, material culture, 31
BaHurutshe, attacked by Sebetwane,
19. Cf. Mangope
BaIla, 30, 176, 184; customs, 32;
dialect, 31; raided by MaKololo,
39, 161; visited by slavers, 43,
126, 129, 131, 178, 179, 228,
233. Cf. Kaingu
BaJoko (BaZonko), see MaZungu
BaKaa, join BaKwena, 304
BaKgalagadi, 50, 305; foods, 45;
method of getting water, 305; village, 37, 130
BaKgatla, attacked by Sebetwane,
19, and by Boers, 85, 89, 90; re-
jection of gospel, 90–1. Cf,
Mosielele, Pilane
BaKhurutshe, raided by Sebetwane,
19. Cf. Tsapo
BaKoba, see BaYeei
BaKwena, attacked by Sebetwane,
18, and by Boers, 2, 85–90, 96;
belief in rainmaking, 239–43,
300–1; idea of God, 301; magical
practices, 297; reaction to mis-
sionary teaching, 91, 99, 131, 300.
Cf. Boers, Dimawe, Dithubaruba,
Kolobeng, Molepolole, Sechele
Balerileng, d. of Sechele, 88
BaLovale, 124. Cf. Lovale
BaLuchazi, 30, 31, 43, 153
BaLunda, 42, 152, 228, 296. Cf.
Kazembe, Mwata-Yamvo
BaMapela, 77, 187; rainmaker,
300
BaMashi, 176
BaNajwa, 14, 15, 51; huts, 14, 53.
Cf. Chombo, Hwange

INDEX

BaNgwaketse, attacked by Boers, 85, 89, 90; rejection of gospel, 91; scarification of warriors, 23. Cf. Makaba, Senthufe

BaNgwato, 1, 9, 27, 91, 100, 300; attack Sebetwane, 19; capital, 4; chieftainship, 300; purification of widower, 76; subject tribes, 4 f. Cf. Sekgoma

BaNyengo, 30, 33, 153; rebel against MaKololo, 125, 140

BaNyeti, 30, 144; medicines, 250; occupations, 197, 203, 214; slaves taken from, 232

Baobab, 10, 101–2, 103–4

BaPhaleng, 5, 26; tribute taken from, 151, 186, 235

BaRolong, steal Boer cattle, 96, 98. Cf. Motshwari

BaRotse, beliefs and practices, 47, 175, 190, 196; capitals, 205; conquest by Sebetwane, 21, 60–1, 203; doctors, 23, 192; dialect, 34, 151, 153, 214; expert watermen, 26, 125, 127–8, 214; maps, 175; physique, 47, 163, 195; rebelliousness, 61, 140, 209; tribal name, 30, 146, 152; villages, 200, 203, 224. Cf. Barotseland, Santudu

Barotseland, climate, 41, 163, 164, 180; crops, 41, 124, 144, 191, 199, 210, 315–16; density of population, 45, 200; description, 46, 204, 224; dialects, 30, 34, 153. Cf. Zambesi

Barth, H., explorer, 127, 151

Bashukulompo, see BaIla

Bashukulompo River, see Kafue

Basiamang, b. of Sechele, 96

BaSotho, 16, 17, 26, 27. Cf. Makololo

BaSubia, 30, 33, 41, 127; chiefs, 40

BaTawana, 1; visit Sekeletu, 142, 150, 151, 160, 235. Cf. L. Ngami, Letsholathebe

BaTlhaping, 88. Cf. Mahura

BaToka (BaTonga), 30, 146, 224; chiefs, 145, 146, 207; customs, 27, 32, 48–9; dialect, 31; musical instruments, 145–6; nudity of women, 184; raided by MaKololo, 234, 235, 252; pay tribute to Sekeletu, 130, 145; slave trade among, 131

BaTswana, 73, 163, 209, 293; character, 12, 17, 96, 98; customs and beliefs, 154, 243, 253, 282, 297; mission work among, 45, 70, 281–2; tunes, 16, 206; villages, 278. Cf. BaHurutshe, BaKaa, BaKgalagadi, BaKgatla, BaKhurutshe, BaKwena, BaNgwaketse, BaNgwato, BaPhaleng, BaRolong, BaTawana, BaTlhaping, infanticide, rainmaking

BaYeei, 55, 62, 68, 120, 147, 306; chiefs, 14, 54, 147, 170; customs and beliefs, 47, 135, 136; foods, 116, 170–1; language, 30. Cf. Matsaratsara, Phalane

Beauty, Native ideas of, 135–6; lacking in Native women, 272

Bechuana, see BaTswana

Bees, 97, 171

Ben-Chombo, Arab trader, 227–30 passim

Benguela, 162, 176, 178, 189, 192, 228, 229

Ben-Habib, Arab trader, 39 n., 228, 252, 291–2

Bié, 177, 178, 179, 189, 192

Birds, 77–8, 108–9, 117, 119, 193, 194, 198, 199, 215, 238, 250–1, 283–4, 286, 306–7, 316; migrations, 38, 97, 163, 198, 199, 251, 316; nests, 77, 78, 109, 119, 123, 284–7. Cf. Ostrich

INDEX

Birth customs, 189, 285

Blaikie, W. G., variant readings of MS., 39, 68, 98, 108, 111, 131, 135, 144, 272, 282, 291, 303

Boatlanama, D.L. at, 3, 100

Boe, Tonga chief, 207

Boers, 49–50, 77, 79, 99, 115, 122, 143; attack BaKwena, 2, 85, 87–90, 96, 154, and other tribes, 177; bar road to interior, 91, 92, 95, 132; buy Native children, 150, 154; character, 84, 85, 161; hostility to D.L., 85, 91, 302, 303. Cf. BaRolong, Kgari, Sechele

Bogwêra (circumcision 'school'), 154

Borotse River, *see* Zambesi

Boshwelakgosi, D.L. at, 77, 78

Botha, A., 81; trial of, 82

Bothithong (Motito), D.L. at, 96

Botletle River, 7, 8, 55, 62, 63, 67, 208, 305, 306

Bowdich, T. E., reference to book, 152, 190

Bruce, J., explorer, quoted, 63

Bubi, Kwena chief, 99

Buckland, Prof. W., xvii

Buffaloes, 109, 124, 216, 263; description, 274; ferocity, 125, 274; food, 275; habits, 274, 275–6

Bührmann, H. T., Boer schoolmaster, 302

Bull-frog, 5, 73

Bumbu Rapids, 194

Burns, Robert, quoted, 167, 210

Bushe, H., traveller, 68, 72, 76

Bushmen, 7, 106, 139, 167, 208–9, 280; appearance and physique, 10, 108, 186; arrow poison, 103; character, 12, 107; divining-bones, 105; foods, 10, 73, 106, 107, 109, 112, 114; guides, 9, 12, 104, 105, 107, 109–16 *passim*, 123; hunting methods, 103, 107, 164, 249, 293; language, 11–12, 30, 209;

thefts of cattle, 79; villages, 11, 14, 62, 78, 305

Campbell, Griqua settlement, 95

Campbell, Dr J., editor, 298

Canoes, 46–7, 125, 131, 234; dimensions, 195; fatal capsizes, 17, 34, 38, 61, 193; ferry wagons across Chobe, 23, 126, 127; royal, 32, 203; speed, 16, 23, 195, 230

Cape Town, D.L. at, 80–3; departure from, 84

Cassantse, Ngala tribe, 294

Cassaquare (Bushmen of Angola), 208–9

Cattle, Native types of, 16, 32, 41, 79, 210, 311

Cattle Posts, 36, 45, 130, 133, 299

Catumbela River, 162

Chapman, J., visits MaKololo, 231, 234

Cheeta village, D.L. at, 63

Chief, authority, 156–7, 160, 161, 299; gifts to subjects, 144, 146, 154, 205, 210, 211, 212; rain-making functions, 242, 300; tribute from subjects, 130, 142, 144, 145, 147, 151, 160, 186, 205, 212

Chō, Yeei chief, 147

Chobe River, 15, 35, 67, 81, 111, 128, 129, 173, 188, 191, 295; branches, 112, 113; course, 23, 130, 147; floods, 46, 47, 72, 112–122 *passim*, 146, 147, 254; sources, 38, 47, 67, 147, 189. Cf. Sansureh, Savuti

Chombo, Najwa headman, 14, 49, 51

Chonwane, mission station, 74

Christianity, Native attitude to, 16–17, 91, 131, 144, 236, 297, 299, 300, 301; misconduct of converts, 83, 281–2, 291, 306

329

Chuaning Pan, D.L. at, 98

Chukutsa Pan, D.L. at, 6, 7, 71, 100, 305

Chwantsa Pan, 8, 70

Civilization, criteria of, 191, 197; develops human faculties, 280; influence on tribal life, 156–7, 159; 'produces beauty', 272

Clothing, Natives adopt European, 16, 41, 42, 45, 46, 124

Codrington, W., sportsman, 89, 91

Commerce, need for development, 43–4, 49, 131, 132, 141, 143

Cotton, wild, 106

Crocodiles, 126, 222

Cruelty, instances of Native, 135, 183, 224, 238

Cubal River, 162

Cumming, R. G., 69, 73, 165

Damaras, see OvaHerero

Dances, described, 147–8, 200, 209; mentioned, 128, 152, 155, 169, 185, 186, 210, 211, 239

Darling, Lieutenant-Governor C. H., 81

Debenham, Prof. F., xvii, xxi

'Dikolobe, River of the', 133

Dimawê, BaKwena move to, 1, 2, 78, 87

Dingalo's village, D.L. at, 54

Dinyanti, 22, 25, 145; D.L. at, 35, 36, 46, 137 ff., 234 ff.; visited by slavers, 123, 176

Diolo-diphephe, plain, 11, 102

Disho (Lishwa), Mbukushu chief, 176

Distances, lists of, 51, 55, 133

Dithakong, defeat of MaKololo at, 18, 22

Dithubaruba, Kwena capital, 99

Divination, Native methods of, 48, 105, 174–5, 184, 185

Doctors, Native, 23, 24, 48, 148, 174, 183, 185, 192, 193, 288

Dolman, A., traveller, 68

Dreams, Native, 239, 290

Drought, 1, 63, 67, 74, 75, 100, 172, 242, 264, 275; cyclical occurrence, 6

Duprat, A., Portuguese consul, 81, 207, 237

Edwardes, (Sir) H. B., quoted, 78

Edwards, R., missionary, 88, 90 n.

Edwards, S. H., trader, visits Ma-Kololo, ix, 7 n., 46

Eland, 74, 112, 221; description, 268–9; food, 271–2; habits, 269–270; measurements, 271

Elephants, 29, 31, 106, 108, 109, 112, 124, 125, 126, 166, 194, 220; description and size, 245, 246; flesh, 250; food, 114, 116, 246; habits, 247–8, 249; tusks, 248, 305

Faure, Rev. P. E., visits Boers, 302

Ferreira, C. J., visits MaKololo, 176–9 passim

Fever, attacks D.L.'s servants, 103, 107, 108, 110, 142, 151, 164, and son, 69; D.L.'s attacks of, 145, 148, 164, 174, 179, 183, 184, 191, 215–16, 226, 231, 276, 283; Native treatment for, 148; remedies for, 132, 149, 164, 176; seasonal incidence, 146, 147, 148, 150, 164, 174, 191; symptoms, 104, 110, 148–9, 150–1, 163, 164, 215–16, 231

Fire, animals 'fascinated' by, 114, 280–1

Fishing, Native methods of, 8, 33, 47, 120, 213

Fitzgerald, Bobby, 'English sportsman', 6

Flood, tradition of, 204

Frédoux, J., missionary, 96 n., 237
Freeman, Rev. J. J., xviii, 307; visits Kolobeng, 306

Ganguela tribes, hostile to travellers, 192
Ganyesa, D.L. at, 96
Garden, made for D.L. by Ma-Kololo, 49, 145, 234; planned by him as experiment, 189, 230, 282, 283
Gelfand, M., variant readings of MS., 13, 66, 70, 74, 108, 111, 148, 149, 253
Geographical discoveries and observations, xv–xviii, 8, 10, 36, 38, 46–7, 77, 79, 110, 121, 147, 190. Cf. Barotseland, Chobe, drought, Gonye Falls, latitudes, Zambesi
Geological observations, 99, 195, 213
George Fleming (Coloured trader with D.L.), 72, 106, 107, 114, 127, 172, 250, 258, 272, 290, 294; attacks of fever, 105, 151, 179; dealings with MaKololo, 141, 146, 158, 191
Giraffe, description, 266–7; food, 266, 268; habits, 267–8; measurements, 101, 266; numbers, 268; mentioned, 140
Goha Hills (Ngwa), 109, 110, 111, 173
Gonye Falls, 195, 204; description, 196–7
Goosimjarrah, 11, 12, 72
Goroje, 'Bushman chief', 9, 10, 101, 102
Grahamstown Journal, 83
Grapes, wild, 106, 109, 110
Green, F. J., trader, 76, 89
Green, H., civil servant, 96
Grey, Earl, Colonial Secretary, 81, 82

Griquas, 45, 88; missions among, 93; repulse Sebetwane, 18; visit interior, 142, 299
Griquatown, D.L. at, 79, 84
Ground nuts, 40
Guizot, F. F. G., 187
Gumkirreh, see Unku
'Gun medicine', 143, 147, 223, 291
Guns and ammunition, desired by Sebetwane, 17; effects on animal life, 134, 266, 279, and tribal warfare, 177; given to Natives by D.L., 7, 128, 140, 150; possessed by Natives, 7, 26, 72, 124, 129, 143, 192, 201; procured by D.L. at Cape Town, xxiii, 81; trade in, 6, 39, 42, 43, 71, 151, 173
Guyot, A., book discussed, 186–7
Gweta, 9

Habit, 283
Hae, Hans, Griqua hunter, 68
Hae, Jakobus, 89
Hair, Native reaction to D.L.'s, 146, 202
Heralds, Native, 212–13, 276. Cf. Mapulanyane
Hippopotamus, 16, 122, 126, 191, 194, 219; appearance and habits, 128, 213–14; hunted by Natives, 197, 214, 217, 218, 305
Hofmeyr, Mr (Cape Town), 237
Holmes, G. S. (Cape Town), 237
Hornets, 273, 287
Horse sickness, 74
Hottentots, appearance, 186; beer, 84; missions among, 307; rebellion, 81, 82
Hughes, I., rejuvenated missionary, 79 n.
Humanity, types of, 186–8
Hunting, animals killed by D.L. and party, 100, 102, 103, 107, 109, 114, 119, 123, 124, 126, 130,

140, 213, 216, 315; Native methods, 124, 125, 305; views on, xix, 124, 140, 172, 174, 249. Cf. Bushmen, hippopotamus, lions, pitfalls

Hwange, Najwa chief, 129, 130–1

Hydrophobia, case of, 99

Imasiku (Masiko), Lozi prince, 209, 210 n., 233

Imbua (Mpoa), Lozi chief, 140

India, 9, 68

Infanticide, 159, 253

Insanity among Natives, 253

Insects, 10, 103, 162, 171, 172, 283, 288–9. Cf. Ant-lion, ants, bees, fire, hornets, mosquitoes, mud-dauber, Ngwa, scavenger, tampan, tsetse

Isaac (Paul's son), misconduct, 304

John, Oswell's servant, 45

Kabompo River, 41 n., 219, 225, 238

Kabonda (Kambonga), chief, 205

Kafue River, 30, 32, 291, 292

Kaingu, Ila chief, 223, 252

Kaisa, Kalaka headman, 11, 101

Kalahari Desert, 14, 63, 74, 98, 292, 299

Kali Rapids, 194

Kalingo River, 37, 130

Kamati, obtains gun by false pretences, 7, 9, 72, 76

Kamati's Ponds, D.L. at, 69

Kandehy valley, 111

Kane, D.L. at, 5, 75, 100

Kangomba, Tonga chief, 207

Kangombe, Mbunda chief, 162

Kasiku, Lozi village, 206

Katimamolelo, D.L. at, 193

Katongo, 193, 220; residence of Silva Pôrto, 204–5, 207, 232; visited by D.L., 226

Kaungara Pan, D.L. at, 10

Kazembe, Lunda chief, 228, 229, 230

Kebopetswe, servant, 104–10 passim, 112, 114

Kgakge, attacked by Sechele, 303

Kgari (Sechele's son), captured by Boers, 88 n., 99

Kgolomadue Pond, D.L. at, 3, 99

Kgwebe Hills, 20 n., 235

Khama-Khama, D.L. at, 11, 72, 102

Kiadjara, see Rapesh

Kidia Hill, elephant killed at, 248, 305

Kingushe, D.L. at, 108

Kobo, Tebele chief, 207

Koboyapudi, mission assistant, 97

Kokonyane Pits, D.L. at, 6

Kolobeng, 3, 99, 168, 304, 306; abandoned by BaKwena, 1, 2, 78; attacked by Boers, 85; D.L.'s house at, 88, 99, 297–8, 307; visited by Sebetwane's messengers, 3, 7, 169

Kolombota, informant, 294

Konate (Connat), servant, 116, 118, 119, 120, 122, 123

Kopong, D.L. at, 3, 99

Korotse's village, 133, 134

Kowrie island, 218

Kruger, G. J., Boer commandant, 302, 303

Kuadzou, D.L. at, 107, 108

Kube, D.L. at, 8, 100

Kudibela, D.L. at, 100

Kumele, Kololo headman, 252

Kunehu, spring, 10

Kuruchwe Pond, D.L. at, 78

Kuruman, 18, 95, 97; birds of, 97, 108, 198, 251; D.L. at, 79, 84, 92, 96; mission, 282. Cf. Servants

Kurutlele, Sebetwane's homeland, 18

Kwenane, Kololo induna, 28, 137, 252, 276, 277

Lake Dow (Kumadow), 69

Lake Maravi, 44

Lake Ngami, xv, 47, 142, 185, 237; journey to, xvii, 304–6

Lake Tanganyika, 229

Langa, Tebele chief, 60

Latitudes and Longitudes, 81, 129, 130, 134, 193, 194, 195, 196, 214, 231, 306. Cf. Astronomical observations, Maclear

Lebeola (Motonka), Kololo headman, 36, 45, 130, 276, 277, 290

Lebompo, aged informant, 210

Lechwe waterbuck, 43, 114, 119, 124, 125, 126, 134, 140

Lechwee, abducts Sebetwane's wife, 27

Leeba River, 219. See Zambesi

Lephephe, D.L. at, 3, 100

Letlhotswe, D.L. at, 5, 100

Letlonkana, Kololo headman, 131, 134, 181

Letsholathebe, Tawana chief, xv, 50, 142; obstructs D.L., 306; provokes MaKololo, 68, 151, 153–4, 235; traffic with Boers, 150, 154

Liambae River, 41, 193. See Kabompo, Zambesi

Liambezi Lake (Nyampetsi), 124

Libebe, Mbukushu chief, 48, 142; country, 67, 144, 147, 152, 176, 235

Libunda, Kololo town, 42; D.L. at, 211, 214, 222

Licuano, see Mpakane

Lilundu, Santudu's capital, 212; D.L. at, 224

Limpopo River, 6, 92, 248, 302; tsetse on, 63, 64 n., 66

Linangelo, Lozi village, 211–12

Linanka, gardener, 197; river, 197, 198

Linyanti River, see Chobe

Lions, 98, 267, 276; cannibalism, 166; encounters with, 3–4, 222, 272, 299; hunted by Natives, 75, 103, 107, 164; roar, 125, 164, 165, 216; timidity, 110, 112, 130, 165–6

Lisibani, Kololo headman, 230

Litufa, D.L. at, 199, 200, 230

Livingstone, Agnes, 295

Livingstone, Charles, 237

Livingstone, David, at Cape Town, 80–3; belief in divine favour and guidance, xxi, 7, 29, 71–2, 85, 106, 108, 111, 123, 124, 133, 142, 147, 162; belief in human progress, 167–8; children, xxv, 71, 105, 295; condemns Native character and practices, xx, 143, 146, 161, 185, 191, 205–6, 209, 223–4, 234, 236, 252, 253; discovers Zambesi at Sesheke, 38; early journeys in Bechuanaland, xi; first journey to MaKololo, 3–16; friendliness and respect of Natives towards, 123, 132–3, 134, 137, 143–4, 147, 224; gifts to MaKololo, 49, 128, 139, 140, 149, 150; gifts from Natives, 16, 17, 29, 36, 37, 40, 49–50, 54–5, 62, 78, 129, 133, 134, 136, 140, 141, 144, 146, 147, 149, 215, 223, 230, 290, 295, 296; illnesses, 188, 190, 191 (cf. Fever); journal, ix f., xi ff., xxii f., xxv, 6, 295, 296; journey to L. Ngami (1849), xv f., 304–6; linguistic studies, xix f., 30–4 passim, 95, 191; literary activities, xvii, 80, 92, 95, 100, 298; love of nature, xix, 171–2, 244, 251, 266, 283, 289; maps, 81; motives for journeys, xv, 2, 3, 16, 46, 161, 162; personal traits, xx f., 250; prayers, 111, 135, 147, 164, 291, 295, 302; preaches to Natives, 23, 40, 62,

129, 134, 144, 160, 166, 169–70, 179, 185–6, 190, 205, 209, 223, 226, 231, 234, 235, 250, 258, 283, 291, 303, 305; proposed journey to Luanda, 192, 233, 237, 281, 290, 294, 296; reasons for leaving BaKwena, 1, 2, 78–9; rebuked by Mrs Moffat, 70–1; religious views, 28, 90–1, 111; return to south (1851), 46, 51 ff.; scientific observations, xvi–xx (cf. animals, astronomical, birds, fever, geographical, geological, humanity, insects, latitudes, maps, salt, temperatures, thermal, trees, tsetse); Sabbatarianism, 193; second journey to MaKololo, 84–122; sense of vocation, xxi, 47, 98, 108, 132–3, 135, 192; speculations about death, 97–8, 108; views on missionary policy, 45, 50, 61–2, 93, 131, 161, 307; visit to Barotseland, 156, 158, 160, 162, 170, 180, 186, 190, 192–230. Cf. Alcohol, Boers, civilization, garden, guns, hair, hunting, magic lantern, Oswell, pontoon, seeds, Silva Pôrto, slave trade, socialism, theft

Livingstone, Mrs D., 13, 70, 141 n., 153, 230, 237, 280, 295, 299, 304; pregnancy and confinements, 24, 68, 71, 72, 304

Livingstone, Robert, 25, 295

Livingstone, Thomas, 295; birth, 304; attacks of fever, 69, 72

Livingstone, William Oswell, 295; birth, 68

Lobotani, 4

Logageng, D.L. at, 98. See Molepolole

London Missionary Society, 'in bad odour', 81–2; missions in Cape Colony, 93, 307

Lonta River, 41, 221. See Zambesi

Lotlhakane, D.L. at, 72, 100

Lovale, 29, 41, 219

Luanda, 189, 192, 229. Cf. Livingstone, D.

Luanginga River (Moenye), 41, 173, 212

Ludorf, Rev. J., at Kuruman, 93

Luete River (Simah), 175, 198

Lui, Lozi capital, 205, 210

Lui River, 199

Lumbi River, 195

Lunga River (Maninche), 43, 205

Lungwebungu River (Loeti), 31, 175, 219

Lwale, D.L. at, 99

Mababe River, 12, 13, 14, 53, 54, 67

Mabe, Tlhako chief, 301, 303

Mabotsa, mission station, 299

McCabe, J., trader, 89; crosses Kalahari Desert, 98

Maclear, T., xi, xviii, 81, 237; 'observations', 308–10

Maditsa, D.L. at, 6, 100

Magic lantern, used by D.L., 273–4, 290

Mahale, Kololo headman, 16, 28, 29, 126, 131, 272; visits Kolobeng, 7, 71; wife's infidelity, 250, 251, 282

Mahonto island, 122 n., 126

Mahura, Tlhaping chief, 96

Maila, D.L. at, 11, 101

Makaba II, slain by MaKololo, 26

MaKalaka, 4, 5, 6, 11, 145, 163, 164; cultural peculiarities, 5; name, 146. Cf. BaNajwa, Kaisa

Makgetho's village, D.L. at, 55, 62

Makgethonyane's Ford, 63

Makishi dance, 209

Makoanyane, Sotho warrior, mentioned, 187

MaKoba, *see* BaYeei

MaKololo, assemblies and social gatherings, 151, 153, 169, 206; character, 155, 191, 223–4, 253, 272–3; diffusion of language, 34, 142; domestic life and customs, 156, 158–9, 276–7; eating habits, 17, 158, 170, 184–5, 206, 273; ethnic composition, 16, 26, 27; health and physique, 47, 134, 136, 163; ideas of beauty, 135–6; migration to Barotseland, xv, xx, 18–22, 203; punishments, 238; raids on neighbouring tribes, 39, 41, 43 (cf. BaIla, BaToka); relations with subject peoples, 142, 259 (cf. BaNyengo, BaRotse); ritual beliefs and practices, 24, 181, 186, 190, 223, 236, 291; social system, 154, 158, 159; status of women, 132, 156; visited by traders, 37, 39, 42–3, 131, 172, 176, 231 (cf. Arabs, Mambari, Portuguese, Thompson, Wilson). Cf. Cattle, chief, clothing, dances, doctors, dreams, guns, heralds, Livingstone, MaTebele, menstruation, MmaMotsisane, Mphephe, names, reading, Sebetwane, Sekeletu, slavery, wild hemp, witchcraft

Makoma River, 212. *See* Luanginga

Malaria, 24, 47. *See* Fever

Malebele, Kololo doctor, 134

Maleke, Kwena chief, 99

MaLozi, *see* BaRotse

Mambari, 37, 45, 137, 151, 153, 161, 173, 214, 226, 227, 231, 277; slavers, 42–3, 123, 126, 131, 134, 144, 203, 205

MaMbowe, 214, 216, 219, 221; robbery by, 217–18, 220

MaMbunda, 30, 32; customs and beliefs, 33, 48; dialect, 151, 153

Mamidi, Kololo nobleman, 236, 252, 276

Mamogale, Tswana chief, 303

Mangana Vlei, D.L. at, 100, 305

Mangope, Hurutshe chief, attacked by Sebetwane, 18, 59

Maninche River, 32, 39. *See* Lunga

Manjor, 'Governor-General' of Angola, 178

Mantlhanyane, Kololo renegade, 151

Maokaneng, Sechele's wife, 299

Maps, 'drawn' by Natives, 31, 33, 40, 173, 175, 294, 295

Mapulanyane, court herald, 169, 274, 290

Mariba, D.L. at, 104

Marije, Sebetwane's wife, 131, 238–9

Marile River, 21, 212, 224, 226

Marshbuck (Nakong), 55

Martinus, servant, 75

Masenyo's village, D.L. at, 305

MaShona, 6, 11

Mashuwe, D.L. at, 4, 77, 100

Masongo River, 199

MaTebele, 5 n.; raids on MaKololo, 18, 20, 23, 25, 26, 27, 30, 60–1, 129, 134, 252, 259; rumoured invasion by, 131, 183–4, 234. Cf. Moselekatse

Matende island, 215

Mathuluane, D.L. at, 74, 100, 305

Matlape's village, 15, 16

Matlomaganyana, springs, 10

Matsaratsara, Yeei chief, 53, 54, 104

MaZungu, slavers, 39, 43

Mbonta River, 23. *See* Chobe

Mbowe island, 194

Mebalwe, evangelist, 2, 299, 301, 304

Mei island, 199

Menstruation, affected by climate, 24, 47

Mirror, Native reactions to, 136

Missionary collections, statistics of, 94–5

Mitchell's Pass, 79

Mmakgari, Sechele's wife, 298, 299

MmaMotsisane, succeeds Sebetwane, 28, 29, 36, 46; abdication, 124, 141, 200, 201, 202; present for, 128; relations with Sekeletu, 143, and Mphephe, 181; visited, 202

Mmanku, Sebetwane's wife, 25, 26, 131, 132; meeting with, 137; village, 16, 17, 181

MmaSebele, Sechele's wife, 89 n.

MmaSekeletu, Sebetwane's wife, 29 n.; village, 201, 202

Mmutlanyane, Kwena tribesman, 71

Moatswi, Ngwato headman, 9

Moçambique, Portuguese seek overland route to, 176, 177, 207, 223

Modimolole, warm bath (Transvaal), 77

Moeng, village headman, 305

Moffat, J. S., 237

Moffat, Mrs R., letter to D.L., 70–1

Moffat, R., 92, 93, 237, 251, 290; visits Kolobeng, 306

Moffat, R., junior, 79

Moikabi, Kwena headman, slain by Boers, 96

Mokantju, Mbunda informant, 32, 36, 42, 43, 137, 239

Mokantsa, Goroje's son, 102

Mokgari, Kololo headman, 276

Mokgatlê, Tswana chief, 301, 302

Mokgokong, Sechele's wife, 88 n., 96, 299, 304

Mokhele, Lozi informant, 291

Mokhutswane, Bushman headman, 11, 102

Mokoko, old river bed, 72, 73, 305

Mokwala's village, 196, 197

Molapo-wa-dikgong, D.L. at, 78

Molepolole (Logageng), 1, 3

Moloi, Talaote chief, 4

Molopo River, D.L. at, 98

Monachahela, Luchazi chief, 31

Montagu, J., civil servant, 81

Months, Native names of, 267–8, 316

Montshiwa, Rolong chief, 98

Morantsiane, headman of Sesheke, 39, 193, 231, 234, 251; proposes raid on BaToka, 252, 258, 259, 272

Moremedi, Kwena tribesman, 71, 72

Moremi, Kololo headman, 129; village, 113, 122, 126, 231

Moremi, Ngwato servant, 5, 9, 72; purification, 76

Morotse, Yeei headman, 14, 53

Moruakgomo, Kwena chief, attacked by Sebetwane, 18

Morwa-Mantshunyane, Kololo messenger, 54

Morwa-Mokondi's village, 55

Morwa-Motonka, Kololo tribesman, 134

Mosadi-wa-Tau, slayer of Makaba, 26

Moselekatse, x, 10, 92, 125, 234; fugitives from, 5, 11; raids on MaKololo, 17, 26, 27, 30, 46, 131, 134

Moshaneng, D.L. at, 99

Moshawana, boatman, 225–6; canoe song, 238

Mosielele, Kgatla chief, 89, 301

Mosquitoes, 14, 53, 112, 237

Mothibe, Kololo nobleman, 200, 201, 212, 213, 222, 223, 236, 291

Motlatsa, D.L. at, 100

Motonka, see Lebeola

Motshipi, Sechele's wife, 96 n., 299

Motshwari, Rolong chief, 96–7

Motswasele, Sechele's father, 90

Mpakane (Licuano), defeated by Sebetwane, 21, 26

Mphephe, 31, 45, 49, 277; charac-

ter, 183, 220, 232, 233; conspiracy against Sekeletu, 143, 161, 181, 183, 184, 200, 210–11, 232–3; execution, 183, 236, 288
Mpololo, 131, 140, 141, 143, 155, 156, 158, 160, 205, 212, 277
Mud-dauber (wasp), 264–6
Mumps, 250
Mulambwa, Lozi chief, *see* Santudu
Mwata-Yamvo, Lunda chief, 228, 229, 230, 294

Naliele, Lozi capital, 202–3, 207, 210, 211, 212
Names, bestowal of, 136, 141, 153
Nameta village, 198, 199
Namissan (Ngabisane), 69, 306
Nata River, 6
Ngambwe Falls, 194
Ngoga River (Cho, Tso, Zo), 26, 47, 67, 147
Ngwa, hill (*see* Goha); poisonous insect, 103, 111, 162
Nifale village, 200
Niger expedition, 139
Njoko River, 194, 195
Nkalange, lake, 176
Nkowane Pan, D.L. at, 5, 6, 100
Nokwane, headman, 155; illness, 236, 237, 239, 250, 288
Ntwetwe Pan, 8, 101, 102
Nuanabotale, Subia chief, 40, 41
Nuana Mei, island, 194
Nuanamoari, Subia chief, 40, 41
Nudity of Native women, 32, 184, 253

Oboia, Silva Pôrto's companion, 151
Oepeng, servant, 105; immorality, 250, 251, 282
Okovango River (Cubango), 188, 189
Ootse, 74
Orapa, D.L. at, 69, 70

Ostrich, 63, 165, 292–4, 311
Oswell, W. C., accompanies D.L. on journeys, 3–80, 304–6; astronomical observations, 34–5, 40; encounter with lion, 3–4; kindness to D.L., 4, 6, 36, 72, 80, 124; plan for extirpating slave trade, 44; references to, 7, 13, 23, 28, 29, 33, 37, 46, 53, 54, 55, 71, 77, 130, 152, 214, 230, 233, 237, 248, 276
OvaHerero, attacked by Sebetwane, 20; visit BaTawana, 235
Overweg, A., explorer, 127, 151
OviMbundu, 153. Cf. Mambari
Oyama River, 199

Pakington, Sir J., written to, 95
Paku, Ngwato guide, 7, 72
Park, Mungo, quoted, 152
Pati, Teti chieftain, 305
Paul, evangelist, 78, 299–303 *passim*, 306
Paulus, death of, 297
Pereira, M. G., travels questioned, 152, 153, 179, 210
Phalane, Yeei headman, 63, 67, 71, 305, 306
Phampa's village, 305
Pienaar, Griqua 'explorer', 142
Pilane, Kgatla chief, 297, 303
Pitfalls, 53–4, 55, 63, 68, 247
Pitsane, Kololo headman, 129, 190
Pitsepedi, spring, 10
Pogo's village, 36, 45
Poisoning of wells, 129
Pontoon, used by D.L., 116, 120, 122, 290
Ponwane, headman, 16, 29, 36, 43, 123, 125, 126, 134, 146, 228
Portuguese, 31, 151, 173, 177, 226, 230; attempts to cross Africa, 205, 207, 223; half castes, 43, 179, 205, 226; slavers, 178; trade in

Barotseland, 39, 42, 185; travels in interior, 41, 152. Cf. Duprat, Ferreira, Moçambique, Pereira, Silva Pôrto

Potgieter, A. H., Boer commandant, 302, 303

Pretorius, A. W. J., Boer commandant, 90, 96

Prichard, J. C., book referred to, 186

Puku antelope, 'probably unknown', 37, 215, 221

Pulane, Kololo headman, 212

Quelimane, 205, 207

Rainmaking, 168, 239–43, 300–1

Rakhobe, Kwena tribesman, 297

Ramocumisi, Kololo tribesman, 134

Ramoshobotwane, Tonga chief, 145, 146

Rapesh, D.L. at, 9, 101

Rasipipi, attacked by Sebetwane, 20

Raunkwe, Mphephe's father, executed, 200–1

Read, J., missionary, 82

Reading and writing, Native views about, 133, 144, 223, 236

Rejuvenation, case of, 79

Renton, Rev. H. J., 83

Rhinoceros, 109, 110, 125, 126, 140, 245, 248; diseases, 74, 262; encounters with, 263, 303; food, 262, 263; habits, 13, 261–4, 281; measurements, 100; species, 62, 259–60, 262, 263

Rio Cuvo, 189

Rio Voma, 229

Robertson, Rev. W., visits Boers, 302

Royal Geographical Society, xvii, xviii, 80, 237

Rramhiko, Kwena headman, 299

Rutherfoord, H. E., merchant, 290

Sable antelope, 130

Salt, ingredient of Native medicines, 177

Salt pans, 8

Samungana, Yeei headman, 306

Sandile, Xhosa chief, views on missions, 83

Sanjamba island, 231

Sansureh River, 115 n., 116, 126, 130, 147

Santudu, 21, 152, 153, 210, 211; character, 203; 'expelled' by Sebetwane, 26, 41, 203; purchases trade goods, 41, 228; relics, 224–225; royal barge, 32, 203; towns, 203, 206–7, 212, 224

Savuti channel (Sonta River), 15, 46, 51, 72

Scavenger beetle, 171, 277–8

Scholtz, P. E., Boer commandant, 90

Sebetwane, xiii, xv, 1, 2, 9, 14, 29, 31, 32, 36, 47, 49, 139, 141, 194, 199, 202, 203, 210, 222, 291, 296, 306; appearance and character, 16–17, 26, 27, 28, 134, 211, 259; campaigns, 26, 27, 30, 41, 60–1; disregard for human life, 27–8, 151–2, 184; history and migrations, 18–22; illness and death, 23–5, 35, 68; invites D.L. to visit him, 3, 7, 71; marriage law, 276; praise-poems, 56–60; sells slaves to Mambari, 39, 42–3; sister, 40; suspects Mphephe, 183, 232–3; wives, 27–8, 35, 39, 131, 137, 141, 238–9

Sebetwane's Ford, 19, 69

Sebolamokoa, 'swamp', 44, 176, 291

Sebubi, evangelist, 91

Sechele, 1, 71, 78, 96, 99, 297, 303; attacked by Boers, 85, 96, 98, 150, 154; belief in use of force, 155; conversion and baptism, 298, 299, 300; letter to Moffat, 85–90; renounces polygamy, 298–9; transgression, 304

Seeds, given to MaKololo, etc., 49, 139, 226; planted by D.L., 116, 282. Cf. Garden

Seepo River, 198

Segeng, 99

Segwagwa, D.L. at, 98

Seipone, Sebetwane's wife, 131, 141

Sekelenke, Mbunda chief, 41

Sekeletu, 29, 124, 125, 131, 140, 146–7, 148, 149, 156, 157, 158, 160, 162, 168, 170, 172, 176, 184, 185, 191, 195, 202, 209, 212, 214, 250, 259, 295; age and character, 129, 137, 141, 144, 161, 211, 252; attitude to slave trade, 123, 178; executes Mphephe and others, 181, 183, 200–1, 232, 236, 288; gifts from D.L., 150; learns alphabet, 273; political troubles, 141, 143, 161; wives, 131, 136, 144, 185

Sekgoma, Ngwato chief, character, 4, 76; illness, 4; mentioned, 9, 72, 304, 305

Sekonyela, drives Sebetwane from homeland, 18

Sekute, Leya chief, 22 n.; attacked by Sebetwane, 60–1, 233

Selinye, D.L. at, 3

Seloenda, Kololo tribesman, 133–4

Selokolela, D.L. at, 99

Senthufe, Ngwaketse chief, 89, 91, 304

Senyenki River, 216

Seriba, D.L. at, 192

Serinane, thermal spring, 77

Serotle, D.L. at, 304

Servants, misconduct of, 281–2, 290, 291, 294

Sesasechoe, D.L. at, 3

Sesheke, 21, 25, 28, 38, 41, 44, 72,

193, 204, 292; D.L. at, 39, 40, 231, 234. Cf. Morantsiane

Sesheke River, see Zambesi

Setefano, Sechele's son, 300

Setlagana, village headman, 51, 130, 134

Setlagole, 96

Setlhongwane, D.L. at, 95, 96

Shashi River, 6, 92

Shelley, E., traveller, 68, 72, 76

Shobo, Bushman guide, 12–13, 63, 72

Shokolo, Luchazi informant, 31, 42

Shokotsa, D.L. at, 77

Sikosi's village, 193, 231

Silva Pôrto, A. F. F. da, 123 n., 156, 160, 177, 179, 185, 210, 219, 223, 228, 290; establishment at Katongo, 204–5, 226, 232, 233; intrigues with Mphephe, 220, 232, 277; meetings with, 188, 189, 190, 192, 205, 207, 232; slaver, 126–7, 129, 137, 144, 151, 178, 205, 232, 233, 277, 281

Sima, Kololo tribesman, 133, 134, 181

Simah River, see Luete

Simpson, J., trader, steals cattle, 95

Sinamane, Tonga chief, 207

Sinangombe, Tonga chief, 207

Sinkatauba, 'Shona chief', 152

Sipopa (Tutanka), Lozi prince, 26, 41

Sitoti Rapids, 198

Skietfontein, D.L. at, 84

Slave trade, 39, 42–3, 123, 126, 129, 131, 134, 144, 178, 179, 205, 220, 227, 228, 232, 277; D.L. protests against, 39, 49, 209; means of counteracting, see Commerce, Oswell. Cf. Arabs, Ferreira, Mambari, Silva Pôrto

Slavery, indigenous, 135, 205, 209, 210, 234, 235, 251–2, 258

Smith, Sir Harry, 82, 83

Snake charmers, 192
Snakes, 162, 280, 281
Snyman, servant, 107, 112, 172
Socialism, 277
Somerset, Colonel H., 83
Sonta River, *see* Savuti channel
Spencer, Rev. T., 92
Steele, Colonel T. M., 68, 72, 237
Stone buildings, 190
Sumagow's village, D.L. at, 55, 62

Tampans, 120, 193
Taoge River, 47, 67
Teeth, evulsion of, 27, 32, 33, 48–9
Temperatures, 98, 100, 101, 102,
    129, 132, 135, 160–1, 162, 163,
    168, 185, 186, 200, 224, 237,
    276, 283
Termites, *see* Ants
Tetemba, *see* Tlole
Thamalakane River (Tamunakle), 7,
    47, 55, 67, 306
Thebe, servant, 116
Theft, case of, 231, 234
Thermal springs, 77
Thompson, F., trader, visits Ma-
    Kololo, 231, 234, 250
Thompson, Rev. W., 87 n., 237;
    sister's gift to MmaMotsisane, 128
Thutsa, well, 70
Tidman, Rev. A., xii, xviii, 237
Tlakatlaka, Kololo tribesman, 134
Tlhabala, 75. *See* Kane
Tlhakgameng, D.L. at, 97
Tloga, D.L. at, 103
Tlole, Shona chief, 6, 11
Tlomha, 'hollow channel', 106, 107
Tlomtla, D.L. at, 9, 101
Tongane island, 216
Tortoise, habits and food, 73, 98
Trees and plants, 10, 38, 75, 77, 78,
    80, 84, 94, 99, 101–2, 103–4, 105,
    106, 107, 109, 110, 119, 121,
    126, 129, 132, 141, 144, 162,

164, 180, 193–4, 198, 199, 200,
    215, 216, 217, 222, 237, 306;
    eaten by Natives, 10, 14, 37, 45,
    47, 51, 75, 106, 107, 109, 111,
    112, 119, 215; eaten by wild
    animals, 73, 246, 262, 263, 268,
    271–2, 275, 292, 311; Native
    names of, 61, 107, 317–19
Tsaeheriga, D.L. at, 109
Tsapo, Khurutshe chief, 6, 7, 68, 69,
    71, 305
Tsara, D.L. at, 15
Tsarologa's village, 305
Tsatsa's village, 192
Tsatsara, D.L. at, 15, 51
Tsetse fly, description, 63; distribu-
    tion, 13, 14, 15, 16, 31, 37, 46,
    51, 53, 54, 63, 65–6, 72, 111,
    116, 130, 139, 144, 161, 162,
    178, 198, 220, 231, 235, 251,
    290; effects of bite, 16, 36, 54, 63,
    64–5, 66–7, 139, 144, 178, 294
Tsodilo Hill (Sorila), 67
Tsonarrah, *see* Maila
Tutanka, *see* Sipopa

Uithaalder, Hottentot rebel, 84
Unku, D.L. at, 11, 101

Vardon, F., sportsman, 64, 276
Vaughan, R., editor, 92
Venereal disease in Barotseland, 184
Victoria Falls (Mosioatunya), xv, 60,
    125; hearsay description, 40

Water, 'value' of, 13, 92
Watt, Rev. D. G., correspondent,
    69, 95, 237
Webb, W. F., sportsman, 89, 91, 95
Wet-nurses, aged, 253–4
Whately, Archbishop R., 6
Wild dogs, 130
Wild hemp, smoked by MaKololo,
    26, 27, 164, 169, 206

Wildebeest, description, 278; habits, 278–9; varieties, 280
Wilson, J. H., trader, visits Ma-Kololo, 7 n., 46, 156; correspondence with, 237
Wine, welcome gift of, 68, 72
Witchcraft, 183, 185, 233, 237, 250, 251
Wylde, Sir J., 'infamous hypocrite', 82

Xhosa tribes, wars against Colonists, 81, 82–3, 92

Zambesi River, 30, 32, 40, 41, 43, 44, 131, 144, 193, 216, 218, 219, 220, 221, 229, 291, 292; annual floods, 37, 38, 42, 46, 47, 147, 195, 203, 204, 254; branches, 30, 294; current, 195, 211, 220; discovered at Sesheke, 38, 41; D.L. travels on, 193–202, 211–31; islands, 198, 214, 218, 219; scenery, 193–4, 195, 197, 198, 199, 200, 215, 216, 217; song about, 237–8; sources, 189
Zambesi valley, 203, 204, 210, 224, 226. Cf. Barotseland
Zanzibar, Arabs from, 228, 229
Zebra, 279, 283
Zimbati River, 229
Zouga River, see Botletle